D1158169

The Art of Agent-Oriented Modeling

Intelligent Robotics and Autonomous Agents
Edited by Ronald C. Arkin

The Art of Agent-Oriented Modeling

Leon Sterling and Kuldar Taveter

The MIT Press
Cambridge, Massachusetts
London, England

For information about special quantity discounts, please email special_sales@mitpress.mit.edu.

This book was set in Times New Roman on 3B2 by Asco Typesetters, Hong Kong.
Printed and bound in the United States of America.

Library of Congress Cataloging-in-Publication Data

Sterling, Leon.
The art of agent-oriented modeling / Leon S. Sterling and Kuldar Taveter.
   p.   cm. — (Intelligent robotics and autonomous agents series)
Includes bibliographical references and index.
ISBN 978-0-262-01311-6 (hardcover : alk. paper) 1. Intelligent agents (Computer software) 2. Computer software—Development. I. Taveter, Kuldar. II. Title.
QA76.76.I58S757   2009
006.3—dc22   2008044231

10 9 8 7 6 5 4 3 2 1

To Miriam, Danya, Sara, and Emily

To Siiri, Eliise, and Sanne

Contents

Foreword

The software systems that we need to run our society in the twenty-first century are becoming increasingly complex. We need to build large systems by integrating existing systems and components from a range of suppliers. These systems have to be responsive, dependable, and secure. Our reductionist, top-down software engineering techniques—which have helped us create the large, reliable software systems that we depend upon—are now struggling to cope. To meet the demands for twenty-first century systems, we need new approaches to software engineering that can cope autonomously with a rapidly changing environment and that can take advantage of new features as they become available. We need systems that can cope with the unexpected—in terms of both reacting autonomously to problems and communicating these problems to other agents in the system. Agent-oriented software engineering is an important emerging technology that can help us build such systems.

In any developing technology, books in the area go through stages. Initially, the only works are the proceedings of specialist conferences for researchers, where the book includes advanced research papers. The second stage is typified by multiauthor books and specialist books aimed at researchers and early adopters, which focus on a specific topic. These works assume that readers understand basic concepts and principles. Finally, student textbooks are written, aimed at people who need to start from the beginning. Agent-oriented software engineering has now reached this final stage of maturity. This book is one of the first textbooks on agent-oriented software engineering. It aims to disseminate knowledge about this important topic to a wide audience.

The Art of Agent-Oriented Modeling is an introduction to agent-oriented software development for students and for software developers who are interested in learning about new software engineering techniques. Although the principal focus of the book is agent-oriented modeling, it is an excellent general introduction to all aspects of practical, agent-oriented software engineering. Building on Leon Sterling's and Kuldar Taveter's courses in this topic, this book uses everyday examples to illustrate the notion of agents and how agents can interact to create complex, distributed systems.

A key difference between this book and other books in the field is that this book recognizes that if agent-oriented development is to enter the mainstream, it must be done with consideration of practical software engineering issues. As well as delivering the required functionality, agent-oriented systems have to be reliable and secure; their development has to fit into a software engineering life cycle, where systems must meet externally imposed requirements and have to be maintained over many years.

This book has many important insights and it is perhaps invidious to pick on only one of them as an example. However, I think the key point that Leon and Kuldar make in this book is that agent-oriented technology is an effective way to construct sociotechnical systems, which take into account organizational and human issues as well as technical issues. Agents are a useful abstraction that helps us think about how sociotechnical systems deliver the services required by their users. We should think about this without regard to whether the agents that deliver these services are people or automated systems. Modeling a system as agents gives us a way of establishing flexible boundaries for the automated system that can be extended as our understanding of human tasks improve. Over time, these systems can evolve with more and more functionality being taken over by automated agents.

Barry Boehm, one of the most respected software engineering researchers and practitioners, has called the twenty-first century the "software century." The challenges for humanity are to improve the lives of people around the world without making unsustainable demands on the environment. We can achieve this only with the help of large and small software systems that coordinate resources from different places and different providers and that break down cultural barriers between different civilizations. Many of these systems will be agent-oriented and Leon Sterling and Kuldar Taveter have made an important contribution in this book to the development of agent-oriented software engineering.

Ian Sommerville, *St. Andrews, Scotland, July 2008*

Preface

The introduction of the personal computer changed society's view of computer systems. No longer was a computer a complicated machine doing a task, tucked away in a separate room or a far-off corner of an office or work environment. A computer was a machine on your desk that was ready for daily interaction. No longer was a computer only for specialist programmers—it was a tool to be used by virtually all office workers.

The rapid rise of the World Wide Web in the mid-1990s changed society's view still further. No longer was the personal computer restricted to a desk or a small office network. The machine on your desk could be part of a global network. In addition, the use of computers at home skyrocketed. Almost every home in the developed world acquired a computer. Laptops were mandated for school children in many schools. The volume and visibility of email addresses and domain names exploded.

In the mid-2000s, as this book is written, our interaction with computers is everexpanding. Businesses depend on software for many—if not most—of their core activities. Cars and appliances have embedded software of which we are barely aware. Teenagers and young adults engage in social networking, and share music and videos on Web sites such as LimeWire and YouTube. We look up knowledge on Wikipedia. Skype is a common method for making telephone calls over the Internet.

So how do we develop computer software to interact with the ever-increasing complexity of the technical world and the increased fluidity of social organizations? It is not an easy task. Having been involved in research and teaching of software engineering and software development projects, we find a need for changing conceptual models. We want to develop software that is open, intelligent, and adaptive. We are becoming convinced that such software needs to be conceived, designed, and developed differently from existing applications that assume fixed requirements and an unchanging environment.

One consideration we believe is important is the need to take a systems view. The system of people and technology has a life cycle of inception, design, implementation, testing, and maintenance. Processes need to be understood for each of the stages of the life cycle. A systems view implies being able to take a holistic approach and to include considerations of all stakeholders.

In this book, we advocate an agent-oriented view. An *agent* is a concept and metaphor that is familiar for people with and without technical background or interest. An agent allows the blurring of the boundary between people and technology to allow more people to be engaged with the process of building software. Thinking in terms of agents can change the way that people think of software and the tasks it can perform.

The concept of an agent is not new to computing. Agents have been discussed in regard to artificial intelligence (AI) from its early days. More recently, agents have been discussed in the context of object-oriented technology, with many researchers and practitioners viewing them as an extension of object-oriented technology. Agent models have been added to established object-oriented modeling approaches, most notably based around UML (Unified Modeling Language). Agent programming extensions have been developed for languages such as Java and Prolog.

We prefer viewing an agent-oriented approach as different from an object-oriented approach. Agent-oriented models need to be described independently of object-oriented models, though sensible reuse of notation is advisable. The reason for differentiation is that people can be sometimes trapped into thinking only in ways familiar to them. As the saying goes, if all you have is a hammer, everything looks like a nail. In our experience, thinking in terms of agents requires a different mindset. Students and practitioners who insist in thinking about building from their existing (object-oriented) methods are less successful in developing agent-oriented applications.

Our interest in writing this book is to encourage a wide variety of stakeholders in the software development process to engage with an agent-oriented approach. This is a challenge. Software developers, software acquirers, software users, and software maintainers have different concerns. Models are needed that are understandable for all stakeholders. The variety of concerns suggests a variety of models. If the models are understandable, the stakeholder is more likely to be engaged. We believe that engagement throughout the process will improve the development of systems consisting of people and software that will interoperate and evolve successfully.

So why another book? One factor in the adoption of a technology is having textbook material in support. There has been an increase in agent-oriented theory, language, and methodology books over the past several years. This progress is to be encouraged. Nonetheless we feel that this book fills a niche not currently being filled.

There are three main features of this book that we feel add significantly to the literature. The first is the presentation of substantial new examples that range from requirements through design to deployment. The more examples that potential users of technology see, the more likely a technology is to be adopted. The second is the use of abstract agent-oriented models at various levels of abstraction and geared to different stakeholders. The models relate to a range of agent-oriented software engineering methodologies that are being actively developed. The third is related— namely, the emphasis on models rather than languages—and the philosophy that models can be mapped to a variety of deployment platforms, possibly including conventional languages, makes the concepts accessible to a wider audience. Our recent discussions with colleagues in both academia and industry have reinforced our appreciation for the need for different models for open, distributed domains.

There are often forces working against trying to show how an approach covers a range of implementation languages. Agent language vendors want companies to be locked into their technology. Indeed, one of the initial motivations for the research underlying this book was a request by an industrial partner on what agent models would be "future-proof." The industry partner had been burned by using an agent-based vendor platform that was no longer supported. Research groups also want to encourage others to use their specific methods. Though this motivation is understandable, the agent community will benefit from broadly supportable models.

Why do we use the word "art" in the title of the book? We have experienced modeling as a creative process that does not always follow clear-cut rules. Many decisions are left to the discretion of the modeler and his or her background and intuition. Modeling is also iterative. Usually one cannot—and should not—end up with final models right away. Even some of the models in the book would improve through further rounds of iteration. Given that we cannot give definitive advice on building "perfect" models, we settle for the more modest aim of providing guidance for creating models.

Having explained some of the motivation that prompted the book, we address the issue of timing. Why now? We have each been working with agent applications for the past ten years. Only now, in our opinion, do we perceive that agent concepts are known widely enough to allow agent-oriented modeling. Modeling tools are emerging: an essential development, if agent concepts are to be used by industry. Also, recent developments in the research areas of autonomic systems, event-based systems, and multiagent systems seem to indicate that the paradigm of peer-to-peer computing in the broad sense is gaining momentum.

Our conclusion that agent concepts have matured sufficiently has been developed through our delivering of seminars and courses on agent technology in academia and industry. We have been involved in teaching graduate students (and advanced undergraduates) for more than ten years. In 2000, Leon was involved in an Australian government project on the rapid diffusion of technology from academia to industry using agent technology as an example. With the benefit of hindsight, the project was premature. Providing students with the models presented in this book has greatly increased their ability to conceptualize and design agent-oriented systems. The models have been progressively polished over the past three years and are now ready for broader engagement. By the time the reader finishes reading this book, we hope that his or her capacity and confidence for the design and modeling of agent-oriented systems will have improved.

Leon Sterling, *Melbourne, Australia, November 2008*
Kuldar Taveter, *Tallinn, Estonia, November 2008*

Acknowledgments

Any book that is of this length and that has taken almost two years to write owes its appearance to many people, events, and circumstances. We gladly take this opportunity to acknowledge and thank the many people who have contributed to this book, in ways both big and small. Doubtless there will be people who have contributed that we have unintentionally omitted from mention. For that we request forgiveness in advance.

First and foremost, we acknowledge the dedication and support of our families. Leon appreciates the love and support of his wife Miriam over his career, and the interactions with his daughters Danya, Sara, and Emily. They have had a positive impact on the book in many ways, including influencing examples.

Kuldar appreciates the love and patience of his wife Siiri, who, not too long after Kuldar's Ph.D. thesis writing process, went through a similar experience. Of enormous importance for the content of this book were Kuldar's interactions with his daughters Eliise and Sanne, now 10 and 7, who at the request of Daddy made experiments with Tamagotchis and consulted Daddy. Kuldar is also thankful to his parents for their prayers and thoughts. And last but not least, Kuldar thanks God for blessing the authors and their families and for providing us with the opportunity to write this book.

We next thank our colleagues who have been instrumental in the appearance of this book. For Leon, the story starts with his return to Melbourne to a professorship in Computer Science and the establishment of the Intelligent Agent Lab, jointly with Professor Liz Sonenberg. Liz and Leon co-taught an Intelligent Agents graduate class in 1996, and to a large extent, the origins of the book lie in the lack of an appropriate textbook for that class. Liz has been a tremendous colleague and indirectly affected the book in many ways. Over the past twelve years, many people have influenced the book's direction. Silvio Salom from Adacel Technologies gave substantial support. The Intelligent Home examples arose from a consulting project with Silvio and many related discussions. The ROADMAP methodology was a response to Silvio's request for a vendor-free agent methodology. There was extensive interaction with the Australian Defence Science and Technology Organisation (DSTO), especially with Simon Goss, and later Clint Heinze and Michael Papasimeon. Adrian Pearce joined the Melbourne Agent Lab in 2000 and formed part of the formative discussions with DSTO. The University of Melbourne Software Engineering group deserves thanks, especially Philip Dart, Ed Kazmierczak, and more recently Shanika Karunasekera. All have been good colleagues who have contributed to Leon's perspective on software engineering. Two software engineering students who later became Ph.D. students, Thomas Juan and Kendall Lister, deserve special mention. This book definitely would not have happened without Thomas's Ph.D. research and surrounding discussions about agent-oriented software engineering methodologies. At RMIT University down the road, Lin Padgham and Michael Winikoff followed some similar paths, and discussions with them have undoubtedly contributed to the book. More recently, we have had helpful interaction with Knobby Clarke from Oakton Computing, previously Agentis, who gave useful feedback on our agent concepts.

Internationally, a special thanks to the Italian Logic Programming Community for inviting Leon to the Italian summer school in 1997, which initiated an ongoing collaboration with researchers at the University of Genoa led by Maurizio Martelli, and supported by Viviana Mascardi and Floriano Zini during their Ph.D. research. Leon has also enjoyed attending two workshops at Dagstuhl in Germany, at the first of which Leon met Kuldar.

For Kuldar, his initial interest in agent-oriented modeling was focused and shaped by Gerd Wagner, currently a professor at Brandenburg University of Technology in Cottbus, Germany. Their collaboration started in 1999 and Gerd later became a co-supervisor of Kuldar's Ph.D. thesis. The cooperation with Gerd over many years has been very influential in the emergence of this book, and is certainly reflected by the contents of the book. It is also not possible to underestimate the contribution of the Academician Boris Tamm, the late supervisor of Kuldar's thesis. He helped Kuldar in getting the real-life case study of manufacturing simulation, which is also present in this book, and was also instrumental in obtaining research funding from the Estonian Science Foundation.

Kuldar would also like to thank his former colleagues at the Technical Research Centre of Finland, VTT Information Technology, who have been involved in forming Kuldar's industry-oriented research attitude. Especially deserves mentioning Aarno Lehtola, now an entrepreneur, who has been very supportive over many years. Other supportive colleagues from VTT Information Technology include Pekka Silvennoinen, Seppo Linnainmaa, and Markus Tallgren.

During the past three years, Kuldar has enormously enjoyed the work atmosphere at the Agent Lab of the University of Melbourne. Particularly his discussions with Leon have been extremely enlightening with respect to the book and to agent-oriented software engineering more broadly. Cooperation with the Lochard and Jeppesen companies in Melbourne has been a good sequel to Kuldar's earlier innovation projects. Kuldar would also like to thank Professors Brian Henderson-Sellers and Aditya Ghose from Australia, Dr. Jens Dietrich from New Zealand, and Professor Eric Yu from Canada for the opportunities to give seminars and receive useful feedback at their universities.

Funding from several research organizations has contributed to Leon's and Kuldar's collaboration. Kuldar was supported as a research fellow through the Australian Research Council Centre for Perceptive and Intelligent Machines in Complex Environments. Funding was also received from the Australian Research Council Discovery and Linkage programs, the Smart Internet Technology Cooperative Research Centre, and Adacel Technology. Earlier, Kuldar's research projects, two of which are overviewed as case studies in this book, were on several occasions supported by the Technology Agency of Finland and VTT Information Technology and once by the Estonian Science Foundation.

Next, we thank research students. In addition to Thomas Juan and Kendall Lister, mentioned earlier, we thank Kevin Chan, Ayodele Oluyomi, Anne Boettcher, Yu Xiu Luo, Bin Lu, Wai Shiang Cheah, Joost Westra, Muthukuruppan Annamalai, Maia Hristozova, and Nicole Ronald. The following research students read drafts of the book and made useful comments: Mohammed Arif, Bin Lu, Yu Xiu Luo, Golriz Rezaei, and Rebekah Velicescu. The coursework and research students who attended the evolving Intelligent Agents class are too many to mention, but their influence is noted. Finally, thanks to Alison Handley who helped with last-minute formatting, and who has been a presence for many years.

We would also like to thank the following external proofreaders who made many useful remarks: Knobby Clarke, Brian Berenbach, Dragan Gasevic, and Jeni Paay. Help with MaSE figures was provided by Scott DeLoach and help with Tropos figures was provided by Anna Perini. A couple of proofreaders deserve special mention. The comments and suggestions by Giancarlo Guizzardi considerably improved the ontological grounding for modeling given in the book. Also, proofreading by the Emeritus Professor Brian V. Hill produced many constructive remarks and proved that the book is also understandable for an audience without a background in information technology.

We would like to thank the publisher and the proofreader for many small improvements. We also acknowledge Skype by Skype Technologies S.A. for enabling us to continue interaction once Kuldar returned to Estonia.

I MODELS

This book presents an approach for modeling complex systems consisting of people, devices, and software agents in changing environments. In part I, a set of models is presented at three levels of abstraction: a motivation layer, where the purpose, goals, and requirements of the system are described; a design layer; and an implementation layer. The first chapter advocates conceiving of the world in which software operates as a multiagent system operating in an environment subject to rules and policies. The conceptual space that we look at will be discussed in more detail in chapter 2. The models themselves will be presented in chapter 3 and applied in later chapters. Chapter 4 focuses on nonfunctional requirements or quality goals. Chapter 5 describes four different platforms, and chapter 6 presents a viewpoint framework that is used in part II to analyze methodologies.

1 Introduction

We live today in a complicated world. Complexity comes in many guises, and ranges from small-scale to large-scale concerns. On the small scale, we interact with an ever-increasing array of devices, most of them new and incompletely understood, such as mobile phones and portable digital music players. On the large scale we live in complex institutions—governments, corporations, educational institutions, and religious groups. No one can understand all that goes on in such institutions.

A sensible response to dealing effectively with the complexity is to seek help. Help can come from other people. We may hire a consultant to help us deal with government. We may get a friend to help us install a home wireless network, or we may use software tools to automate tasks like updating clocks and software. It might even be sensible to combine both people and software. An underlying purpose of this book is to help us conceptualize a complicated environment, where many parts—both social and technical—interact. The key concepts we use are agents and systems.

The underlying question in this book is how to design systems that work effectively in the modern environment, where computing is pervasive, and where people interact with technology existing in a variety of networks and under a range of policies and constraints imposed by the institutions and social structures that we live in. We use the word "system" in the broadest sense. Systems encompass a combination of people and computers, hardware, and software. There are a range of devices, from phones to MP3 players, digital cameras, cars, and information booths.

We are particularly interested in systems that contain a significant software component that may be largely invisible. Why the interest? Such systems have been hard to build, and a lot of expensive mistakes have been made. We believe that better conceptualization of systems will lead to better software.

In this first chapter, we discuss our starting philosophy. There are particular challenges within the modern networked, computing environment, such as its changeability and consequent uncertainty. We discuss challenges of the computing environment in the first section. In the second section we address agents, and why we think they are a natural way to tame complexity. In the third section, we discuss multiagent systems. The fourth section addresses modeling. In the fifth section, we discuss systems engineering, which we believe is a good background for conceptualizing the building of systems. Using multiagent systems to better understand systems with a significant software component is really the raison d'être of the book. The sixth section briefly describes a complementary view of multiagent systems that proceeds "bottom-up," where desired behavior emerges from the interaction of components rather than being designed in "top-down." The final section in the first chapter frames our discussion in the context of the history of programming languages and paradigms over the last fifty years.

An aspect of our philosophy is a strongly pragmatic streak. This book is intended to encourage people to model systems from an agent-oriented perspective. From our teaching experience, we know that describing abstract concepts is insufficient. Clear examples of concept use are extremely helpful, and methods are needed to use the concepts. We strongly believe that developers and students can learn to model by looking at good examples and adapting them. The development of good examples from our teaching and research experience was why we felt ready to write this book. We decided to write this book only when convinced that people could build practical things, and our modeling approach would help people envisage multiagent systems operating in complex environments.

1.1   Building Software in a Complex, Changing World

The task of building software has never been more challenging. There is unprecedented consumer demand and short product cycles. Change in the form of new technology is happening at an increasing rate. Software needs to be integrated with existing systems and institutions as seamlessly as possible, and often in a global network where local cultural factors may not be understood.

In this section, we identify several key characteristics of the modern computing environment for which software must be written. These characteristics suggest five attributes that software should have in order to be effective within the environment. These desirable software attributes are motivating factors for the multiagent perspective being advocated in this book.

Complexity is the first characteristic we highlight. Essentially, the modern world is complicated, and that complexity affects software. As an example, consider a billing system for mobile phone usage or consumption of utilities such as electricity or gas. At first thought, billing may seem reasonably straightforward. All you need is a monitoring mechanism, such as a timer for phone calls or a meter for electricity, and a table of rates. Then it will be a simple calculation to determine the bill. However, billing is not simple in practice. There have been expensive software failures in building billing systems. New taxes could be introduced that change the way billing must be done, and complications when taxes should apply. The government may allow rebates for certain classes of citizens, such as the elderly, with complicated rules for eligibility. There may be restrictions on how such rebates are to be reported. Phone calls that cross calendar days or have differential rates cause complications. International calls have a myriad of other factors. The phone company may decide on special deals and promotions. In other words, the potentially simple billing system is complex, as it is complicated by a range of social, commercial, and technical issues— a common occurrence.

Another characteristic of many modern systems is that they are *distributed*, both computationally and geographically. Web applications are the norm, and they engender a whole range of issues. For example, if the Web application has an international customer base, does it make sense to have mirror sites for storing and downloading information? If the web traffic is high volume, does there need to be load balancing? Are multilingual versions of the interface necessary, or at least a change of terms in different places where the software is delivered? Such considerations change the nature of an application.

Most software applications are *time-sensitive*. Time is an issue both in response to consumer demand and for consumption of resources. For the former, we expect instantaneous responses to our queries. Indeed, too slow a response can cause a product to fail. For the latter, if too many computational resources are necessary to process information, an application may be infeasible. Architectures and designs need to be analyzed for speed and other qualities.

The surrounding environment is *uncertain* and *unpredictable*. Not all of the information that we receive is reliable. Some of the information is caused by genuine uncertainty, like weather predictions or future prices of stock. Some information is fraudulent, such as emails that are part of phishing attacks or scams. Although unpredictability may make life interesting in some circumstances, it is a challenge for software developers. There is no guarantee that the environment can be controlled, which has been the prevailing style for standard software methods. Software has to be developed to expect the unexpected.

The final characteristic of the modern environment that we highlight is that it is *open*. There is new information and new realities. New software viruses are written that must be protected against. There are new policies promulgated by institutions and new legislation developed by governments. And it is not just new information that affects the environment. The external environment is *changing*. Bank interest rates change; mobile phone plans change. To be effective in the environment, behavior must change accordingly.

Having identified these challenging characteristics of the modern environment, let us suggest desirable attributes for software if it is to perform effectively and serve us well.

The first attribute desirable for software is *adaptivity*. As the world changes, we would like our software to reflect the change. As new facts enter the world, the software should not break. Brittleness was a problem with expert systems and has limited their applicability. An obvious area where adaptivity is essential is security. As a new virus or security threat is determined, it would be good if the virus checking/firewall/security system incorporated the information automatically. Indeed, software is beginning to run automatic security updates, and this trend needs to continue.

The second attribute is *intelligence*. Consumer ads already sometimes claim that their product is more intelligent than its competitors—for example, an air conditioning system or a mobile phone. Presumably they mean more features. We would hope that increased intelligence would lead to better integration. We certainly appreciate when a computer clock automatically adjusts for Daylight Saving Time, and when memory sticks and digital cameras work seamlessly across a range of computers and operating systems. Intelligence is a way of dealing with complexity and uncertainty, and being able to determine when knowledge may be false. One dimension of intelligence that we would expect is awareness. A system that was unaware of what was going on around it would not seem intelligent.

A third desirable attribute is *efficiency*. There is a need and expectation for instantaneous responses, which will be achieved only by efficient implementations in light of the complexity. Efficiency may well determine the possibility of solutions—for example, file sharing or downloading large video files.

A more abstract fourth attribute is *purposefulness*. In light of the complexity and changing nature of the environment, it will be difficult—if not impossible—for all requirements to be stated. It is better to work at a higher level and to explain purposes in terms of goals, and, in certain circumstances, to have the system determine the appropriate path of action. This approach can aid system design and clarity, which leads to the next attribute.

The final attribute is a little bit different and perhaps less obvious; namely, the software should be *understandable*, at least in its design and overall purpose. We need ways of thinking about and describing software that simplify complexity, at least with regard to describing behavior. The desire for understandability is influenced by the software engineering perspective undertaken within this book. There are many potential advantages of understandable software, including better instructions for how to use it.

These are a lot of demands, and we need to address them. Let us explore one way of thinking about them. Indeed, the rationale for developing the agent-oriented modeling techniques that form the essence of this book is that they better address the characteristics of the world around us and can meet the desirable software objectives.

1.2   What Is an Agent?

This book advocates adoption of the concept of agents in thinking about software in today's world. Agents are suitable for the current software development challenges outlined in the previous section. In our opinion, the applicability of agents is likely to increase over the coming years.

An agent has existed as a concept for thousands of years. The *Oxford American Dictionary* gives two meanings for the word "agent," both of which are relevant. Perhaps the more fundamental definition of the two is "a person or thing that takes an active role or produces a specified effect." The connotation is that agents are active entities that exist in the world and cause it to change. The phrase "agent of change" springs to mind, and indeed was mentioned in the dictionary entry. The concepts of roles and effects mentioned in the definition are key. They will be discussed in the next chapter and throughout the book.

The more common sense meaning is the other definition: "a person who acts on behalf of another, for example, managing business, financial, or contractual matters, or provides a service."

In human communities and societies, an agent is a person who carries out a task on behalf of someone else. For example, a travel agent can make enquiries and bookings for your holiday; a literary agent interacts with publishers to try and find a book publisher; and a real estate agent helps you buy, sell, or rent a house or factory. In a well-known biblical story from the Old Testament (Gen. 24:1–67), Abraham sends his servant Eliezer to act as a marriage agent to find a bride for his son Isaac.

Computer science researchers have used the word "agent" for more than twenty-five years with a range of different meanings. For the purpose of this chapter, we define an agent as "an entity that performs a specific activity in an environment of which it is aware and that can respond to changes." Depending on their background, readers are likely to bring initially differing emphases and understanding of the word "agent" to the book. We anticipate that the reader will gain an increased understanding of the word "agent" through engagement with this book, its associated exercises, and attempts to construct agent-oriented models.

One obvious consequence of our informal definition that is worth explicitly pointing out is that people are agents. People live in the world, are aware of changes in the world in many different factors and attributes, including weather, politics, and social organizations. People act in the world. For example, they might protect themselves against the weather by carrying an umbrella or putting on sunscreen or a snow suit—usually not all three simultaneously. They might vote in an election to influence politics; they might form networks of friends.

Let us look at some agents from the world of computing over the past decade. Some readers may be surprised at what we consider to be an agent. However, whether you agree or disagree with the classification should not affect your appreciation of the book.

The first successful robot in the consumer market has been Roomba. Its Web site proclaims that Roomba is "the world's top-selling home robot, with over two million sold." Roomba is an automated vacuum cleaner, designed to clean rooms. It senses the shape of your room and determines a cleaning pattern for traversing the room. It is flat and capable of vacuuming under beds and couches. Most models have a charging base to which they return when they are running out of power. Why we describe it as an agent is that it senses its environment, a house, and its own state, and performs a task—namely cleaning a floor. It responds to changes in the environment, such as moving furniture, people, and its own power level. In 2006, the company introduced the Scooba, which washes floors rather than vacuuming, but is otherwise similar. A video clip distributed on the Internet shows it sucking up Diet Coke and "eating" pretzel crumbs.

The next example we consider is a Tamagotchi, a toy developed in Japan and popularized in the late 1990s. In one sense, a Tamagotchi is just a simple interactive simulation. It has "needs": food, bathroom, sleep; its owner, usually a young child, must provide for those needs. If the needs are not met, the Tamagotchi "gets sick" and can even "die." Later models interact with other Tamagotchis, and recently, Tamagotchi Towns have been created on the Internet. We model Tamagotchis in detail in chapter 3.

The most popular robot in Japan is AIBO, a robot produced by Sony Entertainment. Sony marketed AIBO as an electronic pet. AIBO comes with preprogrammed behaviors, including walking, wagging its tail, flashing its eyes, and electronic barking (or making some sound). The behaviors are sophisticated, including a great ability to right itself if it falls over on an uneven surface, for example. Several of the behaviors are affected by its interaction with people, such as being patted on the head: hence the marketing as a pet.

As well as preprogrammed behaviors, Sony provided a programming environment for AIBO. It promoted the use of the programming environment through the addition of a special league to RoboCup, a robot soccer-playing competition held annually since 1997. The Sony dog league, started in 2000, has teams of three AIBO dogs playing soccer on a field larger than two table-tennis tables. The dogs have improved their play over time. While playing a game of soccer, an AIBO dog is certainly an agent. It must sense where the ball is, move to the ball, propel the ball forward toward the goal, and play out its assigned team role—for example, attacker or defender. A photo of an AIBO dog is shown in figure 1.1.

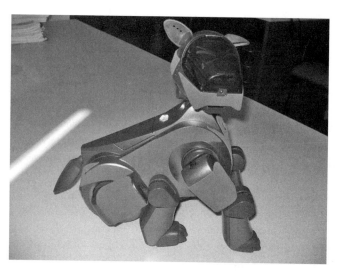

Figure 1.1
The AIBO by Sony

These three examples are tangible. The agents can be identified with a physical device, a vacuum cleaner, a toy, or a dog. Let us be a bit more abstract, as we consider four software examples.

In addition to the so-called gadget-based digital pets mentioned previously, such as Tamagotchis, there are other types of digital pets. They can be Web site–based, such as digital pets that can be obtained and played with in the Neopets, Webkinz, and Petz4fun Web sites. There are also game-based digital pets running on video game consoles, such as Nintendogs by Nintendo and HorseZ by Ubisoft, both for Nintendo DS game consoles.

The second example is a virus of the software kind. Essentially a computer virus is a computer program written to alter the way a computer operates, without the permission or knowledge of the user. We believe a virus should be able to self-replicate and be able to execute itself. Consequently, we regard a computer virus to be an agent because it needs to sense the status of the networked environment that it is in, and to act by affecting files and computers. Viruses can certainly be effective. The MyDoom virus is reported to have infected more than two hundred thousand computers in a single day. Viruses can be regarded as a malevolent agent, as opposed to a benevolent agent.

The next example is one always discussed in the graduate agent class at the University of Melbourne. Consider a program for handling email, such as Microsoft Outlook, Eudora, or the native Mac OS X mail program, Mail. Is such a program an agent? In our opinion, it is. The mail handling program needs to be aware of the network environment, and whether particular hosts are receiving email. If hosts are not receiving mail, messages are queued up and sent later without further human intervention. The email program performs actions such as filtering spam. Further, the email program is an agent in the sense of acting as a person's representative. It has detailed knowledge of network protocols that both Leon and Kuldar would need to research. It knows what networks you are connected with—for example, Ethernet or a wireless network—and chooses which one to use appropriately. Students, however, are initially reluctant to regard Outlook or the other programs as agents, instead regarding them as merely programs.

To consider this issue further, how about a RIM BlackBerry? Is the physical device the agent, or is the software running the device the agent? In our opinion, there is no precise answer. What you are modeling determines the response.

Another standard example used in the agent class at the University of Melbourne is considering whether a Web crawler is an agent. Here, students usually regard the Web crawler as an agent. Certainly a Web crawler takes action in the environment, but whether it is aware of its environment is less clear. There are many more examples that could be explored, but we will encourage further discussion via the exercises at the end of the chapter.

To conclude this section, we note that the agent is not a precisely defined entity. There is an associated metaphor of an agent as a representative that suggests several qualities. We highlight three qualities now. One quality is being purposeful in both senses of agents mentioned earlier. Another important quality of an agent is controlled autonomy, or the ability to pursue its own goals seemingly independently. The third quality is the agent needs to be situated—that is, aware of the environment around it. It must be capable of perceiving changes and responding appropriately. All of the examples that we have discussed are situated in an environment they must respond to, and possess the qualities of purposefulness and autonomy, at least to some extent. We consider this topic in more detail in chapter 2.

1.3   From Individual Agents to Multiagent Systems

Individual agents can be interesting. Interactions between agents can also be interesting, as can interactions between an agent and the environment in which it is situated. Adopting the agent metaphor for developing software raises both the visibility and abstraction level of interactions between agents. To appreciate the value in being able to understand agents and their interactions, we need to consider a broader systems view.

Loosely, a *system* is a set of entities or components connected together to make a complex entity or perform a complex function. If several—or perhaps all—of the connected entities are agents, we have a *multiagent system*. This book is about modeling systems as multiagent systems.

The term *sociotechnical system* is sometimes used to refer to systems that contain both a social aspect, which may be a subsystem, and a technical aspect. Although the term sociotechnical system has some attraction, we prefer the term multiagent system for two reasons. First, it emphasizes our interest in agent-oriented modeling. Second, it avoids any existing associations with different meanings of sociotechnical system. In using the term "multiagent system," we typically convey the sense that the whole is greater than the sum of the parts; also, that the agents interact, and that there will be a focus on interactions.

A note on words: a strength (and weakness) of this book is its attempt to bridge the gap between the everyday world and a strictly formal world. It does so by appropriating terms from our language, such as agent, model, goal, and role, and imbuing them with a technical meaning. Giving precise technical definitions is a mathematical skill, which can be learned but does not come easily, and many people struggle with learning this skill. We aim for accuracy in our use of words, but we do so unobtrusively. We tend not to define terms formally, but will describe specific models carefully. How to progress from general, abstract requirements to precise computer systems is a challenge that will be partly addressed in chapter 7 on methodologies and demonstrated in chapters 8, 9, and 10 on applications.

What is an example of an interaction between agents? A prototypical example from the domestic environment, among others, is an agent encountering and greeting another agent. Microwaves and DVD players often display a welcome message when they are turned on. The message is only for the purpose of interaction. We model greeting in chapters 4 and 9 in the context of a smart home.

Several agents interacting produce interesting behavior that is not predictable. A popular game in the first years of the twenty-first century is "The Sims," which was originally released in 2000 and which comes in several variants. People play the game by controlling activities, appearances, and other attributes of a set of computer-animated characters. The game engine executes the activities, effectively allowing a (simple) simulation of a family. A key feature of the interest in the game is in seeing how the characters interact.

A wonderful example of the power of defining simple characters and activities and letting the interactions produce interesting behavior comes from the movie trilogy *Lord of the Rings*. The movie producers had the challenge of creating realistic large-scale battle scenes between the coalition of the heroes and their followers and the coalition of their enemies. Clearly, participants in a battle are agents, having to observe the actions of others attacking them and having to effect a mortal blow. The key actors of the movie are agents in the battle and need to be filmed. However, it would be expensive getting thousands of extras to enact a battle. Instead, the key human protagonists were superimposed on a computer animation of a battle. The animation of the battle was generated by software agents run under simulation. Each software agent had simple motions defined. It was the interaction between them that made the scene interesting. Very realistic battle scenes were produced.

Simulations are a good source of examples of multiagent systems. The military in Australia and the United States, among other countries, have successfully developed multiagent simulations. We mention here two examples that illustrate possibilities for agent applications.

The Smart Whole Air Mission Model (SWARMM) was developed as a collaborative project between the Air Operations Division of DSTO and the Australian Artificial Intelligence Institute in the mid-1990s. It integrated a physics simulation of flying aircraft with pilot tactics and reasoning. SWARMM was written in the multiagent reasoning system dMARS. The types of tasks modeled in SWARMM were air defense, attack, escort, and sweep (the use of a fighter to clear a path for an incoming fighter plane or planes). SWARMM allowed the pilots' reasoning to be traced graphically during execution of the simulation. The simulation was developed in cooperation with F-18 pilots who liked the rapid feedback and high-level understandability of the simulation. The simulation had tens of agents who formed small teams, and several hundred tactics. The project was very successful. Taking the agent perspective helped develop an understandable system from which the pilots received visual feedback on their tactics, and the interaction between tactics could be seen in the software and understood.

In the late 1990s, the U.S. military conducted Synthetic Theater of War (STOW 97), an Advanced Concept Technology Demonstration jointly sponsored by the Defense Advanced Research Projects Agency (DARPA) and the United States Atlantic Command. STOW 97 was a training activity consisting of a continuous forty-eight hour synthetic exercise. Technically, it was a large, distributed simulation at the level of individual vehicles. Five U.S. sites participated (one each for the Army, Navy, Marines, Air, and Opposing Forces), plus one in the United Kingdom (UK). All told, there were approximately five hundred computers networked together across these sites, generating on the order of five thousand synthetic entities (tanks, airplanes, helicopters, individual soldiers, ships, missile batteries, buses, and so on). Agent-based software controlled helicopters and airplanes in part of the exercise. Eight company-level missions were run, ranging in size from five to sixteen helicopters (plus automated commanders for Army missions), each of which succeeded in performing its principal task of destroying enemy targets.

We conclude this section by considering multiagent systems in two domains: an intelligent home and e-commerce. Both of them are naturally modeled as multiagent systems, and demonstrate both social and technical characteristics. Social characteristics apply to how humans interact with technology and how humans interact with each other by the mediation of the technology, and technical characteristics obviously portray the technology to be used.

Let us consider a smart home where appliances interoperate seamlessly for the benefit of the home occupants, a promising area of application for intelligent agents. According to Wikipedia, the intelligent home "is a technological achievement aimed at connecting modern communication technologies and making them available for everyday household tasks. With intelligent home systems, it becomes possible to call home from any telephone or desktop computer in the world to control home appliances and security systems. Intelligent home systems guide the user to perform any operation, to control lighting, heating, air conditioning, or to arm or disarm the security system, and to record or to listen to messages. Other themes envisioned in intelligent home systems are automation, connectivity, wireless networking, entertainment, energy and water conservation, and information access."

An intelligent home system is easily envisaged with separate agents controlling the separate subsystems such as heating, lighting, air conditioning, security, and entertainment, and the agents interacting to facilitate the comfort and convenience of the home owner. Here are some small examples. When the phone rings, the entertainment agent could be aware and turn down the volume of any loud music in the vicinity. An alarm clock set to wake up the home owner for an early morning flight could reset the alarm after it contacted the airport and discovered that the flight was delayed. A security system could track any person in the house. If the person in the house was not recognized by the system, an intruder alert could be initiated, whereby the home owner and the police were contacted, provided with a photo of the intruder, and any visitors or tradespeople scheduled to visit the house were warned to stay away. Some of these example scenarios will be elaborated in chapter 9.

The intelligent home needs knowledge about the technical devices, including their communication capabilities, parameters that can be set, and functions that they can achieve. The intelligent home also needs to be aware of legal and social restrictions. Examples are not playing music too loudly late at night, and not running automatic watering systems in gardens during times of severe water restrictions. The home also needs considerable general knowledge.

We turn to e-commerce. According to Wikipedia (October 11, 2006), e-commerce "consists primarily of the distributing, buying, selling, marketing, and servicing of products or services over electronic systems such as the Internet. . . . It can involve electronic funds transfer, supply chain management, e-marketing, online marketing, online transaction processing, electronic data interchange (EDI), automated inventory management systems, and automated data collection systems. . . . It typically uses electronic communications technology such as the Internet, extranets, email, e-books, databases, catalogues, and mobile phones."

E-commerce in its broadest sense is already a big business. Buyers and sellers, both institutions and individuals, can and should clearly be modeled as agents. They form organizations such as company hierarchies, virtual enterprises, and markets. Interaction protocols such as auctions are relevant for modeling and understanding the behaviors of such organizations and their constituent individual agents. A key activity to be understood is negotiation, which has been thoroughly studied in the agent community. E-commerce also implies agents' detailed knowledge about their environment, which consists of environment objects, such as Enterprise Resource Planning (ERP) and Enterprise Application Integration (EAI) systems, servers, Web services, and databases. In business processes are also relevant cultural values, products, and their pricing. All these examples show the complexity of multiagent systems. Business-to-business e-commerce is illustrated in chapter 8.

1.4   What Is Modeling?

The underlying motivation of this book is to help people write software that can work effectively in the modern software context, such as a sophisticated smart home or global e-commerce. To deal with the complexities in such environments, we need to model the systems, highlighting which features are important for the software and how they will be enacted and which features can be ignored.

This section addresses modeling, or the construction and description of models. Modeling is empowering in a practical sense. If you can model, you are a significant part of the way to building something useful.

Let us consider the question: "What is a model?" A definition taken from the Web is that a model is a "hypothetical description of a complex entity or process." A model is constructed to aid in building the system that we have in mind. To paraphrase Parnas's well-known characterization of specifications, a model should be as complex as it needs to be to reflect the issues the system is being built to address, but no more complex.

What are some examples of models? A common school project for primary school children is to build a model of the solar system. In such a model, there is at least some depiction of individual planets, and the sun. More detailed models may include moons of planets and asteroids. More advanced students may try and get some idea of distance of planets from the sun, by either placing the planets in an order, or with some scaled representation of distance. Yet more ambitious students may add a dynamic element to the model by having the planets move around their orbit. Building a good model of the solar system clearly stretches the abilities of primary school children—and usually their parents.

Many years ago, Leon had the experience of visiting a steel plant in northern Ohio to pitch a project to build an expert system that could troubleshoot flaws while making steel. He was accompanied by a professor of mechanical engineering, who was offering to build a model of the steel plant. The model would be built at a consistent scale, and would involve pouring liquid from a model of the steel furnace and transporting the molten steel in carts on a track to the location where it would be shaped into sheets. Key discussion points were the layout of the plant, viscosity of the model liquid, and what aspects of the model would be useful for the engineers ultimately designing and building the plant, so that they could be confident the plant would work correctly from the moment it started operating.

Kuldar had the experience of visiting the Melbourne Museum and seeing a display of gold mining. The model of the gold mine at the museum was a useful way of visualizing how the gold mine would have operated in its heyday. Without the model, it would have been difficult to understand.

These examples are of tangible, concrete models. The world of software is more abstract, and accordingly, more abstract models are needed to help envisage and build software systems. We note that software professionals or computing students, the likely readers of this book, possibly spend less time thinking about models than other engineering disciplines or construction areas. Perhaps they don't think in terms of models at all.

One field in which modeling has been used is the development of object-oriented systems. It is usual to build a UML description, which is in fact a model. UML is an acronym for Unified Modeling Language, which reminds us of its modeling nature. UML models can be checked and reviewed to see whether the system is understood and correct before code is generated and the system implemented. Modeling notations for systems built in a procedural style have also been developed, but are perhaps not as widely used.

Models abstract information. For object-oriented programming, interfaces between classes are given, and the actual data passing mechanisms are finalized when the code is implemented. The model limits what we focus on at various stages of the software development life cycle.

To summarize this section, we advocate building appropriate models in order to understand how to design and implement a complex system. It is essential to have intuitively understandable models. The models must have sufficient detail to be useful, but not so much detail as to overwhelm.

1.5   Systems Engineering

How does one build a multiagent system? The research community has diverse opinions on what to emphasize. The conference title of an early set of workshops devoted to all things "agency," ATAL, reflects that diversity of opinion. ATAL is an acronym for Agent Theory, Architecture, and Languages. The theoreticians claim that once the theory is established, the practice will be straightforward to implement, and so emphasis should be on theory. The architects claim that if you have the right architecture, all the rest will follow. The language developers claim that given the right programming language, it is straightforward for agent developers to build multiagent systems.

This book makes a different claim. A multiagent system is a system with a significant software component. We must build on what has been learned about developing software over the last forty years. The perspective that needs to be taken for building multiagent systems is a software engineering perspective, which we loosely identify with a systems engineering perspective. So we choose not to focus on theory, architecture, or language, though of course we don't ignore them. Indeed, chapters 5 and 7 discuss some of the architectures, languages, and tools that have emerged from agent research and development.

In this section, we give some motivation for software and systems engineering, a field often slighted and misunderstood by computer scientists and AI researchers. We mention the software engineering life cycle, which motivates the models that we discuss in chapter 3 and illustrate in our examples. We also relate the software engineering life cycle to the systems engineering life cycle by using the analogy of constructing a building. Chapter 4 discusses quality, an important issue to consider when taking a software engineering perspective.

To gain a perspective of software engineering, we offer the following analogy. Consider the task of building a small shed for storage in the backyard of a house, a common hobby for men, especially in previous decades. Many men and women could be successful with this task, particularly if they have a practical bent. However, just because someone built such a storage shed would not immediately qualify him or her to build a thirty-floor office building. There is extra knowledge needed about building materials, structures, and regulations—to mention just a few issues. Now consider the task of writing a computer program to process data. Many men and women could be successful with this task, particularly if they have a technical bent. However you wouldn't automatically trust that person to program an air traffic control system. The missing discipline and knowledge is loosely covered in the area of software engineering.

A definition of software engineering developed for Engineers Australia is "a discipline applied by teams to produce high-quality, large-scale, cost-effective software that satisfies the users' needs and can be maintained over time."

Significant words and phrases in the definition include *discipline*, which implies an underlying body of knowledge; *users*, which implies the need for requirements; *teams*, which implies the need for communications and interfaces; *over time*, which implies that the system should be able to be changed without becoming brittle; *high-quality*, which suggests performance criteria, not only functional capabilities; and *large-scale*, which means different architectural consideration about performance and other qualities. Understanding costs and trade-offs in design will be important. Also important will be recognizing the needs of stakeholders, not only users.

Although all aspects of software engineering are not explicitly addressed, we have been influenced by taking a software engineering view. Models have been proposed that we believe can be understood by a variety of stakeholders at varying levels of abstraction. We take a systems view because multiagent system designers and developers should have a broad awareness of how the software they are designing and building interacts with other hardware, software, and agents more generally.

We presume that the multiagent system will follow a systems development life cycle. There will be a stage of gathering requirements. Once the requirements have been elicited, they are analyzed. The analysis goes hand in hand with design, where trade-offs are expected to be needed to allow the building of a system that meets users' requirements, both functional and nonfunctional. The system must be implemented, tested, and maintained. Explicit languages, methodologies, and tools for the latter stages are presented in chapters 5 and 7. But the models of chapter 3 and 4 have been developed in the belief that good engineering practices can be followed.

As discussed in section 1.3, this book takes a systems engineering approach by conceiving of the final product as a system. *Systems engineering* has been defined as the process of specifying, designing, implementing, validating, deploying, and maintaining sociotechnical systems. A useful analogy is the process of constructing a building. When someone plans the building of a house, the first thing that needs to be done is a sketch. The sketch roughly specifies the location, size, shape, and purpose of the building and the layout and purposes of its rooms. It proceeds from conversations between the customer and architect.

Next, the architect turns the sketch into the architect's drawings, which include floor plans, cutaways, and pictures of the house-to-be. The purpose of the drawings is to enable the owner to relate to them and either agree or disagree with its different parts and aspects. We can call this process *requirements engineering*, because its main purpose is to understand and specify requirements for the building. Moreover, as the architect normally creates the drawings by using a computer-aided design (CAD) system of some sort, it could also be possible to simulate some aspects of the building, such as how doors and windows are opened, or what kind of interior and functionalities the building should include. Both the sketch and the architect's drawings model the final product—the building—from the *owner's perspective*.

As the next step, the architect's drawings are turned into the architect's plans. The plans constitute the *designer's perspective* of the final product. They consist of detailed descriptions of the building-to-be from different aspects, including site work, plumbing, electrical systems, communication systems, masonry, wood structure, and so forth. The architect's plans specify the materials to be used for construction work and serve as a basis for negotiation with a general contractor.

Finally, the contractor transforms the architect's plans into the contractor's plans, which represent the *builder's perspective*. The contractor's plans essentially provide a "how to build it" description. They define the order of building activities and consider the technology available to the contractor. There can also be the so-called shop plans, which are out-of-context specifications of the parts, or functional areas that are outsourced to subcontractors.

A systems engineering process is in many ways similar to the process of constructing a building. First, we sketch the system as situated in its environment. The models employed for this purpose may, for example, include *use cases*—a means of specifying required usages of a system. This is the system modeled from the *owner's perspective*. The owner's perspective may also comprise scenarios that can be simulated. The *designer's perspective* consists of various models that describe from different aspects how the system should be designed. A standard widely accepted by the software industry for this purpose is UML. The *builder's perspective* is based on the designer's perspective, but considers specific languages, technologies, and tools to be used and defines the order of systems engineering activities. Changing perspectives is not always straightforward. For example, a designer has to consider the languages, technologies, and tools of the problem domain.

The order in which we represent an agent-oriented modeling process in this book has been influenced by the systems engineering perspective. Different kinds of models to be presented in Chapter 3 are to allow inclusion of different perspectives of the system.

1.6   Emergent Behavior

Models proceed from the requirements of an owner to the design expertise of a designer, and are then handed over to a developer to be implemented and deployed. Implicit in this previous sentence, and indeed in our discussion in this chapter, has been that building a multiagent system proceeds from the top down. If the three stakeholders—the owner, the designer, and developer—are different people, it is more natural for the order to proceed top-down. It is possible, though not advisable, for development of a system to proceed from the bottom up. The developer can implement a system, which can retrospectively be designed, and the underlying motivation and purpose be determined through use. This makes some sense if the three perspectives are that of the same person, and the bottom-up approach essentially becomes rapid prototyping. Otherwise, the owner is completely dependent on the will of the developer.

To contrast the top-down and bottom-up approaches, let us reconsider the example of building a house. The top-down approach starts with the goal of building a house with particular objectives. These days, for example, one objective might be to be environmentally friendly. The objectives are explained to an architect, who comes up with a design. The design is then fully specified and agreed upon and given to a builder to construct. The bottom-up approach has builders starting to build. This is presumably what happens in the insect world. Termites build quite complex nests for the termite colony to live in, assembled from the bottom up. To the best of our knowledge, there is no "head termite" with an overall plan. Rather, the nest emerges from the simple behavior of the termites. This is sometimes called *emergent behavior* or *self-organizing behavior*.

Emergent behavior is not just a feature of the insect world. City life or group culture is often emergent. Creative cities work by collocating a group of people and hoping that synergies happen. Several successful cities have developed in this way throughout history.

We are aware of two classes of agent-oriented applications in which an exploratory, bottom-up approach is natural, and in which there has been extensive research. One is the field of mobile robots. Two of the agents discussed in section 1.2, the Roomba vacuum cleaner and the AIBO robotic dog, are essentially mobile robots. Vacuum cleaning can be approached both from the top down and from the bottom up. Top-down, there is a clear overall goal of removing dust, especially from carpets. At the design stage, deciding which agent cleans which surface needs to be determined. Then appropriate devices are deployed. Bottom-up, a vacuuming device is built. How well it works is factored in and other steps may be needed either to improve the overall quality goal, or to augment the cleaning with other devices. Roomba clearly fits in the bottom-up stage. Similarly, AIBO is a robotic pet designed with particular capabilities that it is hoped are entertaining to the owners that buy them. Although Sony, the manufacturer, clearly had design specifications, once they are in an environment, they interact in their own way.

The second class of examples in which emergent behavior is interesting is that of simulation and modeling. To give an example, suppose that one was holding a large sport event with tens of thousands of attendees. One would like to know whether the event was suitably hosted. One way to do this is to build a model and run it to see what behaviors by attendees may emerge.

Many researchers have investigated "ant algorithms," which are essentially bottom-up explorations by simple agents to achieve an objective. Such algorithms are interesting and worthy of further research. We do not explore them, or the larger issue of emergent behavior, any further in this book. For additional information, the reader is referred to De Wolf and Holvoet 2005.

1.7   A Quick History of Programming Paradigms

We used the previous sections to set the development of agent concepts in context.
We mentioned in section 1.2 that agents connote intelligent assistance. The desire to
create intelligence in a computer has been a constant theme for computing, dating
back to Alan Turing, the father of computer science. Sixty years of research on computing, fifty years of research in AI, and forty years of research in software engineering are all relevant to how agents are conceptualized and deployed. We give a brief
history here.

Early computing research focused on programming, not modeling. The earliest
programming languages reflected a procedural view of the computer world. Programmers wrote instructions in the languages for the computer, which was envisaged
as a machine for executing a sequence of instructions. Analysts, perhaps loosely
equivalent to modelers, used flow charts to represent the instructions that needed to
be followed at a more abstract level.

Early computer languages, such as Fortran and COBOL, typify the procedural
view. A business application written in COBOL could be viewed as a collection of
financial agents cooperating to produce a business report. The analyst, however,
had to specify the complete control flow for the coder, and there was no advantage
in the agent perspective. It is worth noting that the SWARMM system mentioned
earlier in this chapter superseded a system written in Fortran. It was hard to maintain the Fortran system and very difficult to engage with the end users—the pilots.
The agent-oriented system worked much better.

Object orientation is an alternate to the procedural view of computing. It views a
program as a collection of objects sending messages to each other rather than as a
sequential list of instructions. Though object-oriented languages such as Simula
appeared as early as the 1960s, the popularity of object-oriented computing grew
through Smalltalk and especially C++ only in the 1980s. By the 1990s, object orientation had become the preferred paradigm for developing applications for a distributed, complex world.

It is plausible to view agent-oriented computing as an extension of object-oriented
computing. Amusingly, agents have been described as "objects on steroids." Such a
description, however, is not helpful for developers, or politically correct in a climate
of cracking down on drugs in sport. In our experience teaching programming, trying
to understand one paradigm in terms of another often limits one's understanding. Indeed, some of the models to be described in chapter 3 were prompted by a need to
differentiate them from object-oriented models that students were using without
gaining an appreciation of how to think from an agent perspective. So although we
do appropriate some object-orientation notation in our models, we downplay the

connection between the agent-oriented and object-oriented ways of thinking in this book.

The meteoric rise of the Internet's popularity and the need to deploy applications on a variety of platforms led to the emergence and popularity of Java. To some extent, Java is an object-oriented applications development language, in contrast to C++, which is more of an object-oriented systems development language. Java's simplification of network interactions has made it popular for developing agent applications, as has its platform independence. It is no coincidence that most of the agent programming languages described in chapter 5 are built on Java.

Having described Java as a language suitable for developing applications, we briefly mention scripting languages. These languages make it quick to develop and deploy applications. Some have been developed for agents such as the now-defunct Telescript and Aglets from IBM. Using a scripting language tends to discourage thinking in terms of systems and models. Although we are not averse to people using scripting languages, such languages are not relevant to the book and are not discussed further.

We turn now to another programming paradigm: declarative programming. The declarative paradigm has been influential in agent research. It is connected with the body of work in formalizing agent behavior using various logics. Early researchers in AI advocated the physical symbol system hypothesis, that a machine manipulating physical symbols had the necessary and sufficient means to be intelligent and exhibit intelligent behavior. Lisp was an early programming language that was adopted in applications that manipulated symbols.

Predicate logic was natural to use when taking a symbolic view. A prototypical AI project conducted from 1966 to 1972 at the Artificial Intelligence Center at what was then the Stanford Research Institute in the United States is illustrative. The project centred on a mobile robot system nicknamed Shakey. Shakey moved around in a physical environment consisting of makeshift "rooms" and blocks that could be pushed from room to room. Shakey can definitely be considered an agent.

Part of the project involved Shakey formulating and executing plans to move blocks from room to room. Shakey's world was described in terms of logic formulae such as `in(room1,shakey)`, denoting that Shakey was in room 1. The planning problem for Shakey was to move blocks from room to room. Knowing which room the robot was in was a challenge for the vision system of the time, but that need not concern us here. The planning problem was formulated in terms of STRIPS (Stanford Research Institute Problem Solver) operators. Operators were expressed in terms of preconditions, which needed to be true if the operator were applicable, and postconditions, which became true after the operator was executed. For example, an operator's instruction `move(block1, room1, room2)` might be invoked to move block1 from room 1 to room 2. The precondition would be that Shakey was in room 1, and the postcondition that Shakey was in room 2 and no longer in room 1. Of course, the operators were expressed more generically. Planning was stringing together a sequence of operators that could achieve a desired state. STRIPS, the planning approach, is intuitive, and has been influential in AI.

Shakey's system is declarative, in the sense that the system developer merely expressed (declared) a set of operators. The underlying planning was left to the system. Declarative programming is ideal in theory. In practice, how the operators are expressed can have considerable influence on the effectiveness of the planner. The analogous declarative view of systems is to express a series of axioms as statements of logic, and leave it to an underlying theorem prover to draw the conclusions or reason appropriately. How axioms are expressed affects how well a system may perform.

Around the time of the Shakey project, experiments with theorem proving led to the development of the programming language Prolog. Prolog is a good language for many AI applications. In particular, Prolog is useful for prototyping logic reasoning systems. Several of the agent programming languages described in chapter 5 build on Prolog, or are at least influenced by it.

Formulating statements in logic and relying on an underlying theorem prover to prove whether they are correct or to generate a plan is orthogonal to the concerns of this book. Declarative programming is a good paradigm. Being precise in one's knowledge is to be commended. Also, it would be helpful, as many researchers advocate, to delegate the reasoning to some interpreter. However, considering the execution as proving a theorem masks the systems approach of how agents interact and whose responsibilities and what constraints there are, which is how we model systems. So despite the large amount of research in logic, we do not take that focus here.

There was a strong reaction to the declarative view of intelligence in the 1980s. The contrasting view was a reactive approach to achieve intelligence. The idea is to build more intelligent activities on top of core functionalities. An analogy can be made with human learning. Infants learn to walk and talk in their first years. Greater intelligence comes later, built on top of our skills in walking and talking. Our robust intelligence depends to a great degree on the robustness of the underlying mechanism. This book is not, however, a book about intelligence, but rather about models, and how they can be developed top-down as part of a systems engineering life cycle.

To summarize the chapter, we advocate conceiving of the world in which software must operate as a multiagent system operating in an environment subject to rules and policies. There will be models to reflect important aspects of multiagent systems to aid understanding. The conceptual space that we look at will be discussed in more detail in chapter 2. The models themselves will be presented in chapter 3, and applied in later chapters.

1.8   Background

The background section at the end of each chapter is where we will supply more detailed information about the references cited in each chapter, a more informal way of handling references than footnotes. It also serves as a place for suggesting further reading. Needless to say, the size and style of the background section will vary from chapter to chapter.

This first chapter sets the scene for agents. The agent paradigm has become much more prevalent over the past decade. For example, the agent metaphor is used as the unifying image for AI in the leading AI textbook by Russell and Norvig (2002).

In the late 1990s, there was a spate of survey articles about intelligent agents, which make useful additional readings. Two of the better known examples are Wooldridge and Jennings 1995 and Nwana 1995. The one most useful in our experience for graduate students is Wooldridge 1999.

A common approach to introducing agents is to spend time discussing definitions. The amusing definition of "objects on steroids" mentioned in this chapter has been introduced by Parunak (2000, p. 13). For those readers seeking a more extensive discussion of definitions, we recommend the article by Franklin and Graesser (1997). In this book, we have not agonized over the definition of an agent. In classes, votes are taken on what people regard as agents. There is always diversity, and usually some change of opinion by the end of the class. Indeed, a popular examination question used in the University of Melbourne agent class is why does it not matter that there is no exact agreed-upon definition of an agent.

The digital pet Web sites for Neopets, Webkinz, and Petz4fun mentioned in the chapter are http://www.neopets.com, http://www.webkinz.com, and http://www.petz4fun.com, respectively.

The analogy between constructing a building and developing a software system is by John Zachman (1987).

UML is defined in OMG 2007.

A place to read more about the SWARMM system is Heinze et al. 2002. More information about the STOW-97 simulation can be found in Laird et al. 1998.

Our understanding of the role of agents in the film trilogy *Lord of the Rings* came from footage on the extended DVDs of the movies. In fact, the film producer Peter Jackson explaining agents is the best endorsement of agents that we have seen.

The leading proponent of the reactive approach to intelligence is Rodney Brooks. One of the most well-known papers by him is Brooks 1991.

Another influential critic of classical AI in the 1980s was Terry Winograd. He published a book with Fernando Flores entitled *Understanding Computers and Cognition* (1986) that argued that there were limits to computer intelligence and that computers should be used to facilitate human communication. Although we don't explore the connection, philosophically, our holistic view of multiagent systems and thinking about roles, responsibilities, and constraints are in keeping with this Winograd and Flores philosophy. Their philosophy also influenced William Clancey, who developed a theory of activity that we draw on in chapters 2 and 3.

Having given the references, we'd like to comment on the following. Many of the references were acquired by searching the Web using Google. For example, the definitions of models were extracted from the answers generated from typing the question "What is a model?" into Google. The exercise was interesting and illustrates well the diversity of the use of a common English word across a range of fields. We encourage readers to try such searches for themselves.

Several of the sources were adapted or quoted directly from Wikipedia articles. Wikipedia's status as a reference of record is admittedly controversial. However, it typically reflects popular opinion, supports the impression that we are imparting of complex distributed sociotechnical systems, and is appropriate for our purposes in this chapter. It would be fun to discuss why aspects of Wikipedia are controversial relating to authorship and the ability to change records, but that is beyond the scope of this book.

The Wikipedia references on e-commerce and intelligent homes are respectively Wikipedia 2006a and 2006b. The Wikipedia reference on computer viruses is Wikipedia 2006c.

Exercises for Chapter 1

1. Discuss which of the following you would consider an agent, and explain why or why not. If you are unfamiliar with the example, try looking it up on the Internet.

• The Furby toy

• The Australian device for autonomously cleaning swimming pools, known as a Kreepy Krauly

• An unmanned aerial vehicle (UAV)

• A search engine such as Google

2. Identify the various agents involved in the following:

• A book publishing company

- A university
- A church or your local religious organization
- Australia, Estonia, or a country of your choice

3. Search the Internet for an application of agents in an area of personal interest.

4. The robotic soccer competition was augmented by having a competition, called RoboCup Rescue, for teams of robots working in a rescue site. This was partly triggered by the devastation caused by the Kobe earthquake in 1995. Discuss what needs to be modeled to make such a competition useful. What features should be included in a model?

5. Consider what would be useful to model in the transportation system of your city.

2 Concepts

The first chapter discussed the complex world in which software and people interoperate and the rationale for agents and a multiagent system perspective. In this chapter, we map out the conceptual landscape that underlies the book. This is not a mathematical treatment, but rather a carefully worded description. We explain concepts descriptively. In chapter 3, we give an extended example that shows how the concepts apply in practice.

After covering the conceptual landscape, we provide some ontological grounding for the chosen modeling notions. This helps the reader to understand how the modeling notions that we have chosen relate to the attempts to represent the real world as precisely as possible using ontologies.

2.1 The Conceptual Space

As introduced in chapter 1, this book is concerned with modeling systems with multiple agents, both human and manmade, interacting with a diverse collection of hardware and software in a complex environment. The term "sociotechnical system" has sometimes been used to indicate such systems. A *sociotechnical system* has been defined as one that includes hardware and software; has defined operational processes; and offers an interface, implemented in software, to human users. However, we prefer to call it simply a "system."

When thinking about the world, people form sets of interrelated concepts. Such concept sets are often implicit. We believe they should be made explicit in designing and building multiagent systems. Prompted by our desire for explicit concepts, we introduce a *conceptual space* within which to view systems. The conceptual space is an open concept set for systems engineering rather than a fixed concept set. By "open," we mean that new concepts can be added and existing ones replaced or deleted.

The conceptual space consists of three layers: a motivation layer, a system design layer, and a deployment layer. They embody the owner's perspective, designer's perspective, and builder's perspective on systems engineering, which were discussed in chapter 1. A design process in systems engineering can be understood as transforming the models of the motivation layer into the models of the system design layer. Likewise, an implementation process is the transformation of design models into the models of the deployment layer—deployment models. A depiction of the conceptual space and the design and implementation processes is given in figure 2.1.

We describe the three layers from the highest to the lowest as drawn in the figure. The *motivation layer* contains abstract modeling concepts needed for defining requirements and purposes of a system. Arguably, the most foundational are the *goals* of the system, which must be modeled, as well as *roles* for achieving the goals. For example, a home security system has the goal "Handle intruder" and the role of Security Manager. Goals and roles are further addressed in section 2.2.

The *system design layer* consists of the notions required for modeling and designing a sociotechnical system. The central one among them is the concept of *agents*. We define an *agent* as an autonomous entity situated in an environment capable of both perceiving the environment and acting on it. Each agent belongs to some *agent type* that in turn is related to one or more roles from the motivation layer. Agent types are determined by the system to be designed; roles belong to the problem domain. Agents enact roles by performing *activities*. Each activity instantiates some *activity type* that specifies functionalities defined by goals at the motivation layer. For example, in a home security system, activities of types "Identify intruder" and "Respond" realize the respective goals. They are performed by one or more agents enacting the role of Security Manager. We further discuss agents and activities in section 2.3.

Agents and activities are situated in an environment that is represented at the *deployment layer* of the conceptual space shown in figure 2.1. For example, greeting someone at home is different from greeting a person in a workplace. On the other hand, agents are not just surrounded by the environment but form parts of it. Environment is thus the real material world inhabited by various kinds of entities. The environment is treated in more detail in section 2.4.

The conceptual space naturally comprises the owner's, designer's, and builder's perspectives on systems engineering and the analysis, design, and implementation processes of systems engineering.

2.2   Roles, Goals, and Organizations

The fundamental concept underlying this book is that of an agent that is actively situated in an environment. The agent is assumed as being purposeful. Where does the purpose come from? The deliberate choice within our conceptual space is that purpose is modeled within the motivation layer. This section describes the concepts from the motivation layer—namely goals, roles, and aggregates such as

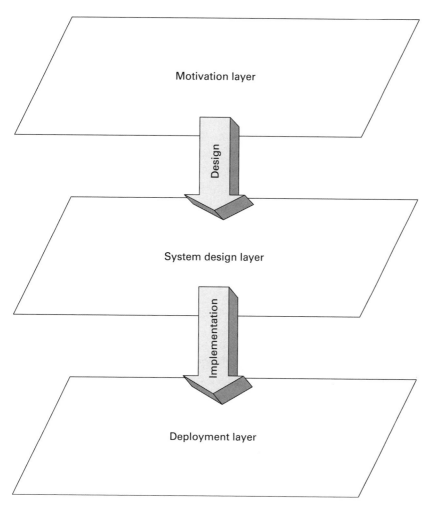

Figure 2.1
The layers and processes of the conceptual space

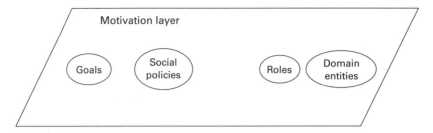

Figure 2.2
The motivation layer

organizations—that determine social policies. The motivation layer is depicted in
figure 2.2.

The models of goals, roles, and organizations refer to knowledge about the problem domain of the system to be designed. At the motivation layer, such knowledge is
represented as a set of domain entities and relationships between them. Though domain knowledge is distributed throughout the conceptual space, we choose to depict
it at the motivation layer; we explain this concept more in chapter 3 when describing
our models in detail.

How does one express the purpose of an agent? This difficult question has
absorbed the attention of many philosophers over thousands of years. For this
reason, we almost called the motivation layer "the metaphysical layer," but later on
decided to downplay the philosophical side.

The two primary concepts that we use throughout the book are goals and roles.
"Goals" and "roles" are both common words. They have been appropriated by
many agent and other computing researchers to use in a technical sense—often in
quite different ways. So we will discuss these terms at some length.

A *goal* can be defined as a situation description that refers to the intended state of
the environment. For example, in the case of dealing with an intruder within an intelligent home, the goal of handling an intruder denotes the state of the environment
where an intruder has been noticed, identified, and the case has been handed over to
the police or security company.

Goals are measurable—how else do you know when you have attained your goal?
However, we still want to express an aspirational side of goals. Reflecting a compromise, a goal has also been dubbed "a dream with a deadline."

Goals are based on *motives*. For human agents, there is a variety of motives. They
are generally divided into *physiological*, *psychological*, *interactional*, and *intellectual*
motives. Examples of physiological motives are hunger, sexual attraction, and fa-
tigue. Examples of psychological motives are stress or other emotions, ambitions,
and aesthetic pleasure. Finally, examples of interactional and intellectual motives are

the respective needs for interpersonal relationships and curiosity. Manmade agents may have simulated motives. For example, a Tamagotchi may perform certain activities out of "hunger" or because it has "pee need." A Tamagotchi may then be seen as having a goal to get its need satisfied by a certain time, or otherwise it will "become sick."

Goals can be categorized into achievement goals, cease goals, maintaining goals, avoidance goals, and optimization goals. *Achievement goals* and *cease goals* are respectively targeted at achieving or ceasing a certain state of affairs or world state, *maintaining goals* and *avoidance goals* respectively aim at preserving or avoiding a certain state of affairs, and *optimization goals* strive for maximizing or minimizing a specific optimization function. For example, in air traffic management, there can be an achievement goal to allocate the airport resources, a maintaining goal to maintain a minimal distance between landing planes, an avoidance goal to avoid simultaneous landings on crossing runways, and an optimization goal to have an optimal mixture of takeoff sequence and departure flow.

Goals can be measurable, to a greater or lesser extent. For example, the goal of playing soccer can be to win a soccer game or to have fun, or both at the same time. We have decided to represent goals that are not easily measured as quality goals. A *quality goal*, as its name implies, is a nonfunctional or quality requirement of the system. For example, in air traffic management, we may have an optimization goal of maximal safety, for which it might be hard to construct an optimization function. However, there may also be a quality goal of achieving maximal throughput of the airport, the attainment of which is easier (but not simple) to measure.

Goals are expressed by using nouns, verbs, and (optionally) adjectives. The noun tends to be more of a state, and the verbs more into the activities that are needed to achieve a goal. For example, there can be a goal to have a million dollars or become rich. However, sometimes it may be reasonable to represent the state to be achieved as a quality goal associated with a functional goal. For example, in the New Testament, Jesus urges us to forgive each other seventy times seven times (according to most translations). Here "to forgive each other" should be modeled as a functional goal and "seventy times seven times" as a quality goal associated with it. We explain this example in more detail in section 4.5.

Goals can have subgoals. For example, in an intelligent home, a goal of handling an intruder might consist of the subgoals of noticing a person, identifying an intruder, responding, and evaluating.

We begin our treatment of roles by considering the question of how to understand behavior of an agent in a complex system. Complexity is best handled if it can be decomposed into simpler pieces. A natural decomposition of agents and their behaviors can be produced by consideration of roles. Therefore, roles characterize the functions that agents perform. To put it in a personal context, people have many roles. Leon and Kuldar are sons, husbands, fathers, teachers, students, and academics, to name just a few. Each role carries expectations. We go through a complicated, largely unconscious evaluation of which of the roles may be appropriate at a particular time, place, and circumstance, and how we fulfil the role(s) in that circumstance.

We emphasize the naturalness of considering roles. We are involved in role-play from an early age. Children play mothers and fathers, house, doctors and nurses, and teachers and school. We will not develop the psychological implications of role-play, but we reiterate that role as a concept is very natural to help understand behavior in simple and especially in complicated systems.

What is a role? This perhaps is the least clear for the reader, as in the agent and computing literatures the term is used in many senses. We define a *role* as some capacity or position that facilitates the system to achieve its goals. In our view, roles express functions, expectations, and obligations of agents enacting them. We encompass these senses in the term *responsibilities*, which determine what an agent enacting the role *must* do in order for a set of goals and quality goals to be achieved. In addition, a role may also have *constraints* specifying conditions that the role must take into consideration when performing its responsibilities. For example, in an intelligent home, the role of home security manager has responsibilities to detect the presence of a person in the environment, to check the house schedule for strangers scheduled to be there, to record an image of the person, and so on. The same role also has constraints that the owner and each person pointed out by him/her needs to provide in advance personal information (face) to be recognized, that a subject to be detected needs to be visible within the camera's image area, and that the owner must maintain the house schedule, among others.

A natural way of expressing some of the behaviors of roles is scenarios. A common game that Leon played with his daughters and that Kuldar occasionally still plays with his daughters, admittedly reluctantly in both cases, is house. How do you play house? You assign roles, such as mother (mummy or mommy depending on your country and culture), daddy, big sister, and so on, and then enact scenarios. For kids, enacting scenarios is a way of coming to terms with things and processes in the world.

We define a *scenario* as the specification of a purposeful sequence of activities by the agents involved. By purposefulness, we mean that a scenario has to achieve a goal specified in the goal model. For example, the intruder-handling scenario includes an activity of type "Handle intruder" performed by the enactor of the role of home security manager and its subactivities of identifying an intruder and responding, which achieve the goal of handling an intruder with its associated quality goals. Scenarios are thus derived from goals by specifying how they map into activities and the order of performing the activities. We talk more about scenarios and propose a way to model them in section 3.8.

Another natural concept that manifests itself from childhood is that of an *organization*. A dictionary (Apple Dictionary 2.0.2) gives the definition of "an organized body of people with a particular purpose." We find ourselves in numerous organizations. Some are inevitable, such as families and schools. Some are optional, such as sporting clubs or religious groups. Some are community-based and provide services, such as police, garbage removal, or, more abstractly, government. Several of the organizations may overlap.

Roles aggregate into organizations, because an agent may need to rely on other agents for fulfilling its responsibilities defined by the goals of the corresponding role. For example, the roles of wife and husband constitute the core of a family organization.

Different kinds of organizations can be distinguished depending on the types of relationships between roles. The three example types of organizations are hierarchies, markets, and networks. In a *hierarchy*, the enactor of a parent role delegates some of its responsibilities to the enactors of its children roles. In this case, the enactor of a child role cannot decide which responsibilities it will get but must accept whichever responsibilities are delegated to it by the agent playing its parent role. An example of a hierarchical organization is a traditional family, in which the husband may delegate responsibilities to a wife, but never the other way round. An organization of this type has the *control relationship* between a parent role and its children roles.

In a *market*, each agent can choose its responsibilities so that they best fit the goals and quality goals applying to the agent. For example, in an auction, the organizer announces the responsibilities to be fulfilled and the participants bid thereafter. This organization type is based on *benevolence relationships* between self-interested roles, in which an agent performing a role offers to fulfil responsibilities for an agent performing another role whenever it appears beneficial to it.

In a *network*, a responsibility can either be delegated by the enactor of a parent role or requested by the enactor of a child role, which means that those roles have equal status. For example, in a modern family, the husband can delegate his responsibilities to the wife, as well as the other way around (with the exception of giving birth to children). This implies *peer relationships* between equal roles.

Scale is a key factor in considering organizational structure. To use a biblical example, the Israelites in the desert had a flat structure for making judgments. All questions were referred to a single judge, Moses. His father-in-law, Jethro, pointed out that a single judge didn't scale if the number of complaints increased, and that Moses was being worn out from all the judgments. This realization led to a hierarchical structure with chiefs for groups of tens, fifties, hundreds, and thousands.

Roles can also be related by means of an *authorization* relationship, in which an agent playing a role needs to be empowered to fulfil its responsibilities by an agent playing another role. For example, there is an authorization relationship between the roles of security manager and owner meaning that the security manager requires an authorization from the owner in order to enter the house.

Responsibilities of roles often map to *social relators*—sets of *commitments* and *claims*—between agents playing the roles. For example, in a modern family, the wife may delegate to the husband the responsibility of looking after their children for a particular time period. This delegation means that the husband has a commitment toward his wife to look after the children in that period and the wife conversely has a claim against her husband to fulfil the responsibility delegated to him. Relationships between roles can thus be described by the sets of commitments and claims that may occur between the agents playing the roles. Checking and enforcing commitments are difficult tasks, and it is really a research topic to see how they might be implemented. However, one of the methodologies to be addressed in chapter 7 provides at least a partial solution to this.

Organizations constrain the achievement of goals, and the formation and satisfaction of commitments and claims by agents within them by means of *social policies*. For example, the social policy of binding commitments may apply to the goal of negotiating a deal. This social policy requires that if agents agree on a deal, they should not be allowed to *decommit* on that deal. Social policies can be modeled as quality goals over functional goals. For example, the social policy of binding commitments can be represented as a quality goal "commitment is binding" attached to the goal to "negotiate a deal." Social policies can be modeled as scenarios, for example, how to greet members of the royal family or behavior patterns at a social event. Social policies can also be embedded in the responsibilities and constraints of roles.

In general, we are influenced by social policies. For example, in different countries, how to tip, an example of a social policy, can pose a real problem for travelers. To make things simpler, in some countries a tip in the form of a service tax is automatically added to one's invoice. In Estonia, there is the social policy of bringing flowers to a wedding ceremony. As another example, in many Asian countries there is the social policy of handling business cards with two hands.

Social policies sometimes are blurred with roles and knowledge. For example, while how much to tip is a social policy, it is also a piece of knowledge relevant for the role of customer. Social policies can be evaluated by different quality attributes attached to them, such as security, privacy, fairness (in the context of a market organization), and efficiency, which affect activities that agents are engaged in.

Social policies can be anything from access rights, to social norms or obligations. Social policies are identified based on the relationships and dependencies between

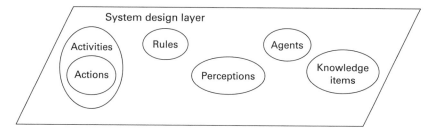

Figure 2.3
The system design layer

roles. When we turn goals and the related responsibilities of roles into scenarios, these scenarios must be defined in a manner consistent with social policies. For example, the scenario of talking to someone may be affected by the social policy about waiting until someone stops speaking. Similarly, the scenario of greeting elders in some Asian societies is very sophisticated, and sometimes opaque. In an intelligent home, the scenario of handling an intruder must include consideration of the safety of the homeowner and his or her family and possible visitors.

Policies of the motivation layer are reflected in the rules of the system design layer. Just having rules may be sufficient for most uses of a system. Having the policy is helpful when knowing whether it is appropriate to break the rules.

2.3 Agents and Activities

Agents and activities are modeled at the conceptual space's system design layer, which is shown in figure 2.3. The system design layer provides the concepts necessary for modeling agents and their activities. The concepts used for modeling at the system design layer are types. Ideally, the instances of these types could be directly implemented. However, to reflect the diversity of implementation techniques, like programming languages and platforms, the types modeled at the system design layer are related to the corresponding types of concrete agents and objects represented at the deployment layer. For example, agent types used in modeling can be related to software agent types represented in a particular programming language. Nevertheless, in modeling it may be useful to talk about hypothetical instances or occurrences of the types modeled at the system design layer. This is reflected by the depiction of the system design layer in figure 2.3 and by the discussion in this section.

Agents are entities that enact roles. Roles are discussed in the previous section. We define an *agent* as an entity that can act in the environment, perceive events, and reason. Events that an agent perceives by, for instance, receiving a message or sensing a

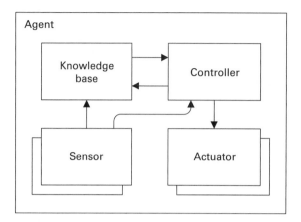

Figure 2.4
An abstract agent architecture

temperature change, are caused by agents or other entities in the environment. Conversely, through acting, agents can affect entities in the environment. By reasoning, we mean drawing inferences appropriate to the situation.

We can ascribe to an agent a *mental state*. By doing so, we can attribute to it *anthropomorphic qualities* like beliefs, responsibilities, expectations, capabilities, goals, desires, and intentions, and *social relators*, such as commitments and claims. An example of an agent with anthropomorphic qualities and social relators is a Tamagotchi, the popular digital pet which was mentioned in section 1.2 and described in more detail in section 3.1. It becomes hungry; it needs to go to the bathroom; it has to be entertained; it needs to associate with other Tamagotchis and humans; and so on. The owner of a Tamagotchi effectively has commitments against it and the Tamagotchi, conversely, has claims against its owner, or otherwise the Tamagotchi—a creature appearing on the screen of the physical toy—ceases to function, or, as the manufacturers describe it, dies. As Kuldar and his daughters Eliise and Sanne have felt, for a human, it is surprisingly easy to begin feeling guilty about his or her behavior toward a digital pet that cannot even speak. Because it is just a toy, however, a new Tamagotchi can be "hatched" within the toy.

We demonstrate our view of agents by presenting a simple abstract agent architecture, shown in figure 2.4. An agent receives information from the environment, including messages from other agents, through one or more *sensors* and stores information received from them in its *knowledge base*. The agent's behavior is determined by a *controller* that performs actions affecting the environment, including messages sent to other agents, through the agent's *actuators*. The controller receives its input knowledge from the knowledge base and from the sensors. Besides acting through

```
while the agent is unfulfilled do
        sense the environment;
    update the knowledge base;
            reason;
        choose actions;
            act;
        end while
```

Figure 2.5
The execution loop of an abstract agent

actuators, the controller also performs local actions that change the knowledge stored in the agent's knowledge base.

The controller performs the execution loop depicted in figure 2.5 while the agent is unfulfilled, the meaning of which is specific to a particular agent. For example, a Tamagotchi performs the loop while it is alive. The loop involves sensing the environment and updating the agent's knowledge base accordingly, reasoning on the newly updated knowledge base, choosing actions based on the information received from the sensors (*perceptions*), the state of the knowledge base, and acting. Perceptions can directly lead to choosing actions, which is represented by the arrow from the sensors to the controller in figure 2.4.

The abstract agent architecture is refined by specific agent architectures, such as the Belief-Desire-Intention (BDI) agent architecture described in section 5.1. In the BDI architecture, an agent's actions are specified as based on its intentions that, in turn, proceed from the agent's desires and beliefs. Alternatively, actions can be specified in terms of the agent's perceptions and beliefs.

We distinguish between various categories of agents. Examples of human agents are the employees Leon and Kuldar of the University of Melbourne, the student Andrea of the same university, and the nurse who treated Kuldar yesterday, where "yesterday" denotes a time span relative to the current time. Examples of manmade agents are the Mars Exploration Rover, a Sim from the Sims game, the software agent that represents a particular company in an automated contract negotiation, an email client, and an industrial robot that performs welding a car body. We can group individual agents into *agent types*. For example, Leon and Andrea are respectively instances of the agent types `Employee` and `Student`. All the human agent examples presented are also instances of the agent type `Person`. Similarly, we can talk about the manmade agent types `ContractNegotiationAgent` and `WeldingRobot`.

The idea for this book arose from research projects devoted to software agents but later on, we have concluded that the distinction between software agents and other kinds of manmade agents can be blurry. For example, should the Mars Exploration

Rover or a Blackberry be categorized as software agents? Therefore, we prefer to talk about agents in general.

The notion of institutional agent serves as a useful modeling abstraction. We define an *institutional agent* as an aggregate that consists of internal human and manmade agents, which share collective knowledge, and that acts, perceives, and communicates through these internal agents. Examples of institutional agents are organizations, such as a bank or a hospital; organization units; and groups. Institutional agents are used in the examples of B2B electronic commerce and manufacturing in chapter 8.

Agents—and especially institutional agents—can relate to each other through commitments and claims. For example, it may be helpful to model that one institutional agent, a factory, has a commitment to provide another institutional agent, a wholesale company, with a product set. Further examples of commitments and claims are provided in chapters 7 and 8.

There is a consensus that autonomy is central to the notion of agency. An *agent* can thus be defined as an *autonomous* device, person, or software component that can interact with its environment. What do we mean by "autonomy" here? Some people define *autonomous agents* as agents that create and pursue their own agendas, as opposed to functioning under the control of another agent. Although a philosophically and psychologically important concept, it is questionable whether manmade agents pursuing their own agendas can efficiently help human agents in their daily activities. In fact, from the numerous industry-related case studies in which Leon and Kuldar have participated, they cannot remember even one where such agents were needed. Moreover, as pointed out in section 1.2, the very term "agent" stands for an entity that acts on someone's behalf rather than in a completely autonomous manner. Industry accordingly prefers to talk about *controlled autonomy*. We can conclude this discussion by saying that autonomy of an agent should be regarded as a relative rather than an absolute characteristic.

More important than the autonomy of an agent from the practical point of view is its situatedness in the environment. Agents are capable of perceiving events that occur in the environment, which includes receiving messages from other agents, and performing actions that affect the environment, which includes sending messages to other agents. This is reflected by the concepts of *perceptions* and *actions* depicted in figure 2.3.

Some authors have emphasized the notion of *intelligent agents*. According to them, an intelligent agent is required to be reactive, proactive, and social. An agent is *reactive* if it is able to perceive its environment and respond in a timely fashion to changes that occur in it. An agent is *proactive* if it does not simply act in response to its environment, but is able to exhibit opportunistic, goal-directed behavior and to take the initiative where appropriate. Finally, an agent is *social* if it is able to interact, when appropriate, with other manmade agents and humans in order to complete their own problem solving and to help others with their activities.

So, is a Tamagotchi an intelligent agent? It is certainly responsive, because it can perceive its environment through two kinds of sensors: infrared sensors and button sensors. A Tamagotchi is also social, because it is able to interact with other Tamagotchis and humans, for example, to play a game, which can be viewed as a problem-solving activity. Is a Tamagotchi proactive, as well? It certainly can exhibit behavior arising from its mental state, for example, by requiring socializing when it "feels lonely." Can this sort of behavior be characterized as goal-directed? Yes, but it is not always necessary to represent goals explicitly for modeling and representing goal-directed behavior. As we argue later in this section, explicit representation of goals is fully justified only for modeling problem-solving activities, which make up only a specific part of human activities. We conclude the discussion on intelligence by saying that Tamagotchi is certainly intelligent according to the definition presented earlier. However, this shows only Tamagotchi's conformance to the definition rather than real intelligence. As a reality check, when Kuldar posed the question "Is a Tamagotchi intelligent?" to his then eight-year-old daughter Eliise, he received a very confident "Yes" in reply!

An agent's knowledge is represented in its knowledge base by *knowledge items*. It may help in modeling to use knowledge items to determine the agent's mental state. For example, a Mars Exploration Rover has knowledge items for representing its state and location.

Agents are engaged in activities. Activities for manmade agents should be designed so that they best support activities performed by humans. Broadly speaking, an activity is what an individual agent does in its role. We daily perform all kinds of activities: sleep, eat, groom, study, write, rest, run, play, explore, swim, worship, wait, sing, clean, and so on. An *activity* can be defined as an agent's engagement situated in a specific social context that takes time, effort, and application of knowledge.

We can distinguish between *private activities*, such as walking, and *collective activities*, such as playing tennis. A *collective activity* can be defined as an activity involving agents performing two or more roles; a *private activity* is performed solely by an agent playing a particular role. As we show in chapter 8, in modeling it can be helpful to consider collective activities as being performed by institutional agents, like organizations and companies, or groups.

In a sociotechnical system, an activity can be performed by a human agent, or more generally by a biological agent, such as a dog, or by a manmade agent, such as a software agent. Sociotechnical systems exist to support human activities, such as guarding of a building, trading, planning a route, and flirting. Various kinds of agents can be involved in sociotechnical systems. For example, a building can be guarded by human(s), dog(s), or software agent(s).

As has been implied, an activity may consist of other activities—*subactivities*. At the most basic level, an activity consists of *actions*. There can be *communicative actions*, like sending a message; *physical actions*, like starting a machine; and *epistemic* (knowledge changing) *actions*, like storing the image of a potential intruder. We thus view an agent's *action* more broadly as something that the agent does and that may be perceived as an event by another agent. In particular, communicative and physical actions can be perceived as events and are thus capable of changing the environment state. For example, as we explained previously, a Tamagotchi is capable of changing the mental states of another Tamagotchi, as well as of its owner.

Each activity belongs to some *activity type*, which we define as a prototypical job function that specifies a particular way of doing something by performing elementary epistemic, physical, and communicative actions. For example, the activity of handling an intruder contains the elementary actions of taking an image of an intruder, storing it, and sending a message to the police.

The quality of performing an activity can be evaluated by *quality attributes*, such as privacy, politeness, appropriateness, and playfulness, which are derived from quality goals. Quality attributes are defined for activities like quoting a price and flirting. Quality attributes may have quantitative values such as that performance of a network was 1 MB/sec, or qualitative values such as that network performance was satisfactory. Quality is discussed in more detail in chapter 4.

Intrinsic to activities is the *context* of their performance. An activity's context can be understood as a subset of the agent's environment that is characterized by the time and space of performing the activity, as well as by other contextual activities that enclose the given activity. For example, for evaluating the quality attribute of appropriateness applied to a greeting, any enclosing activities need to be considered. For a greeting, relevant enclosing activities might be having a business lunch or celebrating a family event.

We use *situation-action rules* or simply *rules* to model when an activity is created and for how long it stays active, as well as what actions are performed in its course. Rules depend on goals and social policies that have been defined for the corresponding role(s). Rules are contained by the controller component of the abstract agent architecture represented in figure 2.4. A rule prescribes an agent's behavior in a given situation that is determined by the agent's perceptions and its mental state. For example, there can be a rule for flirting, which states that if an incoming touch has been registered (perception) and the partner is available (mental condition), the flirting activity is started. This rule may additionally require the mental condition to be true for the whole duration of the flirting activity. This flirting rule comes from the Secret Touch application described in chapter 9.

In modeling, rules are usually attached to agent types. Rules are instantiated for individual agents of these types. For example, the rule for flirting is attached to an agent type `IntimacyMediator` and is instantiated for an agent of type `Intimacy-Mediator` when it receives a message containing a touch from another agent of that type.

In addition to the most common condition-action pattern illustrated previously, there can be other rule patterns. For example, in a manufacturing control system that consists of agents representing manufacturing resources and orders, if too many order agents query a given resource agent for its availability to perform a manufacturing process step, the complete production system may slow down. In order to prevent this situation, a rule is established that measures the response time and if needed, requests the order agents to reduce their query sending intervals to minimize the number of concurrent queries. This rule has two conditions: an *activation condition*, query response time out of bounds, and an *expiration condition*, query response time within bounds.

It is helpful to distinguish between activities and tasks. We understand a *task* as a modeling construct that defines the actions performed by an agent in terms of problem solving with goals and operators—plans. Tasks and plans are further discussed in section 2.6.

2.4   Environment

Agents are deployed in a (usually preexisting) environment. An environment can be either a real physical environment or a virtual one, like a simulated environment. For example, a scenario of intruder detection can take place in a real physical environment where software entities interact with humans and physical devices like sensors and cameras. Alternatively, the same scenario can take place in a simulated environment where some events caused by the physical environment, like sensing an intruder, are simulated by software.

The environment is populated by *concrete agents* and *concrete objects*, which are shown at the deployment layer of the conceptual space in figure 2.6. By concrete agents and objects, we mean entities, which have concrete manifestations—*concretizations*—in the environment. Examples of concrete agents are a human, a robot, a dog, and a software agent, and examples of concrete objects are a book, a car, and a Web service. Concrete agents and objects subsume software agents and objects, even though it may be difficult to understand in which sense a software entity exists in the real world.

A concrete agent like a human may be a concretization of the corresponding agent modeled at the system design layer. Analogously, a concrete object of the deployment layer may correspond to a conceptual object—a kind of knowledge item—modeled at the system design layer. Concrete agents and objects belong to the respective *concrete agent types* and *concrete object types*, such as agent and object

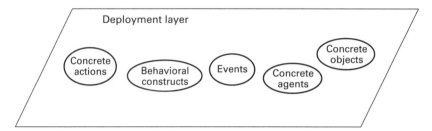

Figure 2.6
The deployment layer

types of a specific software platform. They are derived from the agent types and conceptual object types of the system design layer.

A concrete agent or object can be described by a set of attributes where an attribute is either a *numeric attribute* or a *nonnumeric attribute*. A numeric attribute, like weight, is represented quantitatively as a numerical value, while a nonnumeric attribute, like color, can be subjective and is better represented qualitatively. The ontological grounding of attributes is presented in section 2.6.

Concrete agents perform concrete actions. A concrete action performed by one agent can be perceived as an *event* by other agents. For example, a message sent by one software agent to another is perceived as a "message received" event by the latter. As another example, a security agent can perceive events such as movement in the building.

Behavioral constructs related to a particular concrete agent determine how the environment state is related to concrete actions performed by the agent. For example, a software agent representing a company in electronic trade may have a behavioral construct determining the actions to be performed upon receiving a message from the software agent of another company. The behavioral construct may state that if the message received contains a production order, it should be stored in the agent's knowledge base and a confirmation should be sent to the other agent.

Behavioral constructs of the deployment layer are based on rules of the system design layer. Behavioral constructs are represented in the language of a particular implementation platform. Some examples of agent-oriented implementation languages and platforms are provided in chapter 5.

We distinguish between a *physical environment*, like a factory floor, and a *virtual environment*, like the Internet. From the perspective of a system designer, the environment is not a passive set of entities but rather provides an exploitable design abstraction for building multiagent systems. For this purpose, the environment can be utilized in the following three ways.

First, the environment *embeds resources and services* that can be utilized by agents. For example, in the early days of human civilization, the natural environment immediately provided humans with the natural resources that they required for surviving. In our time, resources and services are provided through mediators, such as producers, wholesale and retail sellers, and service providers. In the virtual Internet environment, resources are various *information resources*, such as databases and Web sites, and services are *Web services* to be accessed by agents.

Second, the environment serves as a *container* and a *means for communication* for agents. For example, a geographical location, like a city, provides a container for human agents and institutional agents (organizations), where they can be found with the help of a phone directory. Human agents and institutional agents represented by them rely for communication on the postal and electronic services. Similarly, a software agent platform provides an agent management system, a directory facilitator, and a message transport system for software agents.

Third, the environment functions as a *coordination infrastructure* for agents. For instance, in a hospital setting, *coordination artifacts*, such as the patient's record, the patient list on the wall, and paper trays, play a crucial role in coordination of work among doctors and nurses. Coordination artifacts are especially important in the context of open systems, where the environment is subject to change, and collective goals, norms, and organizational rules must be adapted accordingly. For example, we as members of an open human society do not memorize all the rules and regulations applying to us at any given moment but instead rely on the information published by authorities, which thus becomes a coordination artefact. In software agent systems, blackboard systems were the first type of mediated interaction models proposed. In addition, tuplespaces can be used as artifacts for communication and synchronization purposes. They essentially function as logic-based blackboards that agents associatively access by writing, reading, and consuming *logic tuples*—ordered collections of heterogeneous information chunks.

We end this section by a definition stating that the *environment* is a first-class abstraction that provides the surrounding conditions for agents to exist and that mediates both the interaction among agents and the access to resources.

2.5 Relationships between the Layers

As is implied by figure 2.1, the concepts at different layers of the conceptual space are related to each other. Abstractly, a design process in systems engineering transforms models of the motivation layer into models of the system design layer. In the design process, the concepts of the motivation layer are related to corresponding concepts of the system design layer. In particular, goals are attached to activities for achieving them and also become parts of agents' knowledge. The activities consist of atomic actions, and rules are required for starting and sequencing the activities. Social policies and the responsibilities and constraints associated with roles are sources for rules. Agents are decided upon based on roles and domain entities (e.g., by coupling and cohesion analysis). Social policies also influence the agent perceptions to be modeled.

Abstractly, an implementation process is the transformation of design models into models of the deployment layer—deployment models. In the implementation process, actions of the system design layer become concrete actions of the deployment layer. Activities and rules of the system design layer are expressed as behavioral constructs that aggregate concrete actions performed by concrete agents. Concrete agents are decided based on the agents modeled at the system design layer. Perceptions of the system design layer are related to the events to be perceived and the behavioral constructs that implement perceiving. The set of knowledge items and their relationships of the system design layer are represented as concrete objects and relations between them.

The relationships between the concepts of the conceptual space are represented in figure 2.7. In chapter 6, we discuss the Model-Driven Architecture and how models can be related across layers in a three-layer conceptual framework. There are useful parallels that can be drawn with the relationships between layers as we have described them, and the relationships between types of models in the Model-Driven Architecture.

2.6   Ontological Foundations of the Conceptual Space

The preceding sections of this chapter introduced a conceptual space within which to view systems. In this section, we provide some ontological grounding for the chosen modeling notions. In the philosophical sense, *ontology* is the study of existence and modes of existence. Going through the grounding presented in this section is not needed for understanding the rest of the book, as the concepts introduced in sections 2.2, 2.3, and 2.4 can be applied to modeling without considering their ontological foundations. We have chosen not to include the formalizations of the ontological grounding, but instead refer the reader to the background information provided in section 2.7 to the sources where the formalization is readily available.

Two kinds of entities inhabit the conceptual space: universals and particulars. *Particulars* are entities that exist in reality, possessing a unique identity. Particulars can also be defined as entities that exist at least in time. They subsume physical entities that exist in both time and space, and virtual entities that exist merely in time. Examples of physical entities are humans and machines, and actions and events are examples of virtual entities. A software system exists in time, but it is debatable whether it also exists in space. On the other hand, *universals* are patterns of features, which can be realized in a number of different particulars. Universals exist neither in space nor

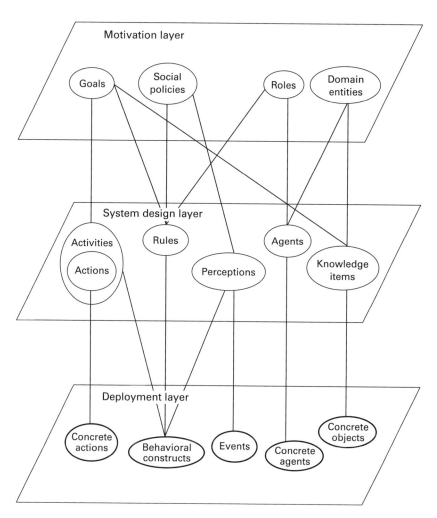

Figure 2.7
The relationships between the concepts

in time; that is, they cannot be localized. Examples of universals are mathematical objects, like numbers and sets; *modeling abstractions*, like goals and roles; as well as *types*, such as agent, object, and activity types. An alternative way of distinguishing between particulars and universals is based on the "causality criterion": universals possess no causal power, and particulars do. In this book, we assume a commonsense understanding of causality as the relationship between cause and effect.

We now describe universals and particulars. It seems to us preferable to understand the real world before attempting to create its abstractions, models. So we will start with particulars. This approach enables us to cover the most fundamental concepts first and subsequently treat the other concepts based on them.

In contrast to universals, particulars are entities and events that respectively exist or occur in the real world. The notion of the "real world" used here includes software systems. Particulars of the conceptual space are represented in figure 2.8. The figure uses the UML notation described in table 2.1 for representing generalization and aggregation relationships, as well as relationships between concepts.

There are two kinds of particulars: endurants and perdurants. The difference between the two is related to their behavior over time. To put it simply, endurants "are in time" and perdurants "happen in time." We presume a commonsense understanding of time. An *endurant* is defined as an entity that persists in time while keeping its identity. Examples are a house, a person, the moon, and a pile of sand. In contrast to this, whenever a *perdurant* is present, it is not the case that all its temporal parts are present. Examples of perdurants are a human race, a conversation, the Second World War, and a manufacturing or business process. The distinction between endurants and perdurants can be understood in terms of the intuitive distinction between things and processes. For example, the book that you are reading now is an endurant because it is present as a whole, while "your reading of the book" is a perdurant, because your reading of the previous section is not present now.

An endurant can be a physical object or an amount of matter. Particulars subsume physical entities and software entities. A *physical object*, like a house, a person, the moon, or a computer program, is a kind of endurant that satisfies a condition of unity, and one for which certain parts can change without affecting its identity. In contrast to this, an amount of matter, like a pile of sand, does not satisfy the condition of unity and, in general, cannot change any of its parts without changing its identity. A *physical agent* is a kind of physical object that can act, perceive, and reason. Physical agents subsume software agents.

To understand software agents, it is useful to compare them with (software) *objects* that are defined as computational entities that encapsulate some state, are able to perform actions or *operations* on this state, and communicate by message passing. An agent's autonomy means that an agent's behavior and its outcome may not be predictable *as observed from the outside*. For example, the criteria for buying a gift

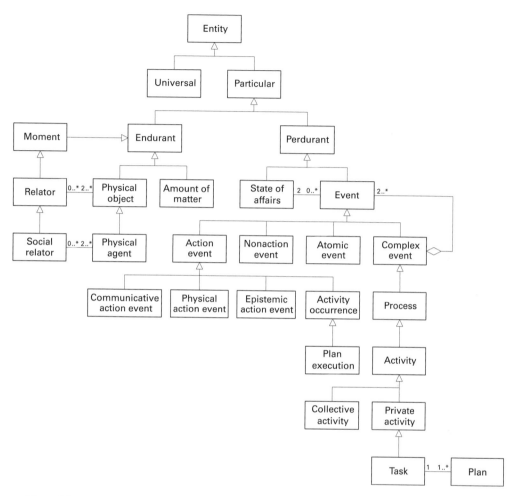

Figure 2.8
Particulars of the conceptual space

given to the shopping agent may not predict exactly what gift it will choose. In contrast, the outcome of invoking an operation attached to some object is usually more precisely defined.

In this book, we frequently refer to resources. A *resource* can be ontologically defined as a physical object used by a physical agent for achieving the goals defined for the system. Resources participate in the actions performed by agents.

Endurants are characterized by *moments*. They are endurants that are existentially dependent on other endurants, which are named their *bearers*. There are two kinds of moments: intrinsic moments and relational moments.

Table 2.1
The UML notation

Symbol	Meaning
————▷	Generalization
————◇	Aggregation
————	Relationship

An *intrinsic moment* is a special kind of moment that is existentially dependent on one single individual. For example, the color of an apple depends upon the existence of the apple itself. Intrinsic moments can be divided into qualities and mental moments.

A *quality*, like the color, height, weight, and electric charge of a physical object, or the age of a software agent, inheres in exactly one endurant and can be represented in several quality dimensions. For example, the color of an apple can be represented in terms of the dimensions of hue, saturation, and brightness. In section 4.1, we discuss the relationship of quality in this sense to the quality goals introduced in section 2.2.

A *mental moment*, like a belief, a thought, a desire, an intention, a perception, a skill, a symptom, or a headache, is a specialization of intrinsic moment referring to mental components of a physical agent. A mental moment can bear other moments, each of which can be a moment or quality. For example, Kuldar's headache can be characterized by the qualities of duration and intensity. In the context of this book, we single out the following mental moments: perception, belief, (logic) goal, desire, and intention.

A relational moment, a *relator*, like a particular flight connection between cities, a kiss, or a handshake, is an endurant that is existentially dependent on more than one physical object. Because of the topic of this book, we are especially interested in relators between physical agents, which we term *social relators*. A social relator is a kind of relator that appears between two or more physical agents. Relators and social relators are shown in figure 2.8.

We now turn to perdurants. The two fundamental types of perdurants are states, which are sometimes termed "states of affairs," and events, also depicted in figure 2.8. The distinction between them can be explained through the notion of their imagined elementary temporal parts, *snapshots*. The *state* of an entity is a perdurant characterizing the entity whose snapshots express the same perdurant (state) type. For example, the state of John can be described as "sitting in a chair." Whenever the snapshot of the state "sitting in a chair" is taken, the state description still holds. On the other hand, "John is running" is the description of a *process* rather than a state, because there are no two snapshots of running that can be described by the same expression. In other words, snapshots taken of the "running" are not themselves examples of "running."

It is important to understand that state and process are modeling abstractions represented at a specific level of granularity. For example, if the functioning of John's internal organs is taken into consideration, one would have to conclude that "John is sitting in a chair" is a process rather than a state.

An *event* is a perdurant that is related to exactly two states—the collective state of the entities of the environment before and after it has occurred. For example, "John rose from the chair" is a description of the event that separates the state of the environment where John was sitting in the chair from the environment state where John is no longer sitting in the chair.

One can distinguish between *atomic events* that are modeled as happening instantaneously, like an explosion or a message reception by a software agent, and *complex events* that are composed of other events, like a storm, a birthday party, or the Second World War. Atomic events and complex events and the relationship between them are depicted in figure 2.8.

Particulars possess causal power. Accordingly, it may be useful to distinguish between action events and nonaction events, depending on the *cause* of an event. An *action event* is an event that is caused by the action of an agent, like sending a message, starting a machine, or storing an intruder description. Three kinds of action events, which correspond to the kinds of actions mentioned in section 2.3, are represented in figure 2.8. On the other hand, there are *nonaction events* that are not caused by actions—for example, the fall of a particular stock value below a certain threshold, the sinking of a ship in a storm, or a timeout in an auction. Action events and nonaction events are shown in figure 2.8.

Some researchers understand action as an intentional event resulting from a social commitment or an internal commitment of the performing agent. We do not subscribe to this definition, because actions performed by a manmade agent or dog, which may form parts of a sociotechnical system, are not necessarily intentional.

An interaction between two physical agents can be ontologically understood as performing an action by one agent that is perceived as an event by the other agent. Turning to software agents, we again use the comparison between software agents and (software) objects for understanding interactions between software agents. Sending a message from one agent to another is different from operation invocation of an object in several important aspects. First, while an object requests another object to perform an operation via a message structured in a very idiosyncratic and accurately specified way, agents communicate by using an agent communication language where message content is a character string. Indeed, the following definition of a software agent has been proposed: "An entity is a software agent if and only if it communicates correctly in an agent communication language." Although we do not subscribe to this definition, it serves as a vivid illustration of the topic.

Another difference between agent and object communication is that the underlying agent communication model is *asynchronous*. Asynchronous communication temporally separates the receiving of a message from the responding to it. For example, if I receive an email, it is up to me to decide when I reply to it. An asynchronous communication model thus implies that an agent may autonomously initiate an activity at any time, not just when it is sent a message. Asynchronous messaging also makes agents suitable for implementing conversations like negotiations. Agent communication languages usually enable the tracking of conversations by assigning each conversation a separate identifier. For the same reason, agents easily lend themselves to facilitating third-party interactions, such as brokering and recruiting.

Figure 2.8 includes the notions of process, activity, task, and plan. A *process* is defined as a complex event that consists of two or more possibly parallel occurrences of events. Examples of process are a storm, a football game, a conversation, a birthday party, and a Web shop purchase. At the system design layer, we model a process that can be attributed to one or more agents as an *activity*. For example, running is an activity because it is performed by an agent (e.g., John), but boiling is a chemical process without any performing agent involved. An activity consists of actions. Figure 2.8 also shows the two kinds of activities—*collective activities* and *private activities*—which were introduced in section 2.3. Collective activities are termed *interactions* by some researchers.

Activity occurrence is an execution of actions comprising the activity. As figure 2.8 reflects, activity occurrence is a special kind of action event. An activity occurrence creates an instance of the activity type.

A problem-solving activity, a *task*, is a private activity related to one or more plans, each of which consists of actions. We can say that for a problem-solving activity, the *postcondition* to be achieved by the activity, which is termed a *logic goal* in the tradition of the logic approach to the formalization of AI, has been defined explicitly before the activity is started. For example, the Mars Exploration Rover may need to perform a planning task with the logic goal to get to a specified location on the Martian surface. Please note that what we generally mean by a goal in this book reflects a state of affairs to be achieved by a sociotechnical system as a whole rather than an expected postcondition of an activity performed by some agent of the system.

For a problem-solving task, a *plan* is the means to achieve a logic goal. A plan consists of actions. Plans may be defined at the time of designing a sociotechnical system or at runtime. For example, a software agent may need to choose between different predefined plans to achieve the goal of allocating a car to the rental order in a car rental company. An example plan is to allocate a car of the given car group, or, if there is no available car in the given car group, to allocate a car of the next higher car group or to allocate a car from another branch. The Mars Exploration Rover again may need, at runtime, to create the plan to get to a specified location on the Martian surface. As is shown in figure 2.8, plan execution is a kind of activity occurrence.

In contrast to tasks, a logic goal associated with an activity is usually implicit rather than explicit. For example, even though a service provider agent may not represent its goals explicitly, it always adopts the whole or part of the customer's goal in attempting to provide the service. For example, given a customer wanting to rent a car, the goal of a car rental company is to provide the customer with a car, which is, of course, a subgoal of the company's overall goal of earning money through renting cars. The car rental company tries to achieve the overall goal by adopting as many customer goals as possible. It does so by performing an activity of the corresponding type that does not need to have as an explicitly defined logic goal providing the customer with a car. More important than explicit representation of goals is an agent's capability to modify its behavior based on the current situation, which entails both the events perceived and the knowledge in the agent's knowledge base. Note that some researchers view all activities as tasks.

We turn our attention now to universals. Figure 2.9 lists the universals that we refer to. As pointed out at the beginning of this section, *universals* are entities that exist neither in space nor in time; that is, they cannot be localized. At all three layers of the conceptual space, modeling is dominantly performed in terms of universals.

Universals are either types or modeling abstractions. A *type* is a universal that carries a *principle of identity* for its instances and whose every instance maintains its identity in every circumstance considered by the model. For example, Intruder is a type, because it carries a principle of identity for deciding who is considered to be an intruder within the system. Additionally, every instance of Intruder handled by the security system is the same person throughout the life span of the system.

Types can also be classified according to the categories of particulars that instantiate the types. The resulting categories of types are depicted in figure 2.9.

Types can be divided into kinds, subkinds, phases, and roles. A *kind* is a rigid type; a *role* and *phase* are antirigid. In simple terms, a type is said to be *rigid* if every instance is necessarily its instance, that is, cannot change its type. For example, Leon and Kuldar can cease being academics (if, for example, we receive better offers from industry) but cannot switch from being persons to beings of some other kind. A type is said to be *antirigid* if its instance can change its type. As another example, Dog is rigid, while Guard is antirigid. The ontological distinction between a role and an

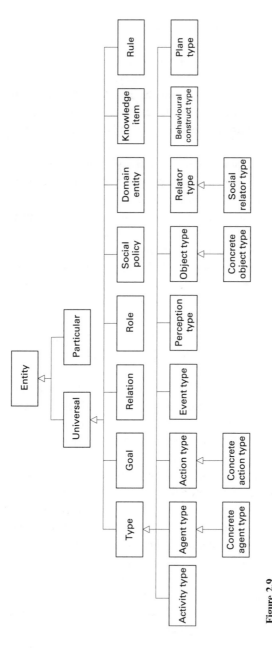

Figure 2.9
Universals of the conceptual space

agent type is that the type of an agent, once fixed, cannot be changed, because it is rigid, yet an agent may change its role because the role is antirigid. We return to roles shortly after explaining relations.

Kinds can be specialized into other rigid subtypes—subkinds. A *subkind* inherits the principle of identity of its parent type and represents its parent type's subset of instances. For example, if we take `Person` to be a kind, then some of its subkinds are `Male Person` and `Female Person`. The subkind relationship expresses that both individual man and woman obey a principle of identity carried by the type `Person`.

Phases, which are also named *states*, are antirigid types that constitute possible stages in the history of a type instance. For example, `Boy`, `Male Teenager`, and `Adult Male` constitute the phases of an instance of `Male Person`. Phases are specializations of kinds. For example, being an adolescent is being a person who is between thirteen and nineteen years old.

In addition to types, important *modeling abstractions* used in this book are goal, relation, role, social policy, domain entity, knowledge item, and rule, all of which are represented in figure 2.9.

A *goal* in the ontological sense is a set of states of affairs or world states intended by one or more agents. This definition reflects how a goal can be achieved by several similar states of affairs. For instance, if Kuldar's goal is to spend holidays on a warm tropical beach, this goal can be satisfied by spending holidays on the Gold Coast as well as on the Sunshine Coast. Goals that we use in modeling are goal types rather than goal instances. A goal can be instantiated for each particular situation at hand.

Another modeling abstraction is relation. *Relation*, also known as *association*, is a type whose instances are tuples of connected by the relation entities. A *formal relation* holds between two or more entities directly, without any intermediating entity. An example of a formal relation is "Leon is older than Kuldar." Conversely to a formal relation, a *material relation* is founded on the existence of an intermediating entity termed as *relator*. *Relator types* occur between object and agent types. An example is the relator type `Marriage` between the roles `Husband` and `Wife`. An instance of the relator type `Marriage` between, say, John and Mary, is created within the wedding ceremony. This instance includes the wedding date and describes the commitments and claims resulting from the marriage between John and Mary. The relator type `Marriage` is therefore a *social relator type*, which is represented as one of the types in figure 2.9.

Goals can be related by various formal relations, which are termed *goal formal relations*. *Goal decomposition* is a kind of goal formal relation between goals. Goal decomposition groups several subgoals related to the same supergoal. Goal decomposition is represented in figure 2.10.

A goal can also be understood as a mental moment. We elaborate on this interpretation further shortly.

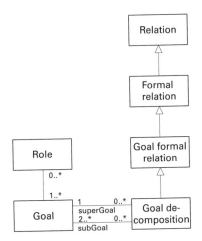

Figure 2.10
Formal relations between goals and roles

The next modeling abstraction to be discussed is role. We define a *role* as an anti-rigid type where agents playing the role need to achieve certain goals. This formal relation between a goal and role is shown in figure 2.10. For example, an agent playing the role `Security Manager`, a human or manmade agent or perhaps a dog, needs to achieve the goal of handling an intruder. To put it more informally, *goals* represent functionalities expected from the system, and *roles* are capabilities of the system required for achieving the functionalities. A role is *relationally dependent*, meaning that the role is defined in the context of its relation to some entity. For example, a student is a person in the context defined by a relation to an educational institution. In the goal and role models presented in this book, relational dependence means that a role is related to the system to be designed. Finally, we understand roles as social roles. A *social role* is characterized by a set of general commitments toward other agents by an agent playing the role. In our role models, these general commitments are represented as responsibilities.

Another modeling abstraction—social policy—can be ontologically defined through the concepts of rights, prohibitions, and obligations. A *social policy* defines the actions that agent(s) subject to the policy may, should not, or must perform on target agent(s) when specific relevant events occur. Social policies constrain the interactions and behavior of agents playing the roles. For example, the social policy of Pareto efficiency requires that the deal achieved by two agents must be Pareto-efficient; that is, there must be no other deal that makes one party better off without making the other party worse off. This policy is a common requirement for automated negotiations between self-interested agents.

The modeling abstraction to be described next is knowledge item. There is the implicit modeling concept of *knowledge*, which permeates the entire conceptual space. It defines the basic concepts of the environments in which the system will be situated. It also includes the definitions of relations between concepts. At the motivation layer, we label these concepts as domain entities. Ontologically, a *domain entity* is an object type.

At the system design layer, the *knowledge* possessed by a physical agent is modeled as a set of knowledge items. In ontological terms, knowledge items are used for representing moments, which were treated previously. A *knowledge item* is either a knowledge attribute or a conceptual object attributed to some agent.

A *knowledge attribute* represents an intrinsic moment. There are two kinds of attributes: numeric and nonnumeric attributes. A *numeric attribute* represents one *quality dimension* quantitatively as a numerical value. For example, the color of an apple can be represented through the numeric attributes of hue, saturation, and brightness. To simplify things, in many cases we represent qualities by means of generalized nonnumeric attributes. A *nonnumeric attribute* represents one or more *quality dimensions* qualitatively, for example, as an enumeration value. For example, there can be a nonnumeric attribute of color with possible values of *red*, *yellow*, *green*, and *black*. As another illustration, the pilot of a combat aircraft may not be interested in the precise number of fuel liters in the tank, but rather in qulitative interpretations of the amount of fuel, which can be *full*, *quarter-full*, *quarter-empty*, and *nearly empty*. Examples of knowledge attributes of a human agent are age, height and address. In modeling, we represent for an attribute its name and type.

Conceptual objects are knowledge items used for representing mental moments. For example, the beliefs of the student Andrea about the subjects she has to take can be represented by the respective conceptual objects. The intrinsic moments of a subject are represented by the attributes attached to the corresponding conceptual object, such as the subject name, lecturer, and the number of credits to be earned. Both conceptual objects and their attributes are characterized by names and types.

Analogously, a goal attributed to a particular agent and its elaborations—desire and intention—can be conceived as mental moments, which are existentially dependent on the agent, forming an inseparable part of its mental state. This special meaning of "goal" is elaborated in chapter 5. However, what we usually mean by "goal" in this book is a set of states of affairs intended by one or more agents.

Relational moments or relators are represented by material relations between conceptual objects. For example, the knowledge of a security agent may include a conceptual object of type `HouseSchedule`. The object type `HouseSchedule` can be related to another object type, `GuestProfile`, through the relator type `ScheduledEvent`, whose instances are material relations representing relational moments.

The behavior of an agent is modeled by *rules*. A rule can be ontologically understood as a relator type between the agent type to which it is attached and types of mental moments, events, and actions. An instance of a rule is evaluated for the combination of a physical agent and specific mental moments, events, and actions. For example, there can be a rule attached to the agent type `SecurityAgent` stating that if a person is detected in the house (event) and the person is not known by the agent (mental moment), the corresponding message is sent to an agent of type `Police` (action).

2.7 Background

This book is concerned with modeling sociotechnical systems with multiple agents. Our definition and understanding of a *sociotechnical system* or simply a *system* is based on Sommerville 2007.

Our treatment of *roles*, *goals*, and *quality goals* emerged from extended discussion within the Intelligent Agent Laboratory at the University of Melbourne, and discussing how to improve the agent-oriented software engineering methodologies Gaia (Wooldridge, Jennings, and Kinny 2000) and Tropos (Bresciani et al. 2004). This particular set of concepts emerged from the ROADMAP metamodel described by Juan and Sterling (2003) and the discussion by Chan and Sterling (2003a). A clear discussion is presented in Kuan, Karunasekera, and Sterling 2005.

The kinds of *motives* behind goals—*physiological*, *psychological*, *interactional*, and *intellectual*—have been defined by Leontief (1979). The distinction between *achievement goals*, *cease goals*, *maintaining goals*, *avoidance goals*, and *optimization goals* has been proposed by Dardenne, Lamsweerde, and Fickas (1993). The quotation that a goal is "a dream with a deadline" comes from Farber 2003.

Social policies have been addressed by Rahwan, Juan, and Sterling (2006). The three basic types of organizations—*hierarchies*, *markets*, and *networks*—have been proposed by Dignum (2004). The *control*, *benevolence*, and *peer relationships* that dominate between roles in the organizations of the corresponding types mentioned previously were conceived by Zambonelli, Jennings, and Wooldridge (2001). Different kinds of organizational relationships—*goal*, *task*, and *resource dependencies*—have been proposed by Yu (1995) and elaborated in the Tropos methodology (Bresciani et al. 2004).

We view agents as active entities with anthropomorphic qualities as contrasted with passive entities—objects. Our abstract agent architecture is rooted in the SMART agent framework proposed by d'Inverno and Luck (2001). The treatment of agents by us encompasses *human agents*, *artificial agents*, and *institutional agents*, as defined by Guizzardi and Wagner (2005b).

We also explain social relators—*commitments* and *claims*. One of the first approaches that addressed commitments was the Action Workflow by Medina-

Mora et al. (1992). It describes commitments in loops representing a four-step exchange between a customer and a performer. Singh (1999) treats commitments as ternary relationships between two agents and a "context group" to which they both belong. For simplicity, we treat commitments in this book as binary relationships between two agents, based on Wagner (2003).

Differently from this book, many other authors confine the treatment of agents to manmade agents of a specific kind—*software agents*. d'Inverno and Luck (2001) have defined *autonomous agents* as agents that create and pursue their own agendas. *Intelligent agents* as *responsive, proactive*, and *social* software systems have been defined by Jennings, Sycara, and Wooldridge (1998). Jennings (2000) emphasizes the importance of agent as a modeling abstraction by arguing that the agent-oriented worldview is perhaps the most natural way of characterizing many types of problems. Odell (2002) argues that agent as a software unit constitutes a natural new step in the evolution of programming approaches due to its unpredictable behavior and asynchronous communication model.

There are different standard proposals for agent communication languages, such as the FIPA ACL (2002) and KQML (Labrou and Finin, 1997). Genesereth and Ketchpel (1994) define agents as entities communicating in an agent communication language.

Taveter (2004a) portrays a sociotechnical system in the sense followed in this book; namely, as a system composed of active entities, agents, that manipulate a number of passive information resources or Web services consisting of conceptual objects.

Because agents as central components of sociotechnical systems need to facilitate different aspects of everyday life, we prefer to talk about activities rather than problem-solving tasks performed by agents. Our treatment of activities is rooted in activity theory put forward by Leontief (1979). We have adopted the definition of *activity* provided by Sierhuis, Clancey, and van Hoof (2003), which emphasizes the context in which an activity is performed. An activity's *context* has been discussed by Clancey (2002) and Lister and Sterling (2003).

Taveter (2004a) provides our definition of "activity type." He also describes the types of human, automated, and semiautomatic activities. We elaborate activities into communicative, physical, and epistemic actions based on Wagner (2003).

The Mars Exploration Rover, which we have used as an example of an agent performing problem-solving activities, is described at http://marsrovers.jpl.nasa.gov.

In general, a *rule* is a sentence of the form "IF condition THEN consequence." Such rules are, for example, the rules of Prolog, as described by Sterling and Shapiro (1994). In the context of this book, rules define behavior patterns of agents. Taveter and Wagner (2001) and Taveter (2004a) have classified *rules* into *condition-action rules* and *event-condition-action-rules*, but our treatment is not confined to these types of rules. Our example of a differently structured rule, which has activation as well as expiration condition, is based on Kasinger and Bauer (2005).

An environment of a sociotechnical system has long been viewed as an implicitly defined container for a multiagent system providing "an infrastructure specifying communication and interaction protocols" (Huhns and Stephens 1999). Only recently, agent research communities have started to view an environment as an essential and utilizable part of every multiagent system. One of the first methodologies that included explicitly defined environment models was ROADMAP, as described by Juan, Pearce, and Sterling (2002) and more extensively by Juan (2008). We view the environment as an exploitable design abstraction for engineering sociotechnical systems. As has been described by Weyns, Omicini, and Odell (2007), the environment embeds resources and services, serves as a container and a means for communication, and functions as a coordination infrastructure for agents.

Because agents are situated in the real world and themselves form parts of the world, our agent-oriented models should be based on descriptions of the world that are as precise as possible. Ontologies are clearly relevant. According to Peirce (1935), the business of ontology is "to study the most general features of reality." However, as opposed to that of ontologists, our purpose is to describe the world in such a way and at the level that it would be useful for engineering sociotechnical systems. To that end, we allow for many simplifications.

Our *conceptual space* is inhabited by two kinds of entities: *universals* and *particulars*, also known as *abstract entities* and *concrete entities*. An ontological distinction between them is made by Masolo et al. (2003) and Guizzardi, Falbo, and Guizzardi (2008). A somewhat similar, but not ontologically founded, conceptual space has been proposed by Kavakli and Loucopoulos (1998).

The notation used by us for representing relationships between particulars in figure 2.8 and between universals in figure 2.9 has been borrowed from UML (OMG 2007).

The foundational concepts for agent-oriented modeling *endurant*, *perdurant*, *physical object*, *physical agent*, *quality*, and *relator* have been defined by Guizzardi and Wagner (2005a, 2005b) and have been refined by Guizzardi (2005). Likewise, the notion of quality dimensions and their relation to attributes as well as the categorization of types into kinds, subkinds, phases, and roles have been borrowed from Guizzardi 2005.

Roles as antirigid types have been defined first by Guarino and Welty (2001) but this notion has been elaborated by "roles as antirigid and relationally dependent types" by Guizzardi (2005) and by Guizzardi et al. (2004) and then by the notion of social roles by Guizzardi and Guizzardi (2008).

Different ontological interpretations of the concept of goal are described by Guizzardi et al. (2007). The concepts of activity and resource have been ontologically characterized by Guizzardi, Falbo, and Guizzardi (2008).

The distinction between *state* and *process* is explained by Masolo et al. (2003). We follow Guizzardi (2005) for the definitions and explanations of types and moments. The ontological definition of *social policy* has been formed after Kagal, Finin, and Joshi (2003). The definitions for the notions of *event, process, action event,* and *nonaction event* are again provided by Guizzardi and Wagner (2005b).

Exercises for Chapter 2

1. Analyze your university, company, or organization as a sociotechnical system and try to identify the following elements for the system:

• goals

• roles

• social policies

• domain entities

• agents

• perceptions by the agents

• knowledge items

• activities and actions performed by the agents

• rules

3 Models

Chapter 2 described a conceptual space for designing and implementing sociotechnical systems. In this chapter, models are defined that fit into the conceptual space. These models are examples of the *types* of models that one would use for developing multiagent systems.

The kinds of models described in this chapter are not intended as the basis of a new agent-oriented methodology. Rather, we present a set of models to reflect the concepts of the conceptual space. We also point out how different types of models are related to each other, but leave specific modeling processes to particular agent-oriented methodologies, some of which are described in chapter 7. For each model type, we provide examples using notation that has been working well, in our experience. As shown in chapters 5 and 7, these models are compatible with a wide range of agent programming languages and agent-oriented methodologies.

3.1 The Running Case Study

We demonstrate and explain our models with a case study of designing digital pets—Tamagotchis, which were mentioned briefly in chapters 1 and 2. We have chosen Tamagotchis as a case study because they are relatively simple and transparent. Nonetheless, they enable the illustration of all types of models needed for designing multiagent systems. As pointed out in section 2.3, a Tamagotchi can be viewed as responsive, as well as social and proactive. Further, the example of Tamagotchis involves both how humans interact with manmade agents and how manmade agents interact with each other. Last but not least, a Tamagotchi toy is widely available, so anyone can build a simple multiagent system with two or more Tamagotchis.

We describe Tamagotchi version 4 in some detail in this section in order to be able to give concrete examples of models in sections 3.2–3.10.

A Tamagotchi is a digital pet that is housed in a small and simple egg-shaped handheld computing environment known as the Tamagotchi's "shell." Three buttons (A, B, and C) on the shell allow the owner to select and perform an activity, including

- hatching a Tamagotchi
- feeding the Tamagotchi a piece of food or a snack
- cleaning up the Tamagotchi's messes ("excrement")
- playing a game with the Tamagotchi
- checking its age, discipline, hunger, weight, and happiness levels
- connecting with other Tamagotchis

A Tamagotchi evolves from egg to baby to child to teenager to adult. It can be female or male. When a Tamagotchi needs something, it calls its owner with a beep and highlights the attention icon on its shell's screen. The owner is then supposed to check what its digital pet needs with the Tamagotchi's health meter and play with it, feed it, or discipline it. A Tamagotchi's shell comes with around ten predefined meals and snacks. The owner can use his or her digital pet's "gotchi points" to buy additional food items from the shop of the Tamagotchi's shell. Up to fifteen kinds of food items can be stored. Overfeeding might make a Tamagotchi sick or overweight, which may also eventually lead to sickness (very realistic and educational, isn't it?). Another basic need of a Tamagotchi is to have its mess cleaned by means of flushing the toilet with the corresponding icon on the screen of the Tamagotchi's shell. When the Tamagotchi becomes sick, the skull icon or tooth icon appears. If the Tamagotchi has not been sick for too long, it can be nursed back to health with the help of one dose of medicine, or occasionally more, provided by the shell.

Sometimes a Tamagotchi might be very naughty and need to be disciplined. This purpose is served by the discipline icon on the shell's screen, which has two options: *time out* and *praise*. For instance, the owner has to discipline his or her Tamagotchi if it calls the owner when it is not hungry or if it refuses food when it is hungry.

A Tamagotchi can be entertained by playing games with it. As the Tamagotchi grows, the number of games that can be played with it increases up to the following five games: *jumping rope*, *mimic*, *shape fit*, *dancing*, and *flag*. Games are also the means by which the Tamagotchi can earn gotchi points. In addition to games, the owner can also let his or her Tamagotchi play with an item, such as a ball or makeup set. Items can be bought from the shop or Tamagotchi Town using gotchi points, as explained shortly.

A Tamagotchi also has social needs, which can be satisfied by connecting it through its shell's infrared port to other Tamagotchis. For connection, the shells of two Tamagotchis are positioned together with the infrared ports at their tops facing each other. Following, the owner of a Tamagotchi can choose to connect with another toy. Upon successful connection, the owner can further choose one of the following three options: *game*, *present*, or *visit*. If the owner chooses *game*, the two Tamagotchis will compete in a randomly chosen game for gotchi points. If the owner chooses *present*, its Tamagotchi gives the other Tamagotchi a gift. Before a present can be given, it needs to be wrapped by selecting the appropriate menu item. If the Tamagotchi gives its friend an unexpected present, such as a *snake*, its training level is not high enough. The owner needs to discipline his or her Tamagotchi then. If the owner chooses *visit*, its Tamagotchi goes to the other Tamagotchi's shell and gives it a present and/or plays a game with it. Relationships between Tamagotchis improve and develop the more connections the owner(s) make between them. A Tamagotchi's level of friendship with another Tamagotchi can develop from *acquaintance* to *buddy* to *friend* to *good friend* to *best friend* to *partner*. After several (at least five) connections, a Tamagotchi may become a good companion with his or her favorite partner of the opposite sex. If this happens, an egg will appear on the screen of the female Tamagotchi's shell. For the first twenty-four hours after the new Tamagotchi hatches, the "mother" Tamagotchi takes care of all the needs of the new Tamagotchi, unless it becomes sick. On such an occasion, the owner must nurse it back to health with a dose or two of medicine. Once the parent leaves, the owner is asked to name his or her new Tamagotchi and must take care of it.

Figure 3.1 shows two interconnected version 4 Tamagotchis, where the top Tamagotchi with the pink shell is visiting the bottom one with the blue shell.

When a female Tamagotchi grows old without finding a partner, another character—a Matchmaker—may appear to suggest a partner for the Tamagotchi. The Matchmaker will go through the Tamagotchi's friend list and ask for each companion "Love? Yes, No". If the owner selects "Yes," a new egg will appear.

In addition to the interaction features, a Tamagotchi can be involved in simulated communication by receiving letters in the mailbox of its shell. The Tamagotchi notifies the owner of receiving a letter by means of the blinking post icon of the shell. A Tamagotchi may, for example, get mail from the Tamagotchi King or may receive a letter if a teacher wants to invite the Tamagotchi to go to school.

The owner of a Tamagotchi can enter the Tamagotchi Town Web site with his or her digital pet. A snapshot of Tamagotchi Town is shown in figure 3.2. In Tamagotchi Town, a Tamagotchi can go to preschool, school, or kindergarten (depending on its age), play games, visit its parents or the Tamagotchi King, and buy food or other items. The owner is able to see its Tamagotchi character on the computer screen and guide it. To visit the Tamagotchi King, the owner has to make a donation, which can be done under the points item of the shell's menu. For logging into the Tamagotchi Town Web site, a Tamagotchi shell generates a fourteen-character alphanumeric password that along with the owner name uniquely identifies each Tamagotchi in Tamagotchi Town. A Tamagotchi shell is paused while visiting Tamagotchi Town. Upon logging out from Tamagotchi Town, the Web site generates another password to be input by the owner into the shell. The password registers that the Tamagotchi has gone to kindergarten or school, has visited the Tamagotchi

Figure 3.1
Two interconnected version 4 Tamagotchis

King, or followed some other option. Tamagotchi Town also generates additional passwords that the owner can input into the shell to receive and store souvenirs that the Tamagotchi has received in Tamagotchi Town. "Souvenirs" are items that the Tamagotchi can collect but cannot play with or eat. Passwords are also used to obtain the gotchi points that the Tamagotchi has earned by playing games in Tamagotchi Town. Passwords also give access to the items and food that the Tamagotchi through its owner has bought for gotchi points in Tamagotchi Town. The Tamagotchi can eat the food and play with the items bought in Tamagotchi Town.

If the owner does not take good care of his or her digital pet, the Tamagotchi will pass away. If this happens, a new egg can be hatched by pressing and holding together the *A* and *C* buttons of the Tamagotchi's shell.

Figure 3.2
A snapshot of Tamagotchi Town

These features we have mentioned do not cover all the features of the version 4 Tamagotchi. However they are more than sufficient for our purposes of demonstrating concretely the range of agent models introduced in the coming sections.

3.2 Goal Models and Motivational Scenarios

A system's *raison d'être* is defined by the goals set for it. For achieving the goals, the system needs capacities or functions, which are described as roles. Goals can also be used for defining social policies, which shape interactions between agents playing the roles. As pointed out in section 2.2, the notions of goals and roles are intended to be intuitive and easy to understand for nontechnical people, such as customers and other kinds of external stakeholders.

Goal models express goals and roles. We explicitly identify a subset of goals called "quality goals." We represent quality goals in the models in this chapter and include a lengthy discussion about them in chapter 4. Goal models describe the goal hierarchy of the system to be developed, starting with the purpose of the system. For our running example, we assume that the overall goal for a Tamagotchi is to *entertain and educate the owner*. The purpose of an intruder detection system presumably is to *handle intruders* and the purpose of an air traffic management system is to *allocate airport resources to arriving and departing flights*. The main objective of goal models is to enable a customer, domain analyst, and system designer to discuss and agree on the goals of the system and the roles the system needs to fulfil in order to meet those goals.

Goal models serve roughly the same function as *use cases* in object-oriented modeling. Indeed, several agent-oriented methodologies have chosen to utilize use cases. However, use cases impose limitations when the system to be developed is a multiagent one. Use cases inherently impose a system boundary. This is unsuitable for several reasons. First, it forces one to distinguish prematurely between which roles might be performed by human agents and which by manmade agents. Second, use cases focus on user actions, which can give only a restricted view of the system. Finally, use cases naturally suggest closed systems, rather than open systems where any number of agents may enter or leave. In our experience, use cases restrict design choices, as they prompt the designer to start thinking about the user interface earlier than needed.

In multiagent systems, unlike in traditional systems, agents or actors appear as proactive components of the system rather than just its users. For example, a Tamagotchi can initiate a behavior based on its needs. Precisely for this reason, we model both Tamagotchi and its owner as roles in our example and model interactions between them. We thus avoid the term "user" and employ the names of appropriate roles like Owner in its place. However, as goal models are at least as simple as use cases, we could regard them as use cases for open and distributed systems.

A goal model can be considered as a container of three components: goals, quality goals, and roles. A *goal* is a representation of a functional requirement of the system. For example, the goal of the example system to be developed is "Entertain and educate owner."

A *quality goal*, as its name implies, is a nonfunctional or quality requirement of the system. For example, the goal "Entertain and educate owner" is associated with the quality goal "The owner has fun."

A *role* is some capacity or position that the system requires in order to achieve its goals. For example, for achieving the goal "Entertain and educate owner" along with its associated quality goal, the roles MyTamagotchi and Owner with specific responsibilities are required. Table 3.1 shows the notation that we have adopted for representing our models. The symbols introduced by table 3.1 have been used in figure 3.3, which depicts the goal model for a system consisting of humans and Tamagotchis.

Goals and quality goals can be further decomposed into smaller related subgoals and subquality goals. This seems to imply some hierarchical structure between the goal and its subgoals. However, this is by no means an "is-a" or inheritance relation-

Table 3.1
The notation for goal models

Symbol	Meaning
(parallelogram)	Goal
(cloud)	Quality goal
(stick figure)	Role
————————	Relationship between goals
– – – – – – – – –	Relationship between goals and quality goals

ship, as is common in object-oriented methodologies. Rather, the hierarchical structure is just to show that the subcomponent is an *aspect* of the top-level component.
For example, the goal "Entertain and educate owner" has the subgoal "Sustain
Tamagotchi," which, in turn, has been decomposed into the subgoals "Cure Tamagotchi," "Clean the Tamagotchi's environment," "Socialize Tamagotchi," and "Entertain Tamagotchi." Each of them represents a different aspect of sustaining the life
of a digital pet by its owner. The hierarchical structure of the goals set for Tamagotchis is reflected by figure 3.3.

Different quality goals have different purposes. For example, the quality goal
"easy and fun-to-use interface" deals with how the Tamagotchi should be designed.
In contrast, the quality goals "My Tamagotchi healthy," "My Tamagotchi happy,"
and "My Tamagotchi well-behaved" describe social policies between the owner and
the Tamagotchi that guide interactions between them at runtime. The quality goals
mentioned are represented in figure 3.3.

Because of the importance of quality goals and their analysis in systems design, we
devote the whole of chapter 4 to discussing quality. Note that we are comfortable

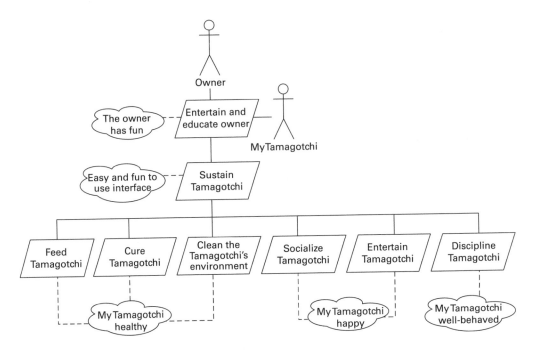

Figure 3.3
The goal model for a system of humans and Tamagotchis

expressing high-level quality goals in goal models to be understood in their own right, without the need to fully define them.

Some agent-oriented methodologies distinguish various kinds of relationships between goals, such as *AND* and *OR* relationships between goals. However, we have deliberately avoided them for the sake of retaining the simplicity of goal diagrams. It is worthwhile to emphasize here that simplicity of models is very important when eliciting requirements in cooperation with nontechnical people.

Roles required in the system are determined from the goals. Each goal is analyzed to ascertain the types of roles needed to achieve it. Roles may share common goals and quality goals. In some situations, comprehensibility of models can be improved by representing a role hierarchy where the capacity of the parent role is divided among its subroles. For example, the role MyTamagotchi has the subrole Matchmaker, which is responsible for finding a partner for the Tamagotchi. Role hierarchies and organization models are discussed in section 3.3.

Who—or which—human or manmade agent fulfils a particular role is not a concern at this stage. An agent may also play more than one role.

Goal models go hand in hand with *motivational scenarios* that describe in an informal and loose narrative manner how goals are to be achieved by agents enacting the

Table 3.2
The motivational scenario of playing with the Tamagotchi

Scenario name	Playing with the Tamagotchi
Scenario description	The owner has to take care of his/her digital pet—the Tamagotchi. This involves the following activities: (a) feeding the Tamagotchi (b) curing the Tamagotchi if it becomes sick (c) cleaning the Tamagotchi's environment if it produces excrement (d) socializing the Tamagotchi by introducing it to other Tamagotchis (e) entertaining the Tamagotchi by, for example, playing games with it and taking it to visit Tamagotchi Town (f) disciplining the Tamagotchi if it is naughty
Quality description	Playing with the Tamagotchi should be fun for the owner. The Tamagotchi should have an attractive and easy-to-operate user interface. If the Tamagotchi is not well taken care of, it will die.

corresponding roles. They are similar to tabular use cases. In contrast to tabular use cases, motivational scenarios model interactions between agents rather than between the user and the system. A motivational scenario consists of a narrative scenario description and a declarative quality description. A quality description reflects qualitative aspects of the scenario. A motivational scenario may also refer to external services employed by agents for achieving the goals. Service models are described in section 3.10. A motivational scenario for the goal model depicted in figure 3.3 is shown as table 3.2. There is considerable overlap between the motivational scenario and the goal model. We envisage that in some circumstances the goal model would be developed first, but in others we would start with the motivational scenario. Motivational scenarios are elaborated by scenarios in section 3.8.

The goal model shown in figure 3.3 can be extended, but we have chosen to represent its extensions as separate diagrams, which are easier to understand. Figure 3.4 refines the goal "Socialize Tamagotchi" that appears in the goal model in figure 3.3. This model reflects the ideas that the customer and designers have about introducing a digital pet to other digital pets of the same kind by using a means of interaction of some kind, which is not refined at this stage. Figure 3.4 includes an additional role FriendTamagotchi, which is required to model socializing. It describes another Tamagotchi with which the agent playing the role MyTamagotchi interacts.

There are two ways of socializing a Tamagotchi. It is natural to model the socializing methods as subgoals of "Socialize Tamagotchi." The subgoals "Visit the friend" and "Find a partner for the Tamagotchi" represent different aspects of socializing. The latter subgoal mentioned—"Find a partner for the Tamagotchi"— is to be achieved by an agent playing MyTamagotchi's subrole Matchmaker. This subgoal is dependent on the "Visit the friend" subgoal in that the Matchmaker finds a partner from among the Tamagotchis with which the agent playing the

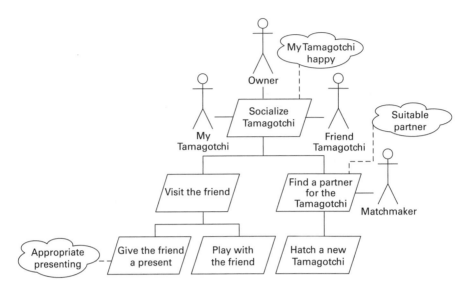

Figure 3.4
The subgoals of socializing a Tamagotchi

MyTamagotchi role has connected. This dependency is an example of a relationship other than *AND* or *OR* between goals that is not refined in goal models. The subgoal "Find a partner for the Tamagotchi" has the next-level subgoal "Hatch a new Tamagotchi," which represents a procreational outcome of matchmaking.

When we visit a friend, we may have a meal together, exchange presents, provide an opportunity for our children to play together, or engage in many other activities. The two options of visiting between Tamagotchis, giving a present and playing together, have been reflected by the corresponding third-level subgoals "Give the friend a present" and "Play with the friend."

The subgoal of giving a friend a present is associated with the quality goal "Appropriate presenting." What is meant by "appropriateness" here? First, this quality goal represents a possible *social policy* that only the visitor can give a present. This social policy in fact applies to interactions between two version 4 Tamagotchis. In our experience, it is more usual for the visitor to bring a present, but hosts can also give presents to visitors. Second, this quality goal means that the Tamagotchi strives to give another Tamagotchi a present that is appropriate. This can be viewed as another social policy guiding the interactions between two digital pets. However, a quality goal does not necessarily guarantee anything but rather serves as a criterion, whose fulfilment can be improved through either designing the system or interacting with it. The given quality goal thus reflects the decision by the stakeholders—customer and designers—to let the owner "discipline" his or her Tamagotchi to

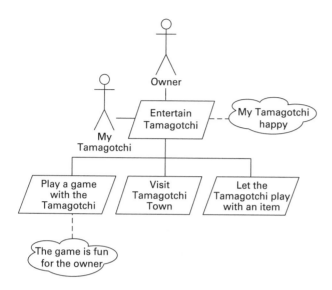

Figure 3.5
The subgoals of entertaining a Tamagotchi

decrease and eventually eliminate the occasions of presenting another Tamagotchi with something like a *snake*. In section 3.3, we show how quality goals can be elaborated as constraints attached to roles.

Figure 3.5 elaborates the goal "Entertain Tamagotchi," which was introduced in figure 3.3. This model reflects the ideas by the customer and designers on how a digital pet could be "cheered up" by its owner. The quality goal "The game is fun for the owner" attached to the goal "Play a game with the Tamagotchi" elaborates the quality goal "The owner has fun" associated with the goal "Entertain and educate owner."

The subgoal "Visit Tamagotchi Town" of the goal "Entertain Tamagotchi" has been elaborated in figure 3.6. This model reflects ideas the customer and designers have about designing the Tamagotchi in such a manner that the owner can visit Tamagotchi Town, the virtual environment in the Internet, with his or her Tamagotchi. That environment contains a virtual school, preschool, workplace, shopping mall, food court, theater, game center, town hall, king's castle, and travel agency. The Tamagotchi Town environment is sketched in section 3.4.

3.3 Role and Organization Models

Section 3.2 focused on describing goals. Roles were also defined, and these are associated with goals. In this section, roles are explained in more detail. In order

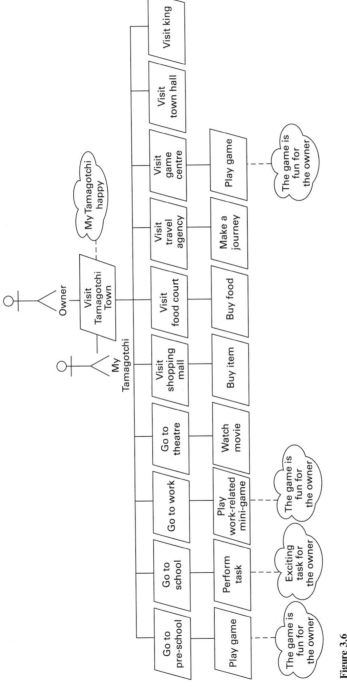

Figure 3.6
The subgoals of visiting Tamagotchi Town

to achieve the goals, the system requires some capacities or positions, which are described as roles. For example, because of the Tamagotchi's purpose to entertain and educate the owner, it has to behave in a certain way to enable the owner to take care of it. At the stage of conceptual domain modeling, we represent this required behavior as a set of responsibilities of the role MyTamagotchi. Similarly, there can also be constraints—conditions that the agent playing the role must take into consideration when exercising its responsibilities. For example, the responsibility to misbehave occasionally is influenced by the constraint stating that the higher the level of the Tamagotchi's training, the less it misbehaves.

The properties of a role can be expressed by a role model. The term "role schema" is used interchangeably with the term "role model."

A *role model* consists of the following four elements:

Role name   A name identifying the role.

Description   A textual description of the role.

Responsibilities   A list of responsibilities that agent(s) playing the role must perform in order for a set of goals and their associated quality goals to be achieved.

Constraints   A list of conditions that agent(s) playing the role must take into consideration when exercising its responsibilities.

Table 3.3 shows a role schema created for the role MyTamagotchi. A role model lists responsibilities of the role without saying anything about the order in which or under which conditions those responsibilities are to be exercised. When we look at the responsibilities of the role MyTamagotchi, we notice that the first six of them model various kinds of proactive behavior by a digital pet, and the rest describe how a Tamagotchi should behave when it is connected to another Tamagotchi. Visiting another Tamagotchi requires an additional role FriendTamagotchi, which is modeled in table 3.4.

As was stated previously, a role model may also include constraints pertaining to the role. For example, the role schema for the role Matchmaker shown in table 3.5 has the constraint "a partner to be proposed must be of the opposite sex," which is a commonsense requirement for hatching a new Tamagotchi.

Because this book is about designing sociotechnical systems consisting of human and manmade agents, the roles played by human agents are also characterized by responsibilities and constraints. Table 3.6 represents the role schema for the role Owner.

Role models are orthogonal to goal models, because although goal models represent the goals of the system to be developed as a whole, role models represent the responsibilities and constraints of individual roles required by the system. In sociotechnical systems, both human and manmade agents have responsibilities. However,

Table 3.3
The role model for MyTamagotchi

Role name	MyTamagotchi
Description	The role of my digital pet.
Responsibilities	Grow from baby to child to teenager to adult.
	Express hunger.
	Become sick.
	Produce excrement.
	Express loneliness.
	Misbehave occasionally:
	• express hunger when not hungry
	• refuse food when hungry
	• present a friend with an inappropriate gift
	Visit a friend.
	Give a friend a present.
	Play with friends.
	Visit Tamagotchi Town.
Constraints	Any present given needs to be appropriate.
	Only the visitor can give a present.
	The higher the level of training, the less the Tamagotchi misbehaves.
	The Tamagotchi needs to be of appropriate age to play with certain items.
	The Tamagotchi must be of the appropriate age to go to preschool or school in Tamagotchi Town.
	The Tamagotchi must graduate from school to go to work in Tamagotchi Town.
	The Tamagotchi must have a sufficient amount of gotchi points to buy items from the shopping mall, food court, or travel agency in Tamagotchi Town.
	The Tamagotchi must donate a certain number of gotchi points to visit the king's castle in Tamagotchi Town.

Table 3.4
The role model for the role FriendTamagotchi

Role name	FriendTamagotchi
Description	The role of a friend to my digital pet.
Responsibilities	Host the visiting Tamagotchi.
	Play games with the visiting Tamagotchi.
	Receive a present from the visiting Tamagotchi.
Constraints	Only the visitor can give a present.

Table 3.5
The role model for Matchmaker

Role name	Matchmaker
Description	The role of my Tamagotchi's personal helper to find a partner.
Responsibilities	Propose a partner from the friends list.
Constraints	A partner to be proposed has to be of the opposite sex.
	The partners should be proposed in order of suitability.

Table 3.6
The role model for Owner

Role name	Owner
Description	The role of the owner of my digital pet.
Responsibilities	Wake up the Tamagotchi.
	Feed the Tamagotchi.
	Cure the Tamagotchi.
	Flush the toilet.
	Discipline the Tamagotchi.
	Play games with the Tamagotchi.
	Let the Tamagotchi play with an item.
	Initiate a visit with another Tamagotchi:
	Take the Tamagotchi to visit Tamagotchi Town:
	• take the Tamagotchi to pre-school
	• take the Tamagotchi to school
	• take the Tamagotchi to workplace
	• take the Tamagotchi to theater
	• take the Tamagotchi to shopping mall
	• take the Tamagotchi to food court
	• take the Tamagotchi to travel agency
	• take the Tamagotchi to the game center
	• take the Tamagotchi to the town hall
	• take the Tamagotchi to the king's castle
Constraints	For interacting with another Tamagotchi, the owner needs to establish infrared connection with correct parameters between the two Tamagotchis.
	To visit Tamagotchi Town, the owner must have a computer with Internet connection.

as we saw in section 3.2, goals of the system are modeled from the perspective of human agents, even though it is conceivable to think about manmade agents performing activities for other manmade agents. Indeed, Isaac Asimov wrote about responsibilities and constraints applying to robots more than fifty years ago.

Clearly, a role model is analogous to the delegation of work through the creation of positions in a human organization. Every employee in the organization holds a particular position in order to realize business functions. Different positions entail different degrees of autonomy, decision making, and responsibilities. Using this analogy, a role schema for a particular role makes up the position description for that role. Indeed, in their interactions with industry, Leon and Kuldar have noticed that positions in organizations are described in terms of responsibilities and constraints.

Being a position, a role is partially defined through its relationships with other roles. For example, the definition of the role MyTamagotchi involves its relationships with the roles Owner and FriendTamagotchi. As we explained in section 2.2, there can be *control*, *benevolence*, and *peer* relationships between roles. Such relationships are represented by organization models and can be helpful for defining interactions between agents. Figure 3.7 depicts an *organization model* for a system consisting of humans and Tamagotchis. This organization model includes control

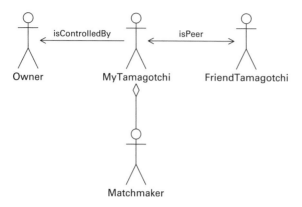

Figure 3.7
The organization model for a system of humans and Tamagotchis

and peer relationships, as well as the aggregation relationship between the parent role MyTamagotchi and its subrole Matchmaker. Organization models will be further illustrated by the case studies of B2B electronic commerce and manufacturing presented in chapter 8.

3.4   Domain Models

When a stakeholder models goals and roles for a system, he or she also has some idea of the environment(s) in which the agents of the system will be situated. Each of those environments comes with particular knowledge that the system is supposed to handle. The model of that knowledge is called a *domain model*. It consists of *domain entities* and relationships between them. A domain entity is a modular unit of knowledge handled by a sociotechnical system. As stated in chapter 2, a domain entity is conceptually an object type. An instance of a domain entity is hence called an environment object. An environment itself can be modeled as one of the domain entities. If the system is related to just one environment, the environment may not be explicitly represented in the domain model.

In our running example, a Tamagotchi is always situated in a local virtual environment, which is embedded in its plastic container. Since the representation of an environment in a domain model should have a name, we call this environment the "Tamagotchi Shell." Section 3.1 also described how an owner can enter with his or her Tamagotchi a global virtual environment in the Internet called Tamagotchi Town. Note that the owners of an increasing number of other physical devices— for example, iPods and other PDAs—can switch between physical and virtual environments.

An important dimension of the environment is time. In our running example, considering changes that happen to all domain entities over time is important for meeting the quality goal "The owner has fun," which is attached to the goal "Entertain and educate owner," as modeled in figure 3.3. Indeed, a prerequisite of having fun is the evolution of Tamagotchis over time. Evolution is also reflected by the responsibility of the role MyTamagotchi "Grow from baby to child to teenager to adult," as depicted in table 3.3. There are a number of ways of modeling time, and we do not claim to be exhaustive here. Our goal models do not represent any temporal sequence or order in which goals are to be achieved. Temporal aspects will be included by interaction and behavior models, described in sections 3.6 and 3.9, respectively.

An environment consists of two kinds of environment objects: services and resources. *Services* are modeled as reactive entities that provide functionality to the agents. Services are discussed in section 3.10.

An environment can produce and store objects to be accessed and used by agents. Such objects are modeled as *resources*. As pointed out in chapter 2, in the context of this book, we are interested in various *information resources* provided by environments. For example, resources of type Letter are produced by the mailbox of the Tamagotchi Shell environment and resources of type Food are provided by both the Tamagotchi Shell and Tamagotchi Town environments. Resources of both types can be stored within the Tamagotchi Shell environment to be used by the digital pet.

Sometimes information resources simulate material resources. For example, rental cars in the information system of a car rental company reflect rental cars used in the company. Similarly, a mold set in a manufacturing simulation system reflects the mold set used in the manufacturing process. An important difference between information resources and material resources is that information resources are infinitely renewable—they do not disappear after consumption—yet material resources will be sooner or later exhausted. This difference also needs to be reflected by the corresponding information resources. For example, after a Tamagotchi has "eaten" a resource of type Food, this resource is removed from its Tamagotchi Shell environment.

Table 3.7 lists the types of resources in the Tamagotchi Shell and Tamagotchi Town environments. For each resource, the table also shows the role(s) with which it is associated. The most essential resource type for a Tamagotchi is Food. Resources belonging to the Meal and Snack subtypes of Food are provided by the Tamagotchi Shell environment. Resources of both types are associated with the role MyTamagotchi and also with the role Owner, because it is the owner's responsibility to feed his or her digital pet. A Tamagotchi, as mediated by its owner, can obtain additional food items from the Tamagotchi Town environment.

In addition to the roles MyTamagotchi and Owner, the resource types Snack and Item are associated with the role FriendTamagotchi, because resources of these

Table 3.7
The types of resources consumed by a Tamagotchi

Resource(s)	Role(s)	Environment(s)
Present (Snack or Item)	MyTamagotchi, Owner, FriendTamagotchi	Tamagotchi Shell, Tamagotchi Town
Food (Meal or Snack)	MyTamagotchi, Owner	Tamagotchi Shell, Tamagotchi Town
Meal (Hamburger, Omelet, Fish, Pizza, . . .)	MyTamagotchi, Owner	Tamagotchi Shell, Tamagotchi Town
Snack (Popcorn, Banana, Grapes, Watermelon, Ice-Cream, . . .)	MyTamagotchi, Owner, FriendTamagotchi	Tamagotchi Shell, Tamagotchi Town
Item (Racing-game, Chest, Flower, Shovel, . . .)	MyTamagotchi, Owner, FriendTamagotchi	Tamagotchi Shell, Tamagotchi Town
Souvenir	MyTamagotchi, Owner	Tamagotchi Town, Tamagotchi Shell
Letter	MyTamagotchi, Owner	Tamagotchi Shell

types can appear as presents given by my digital pet to another. To reflect this, the two types have been generalized into the `Present` resource type.

After a Tamagotchi has entered Tamagotchi Town, that environment can produce resources of the `Food`, `Item`, and `Souvenir` types. These resources can then be transferred into the Tamagotchi's local Tamagotchi Shell environment and consumed from there.

Resources of type `Letter` are associated only with the Tamagotchi Shell environment as they are generated by it.

We conclude this section with a more precise definition of a domain model. *Domain models* represent the environments, the types of resources produced and stored by them, and the relationships between roles, environments, and resources. For example, an agent playing the MyTamagotchi role is situated in the Tamagotchi Shell environment and can enter the Tamagotchi Town environment. Both environments contain resources of type `Present` that can be given by an agent playing the MyTamagotchi role to the agent playing the FriendTamagotchi role. When accessing the environments, a Tamagotchi interacts with its owner. All this is modeled in figure 3.8. The names of both environments have been underlined to denote that there is just one instance of each environment.

3.5   Agent and Acquaintance Models

The models of the motivation layer of the conceptual space—goal models, role and organization models, and domain models—represent the problem domain in abstract terms. Both customers and other external stakeholders on one side and experts in sys-

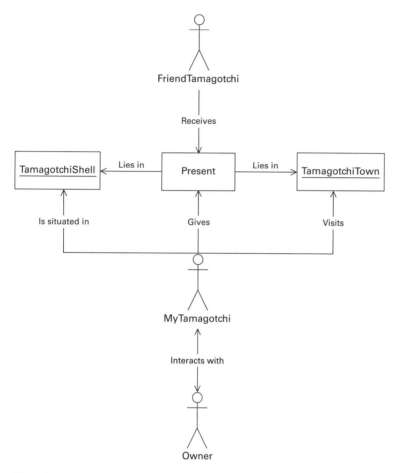

Figure 3.8
The domain model for the Tamagotchi case study

tem design on the other should be capable of understanding these models. The purpose of *agent models* is to transform the abstract constructs from the analysis stage, roles, to design constructs, *agent types*, which will be realized in the implementation process. The agent model outlines the agent types in the system. The *acquaintance model* complements the agent model by outlining interaction pathways between the agents of the system.

The agent model is created by designing agent types to fulfil the roles. Each role may be mapped to one or more agent type(s). Conversely, two or more roles may be mapped to one agent type. Mapping to agent types does not mean disregarding roles, as we continue using roles in design models whenever they enhance the clarity of models.

How to decide agent types? There are no strict rules—only a few guidelines. The agent-oriented methodologies overviewed in chapter 7 discuss deciding agent types in more detail.

First, if two roles are peers, they should probably be mapped to the same agent type. For example, the roles MyTamagotchi and FriendTamagotchi, which are peers according to the organization model represented in figure 3.7, are mapped to the same manmade agent type `Tamagotchi`. Similarly, roles of individuals who are supposed to interact in a peer-to-peer manner, such as TouchInitiator and TouchResponder in the flirting example explained in chapter 9, and institutional roles at the same level, such as Arriving Flights Controller and Departing Flights Controller in air traffic control, are in many cases mapped to the same agent types. The rationale behind this is that individuals or groups of individuals playing those roles may change their roles so that, for example, an agent enacting the role TouchInitiator starts to play the role TouchResponder, or a group of agents enacting the role Arriving Flights Controller starts to play the role Departing Flights Controller. For this reason, it makes sense if an agent type incorporates the responsibilities defined by several roles.

Second, two roles that are related to each other by a control relationship tend to be mapped to different agent types. For example, the role MyTamagotchi is mapped to the manmade agent type `Tamagotchi` and the role Owner—to the human agent type `Person`. In the same manner, roles of individuals where one role is controlled by another, or institutional roles, where one role is subordinated to another, like AccountingDepartment and ManagingBoard in the manufacturing simulation example presented in chapter 8, are usually mapped to different agent types. The reason is that the same agent is not likely to play two disparate roles.

If one role is benevolent toward another, like in market relationships, the roles are generally mapped to different agent types. However, if one agent can play both roles, these roles should be mapped to the same agent type. For example, in the business-to-business e-commerce example in chapter 8, an agent that represents an organization may be involved in both buying and selling. In that case, the roles Seller and Buyer, where a Seller is benevolent toward the Buyer, should be mapped to the same agent type. On the other hand, the same agent cannot play the roles Doctor and Patient in a system created for telemedicine, where medical information is transferred via the Internet for consulting and remote medical examinations and procedures. Consequently, these roles should be mapped to different agent types.

The designer should decide, for each agent type of the system, the number of agent instances of that type at runtime. The agent model can be annotated accordingly. Figure 3.9 shows the agent model produced for the multiagent system of humans and Tamagotchis. The figure reflects that the roles MyTamagotchi and FriendTamagotchi, used in the previous sections, have been mapped to the manmade

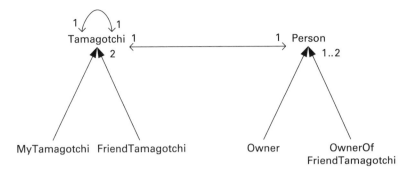

Figure 3.9
The merged agent and acquaintance model

agent type `Tamagotchi`, of which there are exactly two instances. This is because only two Tamagotchis can interact with each other—there is no multilateral interaction between Tamagotchis. This mapping also implies that the responsibilities and constraints attributed to the roles MyTamagotchi and FriendTamagotchi should be amalgamated in the design phase. This is shown in section 3.9.

Additionally, figure 3.9 models that the roles Owner and OwnerOfFriendTamagotchi have been mapped to one or two human agents of type `Person`. It reflects that generally, each Tamagotchi has an owner, but both Tamagotchis may also belong to the same person. We have excluded the cases of shared ownership from our case study for pedagogical reasons. A multiagent system of Tamagotchis and their owners thus consists of two instances of the agent type `Tamagotchi` and one or two instances of the agent type `Person`.

Next, we have to design interaction pathways between agent type*s*. This results in an *agent acquaintance model*. This model is a directed graph between agent types. An arc from agent type A to agent type B signals the existence of an interaction link, allowing an agent of type A to initiate interactions with an agent of type B. An interaction may be sending a message to another agent or performing a physical action affecting it. Information about interactions can be extracted from responsibilities of role models. For example, the responsibilities associated with the role MyTamagotchi, such as expressing hunger, becoming sick, producing excrement, and expressing loneliness, define messages sent from an agent of type `Tamagotchi` to an agent of type `Person`. Conversely, responsibilities of the role Owner define "press-the-button" actions performed by a person toward a Tamagotchi. The purpose of the acquaintance model is to allow the designer to visualize the degree of coupling between agents. Further details such as message types are ignored. Coupling analysis is handled thoroughly in the Prometheus agent-oriented methodology, which we discuss in chapter 7.

The acquaintance model may be merged with the agent model as can be seen in figure 3.9. This model represents how a Tamagotchi may interact with one other Tamagotchi and one person at a time, whereas any party may initiate an interaction.

3.6 Interaction Models

The interaction links described in section 3.5 show only which agents interact with which other agents and which party can initiate an interaction. *Interaction models* represent interaction patterns between agents in more detail. They are based on responsibilities defined for the corresponding roles. As we have repeatedly emphasized, modeling interactions is crucial and central in agent-oriented modeling.

We distinguish between pure interaction modeling and protocol modeling. Pure interaction modeling adopts the perspective of an external observer who is looking at the (prototypical) agents and their interactions in the problem domain under consideration. An external observer just observes what messages flow and interactions occur between agents without knowing anything about how an agent comes to a decision to send a particular message or perform a particular action. We can capture pure interaction models by interaction diagrams, interaction-sequence diagrams, and interaction-frame diagrams. Protocol modeling combines interaction modeling with the modeling of some aspects of agents' behavior.

A (UML-style) *interaction diagram* models (some part of) a prototypical interaction process. It defines the order of interactions by the order of the corresponding graphical arrows. In an interaction diagram, time increases as one moves downward. The fact that the agents involved in the interactions are agent instances rather than types is conveyed by underlining their names. The interaction diagram represented in figure 3.10 models interactions between two interconnected Tamagotchis and the owner of the first Tamagotchi. The diagram represents both physical interactions and communication. The physical interaction modeled in the figure is pushing a button of a Tamagotchi Shell by a human agent, which triggers a visit by the Tamagotchi to the other. Communication is either sending a message by the Tamagotchi to its owner or sending a message to the other Tamagotchi. A visit occurs through the exchange of messages by the two Tamagotchis that results in the visual representation in the Tamagotchi Shells' screens of one Tamagotchi going to the other Tamagotchi's local environment and performing different activities there. The activities can be playing with the hosting Tamagotchi and giving the hosting Tamagotchi a present. A visit in progress is shown in figure 3.10.

The notation employed by interaction diagrams does not distinguish between physical interactions, such as "Please visit your friend" in figure 3.10, and communication. Also, representing the order of interactions by the order of interaction arrows can be tricky for more complicated cases. These deficiencies can be overcome by

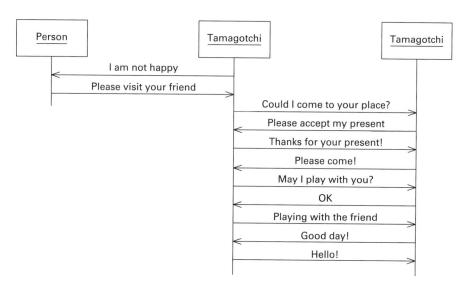

Figure 3.10
An interaction diagram

interaction-sequence diagrams. An *interaction-sequence diagram* models interactions as action events. As is explained in section 2.6, an *action event* is an event that is caused by the action of an agent, like sending a message or starting a machine. An action event can thus be viewed as a coin with two sides: an action for the performing agent and an event for the perceiving agent. A message is a special type of action event—*communicative action event*—that is caused by the sending agent and perceived by the receiving agent. On the other hand, there are *nonaction events* that are not caused by actions—for example, the fall of a particular stock value below a certain threshold, the sinking of a ship in a storm, or a timeout in an auction. In our conceptual space explained in chapter 2, both action events and nonaction events are represented as *perceptions*, because both are always related to an agent that perceives them. The notation for modeling action events is represented in figure 3.11.

An interaction-sequence diagram models a sequence of action events, performed/ sent and perceived/received by agents. The fact that the agents as well as the action events modeled are instances rather than types is conveyed by underlining their names. In the diagram, each action event is characterized by its number. The numbers constitute an *interaction sequence* between the agents involved. It is important to emphasize that an interaction sequence represented by an interaction-sequence diagram is just an example realizing one option out of several possibilities. Figure 3.12 represents an interaction-sequence diagram that is equivalent to the interaction diagram shown in figure 3.10. Differently from an interaction diagram, an

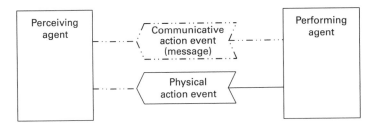

Figure 3.11
The notation for modeling action events

interaction-sequence diagram explicitly represents the order of interactions and distinguishes between messages and physical interactions.

There may be a need to generalize the types of action events occurring between agents and the types of agents themselves. This can be accomplished by interaction-frame diagrams. An *interaction-frame diagram* models possible interactions between two or more types of agents. For example, the interaction-frame diagram represented in figure 3.13 models the types of action events that can occur between two Tamagotchis and the owner of the first Tamagotchi. This interaction-frame diagram consists of two *interaction frames*. The first interaction frame models the types of interactions between a Tamagotchi and its owner and the other one the types of interactions between two Tamagotchis. Please note that all the modeling elements in interaction frames are types: agent types and the types of action events.

As pointed out in section 2.2, greeting and visiting scenarios can be rather sophisticated depending on the age and status of the agents involved. In our example interaction model, represented in figure 3.13, we have reflected this by assuming that a Tamagotchi may refuse a visit by another Tamagotchi younger than he or she is. In our example, it is also assumed that a Tamagotchi can refuse to play with another Tamagotchi.

Interaction-frame diagrams can model all interaction alternatives for both physical interactions and communication. They do not say anything about the order in which the agents interact or about the conditions under which one or another alternative occurs. For example, the interaction frame between two Tamagotchis that is shown in figure 3.13 represents both alternatives: when the second Tamagotchi agrees to host the first one and when it refuses to do so. In other words, interaction frames do not model the behaviors of the agents involved. They view agents as "black boxes" that interact following unknown principles. However, action events in interaction frames are usually represented in the rough order of their sending/occurrence.

Aspects of the agents' behavior are included by mixed interaction and behavior modeling. The resulting models may be termed *protocols*. For example, the UML-

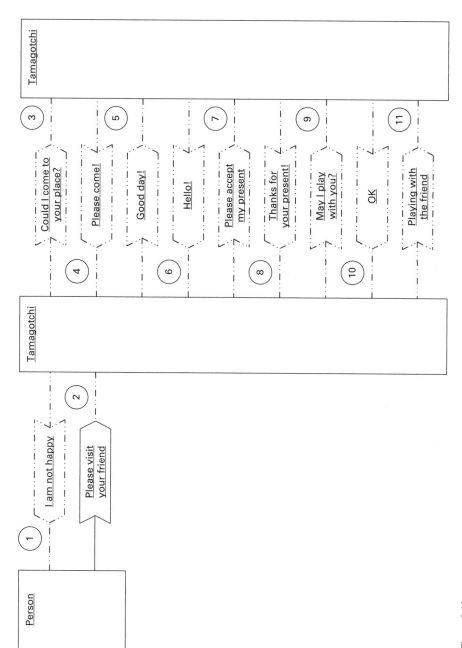

Figure 3.12
An interaction-sequence diagram

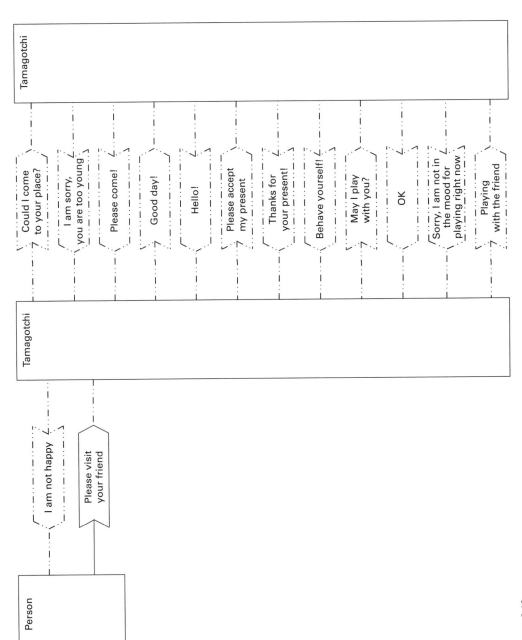

Figure 3.13
An interaction-frame diagram

style sequence diagram depicted in figure 3.14 models the interaction protocol between two Tamagotchis and the owner of the first Tamagotchi, where one Tamagotchi visits the other. This protocol assumes that a visit may include giving a present and playing. The protocol includes four *modeling constructs*: option, alternative, interleaving, and loop, which are specified using boxes. The protocol represented in figure 3.14 uses an *Option box* for expressing how after a human agent initiates a virtual visit between two Tamagotchis, interactions between the Tamagotchis start only if there is an operational connection between the Tamagotchis. The latter condition is modeled as the *guard* [Connection operational]. If the connection is not operational, nothing happens in response to the action by the owner.

In figure 3.14, there is another box labeled "Alternative" nested within the Option box. An Alternative box can have a number of regions, each possibly with a guard, and exactly one region will be executed, depending on the guards, if any. The Alternative box in figure 3.14 has been divided into two regions. The alternative specified by the upper region is that the second Tamagotchi refuses the visit by the first one. We know that this happens if the first Tamagotchi is younger than the second one, even though the modeler has chosen not to represent the corresponding guard in the figure. The alternative specified by the lower region executes the interactions of the virtual visit. The lower region contains the third-level nested box labeled "Loop (1, *), Interleaved" This label models that the regions of the box, two in the given case, should be executed at least once and may be executed any number of times, and can be executed in any order. A Tamagotchi thus has to give the other Tamagotchi a present and play with it at least once. How many times and in which order giving a present and playing are actually repeated is specified by scenarios and behavior models, explained in sections 3.8 and 3.9. Please note that both interleaved alternatives contain boxes labeled "Critical region." This means that no interleaving should take place within the contents of the box. For example, the messages related to giving the other Tamagotchi a present must occur precisely in the order shown within the "Critical region" box. The upper "Critical region" box is also labeled "Option" and has the guard [Enough presents]. The guard denotes that the contents of the box are executed only if the Tamagotchi has enough presents on store. Each "Critical region" box contains another nested box labeled "Alternative." The upper "Alternative" box models that the hosting Tamagotchi either thanks the other for the present or reprimands the visiting Tamagotchi if the latter attempts to present it with something like a snake. The second "Alternative" box indicates that the hosting Tamagotchi either agrees to play with the visiting Tamagotchi or refuses to do so.

A modeler chooses suitable types of interaction models based on the nature of the problem domain and the requirements for the system. For example, if the system to

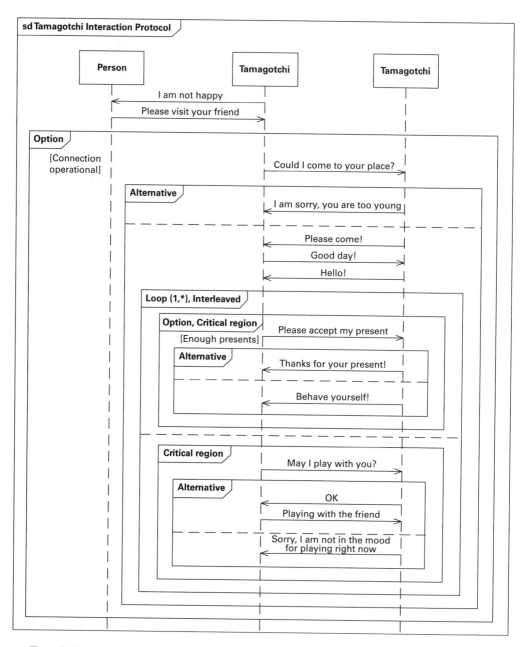

Figure 3.14
An interaction protocol

Figure 3.15
The notation for modeling nonaction events and actions on an environment

be developed does not involve any physical interactions between human and man-made agents, interaction diagrams will do. In a different situation, interaction-sequence and interaction-frame diagrams might pose a better option.

There is one more aspect to interaction modeling. One may need to model events that are not caused by agents or one may not want to include in the models agents causing the events. Such events can be modeled as nonaction events that were briefly explained earlier in this section. Nonaction events are modeled as occurring in an environment in which the agents are situated. For example, receiving a letter by a Tamagotchi should be modeled as a nonaction event, because resources of type `Letter` are generated by the Tamagotchi Shell environment rather than sent by other agents. As another example, a modeler may choose not to represent a human agent performing the role Intruder, who causes by his or her physical movements in the guarded area an action event of type `move`, which is perceived by a home security agent. The notation for modeling nonaction events is represented in figure 3.15. As described in chapter 7, some agent-oriented methodologies model nonaction events as *percepts* from an environment.

A modeler may also need to represent an action performed by an agent on an environment without indicating a specific agent affected by the action. For example, when modeling climate change, it would be sensible to represent the actions of man-made agents affecting the natural environment without singling out particular agents affected. A notation for modeling actions on the environment is depicted in figure 3.15. An example including events originating in an environment and actions performed on an environment will be provided in chapter 4.

3.7 Knowledge Models

Section 3.4 describes *role-based* domain models representing at an abstract level knowledge that the system is supposed to handle. The domain model also identifies relevant parts of the knowledge for roles. This section discusses at a more concrete level how to model the knowledge of agents using *knowledge models*. A knowledge model can be viewed as an *ontology* providing a framework of knowledge for the agents of the problem domain.

Table 3.8
The knowledge attributes of a Tamagotchi

Knowledge attribute	Type
Tamagotchi name	String
Tamagotchi age	Integer
Tamagotchi gender	Enumeration (male; female)
Tamagotchi generation	Integer
Tamagotchi weight	Real
Tamagotchi hunger level	Integer
Tamagotchi happiness level	Integer
Tamagotchi training level	Integer
Tamagotchi life points	Integer
Tamagotchi gotchi points	Integer

Knowledge is carried by agents rather than roles. However, roles may be needed in knowledge models, because the knowledge that is to be represented by an agent depends on the role(s) the agent plays. For example, in the example of business-to-business electronic commerce to be treated in chapter 8, an agent playing the Buyer role needs to represent knowledge about sellers and the types of products sold by them, and an agent of the same type enacting the Seller role needs to know about buyers.

An agent's knowledge model represents knowledge about the agent itself and about the agents and objects in its environment. An agent can represent information about itself by *knowledge attributes*. Recall from chapter 2 that an attribute represents one or more quality dimensions of an entity. For example, each of us can be characterized by the date of birth, height, weight, hair color, eye color, and so forth. The knowledge attributes of a Tamagotchi are represented in table 3.8.

The most frequently used knowledge attribute types are `String`, `Integer`, `Real`, `Boolean`, `Date`, and `Enumeration`. Their meanings should be obvious, but short explanations will follow. An instance of `String` is a sequence of characters in some suitable character set. The types `Integer` and `Real` represent the mathematical concepts of integer and real numbers. The `Boolean` type is used for logical expressions, consisting of the predefined values "true" and "false." The `Date` type represents a day, month, and year. An `Enumeration` type defines a number of enumeration literals that are the possible values of an attribute of that type. For example, the possible values of the attribute Tamagotchi gender listed in table 3.8 are "male" and "female."

An agent can also represent knowledge about itself and about the agents and objects in its environment by means of *conceptual objects* that can be related to each other in a potentially complex way. As an example, an agent's knowledge can be embodied in a relational database that stores conceptual objects representing customers and orders and the relationships between them. Just like agents, conceptual objects can be characterized by attributes, where an attribute describes the quality of an object. For example, the attributes of an order include the type of product ordered and the quantity ordered. Agent architectures, such as the Belief-Desire-Intention (BDI) architecture discussed in section 5.1, generally refer to the knowledge of an agent as its *beliefs*. How some agent programming languages represent agents' beliefs is described in chapter 5.

An agent uses conceptual objects for representing knowledge about resources consumed by it. For example, a Tamagotchi requires knowledge about food items and souvenirs that can be acquired when visiting Tamagotchi Town. There is a conceptual object type corresponding to each resource included in table 3.7, the most generic object types being Food and Item.

Another purpose of knowledge models is to provide different agents with a common framework of knowledge so that they can understand each other in interactions. For instance, two humans need a joint understanding of the terms related to an issue before they can discuss the issue. This knowledge is represented as a set of interrelated conceptual objects shared by several agents.

An example of a shared conceptual object type is Present, which corresponds to a resource shown in table 3.7. This object type is necessary, because two Tamagotchis require common knowledge about the types of presents that one Tamagotchi can give to another. As table 3.7 reflects, this knowledge is also related to the local environments of both agents because a present is transferred from the local Tamagotchi Shell environment of the first agent to the local environment of the second agent. Each Present object has an attribute containing the name of the present, such as "Ice-Cream" or "Flower."

A conceptual object of type Owner represents knowledge a Tamagotchi has about its owner. The attributes of an object of type Owner describes the name and birth date of the owner. The latter is used to ensure a Tamagotchi celebrates its owner's birthday. Note that the conceptual object type Owner and the role Owner are different.

Conceptual objects of types Friend_list and Friend represent the knowledge a Tamagotchi has about other Tamagotchis with which it has connected. A conceptual object of type Friend has attributes describing the name of another Tamagotchi and its friendship level.

Conceptual objects of type Password exchange knowledge between a Tamagotchi and its owner and the virtual environment Tamagotchi Town. As pointed out in section 3.1, Tamagotchi Town identifies each Tamagotchi through a unique fourteen-character alphanumeric password generated by the Tamagotchi Shell of the digital pet and returns another fourteen-character alphanumeric password to be entered by the owner into the Tamagotchi Shell. By means of this password, Tamagotchi Town ensures that a Tamagotchi is at the appropriate age to visit either the school or kindergarten and registers that the Tamagotchi has attended the school or kindergarten. The password thus captures a part of the Tamagotchi's knowledge base, in addition to catering for security. Password is a subtype of the `String` type that was briefly explained earlier.

Finally, a Tamagotchi needs to have knowledge about its environments. Hence we have included the environment objects `TamagotchiShell` and `TamagotchiTown` as knowledge items.

Conceptual objects may be subject to derivations and constraints. A *derivation* is a statement of knowledge that is derived from other knowledge by an inference or a mathematical calculation. An example of a derivation is that the partner of the Tamagotchi is a friend who has connected with it five times. A *constraint* is an assertion that must be satisfied in all evolving states and state transition histories of the system. An example constraint is that to go to school, the Tamagotchi must be from two to five years of age.

Conceptual objects can be related to each other in many ways. The most common types of relationships are generalization and aggregation. *Generalization* is a taxonomic relationship between more general and more specific conceptual object types. For example, there is a generalization relationship between the object type `Food` and the object types `Meal` and `Snack`. *Aggregation* is a binary association that specifies a whole/part relationship between conceptual object types. For instance, there is an aggregation relationship between the object types `Friend_list` and `Friend`.

We are neutral as to knowledge representation languages and notations. For example, one might use the logic programming language Prolog for representing the generalization and aggregation relationships mentioned previously. Possible Prolog code is as follows. The first two clauses express that food is a meal or a snack. The third and fourth clauses for the relationship `friend_list(T, Xs)` expresses that `Xs` is a friend list of `T` if every member of `Xs` is a friend of `T`:

```
food(X) :- meal(X).
food(X) :- snack(X).
friend_list(T, []).
friend_list(T, [X|Friends]) :-
     friend(T, X), friend_list(T, Friends).
```

Knowledge can be represented for an agent as a collection of Prolog facts and rules. We can also create knowledge models by employing a UML-like notation, as has been done in figure 3.16. This figure represents a partial knowledge model for agents of the `Tamagotchi` type. The generalization hierarchy on the lefthand side of

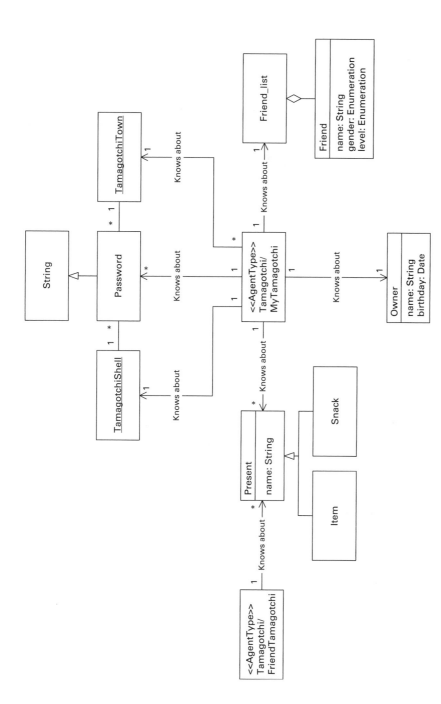

Figure 3.16
A partial knowledge model for agents of the Tamagotchi type

the figure models that a `Present` can be a `Snack` or `Item`. Another generalization hierarchy at the top of the figure represents that an instance of `Password` is of type `String`. The aggregation relationship on the righthand side represents that a `Friend_list` consists of instances of type `Friend`.

In the knowledge model shown in figure 3.16, agent types are distinguished from object types by means of the UML-like stereotype `<<AgentType>>`. The model also shows roles played by different agents of the `Tamagotchi` type by using an `Agent Type Name`/`Role Name` notation inspired by AUML, an extension of UML that is oriented toward agents. This distinction is needed for representing *who knows what*: an agent playing the role MyTamagotchi knows about its owner, friend list, passwords, and environments, and agents playing the roles MyTamagotchi and FriendTamagotchi share knowledge about conceptual objects of type `Present`. In addition, the model includes attributes for the conceptual object types `Present`, `Owner`, and `Friend`.

The model represents *cardinalities* of relationships between entity types, showing how many instances of agents or objects can participate in relationships. For example, a Tamagotchi knows about several presents and passwords but of only one owner and friend list.

3.8   Scenarios

Section 3.6 explained interaction models. Interactions between agents are determined by the activities performed by them. The activities that an agent performs, in turn, depend on the decisions made by the agent. Making decisions and performing activities is addressed by *behavior modeling*. A *scenario* is a behavior model that describes how the goals set for the system can be achieved by agents of the system. Section 3.2 illustrates goal models with motivational scenarios that describe in an informal and loose narrative manner how goals set for the system can be achieved by agents enacting the corresponding roles. In this section, we elaborate motivational scenarios by turning them into scenarios of the multiagent system to be developed.

As shown in chapter 7, several agent-oriented methodologies include scenarios. A *scenario* can be defined as a collective activity that models how a particular goal is achieved by agents enacting particular roles. A collective activity was defined in chapter 2 as an activity involving two or more agents performing several roles. For example, an activity for achieving the goal "Entertain and educate owner" represented in figure 3.3 involves the roles Owner and MyTamagotchi. In contrast, a private activity "Tamagotchi is hatching" is performed solely by an agent playing the MyTamagotchi role. In most cases, goals are achieved through interactions between agents performing the corresponding roles. This is natural, because as we have repeatedly pointed out in chapters 1 and 2 and earlier in this chapter, achieving goals through interactions is intrinsic to multiagent systems.

A scenario may contain subscenarios, which straightforwardly correspond to subgoals. For example, the scenario corresponding to the goal "Sustain Tamagotchi" modeled in figure 3.3 has six subscenarios that realize the respective subgoals "Feed Tamagotchi," "Cure Tamagotchi," "Clean the Tamagotchi's environment," "Socialize Tamagotchi," "Entertain Tamagotchi," and "Discipline Tamagotchi." Among them, the subscenarios "Socialize Tamagotchi" and "Entertain Tamagotchi" include the corresponding third-level subscenarios "Visit the friend" and "Visit Tamagotchi Town." Activities that are not scenarios, such as "Cure the Tamagotchi" or "Give the friend a present," may be called *routine activities*. A clue for deciding which activities should be modeled as routine activities is provided by responsibilites of roles. A routine activity does not have an implicitly assigned goal, but a goal may be assigned to it if the activity is a problem-solving activity. As pointed out in section 2.6, such an activity is termed a *task* and its goal is called a *logic goal*. For example, we can assign a goal to the "Cure the Tamagotchi" activity if curing is modeled as a problem to be solved rather than a simple interaction.

A logic goal associated with a task may be achieved by alternative sets of subactivities and their constituent elementary actions. We can also say that a task may have various *plans* for achieving the goal. As a simple example, the goal of feeding the Tamagotchi can be accomplished through different action sequences, because a Tamagotchi can be fed with sushi as well as with ice cream. It is the Tamagotchi's owner who decides, but a Tamagotchi capable of preferring healthy food to junk food by selecting an appropriate nutrition plan is easily imagined.

A scenario is triggered by a *situation* involving the agent initiating the scenario. For example, the scenario for the goal "Sustain Tamagotchi" is triggered by the actions "Wake up" or "Reset" by the owner, and the subscenario corresponding to the subgoal "Socialize Tamagotchi" is triggered by the expression of a Tamagotchi's state of unhappiness. The former scenario represents a reactive behavior; the latter is an example of a proactive behavior that is initiated by the agent itself. Interestingly and arguably, we claim that any proactive behavior is reactive at some level, because, for example, the state of unhappiness can be reduced to specific events that have caused it. However, this distinction is not relevant for our modeling purposes.

To discover triggers, it is worthwhile to have a look at the rsponsibilities defined for the roles of the system. For example, table 3.3 includes the following responsibilities that have been defined for the role MyTamagotchi: "express hunger," "become sick," "produce excrement," "express loneliness," and "misbehave occasionally."

As shown in table 3.9, a scenario can be modeled as a table showing the scenario's identifying number, goal, initiator, and trigger, and its constituent steps. Some scenarios also show what will happen if the agents involved fail to act as is prescribed

Table 3.9
A scenario for achieving the goal "Sustain Tamagotchi"

SCENARIO 1	
Goal	Sustain Tamagotchi
Initiator	Owner
Trigger	Waking up or resetting by the owner

DESCRIPTION

Condition	Step	Activity	Agent types/roles	Resources	Quality goals
	1	Set the date and time	Person/Owner, Tamagotchi/ MyTamagotchi		
	2	Set the birthday of the owner	Person/Owner, Tamagotchi/ MyTamagotchi		
	3	Choose the owner name	Person/Owner, Tamagotchi/ MyTamagotchi		
	4	A Tamagotchi is hatching	Tamagotchi/ MyTamagotchi		
	5	Choose a name for the Tamagotchi	Person/Owner, Tamagotchi/ MyTamagotchi		
Interleaved	6	Feed the Tamagotchi (Scenario 2)	Person/Owner, Tamagotchi/ MyTamagotchi	Food	My Tamagotchi healthy
	7	Cure the Tamagotchi (Scenario 3)	Person/Owner, Tamagotchi/ MyTamagotchi		My Tamagotchi healthy
	8	Clean the Tamagotchi's environment (Scenario 4)	Person/Owner, Tamagotchi/ MyTamagotchi		My Tamagotchi healthy
	9	Socialize Tamagotchi (Scenario 5)	Person/Owner, Tamagotchi/ MyTamagotchi, Tamagotchi/ FriendTamagotchi	Present	My Tamagotchi happy, Appropriatre presenting

Table 3.10
A scenario for achieving the goal "Feed Tamagotchi"

SCENARIO 2					
Goal		Feed Tamagotchi			
Initiator		MyTamagotchi			
Trigger		The Tamagotchi is hungry.			
Failure		The Tamagotchi dies.			
Condition	Step	Activity	Agent types and roles	Resources	Quality goals
Options, repeat if necessary	1	Have meal	Person/Owner, Tamagotchi/ MyTamagotchi	Food	My Tamagotchi healthy
	2	Have snack	Person/Owner, Tamagotchi/ MyTamagotchi	Food	My Tamagotchi healthy

by the scenario. For example, the scenario represented in table 3.10 specifies in the "Failure" row that the Tamagotchi would die if it is not fed.

Each step of a scenario represents an activity. An activity may be modeled as a subscenario, like the activities modeled as steps 6–9 in table 3.9.

Scenarios identify, for each activity, both the agent type and the role that an agent of that type is playing. For example, we describe the agent types and roles involved in the activity "Socialize Tamagotchi" represented in table 3.13 as Person/Owner, Tamagotchi/MyTamagotchi, Tamagotchi/FriendTamagotchi, and Tamagotchi/ Matchmaker.

When modeling scenarios, we have to decide under which conditions subscenarios and other constituent activities of scenarios are to be performed. For this purpose, the first column in a scenario table is used. For example, the scenario shown in table 3.9 defines the condition "Interleaved" for the steps 6–9, which means that these activities may be performed in any order, depending on the triggers. Similarly, the scenario represented in table 3.10 defines for steps 2–3 the condition "Options, repeat if necessary," specifying that one of the activities is to be performed at a time, and the activity may be repeated. In addition, the keywords "Sequential" and "Loop" can be used for expressing the condition for performing activities. The implicit order of performing activities is sequential. For example, according to the scenario modeled in table 3.14, the activities "Give the friend a present" and "Play with the friend" are performed sequentially. This reflects a design decision that has elaborated the interaction protocol represented in figure 3.14.

The fifth column of a scenario table shows the resources associated with the activity. For example, according to the scenario modeled in table 3.9, the activity "Socialize Tamagotchi" accesses resources of type `Present`.

Table 3.11
A scenario for achieving the goal "Cure Tamagotchi"

SCENARIO 3	
Goal	Cure Tamagotchi
Initiator	MyTamagotchi
Trigger	The Tamagotchi is sick.
Failure	The Tamagotchi dies.

DESCRIPTION

Condition	Step	Activity	Agent types and roles	Resources	Quality goals
Repeat if necessary	1	Nurse the Tamagotchi to health	Person/Owner, Tamagotchi/ MyTamagotchi		My Tamagotchi healthy

Table 3.12
A scenario for achieving the goal "Clean the Tamagotchi's environment"

SCENARIO 4	
Goal	Clean the Tamagotchi's environment
Initiator	MyTamagotchi
Trigger	The Tamagotchi has produced excrement.
Failure	The Tamagotchi becomes sick.

DESCRIPTION

Condition	Step	Activity	Agent types and roles	Resources	Quality goals
Repeat if necessary	1	Flush the toilet	Person/Owner, Tamagotchi/ MyTamagotchi		My Tamagotchi healthy

The last column of a scenario step indicates quality goals relevant for the step. For example, two quality goals, "My Tamagotchi happy" and "Appropriate presenting," are relevant for step 9 of the scenario presented in table 3.9.

The scenarios for achieving the goal "Sustain Tamagotchi" and the first four of its subgoals represented in figure 3.3 are modeled in tables 3.9–3.15. More examples of scenarios are presented in the application chapters in part II.

3.9   Behavior Models

Scenarios focus on how a multiagent system achieves the goals set for it rather than what individual agents do. Behavior models address what individual agents do. We

Table 3.13
A scenario for achieving the goal "Socialize Tamagotchi"

SCENARIO 5	
Goal	Socialize Tamagotchi
Initiator	MyTamagotchi
Trigger	The Tamagotchi is unhappy.
Failure	The Tamagotchi dies.

DESCRIPTION

Condition	Step	Activity	Agent types and roles	Resources	Quality goals
	1	Visit the friend (Scenario 6)	Person/Owner, Tamagotchi/ MyTamagotchi, Tamagotchi/ FriendTamagotchi	Present	My Tamagotchi happy
	2	Find a partner for the Tamagotchi (Scenario 7)	Person/Owner, Tamagotchi/ Matchmaker	Friend_list	My Tamagotchi happy

Table 3.14
A scenario for achieving the goal "Visit the friend"

SCENARIO 6	
Goal	Visit the friend
Initiator	MyTamagotchi
Trigger	The owner has chosen to visit.

DESCRIPTION

Condition	Step	Activity	Agent types and roles	Resources	Quality goals
	1	Connect with another Tamagotchi			
	2	Go to the friend's place	Person/Owner, Tamagotchi/ MyTamagotchi, Tamagotchi/ FriendTamagotchi		My Tamagotchi happy
Loop	3	Give the friend a present	Tamagotchi/ MyTamagotchi, Tamagotchi/ FriendTamagotchi	Present	My Tamagotchi happy, appropriate presenting
	4	Play with the friend	Tamagotchi/ MyTamagotchi, Tamagotchi/ FriendTamagotchi		My Tamagotchi happy
	5	Return home	Tamagotchi/ MyTamagotchi, Tamagotchi/ FriendTamagotchi		My Tamagotchi happy

Table 3.15
A scenario for achieving the goal "Hatch a new Tamagotchi"

SCENARIO 7	
Goal	Find a partner for the Tamagotchi
Initiator	Matchmaker
Trigger	The Tamagotchi has reached a certain age and hasn't found a partner of the opposite sex.

DESCRIPTION

Condition	Step	Activity	Agent types and roles	Resources	Quality goals
	1	Suggest a partner for the Tamagotchi from among his/her friends	Person/Owner, Tamagotchi/ Matchmaker	Friend_list	My Tamagotchi happy, suitable partner
	2	Produce an egg	Tamagotchi/ MyTamagotchi		My Tamagotchi happy
	3	A new Tamagotchi is hatching	Tamagotchi/ MyTamagotchi		My Tamagotchi happy

Table 3.16
Behavioral interfaces for "Have meal" and "Go to the friend's place"

Activity	Trigger	Pre-conditions	Post-conditions
Have meal	Meal selection by the owner	• The Tamagotchi is hungry • The selected meal is in the Tamagotchi Shell	• The Tamagotchi's level of hunger has decreased • The Tamagotchi has consumed the meal from its Tamagotchi Shell
Go to the friend's place	Request to visit by the owner	• The connection to the other Tamagotchi is operational • The Tamagotchi is in its Tamagotchi Shell	• The Tamagotchis is back in its Tamagotchi Shell • The Tamagotchi's happiness level is increased • The Tamagotchi holds any items received as presents

distinguish between two kinds of behavior models: behavioral interface models and agent behavior models. A *behavioral interface model* identifies behavioural units and defines an interface for each behavioral unit. As shown in chapter 7, different agent-oriented methodologies name behavioral units differently—services, activities, capabilities, agents' skills and aptitudes—to mention just a few. For the example models in this section, the behavioral unit is an activity and a behavioral interface is expressed in terms of a trigger, preconditions, and postconditions for performing the corresponding activity. The behavioral interfaces for the activities performed by a Tamagotchi "Have meal" and "Go to the friend's place" are represented in table 3.16. These activities are included in the scenarios presented in tables 3.10 and 3.14.

An *agent behavior model* describes the behavior of an agent of the given type. Because agent behavior models are platform-independent, we cannot make any assumptions about the underlying system architecture. Agent behavior models can thus be expressed only in terms of the abstract agent architecture that was introduced in section 2.3. According to the execution loop of an abstract agent represented in figure 2.5, an agent's behavior is determined by a controller based on the agent's perceptions and knowledge. The controller can be modeled in terms of rules. As explained in section 2.3, a rule is our basic behavior modeling construct.

During each execution cycle of an abstract agent, the rules that can be triggered are found. A rule can be triggered by a perception. An agent can perceive a message sent by another agent or a physical action performed by another agent. An agent can also perceive an event that is not caused by any agent. A rule that is not triggered by a perception is triggered by a *start event* that occurs once per each execution cycle of an abstract agent. The start event activates a rule as soon as the rule's condition becomes true. The condition of a rule checks some aspect of the agent's mental state.

Rules start and sequence activities, which in turn consist of actions. The concepts of rules, activities, and actions were explained in chapter 2. According to chapter 2, there are three kinds of actions: communicative actions, like sending a message; physical actions, like starting a machine; and epistemic actions, like storing a purchase order in the agent's knowledge base.

A visual notation capable of representing rules, activities, and actions is required for behavior modeling. Figure 3.17 introduces a suitable notation. The notation is based on activity diagrams of UML, which are used in several agent-oriented methodologies. The notation also incorporates modeling elements from the Business Process Modeling Notation (BPMN).

A rule is modeled as capable of starting activities and performing actions. In addition, a rule provides a universal modeling element for representing agent behavior modeling constructs such as decisions and forks, and defining the order in which activities are performed.

As opposed to UML activity diagrams and BPMN, we have included agent interactions in behavior models. The notation used for interaction modeling is the one introduced in section 3.6 by interaction-sequence and interaction-frame diagrams. Messages sent or actions performed can be modeled as prescribed by rules, but the modeling notation also enables designers to attach sending of messages or performing of actions to activities.

Agent behavior models focus on a specific agent type. Figure 3.18 represents the behavior of an agent of type `Tamagotchi` who initiates a visit with another Tamagotchi. This involves the routine activities "Express unhappiness," "Connect with another Tamagotchi," "Go to the friend's place," "Give the friend a present,"

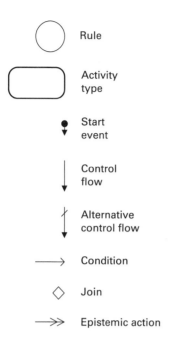

Rule

Activity
type

Start
event

Control
flow

Alternative
control flow

Condition

Join

Epistemic action

Figure 3.17
A notation for modeling agent behavior

"Play with the friend," and "Return home." The first activity is modeled in table 3.13 and the rest are modeled in table 3.14.

Agent behavior models enable both proactive and reactive behaviors to be represented. Proactive behavior is modeled as initiated by values of the agent's knowledge items, representing its mental state, or by values of knowledge items embedded in some environment object computationally accessible to the agent, such as a database. In contrast, reactive behavior is modeled as initiated by some perception by the agent. For example, in figure 3.18, proactive behavior that results in the sending of a message of type "I am not happy" by a Tamagotchi is modeled with the help of rule R1. This rule is triggered by the start event and is activated if the Tamagotchi's mental state is characterized as unhappy. As shown in chapter 5, in practice this is ascertained by the value of the Tamagotchi's knowledge attribute `happinessLevel` being below a certain threshold value. What causes the value of the knowledge attribute to change is determined by other rules briefly illustrated further in what follows. As a result, the behavior of a Tamagotchi can be described as "intelligent," just like Kuldar's eight-year-old daughter Eliise said.

As an example of reactive behavior, in the same figure an activity of type "Connect with another Tamagotchi" is started by rule R2 in reaction to perceiving the corresponding action by a human agent.

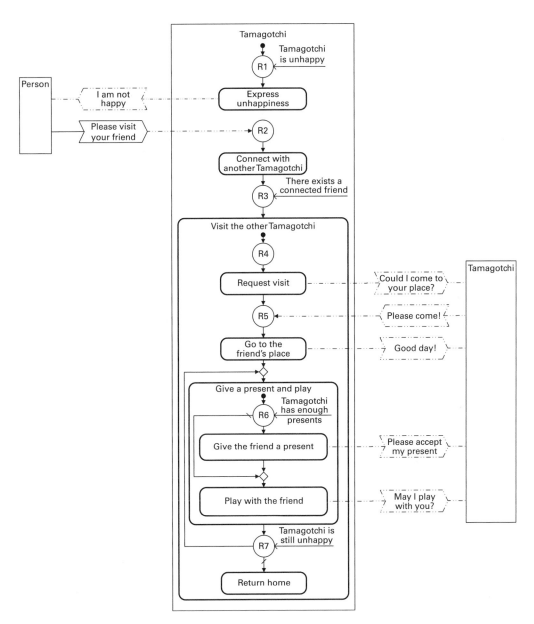

Figure 3.18
An agent behavior model of a Tamagotchi

The condition attached to rule R3 in figure 3.18 means that the rule is triggered only if there exists another Tamagotchi connected to the given one—that is, if an activity of type "Connect with another Tamagotchi" has resulted in an operational connection with another Tamagotchi. When triggered, this rule starts an activity of type "Visit the other Tamagotchi." Returning to the models of interaction protocols explained in section 3.6, rule R3 elaborates the outermost Option box and the respective guard modeled in the interaction protocol in figure 3.14.

Rule R4 models that upon the start of a "Visit the other Tamagotchi" activity, its "Request visit" subactivity is started. After performing that activity, according to rule R5 the Tamagotchi waits for a reply from the other Tamagotchi. Upon receiving a confirmation message from the hosting Tamagotchi, an activity of type "Go to the friend's place" is started. This happens if the visiting Tamagotchi is older than the hosting one. If not, a refusal message is received, which is not shown in figure 3.18.

As an example of a behavior modeling construct expressed by a rule, rule R6 in figure 3.18 represents that upon the start of an activity of type "Give a present and play," if the Tamagotchi has a present, an activity of type "Give the friend a present" is performed. Otherwise, an activity of type "Play with the friend" is performed. Similarly, the condition of rule R7 models that an activity sequence of giving a present and playing is repeated if the Tamagotchi is still unhappy. If the Tamagotchi is happy, an activity of type "Return home" is performed and the enclosing activity of type "Visit the other Tamagotchi" finishes. Rule R7 elaborates the Loop box depicted in the interaction protocol in figure 3.14.

For clarity, rules R1–R7 are modeled in table 3.17. The table shows for each rule its trigger and condition and the action prescribed by the rule.

The behavior of a Tamagotchi within the noninterruptible critical regions of the interaction protocol shown in figure 3.14 is modeled by presenting both "Give the friend a present" and "Play with the friend" as activity types, which must always be executed as units. We have chosen not to represent complete agent behavior models in figure 3.18 for the activity types "Give the friend a present" and "Play with the friend" to demonstrate that behavior modeling is an iterative process where we can model only some parts of the agent's behavior at each step.

As stated previously, actions include epistemic actions that change the agent's knowledge or mental state. We demonstrate in figure 3.19 separately how rules can model epistemic actions by using an example of a rule within the "Give the friend a present" activity type. The notation used in figure 3.19 denotes that when an activity of type "Give the friend a present" is performed, rule R8 increases the value of the Tamagotchi's happinessLevel knowledge attribute by 40.

Alternatively, the agent behavior model represented in figure 3.18 can be modeled as a UML statechart, as is shown in figure 3.20. This notation represents activities as states and rules as state transitions.

Table 3.17
The models for rules R1–R7

Rule	Trigger	Condition	Action if condition true	Action if condition false
R1	Start event	Tamagotchi is unhappy	Send "I am not happy" message to the owner	—
R2	Request "Please visit your friend" by the owner	—	Start "Connect with another Tamagotchi" activity	—
R3	End of "Connect with another Tamagotchi" activity	There exists a connected friend	Start "Visit the other Tamagotchi" activity	—
R4	Start of "Visit the other Tamagotchi" activity	—	Start "Request visit" activity	—
R5	End of "Request visit" activity AND receiving of "Please come!" message from the other Tamagotchi	—	Start "Go to the friend's place" activity	—
R6	Start of "Give a present and play" activity	Tamagotchi has enough presents	Start "Give the friend a present" activity	Start "Play with the friend" activity
R7	End of "Give a present and play" activity	Tamagotchi is still unhappy	Start "Give a present and play" activity	Start "Return home" activity

3.10   Service Models

The fundamental property of an agent is being situated in some environment and being capable of perception and action. Agents have knowledge of environment objects and how to utilize them. Section 3.4 identified two types of environment objects: services and resources. In this section, we discuss services. At the time of writing this book, "service" is an overly hyped term. There are attempts to model nearly everything as a service. However, services do exist for agents and are utilized by them. For instance, consider a taxi hiring system with a centralized service represented by a lady called Kitty.[1] Obvious services that taxi drivers need for their work are getting new customers and providing directions as necessary. Less obvious services that a taxi driver might use are information about traffic conditions and unexpected situations. Such information could be directly exchanged by the taxi drivers in a peer-to-peer or broadcast fashion. It would be unrealistic to have Kitty mediating all that information. Instead, we could regard the service provided by a taxi center as a system supplying a communication infrastructure for taxi drivers and Kitty.

---

1. Kitty is the traditional term used by taxi drivers in Estonia.

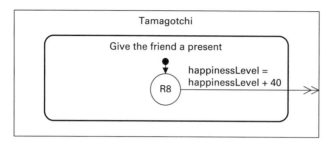

Figure 3.19
Modeling an epistemic action

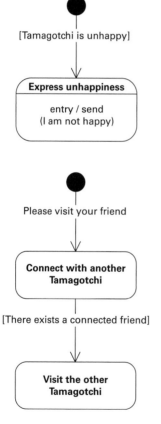

Figure 3.20
An agent behavior model of a Tamagotchi represented as a statechart

Services are modeled as reactive entities that provide functionality to the agents. For example, according to the description presented in section 3.1 and the models given in sections 3.2 and 3.3, a Tamagotchi Shell consists of six important facilities—toilet, shop, storehouse, physician, mailbox, and communicator—that can be manipulated by the Tamagotchi as mediated by the owner. They are modeled as the respective services in the Tamagotchi Shell environment. Similarly, the school and preschool, as well as the workplace, shopping mall, food court, theater, game center, town hall, king's castle, and travel agency are modeled as services in the Tamagotchi's virtual environment—Tamagotchi Town.

As the term "service" implies, only an agent can invoke a service object—never the other way round. For example, a Tamagotchi in Tamagotchi Town can manipulate service objects such as a theater, school, and travel agency. In the domain of intelligent homes, a home security agent can manipulate alarm devices and a face comparison Web service.

As pointed out in section 2.4, an environment can be physical or virtual. For example, a Tamagotchi is placed in a physical environment that is inhabited by its owner and possibly another Tamagotchi. At the same time, a Tamagotchi is always situated in the Tamagotchi Shell virtual environment and can also enter another virtual environment—Tamagotchi Town. In section 3.7, both physical and virtual environments are modeled as environment objects that agents know about.

A physical environment can be made computationally accessible by agents. Computationally accessible environments are called *computational environments*. A physical environment can be made accessible by equipping agents with sensors and actuators. For example, intelligent homes can be furnished with sensors that detect intruders and cameras that take images of an intruder. Similarly, a home security agent can have actuators that enable it to open and shut doors and start alarm devices. Sensors register events occurring in the physical world and transform their occurrences into digital signals. Conversely, actuators transform digital signals into physical actions. The digital signals that are received from sensors and fed into actuators are at a low abstraction level. We therefore need a computational environment layer between sensors and actuators on one hand and agents on the other. The layer consists of services for perceiving events and for performing actions in the physical environment. For example, in the Intelligent Home application in chapter 9, obvious services are detecting and recognizing a possible intruder and greeting the homeowner by voice.

Virtual environments, for example, agent platforms such as JADE and JACK (which are discussed in chapter 5) can be viewed as computational environments. The JADE platform has services `ReceiverBehavior` and `SenderBehavior` for respectively receiving and sending messages. In our running Tamagotchi example, the communicator service of a Tamagotchi Shell environment fulfils a similar purpose.

Services are *stateless*, meaning that a service does not maintain information about its state between its invocations. For example, the communicator service of a Tamagotchi Shell does not check whether a message sent by a Tamagotchi to another one is followed by a reply. This is done by the Tamagotchis involved instead. All the information that a stateless service needs is passed to it by the calling agent or is retrieved by the service from some other environment object, such as a database.

Service models reflect our view of a multiagent system as consisting of agents and services, where services make up a computational environment for the system. What exactly should be regarded as an agent and what as a service? The answers to this question essentially determine the software architecture of the system that is being designed. *Software architecture* defines the structures of the system implemented in software, which comprise architectural elements and the relationships between the elements. Which architectural elements should be regarded as agents and which ones as services depends on the available hardware and software platforms, financial and administrative constraints, and many other factors.

In general, the architecture of a multiagent system can be viewed as consisting of agents and services, as is depicted in figure 3.21. Services, in turn, rely on the lower abstraction layer of functional objects, which are basic software building blocks. In the generic multiagent system architecture, agents interact with each other in an asynchronous manner and invoke services in a synchronous way. A *synchronous invocation* means that an agent waits until the service invoked by it finishes. In the contrary, agents involved in an asynchronous interaction do not have to wait for the replies to the messages sent to each other.

Service objects are passive objects, which are invoked by agents and which do not interact with each other. Different services may, however, be connected at the ab-

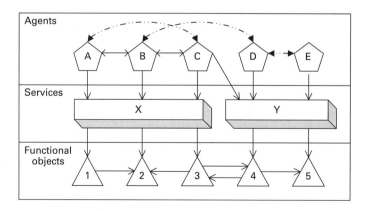
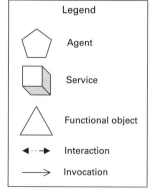

Figure 3.21
The generic architecture of a multiagent system

straction layer of functional objects. For example, the agents B and D in figure 3.21 interact but use different services X and Y that are connected through functional objects 3 and 4 that synchronously invoke each other's operations. The services X and Y may, for example, represent different agent platforms. The layers of service objects and functional objects are sometimes jointly termed as *middleware*. How to engineer service objects and functional objects is beyond the scope of this book and is thoroughly treated in numerous books on object-oriented modeling and design.

In our running example, a Tamagotchi dwells in the virtual environment of the Tamagotchi Shell and can enter the virtual environment of Tamagotchi Town. In the domain model and knowledge model that were created in sections 3.4 and 3.7, we modeled the environments of a Tamagotchi as environment objects `TamagotchiShell` and `TamagotchiTown`. In this section, we elaborate these objects into their constituent service objects. For example, the service objects `Toilet`, `Shop`, `Storehouse`, `Physician`, `Mailbox`, and `Communicator` of the Tamagotchi Shell virtual environment are identified. The resulting service model is given in figure 3.22, using a UML-like notation. An environment is denoted in the figure as an object labeled with the UML-like stereotype <<`Environment`>> and its constituent services are marked with the stereotype <<`Service`>>. The names of service objects depicted in the figure are underlined to convey that there is just one instance of each service. The figure uses the UML notation introduced in table 2.1.

To be manipulated by agents, service objects need *handles* that enable agents to consume resources from the environment and operate on it. For example, a Tamagotchi needs such handles for consuming resource objects, representing food for the Tamagotchi, from the `Storehouse`. We design and implement such handles for service objects as operations, a term that originates in object-oriented design. An *operation* can be defined as a procedure or transformation performed by an object. For instance, the `Toilet` object will be equipped with the `flush` operation for cleaning "excrement" produced by the Tamagotchi. An operation may take arguments and return a value. The types of arguments and the type of the return value are defined by the operation's *signature*. Arguments taken by operations and values returned by them are information resources. For example, the service for greeting the homeowner in the Intelligent Home application by voice has an operation with the signature `speakText (String text, Integer volume, Real readingSpeed, Integer voiceType)`. This operation converts a character sequence into synthesized speech. In the `StoreHouse` service of a Tamagotchi Shell, the operation with the signature `store (Food food)` takes as an argument a resource of type `Food`, and the operation with the signature `Item get()` returns a resource of type `Item`. If the type of the value returned by an operation is not shown in the operation's signature, the type is `Boolean`. For example, the `select(Item)` operation of the `StoreHouse` service returns the value "`true`" if the resource in the storehouse has been successfully

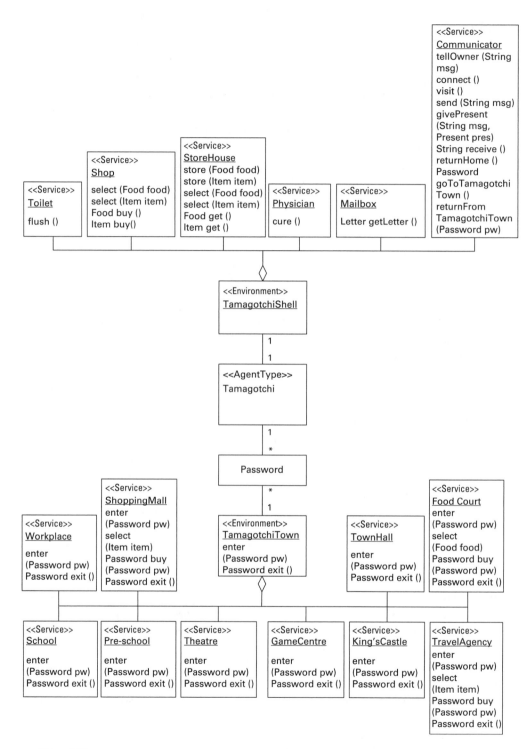

Figure 3.22
The design model of Tamagotchi's computational environments

selected. Otherwise—for example, when the storehouse is empty—this operation returns "`false`". Similarly, the `faceUnknown(CVImage *image)` operation of
the intruder detection and recognition service of the Intelligent Home application
returns the value "true" if a home security agent detects an unknown person in the
room.

Besides being handles for agents, operations may also represent laws that constrain
the effect of the actions performed by agents on the environment entities. For example, a runway allocation service used by an air traffic control agent must consider the
physical laws related to the number of and position of runways, wind direction, visibility, and so on.

An agent may be able to figure out by itself which handles to pull—that is, which
operations of which objects to invoke. For example, a Tamagotchi can be designed
as capable of detecting when its food supply in the storehouse is low and buying
more food from the shop. However, a Tamagotchi of the current version manipulates its environment objects as guided by a human agent.

Figure 3.22 includes operation signatures for both computational environments of
a Tamagotchi. Instead of the operation signature, just the operation name may be
used for referring to it.

The `flush`, `buy`, and `cure` operations of the respective service objects `Toilet`,
`Shop`, and `Physician` of a Tamagotchi Shell do not take any arguments, because
there is only one Tamagotchi for each Tamagotchi Shell environment. It is thus
easy to figure out the Tamagotchi to which these operations apply. The operations
of the `StoreHouse` service enable the Tamagotchi to store a resource, and select a
resource stored and fetch it so that, for example, the resource could be given to the
other Tamagotchi as a present when visiting. The `tellOwner` operation of the
`Communicator` service is used by the Tamagotchi for informing its owner about hunger, sickness, or unhappiness. The `connect`, `visit`, `send`, `givePresent`, `receive`
and `returnHome` operations of the `Communicator` service are used for visiting. The
`getLetter` operation of the `Mailbox` service retrieves resources of type `Letter` that
the Tamagotchi has received by "mail."

As explained earlier, when entering the Tamagotchi Town environment, a Tamagotchi Shell transforms the Tamagotchi's knowledge base into a fourteen-character
alphanumeric password that the owner inserts into Tamagotchi Town. This is done
by calling the `goToTamagotchiTown` operation of the `Communicator` service. Upon
the Tamagotchi leaving Tamagotchi Town, the environment generates another password that is to be inserted by the owner into the Tamagotchi Shell. The password
reflects the changes to the Tamagotchi's knowledge items. The password is
"decoded" for the Tamagotchi by calling the `returnFromTamagotchiTown` operation defined for the `Communicator` service. Figure 3.22 represents through cardinalities that each password generated is unique.

Table 3.18
Service invocations by a Tamagotchi while visiting another Tamagotchi

Activity	Service invocation
Connect with another Tamagotchi	`Communicator.connect()`
Request visit	`Communicator.send("Could I come to your place?")`, `Communicator.receive()`
Go to the friend's place	`Communicator.visit()`, `Communicator.send("Good day!")`, `Communicator.receive()`
Give the friend a present	`Communicator.givePresent("Please accept my present", Present)`, `Communicator.receive()`
Play with the friend	`Communicator.send("May I play with you?")`, `Communicator.receive()`
Return home	`Communicator.returnHome()`

Each service object of Tamagotchi Town has `enter` and `exit` operations for entering into the service a password generated by the Tamagotchi Shell and for retrieving the password generated by the service. The latter password reflects changes caused by the service to the knowledge items of the given Tamagotchi. In addition, the service objects `ShoppingMall`, `FoodCourt`, and `TravelAgency` have an operation with the signature `Password buy (Password pw)` that is used by an agent for buying food and items for its gotchi points.

Service invocations by agents can be modeled by attaching them to activities in agent behavior models. Table 3.18 shows what operations of various services of a Tamagotchi Shell are called when the Tamagotchi visits another Tamagotchi. Alternatively, interactions between agents and environment objects can be captured by sequence diagrams of UML.

In section 5.5 we refine the description given in table 3.18 by demonstrating how a Tamagotchi implemented on the JADE agent platform employs some of the operations provided by the `Communicator` service.

As computational environments are essentially designed in an object-oriented way, there is no need for us to go into more detail with environment design. We have by now performed enough analysis for developing the system and have got a sufficient set of models that can be handed over to developers for implementation.

3.11 Background

Our description of Tamagotchis derived primarily from the use of the toys by Kuldar and his daughters, aged 6 and 9. We also used information from the Tamagotchi Web site (Tamagotchi 2008) and the relevant article on Wikipedia (2008a).

The use of goals in requirements acquisition was pioneered by Dardenne, Lamsweerde, and Fickas (1993). The notion of goal is employed for requirements engineering by several agent-oriented methodologies, notably as goal diagrams by Prometheus (Padgham and Winikoff 2004), as goal hierarchy diagrams by MaSE (DeLoach and Kumar 2005), and as goal cases by MAS-CommonKADS (Iglesias and Garijo 2005). Goals were the key concept in the ROADMAP methodology as described in (Juan, Pearce, and Sterling 2002). The ROADMAP notation, which has been adopted for our goal models in chapter 3, emerged from discussions at the Intelligent Agent Lab at the University of Melbourne, with the leading voices being Thomas Juan and Leon. The notation is clearly described in (Kuan, Karunasekera, and Sterling 2005).

Our example notation for goal models evolved over several years. It is worth stating the history in a little more detail as to avoid repeating ourselves later. Leon's interest in models for agent-oriented systems started with Gaia as described in (Wooldridge, Jennings, and Kinny 2000). The interest was spurred by Thomas Juan, who began his Ph.D. on agent-oriented software engineering under Leon's supervision in 2001. Thomas analyzed the need for additional models in Gaia, such as for the environment, and presented this analysis as an initial set of models for the ROADMAP methodology extension to Gaia in Juan, Pearce, and Sterling 2002. Gaia itself evolved as described in Zambonelli, Jennings, and Wooldridge 2003. ROADMAP became a separate methodology and Thomas was the primary influence in shaping it. The REBEL tool for ROADMAP was developed and described in Kuan, Karunasekera, and Sterling 2005. This latter paper also gave a clear description of the principal ROADMAP models at the motivation layer—namely, goal and role models. The most extensive description of ROADMAP so far is by Juan (2008).

Related to goals are quality goals or soft goals. Our modeling notation for quality goals was suggested by Thomas Juan based on the extensive treatment of quality by Chung et al. (2000). Quality goals form a prominent part of the Tropos methodology (Bresciani et al. 2004). Following the principles described by Rahwan, Juan, and Sterling (2006), quality goals can be used for representing social policies.

The modeling concept of role is a major distinguishing factor between agent-oriented and object-oriented modeling. Among the first researchers applying roles to agent modeling was Kendall (1999). Separate role models are featured by the Gaia (Wooldridge, Jennings, and Kinny 2000) and MaSE (DeLoach and Kumar 2005) methodologies. The MESSAGE methodology (Caire et al. 2004) identifies roles and attaches them to goals in its delegation structure diagrams. The INGENIAS methodology (Pavón, Gómez-Sanz, and Fuentes 2005) identifies roles within use cases. In the PASSI methodology (Cossentino 2005), roles are identified after deciding agent types. Our example representation format for role models originates in the ROAD-MAP methodology introduced in Juan, Pearce, and Sterling 2002 and refined by Chan and Sterling (2003a).

The following famous Three Laws of Robotics coined by Asimov (1950) may also be regarded as a role model for a robot:

· A robot may not injure a human being or, through inaction, allow a human being to come to harm.

· A robot must obey orders given to it by human beings, except where such orders would conflict with the First Law.

· A robot must protect its own existence as long as such protection does not conflict with the First or Second Law.

Organization models, representing relationships between roles, appear as organization diagrams in the MAS-CommonKADS (Iglesias and Garijo 2005), MESSAGE (Caire et al. 2004), RAP/AOR (Taveter and Wagner 2005), and INGENIAS (Pavón, Gómez-Sanz, and Fuentes 2005) methodologies. Based on the OpeRA methodology proposed by Dignum (2004), we regard the control, benevolence, and peer relationships between roles as the most essential ones. These relationship types were conceived by Zambonelli, Jennings, and Wooldridge (2001). Differently, the Tropos methodology (Bresciani et al. 2004) has been built around four types of dependencies between agents: goal dependencies, task dependencies, resource dependencies, and soft goal dependencies.

A domain model represents the knowledge that the system is supposed to handle about its environments. A domain model also includes roles, because agents playing these roles function based on their knowledge about their physical and virtual environments. Domain models are rooted in knowledge models of the ROADMAP methodology and environment models. Knowledge models were proposed as a part of the ROADMAP methodology by Juan, Pearce, and Sterling (2002). Their constituent parts—knowledge components—were defined by Juan and Sterling (2003). Environment models were introduced in the ROADMAP methodology (Juan, Pearce, and Sterling 2002) and added to the later version of Gaia (Zambonelli, Jennings, and Wooldridge 2003). Environment-centred domain analysis forms a part of the MAS-CommonKADS methodology (Iglesias and Garijo 2005), where environment objects are modeled as clouds in use case diagrams. Objects of a conceptual environment, such as servers and databases, can be represented by diagrams of the types offered by INGENIAS (Pavón, Gómez-Sanz, and Fuentes 2005) and Prometheus (Padgham, and Winikoff 2004). The ADELFE methodology (Picard and Gleizes 2004) describes environment by environment definition documents, which are created at various stages of developing a multiagent system. The example notation that we use in domain models is based on the Entity-Relationship Model (Chen 1976) and UML (OMG 2007).

Mapping roles to agent types is handled by the following types of models in the respective agent-oriented methodologies: by agent models in Gaia (Wooldridge, Jennings, and Kinny 2000), MAS-CommonKADS (Iglesias and Garijo 2005), and INGENIAS (Pavón, Gómez-Sanz, and Fuentes 2005), by agent/role models in MESSAGE (Caire et al. 2004), by agent class diagrams in MaSE (DeLoach and Kumar 2005), and by agent society models in PASSI (Cossentino 2005). In the Prometheus methodology (Padgham and Winikoff 2004), agent types are decided based on thorough coupling and cohesion analysis.

Interaction pathways between agent types can be decided with the help of acquaintance models, which were first proposed by Wooldridge, Jennings, and Kinny (2000) as a part of the Gaia methodology. The MaSE methodology (DeLoach and Kumar 2005) uses agent class diagrams for the same purpose and the MESSAGE methodology (Caire et al. 2004)—organization diagrams.

As interaction modeling is crucial and central in agent-oriented modeling, interaction models of some kind are used by all agent-oriented methodologies. The following methodologies rely on UML or its derivation AUML (Bauer and Odell 2005) for interaction modeling: Tropos (Bresciani et al. 2004), Prometheus (Padgham and Winikoff 2004), PASSI (Cossentino 2005), and ADELFE (Picard and Gleizes 2004). The MESSAGE (Caire et al. 2004), INGENIAS (Pavón, Gómez-Sanz, and Fuentes 2005), MaSE (DeLoach and Kumar 2005), and RAP/AOR (Taveter and Wagner 2005) methodologies have conceived their own notations for interaction modeling. In the chapter, we provide examples of UML-based and other kinds of interaction modeling.

GAIA (Zambonelli, Jennings, and Wooldridge 2003) models the environment in terms of abstract computational resources, such as variables or tuples. The agent-environment interactions are accordingly modeled as performing the following actions on the environment variables: sensing (reading their values), effecting (changing their values), and consuming (extracting them from the environment). Prometheus (Padgham and Winikoff 2004) models agent-environment interactions in terms of the percepts from the environment available to the multiagent system and the actions on the environment that the system is able to perform. Interactions between environment objects and agents are addressed by the MAS-CommonKADS methodology (Iglesias and Garijo 2005) as reactive cases, which are refined by textual templates. The INGENIAS methodology (Pavón, Gómez-Sanz, and Fuentes 2005) represents the agent's perception mechanism as a type of association relationship between the agent and an application in its environment. Recently, the MaSE methodology was complemented by DeLoach and Valenzuela (2007) with environment models. Our example notation for modeling interactions between an agent and its environment is based on the RAP/AOR methodology (Taveter and Wagner 2005).

The development of a multiagent system deals with the knowledge that each agent of a multiagent system has about its environment consisting of other agents and environment objects. The most extensive knowledge modeling framework is featured by the MAS-CommonsKADS methodology (Iglesias and Garijo 2005). The expertise model included by this methodology provides means for modeling domain knowledge, inference knowledge, and task knowledge. The PASSI methodology (Cossentino 2005) models knowledge by domain and communication ontologies. The Tropos (Bresciani et al. 2004), and RAP/AOR (Taveter and Wagner 2005) methodologies represent knowledge models as UML (OMG 2007) class diagrams. Our treatment of derivations and constraints originates in (Taveter and Wagner 2001). Our example notation for knowledge modeling is based on UML (OMG 2007), but also makes use of AUML (Bauer and Odell 2005) for joint representation of agent types and roles.

Most agent-oriented methodologies include a system-level behavior model of some kind. Examples are strategic rationale diagrams in Tropos (Bresciani et al. 2004), task models in MAS-CommonKADS (Iglesias and Garijo, 2005), domain requirements description diagrams in PASSI (Cossentino 2005), use case models in ADELFE (Picard and Gleizes 2004), and use case diagrams in INGENIAS (Pavón, Gómez-Sanz, and Fuentes 2005) and MaSE (DeLoach and Kumar 2005). Scenarios as system-level behavior models are included by the Prometheus (Padgham and Winikoff 2004) and RAP/AOR (Taveter and Wagner 2005) methodologies.

Behavioral units are identified by behavioral interface models as services in the GAIA (Zambonelli, Jennings, and Wooldridge 2003) and MAS-CommonKADS (Iglesias and Garijo 2005) methodologies, as capabilities in Prometheus (Padgham and Winikoff 2004) and PASSI (Cossentino 2005), as activities in RAP/AOR (Taveter and Wagner 2005), and as agents' skills and aptitudes in ADELFE (Picard and Gleizes 2004).

After a behavioral interface model has been created for an agent, its behavior can be modeled. In Gaia (Wooldridge, Jennings, and Kinny 2000), agent behavior is modeled by liveness and safety properties. In the MAS-CommonKADS methodology (Iglesias and Garijo 2005), agent behavior is defined by an agent model that, in turn, utilizes the agent's expertise model. The PASSI methodology (Cossentino 2005) models agent behavior by activity diagrams of UML (OMG 2007). The MaSE methodology (DeLoach and Kumar 2005) uses for the same purpose concurrent task models, which are based on state charts. The INGENIAS methodology (Pavón, Gómez-Sanz, and Fuentes 2005) represents agent behavior in terms of the agent's mental attitudes that trigger interactions. The Prometheus (Padgham and Winikoff 2004) and Tropos (Bresciani et al. 2004) methodologies assume BDI to be the agent architecture and model agent behavior accordingly in terms of capabilities and plans. Prometheus represents plans using a derivation of UML activity diagrams. The example notation that we have adapted for agent behavior modeling is based on UML activity diagrams (OMG 2007) and BPMN (OMG 2006). They have been complemented with rules as proposed by Taveter and Wagner (2005), who promote rules as a generic agent behavior modeling construct.

The design also includes modeling service objects provided by computational environments. These objects are known and manipulated by agents. The motivation for the modeling paradigm encompassing objects that are subordinated to agents was explained by Høydalsvik and Sindre (1993) and Metsker (1997). Both argued for the need for ontologically oriented modeling and programming languages that would allow "thinking over objects." The idea was put into the agent-oriented context by Taveter (1997) and Oja, Tamm, and Taveter (2001). Similar in sprit is also the treatment of environment variables in the Gaia methodology (Zambonelli, Jennings, and Wooldridge 2003), where each variable is associated with a symbolic name, characterized by the type of actions that the agents can perform on it. The concept of stateless services has been introduced by Fielding (2000).

In our example models, operations are attached to service objects that can be accessed by agents. Service objects and the operations attached to them are modeled in an object-oriented way, which has been described in numerous books devoted to object-oriented modeling. In particular, we have relied on Blaha and Rumbaugh (2005). We have used for representing service models an example notation based on UML (OMG 2007). Services employed by agents also comprise Web services. How a Web service should be invoked is described using the Web Services Description Language (WSDL; W3C 2007). Conversely, an agent can be embedded in a Web service.

Exercises for Chapter 3

1. Create an acquaintance model for the case when one or both interacting Tamagotchis are owned by more than one person.

2. Create an acquaintance model and an interaction model for multilateral interactions between three or more Tamagotchis.

Extend exercise 2 so that behaviors of one or more agents are modeled.

3. Create the following types of models for your university, company, or organization, where agents would automate some of the activities performed by humans:

· goal model

· role models

· domain model

- agent and acquaintance model
- interaction models
- knowledge model
- scenarios
- behavior models
- service models

4 Quality

Chapter 3 focuses on an agent-oriented approach to describe the functional requirements of a system, using concepts such as goals, roles, and agents. Just concentrating on functionality is insufficient to develop systems. Nonfunctional requirements are essential. An agent greeting system is not useful if it is too slow. For example, being greeted one hour after you arrived in a room would provide comic value at best. If an alarm clock scheduled to wake you is unreliable, it is not useful. If an automated banking system is insecure, it is not good for the bank that deploys it or the customer who might want to use it.

The models we introduced allow the expression of nonfunctional requirements by attaching quality goals to goal models, and constraints to role models. Our motivation in encouraging explicit quality goals is to affirm the importance of quality concerns. Quality considerations should not be an afterthought during system development.

This chapter takes a more detailed look at incorporating quality considerations within agent-oriented modeling. We believe that agent-oriented concepts enhance the handling of quality requirements in open, distributed sociotechnical systems. The first section discusses different meanings that people ascribe to the term quality to clarify the sense in which we use the term. Sections 4.2, 4.3, and 4.4 give three different specific examples of quality concerns: performance, safety, and security. None of the discussions provide a definitive account of the particular quality attribute. Rather, they show how to incorporate quality requirements effectively into agent-oriented models, usually by introducing appropriate additional concepts. Section 4.5 looks at more abstract and creative requirements such as being fun or playful. Having an explicit quality goal can spark useful discussions during requirements analysis and design. Section 4.6 discusses analyzing and elaborating multiple quality requirements recognizing the need for trade-offs between competing requirements.

4.1   Considerations of Quality

The word "quality" has at least three distinct meanings that we wish to point out. The first meaning of quality is as a standard of excellence. Artifacts such as manufactured items or pieces of writing can be rated according to an assumed standard: being described, for example, as of poor, excellent, or sterling quality. The word "quality" itself usually suggests a high standard.

The second meaning of quality is "fit for purpose." Quality standards such as ISO 9001, SPICE, and Six Sigma are based around this meaning. The quality movement that emerged in the United States in the twentieth century is concerned with this meaning of quality. The idea was to take a scientific approach and measure processes. Quality for manufacturing was mastered within postwar Japan and was a factor in its transformation as a manufacturing power.

A good example of a quality process in this sense comes from the McDonald's fast-food chain. For more than fifty years, in a wide range of locations across the world, McDonald's franchisees control how hamburgers are made in their premises. Consequently, a customer purchasing a McDonald's hamburger will know exactly how the hamburger will taste. Saying that McDonald's has an excellent quality process does not mean that the hamburgers are of the highest quality in the first sense of the term, but rather that the process is completely repeatable, so that a McDonald's restaurant anywhere in the world can produce an identically tasting hamburger.

The third meaning of quality is as an attribute. This meaning is exemplified by the well-known Shakesperean quote "The quality of mercy is not strained." We are interested in addressing a wide variety of quality attributes of software, including speed, reliability, scalability, maintainability—to name just a few from the engineering mindset. We also want to include other quality attributes to cover desired requirements such as that playing with a Tamagotchi should be fun, a game should be entertaining, and flirting with a friend using an online device should be exciting.

In this book, we primarily use quality in the third sense of trying to add properties and attributes to software. We use the term *quality requirement* to refer to any requirement about the quality of the software, as opposed to its functionality. We want to embed consideration of quality requirements in a systems engineering process, and by doing so to produce software that is excellent, that is high-quality (in the first sense of the term), as well as that has the desirable attributes.

Focusing on quality is a well-established procedure within software and systems engineering. Software engineers are aware of the need to express quality attributes of software as well as functional capabilities of software. Sometimes, the phrase "nonfunctional requirements" is used. We prefer the term "quality requirements" for its more positive connotations.

Some people advocate that all quality requirements, which we express as quality goals within goal and role diagrams, should be turned into measurable goals and specific functional requirements during requirements analysis. We do not favor such a unilateral approach. We believe that qualitative descriptions are often more intuitive for stakeholders. Although some quality goals, such as performance targets or system availability, are readily quantifiable, others—such as a system being secure or a game being fun—are less so.

Keeping a qualitative description of a constraint at the motivation layer aids future system evolution and adaptability. We believe that it is often valuable to delay specifying quality requirements as explicit numeric constraints to allow designers to be able to make trade-offs. Indeed, there are many considerations that could affect the final design decisions that get embedded in the system specification. Human factors are an issue. The choice of implementation language may well have an impact on quality attributes such as performance. Making a decision before all the factors are known might lead to overspecification, and might disengage key stakeholders from the process.

Another term that has been used to describe the type of quality goals we are discussing is *soft goal*. Soft goals can clearly be relaxed during design trade-off discussions. This term contrasts with a hard goal, which is explicitly quantifiable. We prefer the term "quality goals" to connote subtly that we advocate an engineering approach and want to build high-quality systems.

Quality considerations can be expressed in several of the models that we introduced in the previous chapter. They are most visible in goal models in which quality goals are represented as clouds. They are also present as constraints in role models. They can also be attached to scenarios in which it is desirable to identify the key step where the particular quality attribute is important. Quality considerations may also affect knowledge models, as discussed in section 4.4.

In the sections that follow, we present a range of examples of quality goals being attached to goal and role models. Although the same qualitative notation can be used to describe different quality attributes at a high level, detailed analyses of different quality requirements typically need different methods. Addressing safety concerns about personal injury naturally has a different process from analyzing a system to guarantee speed of response, which is different again from being aware of and taking steps to avoid hacker attacks. In complex systems with several competing quality concerns, there may well be a need for composite methods.

To conclude this section, we reiterate the importance of explicit expression of quality requirements as quality goals. Quality attributes are often forgotten about during software development, but are a major factor in determining system success. Quality requirements are an important part of any software project. They are often built with a completely independent method of assessment. We believe it is important to take a holistic approach, thinking about quality requirements from the earliest stages of requirements elicitation and analysis. We represent quality requirements in such a way that considerations of assessment arrive early. Assessing quality will require specific expertise, as becomes apparent in the next few sections.

4.2   Performance

The first and probably the most fundamental quality goal that we want to discuss is *performance*. Performance is a general term that can cover a range of quality attributes, including responsiveness, availability, reliability, and usability. We do not attempt to define performance, but rather give examples. Performance is a key consideration for the extended Tamagotchi example of chapter 3. If a Tamagotchi doesn't respond quickly enough, children will lose interest. If the interface is difficult to use, children won't play with it.

We first observe that some aspects of performance can be handled in a straightforward manner. We illustrate with an example to be elaborated upon in section 4.3 when discussing safety. Consider an automated system for palletizing fruit to be transported to market. The palletizer has two main functions. The first function is to pack fruit into boxes without damaging the fruit. The second function is to stack boxes onto a pallet. Once thirty-six boxes have been placed onto a pallet, the palletizer covers the packed boxes with a plastic sheet and nails the four corners of the sheet onto the pallet. After the boxes have been covered, the pallet is moved to a storage area, and the packing into boxes starts again.

Figure 4.1 gives a goal model for the palletizer. The overall goal for the palletizer, "Palletize," is broken down to three subgoals: "Pack," "Stack," and "Store." The goal model includes two roles: Palletizer and Operator. The first represents the automated component of the system and the second represents a human operator required for providing the system with fruit and boxes, as well as for collecting the pallets. The role models for Palletizer and Operator are given as tables 4.1 and 4.2, respectively.

In this chapter, we are interested in the quality goals. The two quality goals attached to the left of the "Palletize" goal express that the palletizing should be efficient and reliable. These two quality goals can be translated into specific constraints on performance, which clearly need to come from a domain expert. In this case, our local domain expert has stated that to be efficient, the palletizer should pack six pallets per hour without damaging the fruit. Whether this is a sensible number requires engineering knowledge of what is possible.

Let us do some quick calculations. Ignoring any moving time translates into taking ten minutes per pallet. For thirty-six boxes to be packed in ten minutes, assuming

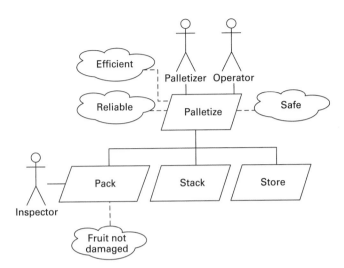

Figure 4.1
A goal model for the palletizer

Table 4.1
The role model for Palletizer

Role name	Palletizer
Description	Store fruit on a pallet to be ready for market.
Responsibilities	Get boxes.
	Place the boxes for packing.
	Pack fruit into the boxes.
	Stack the boxes onto a pallet.
	Get plastic sheet.
	Cover the boxes with the plastic sheet.
	Nail the corners of the sheet onto the pallet.
	Store the pallet.
Constraints	Place a box in a correct position for packing.
	Do not place more than 36 boxes on a pallet.
	Pack a box in 17 seconds. (Efficiency)
	Be available for at least 167 hours with one hour down time for each week. (Reliability)
	Don't damage fruit.
	Palletize safely.

Table 4.2
The role model for Operator

Role name	Operator
Description	Provide boxes and fruit and collect the pallets.
Responsibilities	Operate the palletizer. Provide boxes. Provide fruit. Collect the pallets.
Constraints	Place boxes so that the palletizer can find them. Place fruit so that the palletizer can find it. Collect the pallet as soon as it is loaded with boxes.

that they are packed sequentially, each box should be packed in approximately 0.28 minutes, or 17 seconds. Constraining a box to be packed in 17 seconds would be added to the Palletizer role. The corresponding constraint has been included in the Palletizer role in table 4.1.

Reliability can be handled similarly to efficiency. According to our local domain expert, to be reliable, the palletizer should be available for at least 167 hours, with one hour down time for each week. The appropriate constraint has been added to the Palletizer role in table 4.1. Adding both these constraints sets up the expectation that they will be monitored. Output of the palletizer and its availability will need to be measured, automatically or manually, to see whether the constraints can be met.

Reviewing the simple description of the efficiency requirement suggests that another role is needed. Placing boxes on the pallet speedily has to be achieved without damaging the fruit. How do we know if fruit is damaged? An inspection role is needed, as depicted in the goal model in figure 4.1. Whether the inspection will be done by a human or an automated inspection system is indeed a question; this issue will be determined by cost considerations. The point is that in general, discussing performance requirements can suggest roles.

Let us consider performance requirements in the context of an intelligent home, an application to be discussed in chapter 9. One scenario that we investigate is being greeted when entering the home. Here are some plausible constraints. An agent greeter needs to respond within three seconds of someone entering a room. Face identification needs to decide whether a face captured on a camera is a friend or an intruder within 15 seconds. An automated music player needs to start playing an appropriate piece of music within 5 seconds. Each of these is an explicitly quantified constraint related to performance.

Let us investigate the example of recognizing a face from an image captured on a camera a little more closely. Factors such as the necessary level of recognition accuracy or the size of the database of known faces against which the face is matched can have a very large impact on performance. To be extreme, if only five members of a household need to be matched against, screening might be very rapid. Trying to match a face against an internationally distributed collection of faces of people with a criminal background would take a large amount of processing. Not the least consideration would be negotiating appropriate permission and access issues.

It is unlikely that face recognition in an intelligent home security system would need to be very elaborate and consult a worldwide database of known criminals. What our consideration demonstrates is that a lot more needs to be known about a specific application before the specification of performance can be finalized. The architecture of the home network, its connectivity to the Internet, and the volume of transactions needed to be considered, as they are all issues that potentially affect performance.

In section 3.10, software architecture is briefly discussed. Note that software architecture is a key determinant of attributes such as performance and scalability. It is also a factor that is not well understood by many developers and is often neglected. We don't say a lot about architecture in this book. However we are aware of its importance, and the need to consider architecture in detail during design, which will affect implementation.

To conclude this section, we note that experience and knowledge are needed to address performance properly. The experience might be expressed in rules of thumb, for example, how long an average message sent between two machines might take. Our examples described here and elsewhere only start a way of thinking about performance. It is beyond our scope, knowledge, and experience to give a complete analysis of performance, or any other quality attribute. Our purpose is rather to raise issues so that quality requirements are taken seriously and integrated holistically into system development. Each quality requirement should ideally lead to an informed discussion with an appropriate expert or experienced developer.

4.3   Safety

The next quality attribute we consider—safety—seems a less obvious concern than performance, the quality attribute addressed in the previous section. Indeed, in many systems, safety is not a concern at all. However, multiagent systems have tragically been involved in loss of life. The explosion of the space shuttle *Challenger* in 1986 and the fatal dosage of radiation delivered by the Therac-25 X-ray machine in the 1980s are two that readily come to mind.

The term *safety-critical systems* has been coined to cover systems where safety is a critical concern. Within software and systems engineering, many methods and processes have been developed for the analysis, modeling, and evaluation of systems that of necessity must consider safety. The methods and processes are applied to increase assurance that accidents will not happen or are mitigated when they do.

In this section, we show how safety analysis methods may be incorporated within agent-oriented modeling. We reiterate our observation of the previous section. Outside expertise will usually be needed to decide on the appropriate quality approach; in this case, safety methods. We believe that agent-oriented models potentially have an advantage over more traditional software engineering methods with respect to safety requirements. The reason is twofold. First, integration will be easier, because of the more abstract concepts such as goals and roles that can be used to connect with safety requirements. Second, safety often needs to be considered in the interactions between people and technology. Because our conceptualization of multiagent systems encompasses people and manmade agents, the consideration of interaction is natural.

To address safety as a quality attribute, some definitions are needed. In general, defining appropriate terminology is a common feature of incorporating any quality attribute into requirements elicitation and analysis.

An *accident* is an event that results in harm, injury, or loss. A system is regarded as *safe* if the likelihood of the system causing an unacceptable accident is acceptably low. The meaning of the term *unacceptable* depends on how events that trigger accidents are perceived. This concept is not just related to the consequences but also related to context and culture. A *hazard* is a potentially harmful situation, where an accident is possible. A *hazard analysis* is an analysis of a system and its environment to identify potential hazards.

A role is *safety-critical* if responsibilities attached to the role will affect the safety of the system. Current standardized hazard analysis and safety engineering approaches accomplish a high level of safety assurance by identifying the hazards for a system and then meticulously monitoring the identified hazards during design and development. The aim is to assure that each hazard is either neutralized or mitigated to the extent required by the severity of the hazard. If the system's requirements change or if there is a change to design or to the manner in which the system must interact with its environment, then the hazards and design must be reanalyzed for safety.

We introduce a modified method for analyzing multiagent systems influenced by Hazard and Operability Studies, or HAZOP for short. HAZOP was initially developed for the chemical industry, but has been widely applied to different areas over the last thirty years. The aim is to explore potential deviations from the specified or intended behavior of the system and determine whether a deviation can lead to harm, injury or loss in some way. HAZOP requires a sufficiently detailed understanding of the system, its components, and the attributes of the components. HAZOP uses *guidewords* to prompt the exploration of system behavior. A team of system and domain experts interpret the guidewords in the context of the system.

The output from a HAZOP study is a list of hazards, their causes, and the consequences of each hazard. There are three typical outputs. The first is details of the hazards identified, and any means within the design to detect the hazard and to mitigate the hazard. The second is recommendations for mitigation of the hazards or their effects based on the team's knowledge of the system and the revealed details of the hazard in question. The third is recommendations for the later study of specific aspects of the design when there are uncertainties about the causes or consequences of a possible deviation from design intent.

We now elaborate the palletizer model depicted in figure 4.1 that identified the palletizer's goals "Pack," "Stack," and "Store." Let us do a simple safety analysis for the palletizer example given in the previous section. The analysis is in terms of roles and agents, interactions between agents, and between agents and the environment, activities performed by agents, and resources in the system. The palletizer must be safe when there are humans in its vicinity.

To understand the problem domain, we first create a domain model for the palletizer. As discussed in section 3.4, a domain model represents knowledge about the environment that the system is supposed to handle. The entities of the environment that the palletizer needs to be aware of are Pallet, Box, and Fruit. More specifically, an agent playing the Palletizer role, itself situated in the environment, packs fruit into boxes and loads the boxes onto pallets. This is modeled by the domain model shown in figure 4.2. We can conclude that Fruit, Box, and Pallet constitute *resources* that the palletizer needs for its functioning. The model also reflects that a human operator perceives the operations of the palletizer via the environment.

Our analysis elicits hazards of the system by exploring activities performed by an agent and the agent's manipulation of its resources using HAZOP-style guidewords. If the environment changes, then the changes that need to be made to the activities performed by an agent can be determined by simply looking at how the agent manipulates its resources. If an agent deviates from its role, then the effect on other agents or the environment can be determined by considering the agent's interactions with other agents or its effects on other agents via shared resources.

Because agents situated in the environment pose potential safety hazards rather than the roles, we need to develop a design in order to do the safety analysis. As the Palletizer role contains the distinct groups of responsibilities respectively related to packing and stacking, it is a natural decision to map the role to two agent types: Packer and Stacker. The design is reflected by the agent and acquaintance model shown in figure 4.3. The model represents that a Stacker agent may interact with one Packer agent at a time, whereas either agent may initiate an interaction. The role Operator from figure 4.1 has been mapped to the human agent type Person. In figure 4.3, there are no interaction pathways between the Packer and Stacker agent types and a human agent type, because they interact via shared resources—fruits, boxes, and pallets—in the environment.

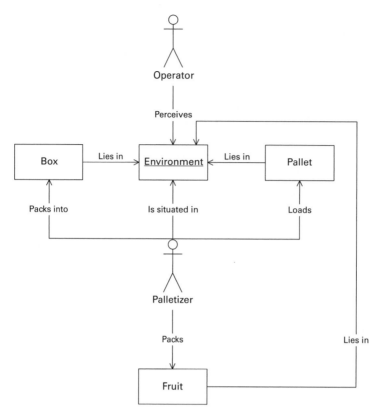

Figure 4.2
The domain model for the palletizer

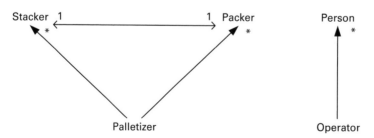

Figure 4.3
The agent and acquaintance model for the palletizer

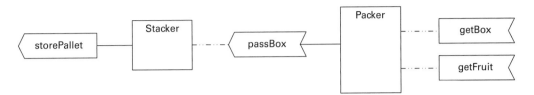

Figure 4.4
The initial interaction model for the palletizer

We next model the interactions in more detail to learn about possible hazards within the system. The interaction model for the palletizer is represented in figure 4.4 by means of an interaction-frame diagram. As shown in section 3.6, interaction-frame diagrams distinguish between physical and communicative actions that may be perceived as events by agents. Interaction-frame diagrams also enable the modeling of events caused by the environment and actions performed on the environment. Figure 4.4 models a `Packer` agent as getting both a box and fruit from the environment. These are represented as `getBox` and `getFruit` environment events. After packing, a `Packer` agent passes the box to a `Stacker` agent. The passing is modeled as a `passBox` physical action by the `Packer` agent that is perceived as an event by the `Stacker` agent. Finally, the `Stacker` agent stores the loaded boxes on the pallet which is modeled as a `storePallet` action on the environment. Because physical actions by agents of the system pose possible hazards for humans near the system, we are now better equipped for analyzing possible hazards in the system.

The final design step to be taken before the HAZOP analysis can be performed is mapping the responsibilities of roles to the types of activities performed by agents. In the given case, this is straightforward. The first four responsibilities of the Palletizer role modeled in table 4.1 are mapped to the "Get boxes," "Place the boxes for packing," and "Pack the boxes" activity types attached to the `Packer` agent type. In addition, a `Packer` agent performs activities of the "Pass the boxes" type that results in passing the packed boxes to the `Stacker` agent as is modeled in figure 4.4. The final four responsibilities from table 4.1 are mapped to the "Check the boxes," "Get plastic sheet and cover the boxes," "Nail the corners of the sheet onto the pallet," and "Store the pallet" activity types attached to the `Stacker` agent type.

Next, we need to identify the constraints applying to the activities. We find them from the constraints given in the Palletizer role model in table 4.1, refining them if necessary.

Now we are ready to perform a HAZOP-style analysis for the `Stacker` and `Packer` agent types. To do so, the activities performed by agents of these types and the associated constraints are listed in the respective tables 4.3 and 4.4. The tables identify which guidewords are applicable to the activities and the constraints. For

Table 4.3
The HAZOP guidewords analysis of the `Packer` agent

Activity type	Constraint	No	More	Less	Oppo-site	Part of	As well as	Early/ Late	Other than
Get boxes			X		X			X	X
Place the boxes for packing	Place a box in a correct position	X			X		X	X	X
Pack the boxes	Stop when thirty-six boxes have been packed	X			X			X	
Pass the boxes		X					X	X	

Table 4.4
The HAZOP guidewords analysis for the `Stacker` agent

Activity type	Constraint	No	More	Less	Oppo-site	Part of	As well as	Early/ Late	Other than
Check the boxes	Thirty-six boxes should be packed correctly	X	X	X	X			X	X
Get plastic sheet and cover the boxes		X			X	X	X	X	X
Nail the corners of the sheet onto the pallet		X	X	X	X			X	X
Store the pallet		X						X	X

example, it can be realized from the guidewords for the "Get boxes" activity type that there are hazards if an agent gets too many boxes at a time, if an agent places a box instead of getting one, if an agent gets a box too early or late, or if an agent performs an activity other than "Get boxes." Similarly, the guidewords for the activity type "Place the boxes for packing" and the related constraint of placing a box in a correct position mean that hazards are posed by the situations where a box is not placed for packing or is not placed in a correct position, or a box is fetched instead of placing it, or some of the boxes are fetched and some are placed, or a box is placed too early or too late, or some activity other than placing the boxes for packing is performed.

Table 4.5
A refined analysis for getting boxes by the `Packer` agent

Guide word	Activity type	Deviation	Possible causes	Consequences	Mitigations
More	Get boxes	Getting more boxes than the agent can carry	Box arrangement or sensor error	There is a risk of box falling and injuring someone	Get only one box at a time
Opposite	Get boxes	Releasing a box instead of getting it	Controller error	A human may get hurt	Ensure that the activity is carried out correctly
Early/Late	Get boxes	Getting a box in wrong time	Sensor error or controller error	The early or late movement may hurt a human	Perceive humans in the proximity of the agent or use barriers
Other than	Get boxes	Perform other activity instead of "Get boxes"	Controller error	The unexpected activity may hurt a human	Ensure that the activity is carried out correctly

Looking at the HAZOP-style results for a `Packer` agent, a number of further constraints can be identified. For example, the realization that there are hazards if an agent gets too many boxes at a time can lead to the conclusion that an agent should get just one box at a time. A new constraint of only getting one box at a time is accordingly created for the `Packer` agent type. By going through the list of guidewords in table 4.3, additional constraints of getting a box in time, and not putting a box back when getting a box are identified. They can be generalized into corresponding constraints for the Palletizer role and to an elaboration of the overall quality goal of safety shown in figure 4.1. One could have a subgoal of the safety quality goal with a name, such as handling boxes correctly, for example, and refine the goal model appropriately. Constraints can be similarly identified for the `Stacker` agent type and generalized for the Palletizer role and into the corresponding quality goals.

In general, identifying a potential hazard might add a constraint for the corresponding role so that an agent playing the role should avoid the potential hazard. A new role might be introduced to monitor and mitigate the potential hazard.

The refined analysis for the `Packer` agent getting boxes is shown in table 4.5. For each guideword, it includes the associated deviation, and its possible causes, consequences, and mitigations. Causes can be external or internal to the agent. The source of each internal cause is represented in terms of the abstract agent architecture depicted in figure 2.4. For example, the reason for getting a box at the wrong time may lie in a sensor or in the controller.

It is interesting to note that most safety analysis methods assume that the system, once built, does not change the way it interacts with its environment. That is, the hazards, once identified, do not change. Removing an assumption that the system is static raises some interesting questions and possibilities for agent-oriented systems. When safety analysis methods are integrated with agent-oriented software engineering models, hazard analysis can be carried out at different levels of abstraction and on different artifacts to those in currently used processes. If a system changes over time, and in particular changes the way it interacts with its environment, then the safety reanalysis will depend on the level at which changes impact the system behavior. But, at higher levels in the agent hierarchy where the impact of changes is absorbed, the existing safety analysis still holds.

We trust the reader can see the applicability of safety analysis in terms of agents performing activities while playing roles to achieve goals set for the system. The example in this section is clearly simplified. However, there are many related systems. Leon visited a fruit canning factory in Victoria's Goulburn Valley, where an automated pear sorting machine had been prototyped. Modeling the system in terms of agents and using the roles, responsibilities, and the environment to guide a safety analysis is definitely relevant in the real world.

4.4 Security

Security has become increasingly critical for multiagent systems. Security is intricately connected with a system's physical constraints and organizational needs, and is affected by requirements of compliance to laws and standards. There are growing concerns over unauthorized access, confidentiality, data integrity, and system availability. Security can be viewed as an umbrella term for a range of quality attributes, including confidentiality, integrity, availability, nonrepudiability, accountability, and authenticity.

We believe that the models presented throughout the book are suitable for incorporating security requirements into systems. The concepts of goal, role, and agent are intuitive for people, helping to model security requirements. Roles facilitate administration of security that greatly reduces security risks. Roles also help to bridge the gap between the business and technical sides of security administration. In this section, we give the flavor of how agent-oriented models can be integrated with security considerations.

Before looking at security as a quality attribute, we note that aspects of security can be modeled directly as functional goals. Chapter 9 discusses an intelligent home example that models a scenario of handling an intruder. Security is expressed through functional requirements in that example instead of quality goals.

Consider an application where security concerns are paramount—Internet banking and commerce. The security of people's money and their personal information is an essential quality attribute of any e-commerce system. A security quality goal expressed at the motivation layer can and should be translated into a wide range of measures at the system design layer, which may extend the original set of goals.

To show the need for extended thinking, let us contemplate a major challenge that banking applications face today. There has been a rash of "phishing" attempts, that is fake emails that ask users to disclose user information under the pretence of being needed for some maintenance operation. Amazingly, some people must respond, because the flood of phishing attempts has endured. So the banks need to be extra clear in their instructions. For example, banks have stated categorically that they will not ask for information over the Internet. Furthermore, users need to be reminded not to divulge their passwords. Now in a naïve formulation, phishers would not be modeled. However phishers are a real security threat needed to be taken into account. Note that modeling an electronic banking system with both humans and software makes it easier to clarify responsibilities. For example, care with passwords is an explicit responsibility of a user.

To be more concrete, we now look at a simple online shopping example, buyers and sellers using an online Web auction site. The overall goal is to sell goods online. There are three roles: Seller, Buyer, and Online Shopping Manager. The selling goal can be expanded into managing ads, viewing ads, bidding for goods, and managing trading. This goal is depicted in figure 4.5.

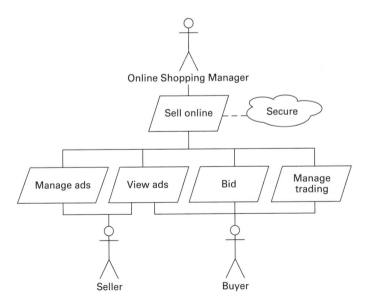

Figure 4.5
Goals for an online auction

Let us analyze security issues surrounding the situation. In practice, security experts would be consulted. Here, our knowledge of the Internet context is sufficient to suggest what needs to be done. There are several issues that can be raised. Is the conducting of commerce appropriate for the domain? For example, students at the University of Melbourne are not permitted to conduct personal business on the university network when it is not a part of the specific educational objectives of the course being studied. Whose responsibility is it to monitor specific users and their behavior? Who needs to worry about the possibility of intruders compromising the system? What degree of authorization is needed to use the relevant services? What are the appropriate encryption standards when any financial information is transmitted such as credit card details? What degree of privacy is required to be supported? What degree of accountability is needed in case something illegal is happening, such as trading child pornography? What current scams are potentially relevant and need to be guarded against?

Questions such as these could be gathered into a checklist for developers to be raised with security experts. Such questions can serve as a prompt, analogous to how guidewords were used within safety analysis in the previous section. Much of this knowledge should also be incorporated in explicit domain and knowledge models both at the motivation and system design layers. Domain entities and roles such as attack, vulnerability, hacker, and unauthorized user should be included in the domain model. Knowledge of encryption standards, hacker exploits, and relevant organizational policies all need to be included in the knowledge model. Knowledge of the right security techniques to use for specific hacker attacks is also needed, and what protections should be invoked if a particular type of attack is detected, such as denial of service. This knowledge should be included in the behavior and service models.

Are there any new roles that need to be added? Should there be an auditing role and an auditing agent to check that security policies are being followed, and to help prevent future attacks? Does there need to be a logging facility? Should there be separate authentication services or accountability services? Should these services and capabilities be in the system or outsourced?

We look at one aspect in a little more detail: interaction protocols between agents. Suppose we have two human agents, Alice and Bob, as the seller and buyer, respectively, and an Auction Web site as the online shopping manager. A simple communications protocol can be designed as depicted in the interaction diagram in figure 4.6. Alice submits information, including the ad, the due date for the auction, credit card information, and the minimum acceptable price, denoted as `Limit` (Step 1). Bob requests ad information (Step 2), which is supplied by the Auction Web site (Step 3). Bob then makes a bid for the product using his credit card (Step 4) which is accepted by the Auction site (Step 5). Finally, Alice is notified of the successful transaction (Step 6).

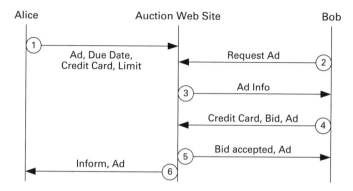

Figure 4.6
An interaction diagram for an online auction

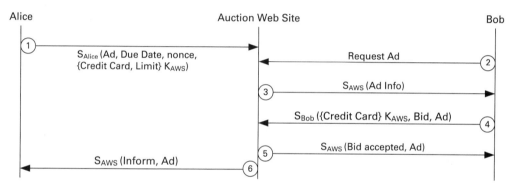

Figure 4.7
An encrypted interaction diagram for an online auction

What are the security requirements? We need to think of the security attributes: for example, which of the exchanged messages need to be protected, and how the security requirements can best be incorporated into the protocol using the appropriate security technique. For the example of an online auction, we might use a symmetric encryption technique where each agent has its own key. Certainly any transmission of credit card information or sensitive information would be encrypted. That leads in our example to five of the six steps being encrypted, with each of Alice, Bob, and the Auction Web site invoking encryption as needed. The resulting interaction diagram is represented in figure 4.7.

Please note that figures 4.6 and 4.7 combine elements of interaction diagrams and interaction-sequence diagrams introduced in section 3.6, thereby emphasizing our neutrality as to particular modeling notations.

Sending encrypted messages for e-commerce is a real issue, though our treatment is simplified for the pedagogical purposes of the book. Whether a message was encrypted properly was the focus of a consulting job that Leon undertook. It related to the use of traffic cameras to enforce compliance to speed limits on highways. The particular system took an image of a car speeding past. The image was downloaded to a central processing facility where the car was identified and a fine issued. The system of cars, motorists, police, and traffic cameras is a good example of a socio-technical system best modeled in terms of agents.

The consulting job was to independently confirm that a specific cryptographic protocol was applied correctly according to the traffic camera tender, and circumvent claims by motorists denying their cars were speeding. Rather than requiring a specific cryptographic algorithm be used, a better system requirement would be to specify that the communication between the camera and the central processing facility be secure. Should the particular cryptographic encryption method be broken, it would be clear that the agent should change the encryption method. This approach would have been far better in terms of purpose and adaptability than insisting on a possibly outdated standard.

4.5   Socially Oriented Quality Goals

The previous three sections covered common quality attributes of systems with an engineering focus. The qualities they represent are necessary for the systems being built. The intent is to have measurable, or at least traceable, goals that embody the quality with which the software is being imbued.

This section discusses quality goals that have a more social dimension. Social descriptions have been used for quality goals in previous chapters. Examples are having fun in a soccer game, having fun playing with a Tamagotchi, being flirtatious, and showing forgiveness. A user interface should be polite. Allowing such qualities makes a challenge for measurement, as it is not obvious how to quantify and measure them.

Socially oriented quality goals are relevant for multiagent systems in which some of the agents are humans and some are pieces of software. Most of our examples in this section concern human experience. We include these examples to better illustrate the qualitative nature of quality goals and why they are important. Although it would be intriguing to contemplate whether an email client was having fun while taking care of email, seriously addressing such a question is beyond scope.

Consider the goal of having fun while playing soccer, a definite goal of Leon's daughter Emily over several years. Clearly the goal has been satisfied, or Emily would not have kept playing. But there was no objective way to determine in advance what would turn out to be fun. You might think scoring a goal would be fun. It probably is, but may not be, depending on circumstances. The day Emily made a spectacular save as a goalie and got covered in mud was fun, but only because of the comments of her team members. The comments were not predictable in advance. Indeed, how the team members interacted contributed to the level of enjoyment and fun. The team dynamics were not always predictable, either. At the end of each game, however, we would have a constructive review of what had happened, and whether it had been fun was part of it.

The quality goal of "being fun" was also raised in the context of interaction with a Tamagotchi. Kuldar and his daughter Eliise could, and did, judge whether her interaction with the Tamagotchi was fun. Again, it would not be easy to write down in advance what would constitute fun. Neither would it be possible to decompose the goal of being fun into a set of smaller goals that, if met, would guarantee that the experience is fun.

These two examples suggest that user studies could be helpfully involved in determining the achievement of socially oriented quality goals. Indeed, the area of usability requires users to be assessed in their use of software. User involvement is an important issue. As well as direct user measurement, indirect measures such as markets can be used. If a computer game is not fun to interact with, it is extremely unlikely to be successful.

Another quality goal that one might be tempted to add to a Tamagotchi or to a computer game is adaptability. If a toy or game behaves exactly the same way every time, it is usually less interesting. One can envisage having a Tamagotchi adapt to the behavior of its owner. There is no single best way as to how this might be achieved. For example, one might want to develop adaptation rules, and add them to the Tamagotchi's design. Or one might want to have a service that learns the owner's behavior preferences, such as playing with the Tamagotchi in the morning, or spending more time on the weekend. The Tamagotchi might then be able to customize its behavior based on the results of the service.

Let us reconsider the urging of Jesus to forgive each other seventy times seven times. There is a quality of forgiveness. The measure of it is to be taken figuratively, rather than literally. The number 490, or 7×70, is a large number, and the religious sentiment to be drawn from Jesus' teaching is to be infinitely forgiving.

We believe that socially oriented quality goals should not necessarily be reduced to measurable goals. They can remain as attributes to be evaluated after a system has been deployed, perhaps in a user study. Socially oriented quality goals can be useful for another purpose within the software engineering life cycle—namely, in stimulating discussions as to whether a particular design meets requirements.

Chapter 9 contains an extended example where abstract quality goals work well with role and goal models. The project involved technology solutions for mediating intimacy. The quality goals usefully complement the motivation and design models that were developed and allowed nontechnical people to engage with requirements and design. This project has led to a new Australian government–supported project on socially oriented requirements engineering for people in the domestic space, as opposed to the office space. The use of nonstandard quality goals in the domestic space is the key.

Sometimes a nonstandard quality goal may trigger a new (functional) goal. As we were writing this book, we wanted the process to be enjoyable. We discovered that we both like sweets such as cake and chocolate. Each of us has brought different cakes to share with morning coffee or tea, and an informal protocol of bringing cake was introduced to achieve a new goal. Bringing cake wasn't a book-writing requirement, but emerged from the quality goal of the book writing process being enjoyable.

4.6   Elaborating and Analyzing Quality Goals

The quality goals that have been described so far have not been presented with much analysis. They have been intended to reinforce the need to be explicit about quality requirements, and to consider quality requirements alongside functional requirements. This section tackles analyzing and elaborating quality goals.

The simplest quality modeling case is a single quality goal attached to the top-level goal in the overall goal model. For example, we might say that the e-commerce system needs to be secure. As discussed in section 4.4, this would be elaborated upon in the design stage to handle issues like intrusion detection in a piece of software or encrypting messages sent as parts of protocols.

Sometimes it may be desirable to elaborate quality goals within the motivation layer. For example, consider the greeting system whose goal model is represented in figure 4.8. (This example is discussed in more detail in section 9.1.) A person arriving at an intelligent home might expect to be greeted. In a greeting scenario, when a person arrives at the intelligent home, the system must realize his or her presence and be prepared to offer personalized services. The system then greets the person by his or her name to acknowledge her presence, so that he or she knows the system is ready to serve. Such greeting might happen when the owner wakes up in the morning and also when a family member comes from work or other activities. The greeting subsystem of the intelligent home should offer personalized greetings to friends, family members, and visitors as they enter.

Whether a greeting is appropriate depends closely on its *context*. For example, in the presence of the home owner's—say Jane's—parents or distinguished guests, the greeting should be more formal and polite. If Jane is alone, the greeting can be

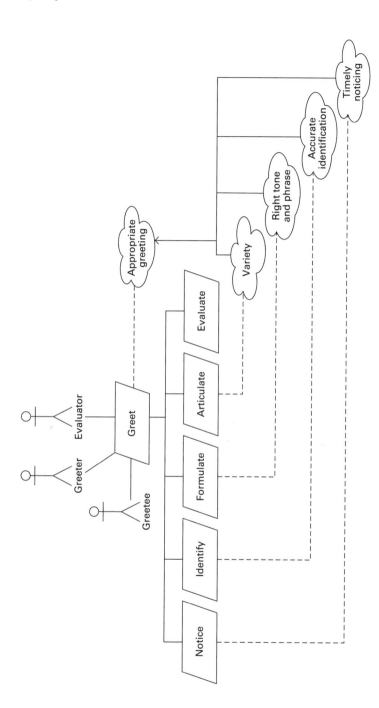

Figure 4.8
The goal model of greeting

more casual and playful. On the other hand, if something unfortunate has happened, the greeting should certainly not be playful, but instead offer more support.

The model depicted in figure 4.8 reflects that greeting consists of noticing and identifying the person to be greeted, formulation of the greeting, articulation of the greeting, and evaluation of the greeting process. There is the "Appropriate greeting" quality goal pertaining to the "Greet" goal. The diagram contains four other quality goals—"Variety," "Right tone and phrase," "Accurate identification," and "Timely noticing." How do these goals relate to the overall quality of appropriateness? In a word, positively, in the sense that increased variety increases appropriateness and more accurate identification also increases appropriateness, as does timely noticing. Some quality goals might contribute negatively. For example, a possible quality goal—speed of greeting—might detract from appropriateness, because the faster the response the less opportunity there is for considered reflection of appropriateness. Some software engineering notations indicate positive or negative contributions by annotating the appropriate visual model with "+" or "−". We prefer to leave annotations to the context of specific analysis methods rather than complexify the goal model.

The palletizer example in figure 4.1 has three quality goals: that the palletization be efficient, reliable, and safe. We treated each of these quality goals independently. The efficiency and reliability goals were addressed by translating the quality goal into a constraint in the role model. The safety goal was handled by a safety analysis of the activities of the agents such as stacking and packing.

The independent treatment of the three quality goals masks an implicit assumption—namely, that the three quality goals would not interfere with each other, or that any interference would be minimal. However, a safety measure that is introduced as a result of the safety analysis may have a negative effect on the system efficiency, and may lead to lower throughput of packing fruit in boxes. For another example, the user interface for a Tamagotchi being fun and interactive may cause the system to be unacceptably slow in consequence.

Handling the interactions between quality goals can sometimes be done with qualitative analysis. The idea is to decompose quality goals into factors that affect them and to express dependencies between the factors. If two factors both positively affect the quality, then the quality will be fine. If one factor affects the quality strongly and positively and the other factor weakly and negatively, the design needs to address the impact of the combination of the factors accordingly. For example, an automated teller machine needs to be secure and quick in response. Adding security encryption adversely affects performance, as more computation needs to be done. A trade-off needs to be made as to the overhead of adding encryption to the downgrading of performance. Such trade-offs can be viewed as qualitative analysis.

4.7 Background

A good account of quality from an IT perspective can be found in Marchewka 2006. The Shakespearean quotation is from *The Merchant of Venice* (act IV, scene 1).

The handling of quality requirements as an entity in their own right was pioneered by Chung et al. (2000). The notation in that book influenced the clouds we use to denote quality goals.

The palletizer example comes from the research of Louis Liu, who provided us with an initial safety analysis which we adapted for section 4.3. Louis is working on a master's thesis at the University of Melbourne under the supervision of Dr. Ed Kazmierczak. Leon is on Louis' supervision committee. Ed and Louis have coined the term Agent Hazard and Operability Analysis (AHAZOP). It is noteworthy that the analysis presented in section 4.3 was done by Kuldar, who has little background in safety, but who found that the safety concepts could be understood easily in terms of the agent models.

The online shopping example is thanks to Giannakis Antoniou and Andrea Luo, both Ph.D. students working with Leon and Kuldar at the University of Melbourne. It is described in Luo, Antoniou, and Sterling 2007. More generally, Andrea is looking at a framework for considering quality requirements as a key part of her Ph.D. work. Using agents for security was also the subject of the Computer Science honors thesis of Arash Arian under Leon's supervision. The agent metaphor fitted the security model, and Arash was able to both design and prototype a multiagent system on the lookout for external attacks.

The title of section 4.5 comes from a project conducted with support from the Australian Smart Internet Cooperative Research Centre. A useful discussion linking ethnography with design can be found in Martin and Sommerville 2004.

A calculus for qualitative analysis of quality requirements is described by Chung et al. (2000). Thomas Juan adapted it for agent concepts in his Ph.D. thesis (Juan 2008). It was also presented in a tutorial by Leon and Thomas on agent-oriented software engineering at the 27th International Conference on Software Engineering (Sterling and Juan 2005).

Exercises for Chapter 4

1. Add quality goals for one of the agents you discussed in chapter 1.

2. Consider a factory operating an automated machine such as a lathe. Do a simple agent-oriented hazard analysis.

3. Consider the security of your home computer network using agent-oriented models.

4. Model another quality requirement for an application of your choice.

5 Agent Programming Platforms and Languages

Chapter 2 described a conceptual space consisting of the motivation, system design, and deployment layers. Chapter 3 introduced models from the motivation and system design layers of the conceptual space. As pointed out in chapter 2, an implementation process conceptually involves mapping the concepts of the system design layer to the concepts of the deployment layer. In other words, models from the system design layer—knowledge models, interaction models, and behavior models—are mapped onto the constructs of some programming platform or language.

The purpose of agent programming languages and platforms is to facilitate the building of systems incorporating agent concepts. In this chapter, we look at several agent programming platforms and languages to demonstrate how the modeling concepts manifest themselves in the implementation constructs employed by those agent programming platforms and languages. Although we believe that models are more important than languages in developing multiagent systems, we acknowledge that other researchers have a different view. We explain how the types of models based on the conceptual space can be implemented in the languages.

Design models—behavior models, interaction models, and knowledge models— are expressed in terms of concepts from the system design layer of the conceptual space. In the system design layer, we defined types of activities and their constituent actions. Two types of events perceived by agents—action events and nonaction events—are introduced. They are subsumed under the common design term of perceptions. Actions and events occur in a concrete environment existing in the deployment layer of the conceptual space shown in figure 2.6. An environment can be physical or virtual.

In the deployment layer, concrete agents perform concrete actions that can be perceived as events by other concrete agents. Concrete agents also perceive other events that are caused by environment objects rather than agents. Concrete agents manipulate concrete objects, such as service objects. Performing actions and manipulating objects occur as specified by behavioral constructs, which have been derived from rules defined at the system design layer.

It is useful to distinguish between platform-independent and architecture-independent design models. The models introduced in chapter 3 are *platform-independent*; that is, they describe the design independently of any specific programming language or platform. Platform-dependent parts of design models are encapsulated by services that are invoked by an agent's actions. For example, an agent can invoke a service for sending a message or perceiving its environment.

All the models introduced in chapter 3 are also *architecture-independent*; that is, they do not prescribe or imply the usage of any specific agent architecture for implementing manmade agents. Sometimes it is helpful to use *architecture-dependent* design models. Examples of architecture-dependent design models are capability and plan models, which are oriented toward the well-known BDI agent architecture.

This chapter is structured as follows. Section 5.1 introduces the BDI architecture. Sections 5.2 and 5.3 describe two agent platforms and the accompanying languages that are (to varying degrees) based on the BDI paradigm on one hand and logic programming on the other. These platforms are Jason and 3APL. Sections 5.4 and 5.5 describe two platforms based on the Java programming language: JACK and JADE. JACK relies on the BDI architecture, and JADE has its own execution mechanism, as explained in section 5.5.

To enable comparison of agent platforms and languages, we have implemented the behavior described by the Tamagotchi behavior model (shown in figure 3.18) in each of them. This behavior can be achieved by different implementation techniques. In this chapter, we demonstrate some of the techniques.

Because agent programming languages historically precede agent-oriented modeling, several concepts in agent programming are used in a similar sense but at a lower level of abstraction. The most fundamental such concept is a rule that in several agent programming languages is used as a behavioral construct. Rules, in turn, refer to goals and plans.

A goal at the deployment layer is understood as a condition referring to the state of the environment intended by the agent. However, at the system design layer goals are modeled as achieved through interactions between agents comprising a multiagent system. At the deployment layer, a goal is modeled as being achieved by a set of concrete actions by a concrete agent. Such an action set is called a *plan*. There can be several alternative plans for achieving a goal. Though at the system design layer goals and plans are only used for modeling problem-solving activities, at the deployment layer they constitute universal behavioral constructs for concrete agents.

The reader interested in using the languages described for practical applications needs to be aware that characteristics of the languages will almost certainly affect quality attributes discussed in the previous chapter, such as performance and security. We do not discuss these characteristics in this book.

5.1   The BDI Agent Architecture and Execution Model

Within the agent community, one architecture stands out as having had a large influence on agent development over the past twenty-odd years. That architecture, articulated for individual agents, is the previously mentioned BDI (Belief-Desire-Intention) agent architecture. Key to the popularity of BDI has been its use of folk psychology terms, such as beliefs, intentions, goals, and plans. Appropriating terms in common parlance has been appealing for those from the AI community, as they have attempted to popularize agent systems.

The BDI agent architecture is primarily conceptual and not precisely defined. Indeed many researchers claim that their (quite diverse) systems have BDI architecture. One system universally agreed to accord to the BDI architecture is the Procedural Reasoning System (PRS) which was developed in the 1980s. We describe the essential PRS architecture in this section.

The internal architecture for an agent within a PRS system can be described as having five major components. The first is a set of facts representing knowledge about the world that the agent currently holds. These facts get updated as the agent experiences the world. These facts are regarded as beliefs and are the "B" in the architecture. We observe that it is possible, and mostly desirable, for individual agents in a multiagent system to have differing beliefs, sometimes conflicting. In the conceptual space of chapter 2, beliefs correspond to concrete objects and associations between them. An agent's beliefs are derived from knowledge items at the system design layer.

The second component of the agent is a set of goals that the agent is trying to achieve. The goals are regarded as desires and are the "D" in the architecture. Note that the terms of the conceptual space of chapter 2 do not exactly match the BDI concepts. The BDI architecture takes an internal agent view, rather than a system view, and does not really have a motivation layer. Goals in the BDI architecture can reflect a high-level purpose or motivation. More typically, however, the BDI goals are used as behavioral constructs. They are derived from activities and rules of the system design layer.

The third component is the "I" component and represents the set of goals the agent is currently trying to achieve—its intentions. This intention structure is the mechanism for instantiating, scheduling, executing, and monitoring plans (to be described next). It needs to keep track of which plans are still needed as intentions as goals are achieved and the world changes.

The fourth component is a library of plans. Plans are sequences of concrete actions for achieving the agent goals. Plans are derived from activities and their constituent actions from the system design layer. Having plans available means that the agent

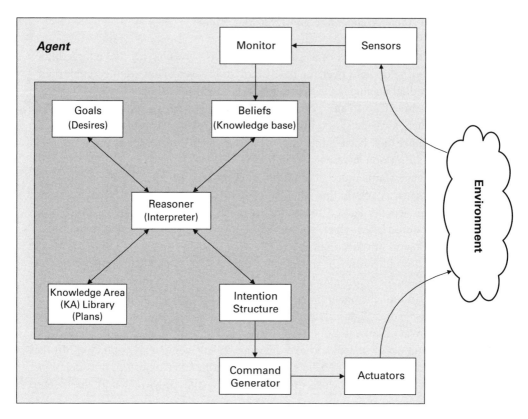

Figure 5.1
The BDI agent architecture (Wikipedia 2008b)

can be more reactive to changes in the environment. While fundamentally static, plans can be updated during agent execution.

The fifth component is a reasoner or interpreter. The role of the reasoner is to orchestrate the overall behavior of the agent. It coordinates sensing and acting, updates beliefs about the world, and chooses which plan to invoke. A diagram showing the five components is given in figure 5.1 in the shaded box. The figure also depicts the agent situated in an environment being monitored with sensors and planned actions being carried out through actuators.

The BDI architecture is a refinement of the abstract agent architecture explained in section 2.3. The reasoner of a BDI agent corresponds to the controller of an abstract agent. Its desires and intentions form part of the knowledge base of an abstract agent.

Let us conceptualize the BDI agent reasoner. Recall from section 2.3 that each agent is responsible for monitoring the state of the environment, choosing how to respond, and acting in the environment. The simplest BDI interpreter realizes that

while there are unachieved goals **do**
    observe the environment;
        update beliefs;
   prioritize intentions to achieve;
   choose a plan for the intention;
   execute and monitor the plan;
        end while

Figure 5.2
The execution loop of a basic BDI reasoner

responsibility in terms of the BDI constructs. Figure 5.2 describes a simple BDI agent reasoner. It consists of a loop of observing the world (through its sensors), updating its beliefs, prioritizing on its intentions, choosing a plan to achieve its prioritized intention, then executing the plan and monitoring its progress. The condition on the while loop is that there are unachieved goals. If "to exist" is one of the agent goals, then the cycle of observing the world, updating beliefs, choosing and executing plans, and monitoring progress continues.

The execution loop performed by the BDI agent reasoner refines the one carried out by the controller of an abstract agent. The main differences are that the BDI agent views the world in terms of the goals to be achieved and has predefined plans for achieving them.

The reasoner in figure 5.2 is very abstract and leaves many decisions for the implementer. In the languages to be described, the processing of the control loop must be done efficiently. Most BDI systems take an event processing approach. Updates to the agent's beliefs are indicated by events.

Another issue is the relative time spent between observing the world, reflecting, and acting. The reasoner gives no guidance on how to allocate time between observing, reflecting, and acting. A concrete allocation policy is needed for practical implementations.

Note that the BDI agent architecture given in figure 5.1 is concerned with a single agent. A system view of a multiagent system would need to coordinate the individual agent interpreters. The coordination needs to be practical for it to work for nontrivial applications.

In the usual scenario, each agent updates its own view of the world. However, if one is performing a simulation, there needs to be an environmental reality. A separate environment simulator with interface to the agents is needed. The case study we describe in section 8.2 provides some insight into how an environment simulator can be implemented.

Many agent platforms and languages have developed these ideas into systems, three of which are described in the following sections. The original PRS system was developed in Lisp at NASA. It was redeveloped in C++ as the Distributed Multi-agent Reasoning System, better known as dMARS, at the Australian Artificial Intelligence Institute. dMARS was used for a range of applications, including the SWARMM system mentioned in chapter 1. Developing in dMARS was accessible to at least some developers. Graphical editors were a useful bridge between users, who were the pilots in the SWARMM example, and developers. In order to be practical, the dMARS implementation was platform-specific, which limited widespread availability.

It is hard to relate the abstract BDI architecture to the dMARS implementation. A clearer mapping from the abstract BDI execution model to the implementation has been proposed with the abstract AgentSpeak programming language. There have been several attempts to make a practical language from the AgentSpeak model. The most successful of them is Jason, which we describe in the next section.

5.2 Jason

Jason is the interpreter for an extended version of AgentSpeak, which is a logic-based language for programming BDI agents. Jason allows agents to be distributed over the Internet. It includes features for agent communication based on speech acts, such as inform and request, and has a clear notion of environments of multiagent systems. Jason is available as open source software.

A Jason agent includes a set of beliefs, making up the agent's belief base, and a set of plans which form its plan library. It corresponds to a concrete agent in the conceptual space shown in figure 2.6. Beliefs express relationships between concrete objects, and plans are sequences of concrete actions of the conceptual space.

The behavioral constructs of Jason agents include goals. A goal declares that the agent wants to achieve a state of the world where the associated predicate is true. All plans are associated with goals in Jason.

A Jason agent reacts to two kinds of triggering events. They correspond to events in the conceptual space. The first kind of triggering event is a change of an agent's beliefs through perception of the environment. Perceptions include messages received from other agents. A Jason agent perceives its environment by first storing all its perceptions as its beliefs and only then choosing the perceptions to which it will react.

The second kind of triggering event is a change in the agent's goals. The change originates from the execution of plans triggered by previous events. Both goals and events are architecture-dependent design and implementation constructs.

A triggering event specifies which events can initiate the execution of a particular plan. The plan of a Jason agent has a head, specifying the events for which that plan is relevant, and a conjunction of beliefs representing a context. The context must be a logical consequence of the agent's current beliefs if the plan is to be considered applicable at that moment in time. A plan also has a body, which is a sequence of atomic actions to be performed when the plan is triggered. Figure 5.3 contains ten Jason plans. As the figure shows, the general pattern for representing Jason plans is:

```
event : context -> body;
```

Atomic actions correspond to concrete actions of the conceptual space. The following kinds of actions can be distinguished in Jason:

- internal actions provided by the software platform in use, denoted by .action name, for example, .print("I'm not happy!")
- adding a goal, denoted by !goal, for example, !givePresent(H)
- removing a goal, denoted by -!goal, for example, -!play(Friend)
- evaluating a predicate, denoted by ?predicate, for example, ?happyLevel(K)
- replacing a belief, denoted by -+predicate, for example, -+presentList(T)

In terms of service models, described in section 3.10, internal actions are the actions that invoke services provided by the software platform in use. In addition, there can be *external actions* that invoke services provided by an external environment to perceive and change it. Jason enables the implementation of such environments in the Java programming language.

At each execution cycle of a Jason program, the Jason interpreter updates a list of events, which may be generated from perception of the environment, or from the execution of plans. Next, the interpreter unifies each event with triggering events in the heads of plans. This generates the set of all *relevant plans* for that event. By checking whether the context part of the plans in that set follows from the agent's beliefs, the set of *applicable plans* is determined. Thereafter, the interpreter chooses a single applicable plan from that set and executes it.

We demonstrate in figure 5.3 how the Tamagotchi behavior model, represented in figure 3.18, can be expressed in the Jason language.

First, we need to express an agent's knowledge base. There are a range of facts about the state of the Tamagotchi, each expressed as a unary predicate. For example the fact happyLevel(10) indicates that the happiness level of the Tamagotchi is 10. A predicate present_list would indicate the presents available to the Tamagotchi. For example, presentList([toy,candy]) would indicate that the Tamagotchi can give a toy or candy. We do not comprehensively list all of the predicates that might be needed here.

Second, we need to express that if a Tamagotchi is unhappy, it will tell its owner. We do this by using the corresponding internal action of the .send type. In

```
happyLevel(0).
myFriend(tamagotchi2).
myMaster(person).
!checkHappyLevel.
presentNumber(2).
presentList([toy,candy]).

@p1 //check own happiness level
+!checkHappyLevel: happyLevel(M) & M <=20
          <- .print("I'm not happy!");
             .my_name(I);
             ?happyLevel(K);
             ?myMaster(P);
             .send(P, tell, unhappy(I,K)).

+!checkHappyLevel.

@p2
+visitFriend: true
          <- .print("Could I come to your place?");
             ?myFriend(Friend);
             .my_name(I);
             .send(Friend,tell, could_I_come_to_your_place(I)).

@p3
+please_come(P): true
          <- .print("Good day!");
             .my_name(I);
             ?myFriend(Friend);
             .send(Friend,tell, good_day(I)).

@p4
+hello(Friend): true
          <- !visit(Friend).

@p5
+!visit(Friend): presentNumber(M) & M >0
          <- ?presentList([H|T]);
             -+presentList(T);
             !givePresent(H).

@p6
+!visit(Friend): presentNumber(M) & M =0
          <- !play(Friend).
```

Figure 5.3
A Jason program for Tamagotchi behavior

```
@p7
+!givePresent(Present): true
        <- ?happyLevel(L);
            .print("Please accept my present,",Present,"!(",L,")");
            ?presentNumber(N);
            -+presentNumber(N - 1);
            -+happyLevel(L + 4);
            ?myFriend(Friend);
            .my_name(I);
            .send(Friend,tell,accept_my_present(I,Present)).

@p8
+!play(Friend): happyLevel(M) & M <=20
        <- .print("May I play with you,",Friend,"?(",M,")");
            .my_name(I);
            .send(Friend,tell,play_with_me(I,M)).

+!play(Friend).

@p9
+thanks(Friend,Present): true
        <- !play(Friend).

@p10
+ok(Friend,M): happyLevel(M) & M <=20
        <- ?happyLevel(L);
            -+happyLevel(L + 2);
            !visit(Friend).
```

Figure 5.3
(continued)

accordance with the principles of the BDI agent architecture, we include this action in the body of the plan @p1 shown in figure 5.3. This plan is invoked when its context indicates that the Tamagotchi's happiness level is less than or equal to 20.

The plan @p2 shown in figure 5.3 conveys that if the Tamagotchi's owner requests it to visit another Tamagotchi, which results in adding the visitFriend belief, the Tamagotchi asks its friend to accept the visit. The value true in the plan's context means that there are no preconditions for executing the plan. A request to accept a visit is expressed as performing another internal action of the .send type.

For simplicity, we have omitted establishing a connection with another Tamagotchi from the Tamagotchi's behavior. It should be expressed as the invocation of an external connectTamagotchi() action.

The plan @p3 is invoked when another Tamagotchi accepts the visit, which is reflected by adding the corresponding please_come belief to the Tamagotchi's knowledge base. The body of the plan sends to the other Tamagotchi the greeting message "Good day!"

Plan @p4 is invoked when the response "Hello!" is received from the other Tamagotchi. Having received from the friend consent for a visit, this plan sets the visit(Friend) goal for the Tamagotchi. In response to adding this goal, either plan @p5 or @p6 is invoked, depending on their context conditions. If the Tamagotchi has presents left in its knowledge base, plan @p5 is invoked. If the Tamagotchi does not have any presents, plan @p6 is invoked. Plan @p5 sets a goal to give the other Tamagotchi a present, and plan @p6 sets a goal to play with the friend. These goals are achieved by plans @p7 and @p8, respectively.

The goal of giving a present is achieved by plan @p7. The body of this plan deletes the present from the Tamagotchi's knowledge base, increases the Tamagotchi's happiness level by 4, and sends a message to the other Tamagotchi of giving it a present. Plan @p9 expresses that after a present has been accepted by the friend, a goal to play is again set. This plan ensures that the Tamagotchis will play after giving a present.

Achieving the goal of playing with the friend consists of sending a "May I play with you?" message to the other Tamagotchi according to the body of the plan @p8 and receiving a reply according to the body of plan @p10. After the reply has been received, the Tamagotchi increases its happiness level by 2. As Jason does not allow loops to be explicitly used as behavioral constructs within plan bodies, the visiting goal is reset at the end of each execution of @p10, until the value of the Tamagotchi's happyLevel is greater than 20.

The plans @p1 to @p10 are shown in figure 5.3. A snapshot reflecting the interactions between Tamagotchis and the agent simulating the owner of the first digital pet is depicted in figure 5.4.

Jason is distributed within an Integrated Development Environment (IDE), which comes with a number of useful tools, such as the Jason Mind Inspector. The Jason Mind Inspector allows for checking of the agent's mental state throughout its execution. The result of running the Jason Mind Inspector on a Tamagotchi simulated in Jason is depicted in figure 5.5.

5.3   3APL

The Artificial Autonomous Agents Programming Language, better known as 3APL and pronounced "triple-APL" is an agent programming language based on modal agent logics. A 3APL agent consists of beliefs, plans, goals, and reasoning rules. A 3APL multiagent system consists of a set of concurrently executed 3APL agents that can interact either directly through communication or indirectly through the shared environment.

In order to implement 3APL multiagent systems, the 3APL platform has been built. It allows the implementation and parallel execution of a set of 3APL agents.

Figure 5.4
A Jason snapshot of the interactions between two Tamagotchis

The platform includes a directory facilitator called the "agent management system," a message transport system, a shared environment, and an interface that allows agents to execute actions in the shared environment.

A 3APL agent is a concrete agent in terms of the conceptual space shown in figure 2.6. The components of a 3APL agent are a belief base, a goal base, an action base, and two rule bases: one for goal planning rules and the other one for plan revision rules.

The *beliefs* of a 3APL agent describe information the agent believes about the world. The belief base of a 3APL agent is implemented as a Prolog program consisting of Prolog facts and rules. The belief base is conceptually a set of concrete objects and relationships between them.

The *goal* of a 3APL agent denotes the situation the agent wants to realize. The goal is one of the behavioral constructs of a 3APL agent. The goal base of the agent is a set of goals, each of which is implemented as a conjunction of ground Prolog atoms—that is, atoms with no variables. Goals defined in a 3APL program are persistent throughout the whole execution of the program. We demonstrate shortly how this feature is used for programming loops.

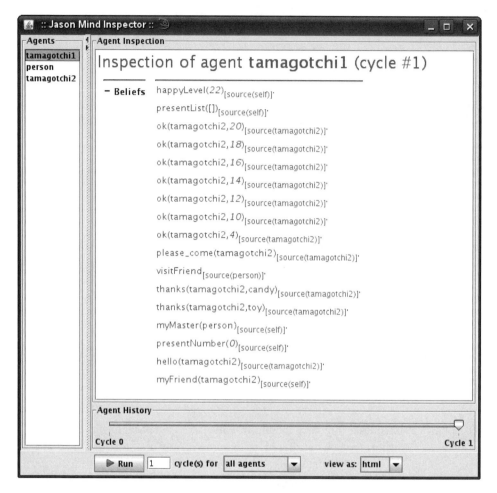

Figure 5.5
A snapshot of running the Jason Mind Inspector on a Tamagotchi

Other behavioral constructs of a 3APL agent are *program operators*. They are used for composing plans from basic actions. The three 3APL program operators are a sequential operator, an iteration operator, and a conditional choice operator.

Basic actions correspond to concrete actions of the conceptual space. In 3APL, five types of basic agent actions are distinguished. They are mental actions, communicative actions, external actions, test actions, and abstract plans.

A *mental action* results in a change in the agent's belief base, if successfully executed. In a 3APL program, a mental action has the form of an atomic formula consisting of a predicate name and a list of terms. The preconditions and postconditions of a mental action should be specified in the 3APL program.

A *communicative action* is used to pass a message to another agent. A message contains the name of the receiver, the type of the message (e.g., inform or request), and the content.

External actions are used to change an external environment in which the agents operate. The effects of external actions are determined by the environment and might not be known to the agents. The agent can come to know the effects of an external action by performing a sensing action. External actions are performed by 3APL agents with respect to an environment, implemented as a Java class. In particular, the actions that can be performed on this environment are determined by the operations of the Java class. This is completely consistent with our general modeling approach taken in section 3.10, where external actions invoke services provided by an external environment to perceive and change it.

A *test action* checks whether a logical formula is derivable from the agent's belief base. Finally, an *abstract plan* is an abstract representation of a plan that can be instantiated with a more concrete plan during execution.

In order to reason with goals and plans, 3APL has two types of *rules*: goal planning rules and plan revision rules. *Goal planning rules* are used to adopt plans to achieve goals. A goal planning rule indicates the goal for which the plan should be adopted and the belief precondition for executing the plan. If the goal is omitted from a rule, the rule simply specifies that under a certain belief condition, a plan can be adopted. *Plan revision rules* are used to revise plans from the plan base.

The execution cycle of a 3APL agent starts with searching for an applicable goal planning rule to adopt a plan for one of its goals and applies the first applicable goal planning rule it finds by marking the plan as executable. The agent then continues with searching for an applicable plan revision rule and applies the first applicable plan revision rule that it finds by first revising the plan and then marking it as executable. After that, the agent continues searching for the executable plans in the order of their occurrence and executes the first plan it finds. Finally, the agent repeats the same cycle or suspends its actions until a message arrives.

In figure 5.6, we present a 3APL implementation of the Tamagotchi behavior model shown in figure 3.18. The initial belief base of the agent is preceded by the BELIEFBASE keyword. As in the Jason language example provided in section 5.2, a Tamagotchi's beliefs include the presents available for it. The belief base also includes two derivation rules, which have been expressed in Prolog. The first of them states that a Tamagotchi is unhappy if the value of the variable indicating its happiness level is less than or equal to 20. The second rule logically defines the meaning of having a present to give away.

The pre- and postconditions of mental actions are specified through *capabilities*. A capability consists of three parts: the precondition, the mental action itself, and the postcondition. In a 3APL program, the specification of capabilities is preceded by the CAPABILITIES keyword. The 3APL program presented in figure 5.6 includes

```
PROGRAM "tamagotchi1"

CAPABILITIES{

    {presentList([H|T])}
                       Extract([H|T])
                       { not presentList([H|T]),
                         presentList(T),
                         present(H),
                         give(H)
                       },

    {TRUE} Info(X) {not notInfo(X)},

    {TRUE} GivePresent(P) {give(P)},

    {happinessLevelNum(Z) AND gap1(Gap1)}
                       Give(X,Y)
                       { not give(X),
                         not present(X),
                         not givenPresentNum(Y),
                         givenPresentNum(Y+1),
                         not happinessLevelNum(Z),
                         happinessLevelNum(Z+Gap1),
                         happinessLevel(Z+Gap1)
                       },
    {happinessLevelNum(Z)}
                       CheckHappinessLevel(N)
                       { checkHappinessLevel(N)
                       },
    {TRUE} DropCheckHappinessLevel(Me) { not checkHappinessLevel(Me)},
    {TRUE} RequestPlay(H) {requestPlay(H)},
    {me(Me)}
                       DropRequestPlay(Me)
                       { drop(me),
                         not requestPlay(Me)
                       },

    {happinessLevelNum(Z)}
                       HandleThank(Friend,P)
                       { not received(Friend,inform,thank_for_your(P))
                       },

    {me(Me) AND gap2(Gap2)}
                       HandleOk(Friend,N)
                       { not received(Friend, inform, ok(N)),
                         handleOk(Friend,N),
                         not happinessLevelNum(N),
                         happinessLevelNum(N+Gap2),
                         checkHappinessLevel(N+Gap2),
                         happinessLevel(N+Gap2)
                       }
}
```

Figure 5.6
A 3APL program for Tamagotchi behavior

```
BELIEFBASE {
 me(tamagotchi1).
 friend(tamagotchi2).
 person(person).
 happinessLevel(0).
 happinessLevelNum(0).
 notInfo(happyinessLevel).
 presentNum(2).
 givenPresentNum(0).
 presentList([toy,candy]).
 gap1(4).
 gap2(2).
 unhappy(X):-X =<20.
 haspresent(X):-presentNum(Y),X<Y.
}

GOALBASE {
 request_visit(),
 govisit(),
 add(),
 checkHappinessLevelGoal(),
 give_present(),
 play_request(),
 play()
}

PLANBASE {
}

PR-RULES{
}

PG-RULES {
 checkHappinessLevelGoal()
    <- happinessLevelNum(H) AND unhappy(H) AND notInfo(V)
     | {
         Info(V);
         person(Person)?;
         Send(Person, inform, i_am_not_happy(Person))
        },

 checkHappinessLevelGoal()
    <- checkHappinessLevel(H) AND unhappy(H) AND
       givenPresentNum(G) AND haspresent(G)
     | {
         DropCheckHappinessLevel(H);
         presentList(K)?;
         Extract(K);
        },

 checkHappinessLevelGoal()
    <- checkHappinessLevel(H) AND unhappy(H)
     | {
```

Figure 5.6
(continued)

```
            DropCheckHappinessLevel(H);
            me(Me)?;
            RequestPlay(Me);
            },

    request_visit()
        <- me(Me) AND friend(Friend) AND received(Person, inform,
           visit_your_friend(Me))
           AND NOT sent(Friend,inform,could_I_come_to_your_place(Friend))
        | {
           Send(Friend, inform, could_I_come_to_your_place(Friend))
           },

    govisit()
        <- me(Me) AND received(Friend, inform, please_come(Me)) AND NOT
           sent(Friend,inform, good_day(Friend))
        | {
           Send(Friend, inform, good_day(Friend));
           presentList(K)?;
           Extract(K);
           },

    give_present()
        <- give(P)
        | {
           givenPresentNum(R)?;
           Give(P,R);
           friend(Friend)?;
           Send(Friend, inform, accept_my_present(P))
           },

    play_request()
        <- received(Friend, inform, thank_for_your(P))
        | {
           HandleThank(Friend,P);
           happinessLevelNum(N)?;
           Send(Friend, inform, play_with_me(N));
           },

    play_request()
        <- requestPlay(R) AND happinessLevelNum(N) AND friend(Friend)
           AND NOT sent(Friend, inform, play_with_me(N))
        | {
           DropRequestPlay(R);
           Send(Friend, inform, play_with_me(N));
           },

    play()
        <- received(Friend, inform, ok(N))
        | {
           HandleOk(Friend,N);
           }
}
```

Figure 5.6
(continued)

capabilities for retrieving a present from the list of presents and for increasing a Tamagotchi's happiness level.

The initial goal base of a 3APL agent is preceded by the GOALBASE keyword. The initial goal base shown in figure 5.6 includes the goals of requesting a visit, going for a visit, giving a present, and playing.

There may be an initial plan base specified for a 3APL agent. The initial plan base is preceded by the PLANBASE keyword and consists of a number of plans separated by a comma. However, the initial plan base in figure 5.6 is empty, because the plans are instead expressed in the goal planning rules section of the Tamagotchi code.

As mentioned earlier, 3APL has two kinds of rules: plan revision rules and goal planning rules. The set of plan revision rules is preceded by the PR-RULES keyword. Figure 5.6 reflects that a Tamagotchi has no plan revision rules.

The set of goal planning rules is preceded by PG-RULES. Each rule is of the following form:

```
goal
    <- pre-condition
    | { plan to be adopted }
```

The first three goal planning rules in the goal base in figure 5.6 deal with checking the Tamagotchi's happiness level. The rules adopt different plans to achieve the goal checkHappinessLevelGoal(). The first goal planning rule expresses that if the Tamagotchi is unhappy, it informs its owner about this. The second rule relates checking the Tamagotchi's happiness level to giving a present to the Tamagotchi to which it is connected and the third rule relates checking the happiness level to playing with the other Tamagotchis. All of the rules include the precondition of unhappiness, meaning that the rule is applied only if the Tamagotchi is unhappy. Because the goal checkHappinessLevelGoal() to be achieved by the plans adopted by the three rules is persistent, the rules are applied in a loop until the Tamagotchi is happy.

The next two goal planning rules with the respective goals request_visit() and govisit() address visiting. According to the first rule, if going for a visit is requested by the owner of the first Tamagotchi, the Tamagotchi sends a message to its friend with a request to accept a visit. The latter rule expresses that if the other Tamagotchi accepts the visit, it is greeted by the first Tamagotchi.

The rule with the give_present() goal defines giving a present. This rule expresses that if the visiting Tamagotchi has enough presents, it gives one to the hosting Tamagotchi. To increase the Tamagotchi's happiness level by a value of 4 as a result of giving a present, the plan generated by this rule invokes the Give capability defined in the CAPABILITIES section of the program.

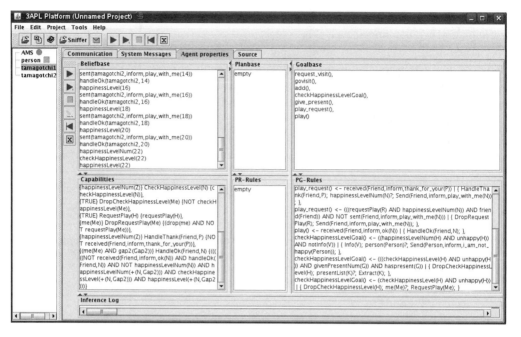

Figure 5.7
Developing the Tamagotchi code with the 3APL platform

The last group of rules deals with Tamagotchis playing. The plan adopted by the rule with the `play()` goal increases the happiness level of a Tamagotchi by 2 by invoking the `HandleOK` capability defined in the `CAPABILITIES` section of the program.

We have omitted from the example program the establishment of a connection between the two Tamagotchis. Connection can happen through invoking the `connect()` operation of the corresponding environment object, which we regard as a service.

The 3APL platform provides a graphical interface for developing and executing 3APL agents. Figure 5.7 exemplifies how the platform was used for developing the Tamagotchi code in figure 5.6. The snapshot of the 3APL platform shown in figure 5.8 demonstrates the interactions between the two Tamagotchis and the agent simulating the owner of the first Tamagotchi.

5.4   JACK

JACK™ Intelligent Agents (JACK) is an agent platform built on top of and integrated with the Java programming language. It includes an agent-oriented program-

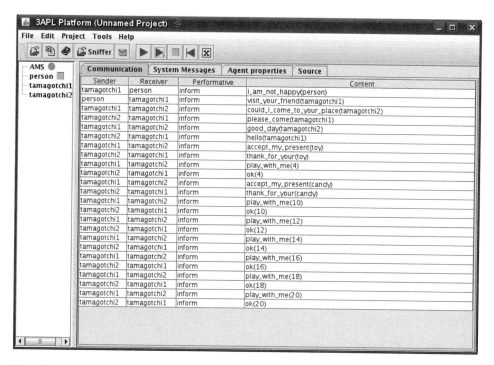

Figure 5.8
A 3APL snapshot of the interactions between two Tamagotchis

ming language, a platform with infrastructure for agent communication, and a development environment with graphical design and debugging tools. JACK also has additional functionality to construct hierarchical teams of agents.

JACK defines a number of concepts. *Agents* in JACK correspond to concrete agents of the conceptual space depicted in figure 2.6. They are defined by the data they have, by the events they handle and send, and by the plans and capabilities they use.

The data a JACK agent has is expressed in terms of beliefsets. A *beliefset* is effectively a small relational database that is stored in memory, rather than on disk. A beliefset can also post events when it is modified. Beliefsets correspond to interrelated concrete objects of the conceptual space.

An *event* is an occurrence in time representing some sort of change that requires a response. Events in JACK represent messages being received, new goals being adopted, and information being received from the environment. Events straightforwardly correspond to the events of the conceptual space.

A *plan* is a process for dealing with events of a given type. A plan includes an indication of which event type it handles, a context condition describing in which

```
import aos.jack.jak.core.*;

public agent Tamagotchi extends Agent {

#handles event VisitYourFriend;
#uses plan VisitYourFriendReact;

#handles event RequestVisit;
#uses plan RequestVisitReact;

#handles event VisitAcceptance;
#uses plan VisitAcceptanceReact;

#handles event Visit;
#uses plan VisitReact;

#handles event Greeting;
#uses plan GreetingReact;

#handles event GivePresent;
#uses plan GivePresentReact;

#handles event Thank;
#uses plan ThankReact;

#handles event Play;
#uses plan PlayReact;

#handles event Ok;
#uses plan OkReact;

#sends event HappyLevel unhappy;
#sends event RequestVisit;
#sends event VisitAcceptance;
#sends event Visit;
#sends event Greeting;
#sends event GivePresent;
#sends event Thank;
#sends event Play;
#sends event Ok;
#private data PresentList presentList();
#private data HappinessLevel happinessLevel();
}
```

Figure 5.9
A core definition of the Tamagotchi agent type in JACK

situations the plan can be used, and a plan body, which can include JACK constructs as well as Java code. In terms of the conceptual space, plans are behavioral constructs.

A *capability* in JACK is a modularization construct, corresponding to a coherent ability of an agent. Capabilities contain beliefs and plans, and specify which events they handle and post. As such, the concept of capability is an amalgamation of the concrete object, event, and behavioral construct concepts of the conceptual space.

The execution cycle of a JACK agent refines the execution cycle of a BDI agent described in section 5.1. Events, which include goals adopted by the agent and messages received from other agents, trigger plans. Each event normally has a number of plans that handle that event, which are called the relevant plans. From among the relevant plans, plans applicable to the agent's current situation are determined by evaluating the plans' context conditions. Thereafter, an applicable plan is selected and run. If the plan fails, its triggering event is reposted and an alternative plan is selected and run. This pattern is repeated until an applicable plan is found or achieving of the goal fails.

We now demonstrate different features of the JACK programming language. We do this by introducing in a step-by-step way the JACK implementation of the Tamagotchi behavior model shown in figure 3.18.

The JACK programming language extends Java in a number of syntactic and semantic ways. First, it adds declaration types which are used to declare agents and their beliefsets, events, plans, and capabilities. Each of the declarations is preceded by "#." We first provide in figure 5.9 a core definition of the Tamagotchi agent type in JACK. The definition includes event and plan declarations that determine which plans handle which events and which events are posted by a Tamagotchi. The definition of the Tamagotchi agent type given in figure 5.9 also includes the declarations of the `PresentList` and `HappinessLevel` beliefsets.

Beliefsets, events, and plans are each defined in a separate file with the corresponding extension. We next provide examples of the beliefset, event, and plan declarations of the `Tamagotchi` agent type.

The `PresentList` beliefset presented here contains the list of the presents that a Tamagotchi has ready for giving to other Tamagotchis. The beliefset is defined as follows:

```
public beliefset PresentList extends ClosedWorld {
#key field int presentId;
#value field String present;
#indexed query getPresent(int id, logical String p);
    PresentList(){
        try {
```

```
                    add(1,"candy");
                    add(2,"toy");
           } catch(BeliefSetException e) {
                        System.err.println
                        ("Add Present Belief
                    failed");
             }
         }
    }
```

The ClosedWorld keyword in the previous definition identifies the beliefset relation as a *closed world* relation that stores true tuples and assumes that any tuple not
found is false. The definition also shows that the beliefset consists of members of the
Present type and provides operations for performing queries on the beliefset. The
getPresent(int id, logical String p) operation assigns to the output parameter the name of a Present in the beliefset.

In addition to the PresentList beliefset, the beliefs of a Tamagotchi include
a beliefset of the HappinessLevel type presented here, which stores the happiness
level of the Tamagotchi and initializes it to 0:

```
public beliefset HappinessLevel extends ClosedWorld {
#value field int h;
#indexed query getHappinessLevel(logical int i);
     HappinessLevel(){
          try {
               add(0);
          } catch(BeliefSetException e) {
               System.err.println
                    ("Add HappinessLevel Belief
               failed");
          }
     }
}
```

A value change of the HappinessLevel beliefset results in posting an event of the
HappinessChanged type. The HappinessChanged event type is defined as shown in
what follows. The definition expresses that an event of the HappinessChanged type
is posted whenever the value of the Tamagotchi's happinessLevel variable drops
below 20:

```
event HappinessChanged extends Event {
#uses data HappinessLevel happinessLevel;
```

```
logical int $x;
#posted when
        (happinessLevel.getHappinessLevel($x) &&
                $x.as_int() <=20 &&
                $x.as_int() >0);
}
```

When an event of the `HappinessChanged` type is posted, the Tamagotchi sends the corresponding message to the agent simulating the Tamagotchi's owner. The owner's agent replies by a message containing an event of the `VisitYourFriend` type. This event invokes the Tamagotchi's `VisitYourFriendReact` plan that sends to the other Tamagotchi a request to accept a visit. If the other Tamagotchi accepts the visit, the plans of sending a greeting, receiving a reply, giving a present, and playing are invoked.

For giving a present, an event of the `GivePresent` type is posted. The `GivePresent` event type is given next. A `GivePresent` event forms the content of a message from a Tamagotchi to the one to which it is connected. The name of a present appears as the content of the present field in the event. An event of this type is posted by invoking the event's `givePresent` operation:

```
event GivePresent extends MessageEvent {
        String present = "";
        #posted as givePresent(String present) {
                this.present = present;
        }
}
```

JACK extends Java by a number of statements to be used within plan bodies. Such statements are preceded by "@." In addition, Java statements can be used in plan bodies. For example, the `@send` statements post events for agent communication and the `@achieve` statements post events for setting goals. An event of the `GivePresent` type is posted by executing the `@send` statement included by the plan presented in figure 5.10. This plan prescribes giving a present to the hosting Tamagotchi, provided that the visiting Tamagotchi has a present to give.

In the JACK programming language, loops can be accomplished through repetitive event postings. For example, the plan represented in figure 5.11 is invoked in response to receiving an "OK" message from the other Tamagotchi, which results in posting of the corresponding event. The plan's body first checks to see whether the Tamagotchi has presents left. If it does and the Tamagotchi is still unhappy, a new present is given to the other Tamagotchi. If the Tamagotchi is still unhappy, a request to play is sent to the other Tamagotchi. As a result, the Tamagotchi is in a behavioral loop of giving a present and playing until it is happy again.

```
plan GreetingReact extends Plan {

#handles event Greeting event;
#uses agent implementing Tamagotchi tama;
#sends event GivePresent ev1;
#modifies data PresentList presentList;

logical String p;

        body() {
                int presentNumber =presentList.nFacts();
                if (presentNumber >0){
                    presentList.getPresent(presentNumber,p);
                    String pp;
                    pp=p.toString();
                    presentList.remove(presentNumber, pp);
                    System.out.println
                        (tama.getMyName() +
                            " :Please accept my present: " +
                            p +".");
                    @send(event.from, ev1.givePresent(pp ));
                }
        }
}
```

Figure 5.10
A JACK plan of giving a present

A snapshot of the interacting Tamagotchis and the agent simulating the owner of the first Tamagotchi is presented in figure 5.12.

Because JACK was built on top of Java, environment objects, which are used as services by JACK agents, are implemented in Java. How service objects can be invoked is shown in section 5.5, which provides an overview of another Java-based agent platform: JADE.

5.5   JADE

The JADE (Java Agent Development Environment) agent platform is a software framework to build agent systems in the Java programming language in compliance with the standards developed for multiagent systems by the Foundation for Intelligent Physical Agents (FIPA). In addition to providing an agent development model, JADE deals with domain independent infrastructure aspects, such as agent life cycle management, and message transport, encoding, and parsing. JADE offers the following features to the agent programmer:

• A FIPA-compliant distributed agent platform that can be split among several hosts

• The Java Application Programmer's Interface, to exchange messages with other agents

• A graphical user interface, to manage several agents from the same Remote Management Agent

• A library of FIPA interaction protocols, such as Contract Net

A JADE agent is implemented as an instance of the `jade.core.Agent` Java class provided by the platform. A JADE agent is a concrete agent in terms of the deployment layer of the conceptual space depicted in figure 2.6.

The knowledge of a JADE agent is represented as a set of interrelated concrete objects implemented in the Java programming language. They may be associated with some persistent data storage, such as a relational database.

```
plan OkReact extends Plan {

#handles event Ok event;
#uses agent implementing Tamagotchi tama;
#sends event Play ev1;
#sends event GivePresent ev2;

    body()
        {
          int i=tama.getHappinessLevel()+ 2;
          tama.setHappinessLevel(i);
          int presentNumber = tama.getPresentNumber();
          if (presentNumber >0 && i <=20){
                tama.setPresentNumber(presentNumber -1);
                String[] present=tama.getPresent();
                System.out.print(tama.getMyName() +
                    " :Please accept my present: " +
                    present[presentNumber -1] +".(");
                System.out.print(i);
                System.out.println(")");
                @send(event.from,
                    ev2.givePresent(present[presentNumber -1]));
          }

          if (presentNumber ==0 && i <=20){
                System.out.print(tama.getMyName() +
                    " :May I play with you?(");
                System.out.print(i);
                System.out.println(")");
                @send(event.from, ev1.play());
          }
        }
}
```

Figure 5.11
A JACK loop of giving a present and playing

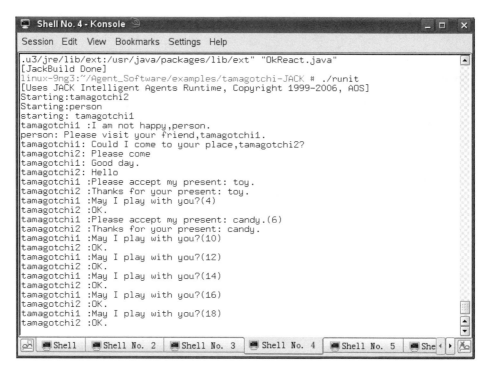

Figure 5.12
A JACK snapshot of the interactions between two Tamagotchis

A JADE agent is capable of performing several concurrent tasks in response to different *events*, either external or internal to the agent. JADE calls these tasks *behaviors*. Events and behaviors respectively correspond to behavioral constructs of the conceptual space. At the elementary level, behaviors consist of *actions* expressed in the Java programming language. In terms of the conceptual space, these actions are concrete actions.

JADE agents register events through internal services provided by the JADE platform, such as the Java Application Programmer's Interface for message exchange between agents, and external services implemented by developers. Behaviors are invoked and sequenced by means of other Java-based behavioral constructs provided by the platform.

The agent platforms overviewed in sections 5.2, 5.3, and 5.4 all relied on the BDI agent architecture and execution model described in section 5.1. The execution model employed by JADE is different.

Each JADE agent is composed of a single execution thread and all its behaviors are implemented as instances of the Java object class jade.core.behaviours

`.Behaviour` provided by the platform. The developer implementing an agent-specific behavior needs to define one or more subclasses of `jade.core.behaviours` `.Behaviour`. JADE has a queue of behaviors to be executed. During execution, behavior classes are instantiated and the resulting behavior objects are added to the queue. The scheduler is implemented by the base `jade.core.Agent` class and is hidden for the programmer. It carries out a round-robin scheduling policy among all behaviors available in the queue. Scheduling is performed by starting, blocking, and restarting behavior classes derived from `jade.core.behaviours.Behaviour`.

The abstract class `jade.core.behaviours.Behaviour` has predefined subclasses `SimpleBehaviour` and `CompositeBehaviour`. The `SimpleBehaviour` class is further divided into the subclasses `OneShotBehaviour` and `CyclicBehaviour`, and the `CompositeBehaviour` class has the subclasses `SequentialBehaviour` and `ParallelBehaviour`. The functionality of a behavior is included in its `start()` operation. Another important operation of a behavior is the `block()` operation, which allows a behavior object to be blocked until some event happens (typically, until a message arrives). The `jade.core.behaviours.Behaviour` class also provides the `onStart()` and `onEnd()` operations. These operations can be overridden by user defined subclasses of `Behaviour` when some actions are to be executed before and after running the behavior. The functionality of `SequentialBehaviour` and `ParallelBehaviour` is included in the operation `onStart()` in place of `action()`.

Because JADE is a lower-level platform than the platforms described in sections 5.2, 5.3, and 5.4, we have included platform-dependent implementation details related to the sending and receiving of messages within the <u>Communicator</u> service of the Tamagotchi Shell environment, which was introduced in section 3.10. This demonstrates how external services can be implemented by the developer. The <u>Communicator</u> service has been implemented as the corresponding `Communicator` Java class. In particular, the `send(String msg)` and `String receive()` service operations modeled in figure 3.22 have been implemented in JADE as shown in figure 5.13. The `String receive()` operation waits for a message until it arrives.

A Tamagotchi can be implemented as an instance of the agent class `Tamagotchi` extending the `jade.core.Agent` class provided by JADE. The knowledge of a Tamagotchi is implemented as a set of Java variables and objects. The following example shows that a Tamagotchi's happiness level is encoded as the `happinessLevel` variable of type `int` and a Tamagotchi's list of presents is represented as a JADE collection accessed through the `Queue` interface:

```
/* The Tamagotchi's level of happiness */
private int happinessLevel = 0;
/** The Tamagotchi's list of presents */
Queue<Present> presentList;
```

```
public void send(String content) {
    /** Prepare and send the INFORM message */
    ACLMessage msg = new ACLMessage(ACLMessage.INFORM);
    msg.setSender
        (new AID("myTamagotchi", AID.ISLOCALNAME));
    msg.addReceiver(getFriend());
    msg.setContent(content);
    tamagotchi.send(msg);
    tamagotchi.getUserInterface().appendMessage("Sent: " + content);
}

public String receive() {
    ACLMessage msg = tamagotchi.blockingReceive();
    return (msg.getContent());
}
```

Figure 5.13
Service operations for sending and receiving messages implemented by JADE

According to the previous code fragment, the collection consists of objects of the `Present` class. As Tamagotchis exchange presents, `Present` has to be a shared object class of which both interconnected Tamagotchis are aware. Shared object classes can be represented by JADE ontologies. A JADE ontology includes a set of element schemas. Element schemas describe the structure of concepts, actions, and predicates that are allowed in agent messages. Concepts are implemented as shared object classes like `Present`.

Ontologies need to be retrieved by agents. The `Tamagotchi` agent class defines in the following way the retrieval of the instance of the `TamaOntology` class, which extends the `jade.content.onto.Ontology` class provided by JADE:

```
/** Information about ontology */
private Ontology ontology = TamaOntology.getInstance();
```

Each agent class of JADE has the `setup()` operation, which performs the agent initialization, and the `takedown()` operation, which performs cleanup operations at the end of its execution. The code fragment presented in figure 5.14 shows the `setup()` operation for the Tamagotchi agent class. The `setup()` operation first registers the ontology instance retrieved as shown earlier with the JADE agent platform. Next, the operation creates a new present list for the Tamagotchi and instantiates the list with three presents. The operation then adds the cyclic behavior of the `Mood_checker` class, which keeps executing continuously. The `Mood_checker` behavior monitors the Tamagotchi's knowledge, and if necessary, proactively initiates new behaviors. Next, the `setup()` operation creates an instance of the Tamagotchi's local Tamagotchi Shell environment as an instance of the corresponding `TamagotchiShell` class. The Tamagotchi Shell environment contains services that are

```
protected void setup() {
    /** Register the ontology used by this agent */
    getContentManager().registerOntology(ontology);

    presentList = new LinkedList();

    presentList.add(new Present ("food"));
    presentList.add(new Present ("chocolate"));
    presentList.add(new Present ("toy"));

    // Adding cyclic behaviours
    addBehaviour(new Mood_checker(this));

    /** Create the Tamagotchi Shell for this Tamagotchi */
    setTamagotchiShell(new TamagotchiShell(this));

    // Creating a new User Interface
    ui = new UserInterface(this);
    ui.show();
}
```

Figure 5.14
The JADE `setup()` method for the `Tamagotchi` agent class

used by the Tamagotchi. Finally, the `setup()` operation creates a user interface for the Tamagotchi.

If the `Mood_checker` behavior detects that the Tamagotchi is unhappy, it informs the owner by means of the Tamagotchi's user interface. To cheer up her or his Tamagotchi, the owner initiates a visit by connecting the Tamagotchi Shells of two digital pets. If the connection is successful, the visit starts. Visiting is implemented by the `Visit_the_other_Tamagotchi` behavior presented in figure 5.15. As the figure reflects, the Tamagotchi first asks the Tamagotchi connected to it for permission to come for a visit. This occurs within the `Request_visit` subbehavior. To receive the reply from the other Tamagotchi, the Tamagotchi retrieves the reference to its local Tamagotchi Shell environment, which is represented in JADE as an instance of `TamagotchiShell` class, and invokes the `receive()` operation of its `Communicator` service object. As an autonomous entity, the second Tamagotchi can refuse to host a visit for various reasons, for example, by stating that the proposing Tamagotchi is too young to visit it, as is modeled by the interaction protocol in figure 3.14. As shown in figure 5.15, after a successful "handshake," the second Tamagotchi replies to the first one with a "Please come!" message and the visit starts. The visiting Tamagotchi is transferred to the hosting Tamagotchi's environment by performing the `visit()` operation of its environment's `Communicator` object. A successful environment change, indicated by the value `true` returned by the `visit()` operation, results in the first Tamagotchi informing its owner that it is away from home, similarly to as is shown in figure 3.1. This is followed by the Tamagotchis

```
class Visit_the_other_Tamagotchi extends SequentialBehaviour {
/**
 * Implements a visit between the two interconnected Tamagotchis
 * where the initiating Tamagotchi goes to the hosting
 * Tamagotchi's environment.
 */

/** The "host" Tamagotchi of this behaviour */
Tamagotchi thisTamagotchi;

/** The message to be sent */
private ACLMessage msg;

/** Constructor of the behaviour */
public Visit_the_other_Tamagotchi(Tamagotchi tamagotchi) {
    super(tamagotchi);
    thisTamagotchi = tamagotchi;
}

/** Actual implementation of the behaviour */
public void onStart() {
    Request_visit rv = new Request_visit(thisTamagotchi);
    addSubBehaviour(rv);
    rv.action();
    removeSubBehaviour(rv);

    /** Retrieves the local environment */
    TamagotchiShell shell = thisTamagotchi.getTamagotchiShell();

    String reply = shell.getCommunicator().receive();
    thisTamagotchi.getUserInterface().
        appendMessage("Received: " + reply);
    if (reply.equals("Please come!")) {
        /** Invoke the visit() operation of the Communicator
         * service */
        if (shell.getCommunicator().visit()) {
            /** If going to the other Tamagotchi's environment
             * was successful */
            /** Inform the owner that the Tamagotchi is away from its
             * shell */
            thisTamagotchi.getUserInterface().appendMessage("Away");
            Go_to_the_friends_place eg = new Go_to_the_friends_place
                (thisTamagotchi);
            addSubBehaviour(eg);
            eg.action();
            removeSubBehaviour(eg);
        }
```

Figure 5.15
The Visit_the_other_Tamagotchi JADE behavior

```
        while (thisTamagotchi.getHappinessLevel() < 20) {
            Give_a_present_and_play b = new Give_a_present_and_play
                (thisTamagotchi);
            addSubBehaviour(b);
            b.onStart();
            removeSubBehaviour(b);
        }
    }
    Return_home rh = new Return_home(thisTamagotchi);
    addSubBehaviour(rh);
}
}
```

Figure 5.15
(continued)

exchanging greetings by executing the Go_to_the_friends_place behavior. After that, the Give_a_present_and_play subbehavior is repeatedly invoked until the Tamagotchi's happiness level becomes 20 or more. Finally, the Tamagotchi returns to its own shell by executing the Return_home subbehavior.

The sequential Give_a_present_and_play behavior has two sub-behaviors: Give_the_friend_a_present and Play_with_the_friend. The first sub-behavior implements the visiting Tamagotchi giving a present to the hosting one provided that the visitor has enough presents. The second subbehavior implements the two Tamagotchis playing. For simplicity, we have replaced several interactions between the playing Tamagotchis with a single message exchange. Sending and receiving messages and giving presents are implemented by invoking the respective operations of the Communicator object.

A snapshot of the prototype of a Tamagotchi implemented by JADE is shown in figure 5.16.

5.6 Background

The BDI model has some philosophical basis in the Belief-Desire-Intention theory of human practical reasoning by Bratman (1987). The BDI agent architecture and execution model was proposed by Rao and Georgeff (1991). The first practical implementation of the BDI agent architecture—Procedural Reasoning System (PRS)—was developed by a team led by Georgeff and was described by Ingrand, Georgeff, and Rao (1992). The figure that illustrates the BDI agent architecture and execution model in section 5.1 is based on the Wikipedia (2008b) article on PRS. The procedural reasoning loop is adapted from Wooldridge 2002. The dMARS implementation is described by d'Inverno et al. 2004. One of the pilot applications was SWARMM. A place to read about it is Heinze et al. 2002.

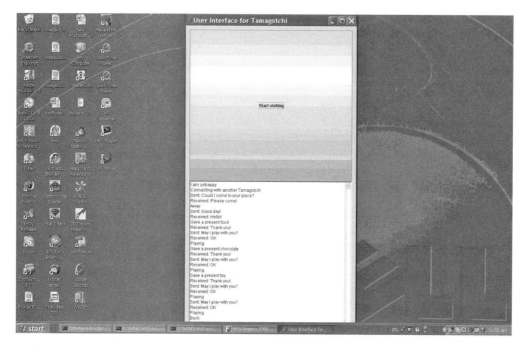

Figure 5.16
A snapshot of a Tamagotchi prototype implemented by JADE

The term *agent-oriented programming* was coined by Shoham (1993). In this influential article, the agent programming language AGENT-0 is described, along with an architecture for its execution. Agents following this architecture are programmed in terms of beliefs, commitments, and rules.

The descriptions of the Jason, 3APL, and JACK agent platforms are based on Bordini, Hübner, and Vieira 2005; Dastani, van Riemsdijk, and Meyer 2005; and Winikoff 2005, respectively. Padgham and Winikoff (2004) show how the modeling process defined by the Prometheus agent-oriented methodology results in a JACK implementation of an electronic bookstore. The JADE agent platform, including its JADEX extension for BDI agents, is comprehensively described by Bellifemine, Caire, and Greenwood (2005). Earlier descriptions include Bellifemine, Poggi, and Rimassa 2001.

Most agent platforms are either implemented in Java or can be interfaced to Java programs. Of the agent platforms overviewed in this chapter, Jason, JACK, and JADE have been implemented in Java. All the platforms covered by this section enable the definition of external environments that consist of Java objects and can be accessed from within agent programs. Many books have been published on the

Java programming language, one of the most prominent among them being Arnold, Gosling, and Holmes 2005.

Several agent programming languages enable the inclusion of Prolog constructs. Among the languages described by this chapter, Jason accommodates Prolog lists. The belief base of a 3APL agent is implemented as a Prolog program consisting of Prolog facts and rules. A good overview of Prolog is provided by Sterling and Shapiro (1994).

Many agent-programming languages claim to use BDI architecture. A lesser known one is Attitude, which was used by Don Perugini in his Ph.D. thesis under Leon's supervision (Perugini 2007) on applying agents for logistics.

The code for all examples is available from the authors on the book's Web site.

6 Viewpoint Framework

Chapter 2 described a conceptual space for designing and implementing sociotechnical systems. The conceptual space consists of three horizontal abstraction layers. In this chapter, we overlay a conceptual framework on top of the conceptual space. A conceptual framework addresses concerns that cross the three layers of the conceptual space. We also analyze how our conceptual space corresponds to the increasingly popular Model-Driven Architecture (MDA).

6.1 Conceptual Frameworks

Before introducing the viewpoint framework, a specific example of a new conceptual framework, we explain conceptual frameworks more generally. The conceptual space introduced in chapter 2 identifies the motivation layer, the system design layer, and the deployment layer. Orthogonal to these layers are vertical concerns that cross the layers. The vertical concerns, sometimes referred to as aspects, are needed for a clear understanding of the issues to be addressed when designing and implementing a system. The models required for design and implementation lie at the intersections of abstraction layers and cross-cutting concerns. Such vertical concerns are provided by conceptual frameworks. Conceptual frameworks incorporate ideas from the software engineering life cycle originating in software and information systems engineering.

In section 1.5, we identify the owner's, designer's, and builder's perspectives to systems engineering. We also describe stages of systems engineering that reflect these perspectives. Illuminated by these perspectives, we now look at four conceptual frameworks: the Information Systems Architecture framework, the Reference Model for Open Distributed Processing, the Enterprise Model, and the process modeling framework. In our treatment of conceptual frameworks, we have adjusted some of the terminology used by the frameworks to the terminology used in this book. In particular, we prefer to talk about agents rather than actors.

One of the earliest and most extensive conceptual frameworks is the Information Systems Architecture (ISA) framework, also known by its author as the Zachman framework. The ISA framework refines the owner's, designer's, and builder's perspectives into six abstraction layers: the system's scope, enterprise or business model, system model, technology model, models of components, and the functioning system. These layers reflect the stages of systems engineering.

In addition to the abstraction layers, the ISA framework defines six orthogonal aspects of a target system being described. The *concepts or data aspect* represents the relevant conceptual objects and relationships between them. The *function aspect* describes the activities performed within the problem domain. The *network aspect* is concerned with the geographical distribution of the activities and interactions between them. The *agents or actors aspect* describes what human or manmade agents perform which activities. The *time aspect* describes events significant to the problem domain. The *motivation aspect* describes the goals of the organization owning the system to be created and is also concerned with their translation into specific ends.

The ISA framework is best conceived as a table. Accordingly, we have presented the framework in table 6.1. Many of the table cells reflect the historical development of the ISA framework in the context of mainframe-based client–server systems.

It is worthwhile to remark that Kuldar got attracted to conceptual frameworks in 1987, living in Estonia under the Soviet regime. Under conditions where the only philosophy tolerated was Marxism, associate professor Toomas Mikli teaching the subject of information systems explained the need for thinking at different abstraction levels and from different perspectives by relying on the theory of logical positivism by Rudolf Carnap.

The next conceptual framework we consider, albeit briefly, is the Reference Model for Open Distributed Processing (RM-ODP). It defines five viewpoints: enterprise, information, computational, engineering, and technology. The *enterprise viewpoint* addresses the purpose, scope, and policies for the organization that will own the system to be developed. The *information viewpoint* covers the information handled by the system and constraints on the use and embodiment of that information. The *computational viewpoint* deals with the functional decomposition of the system into components suitable for distribution and describes how each component works. The *engineering viewpoint* covers the interactions between the components of the system. Finally, the *technology viewpoint* addresses the hardware and software required by the system. Each viewpoint of RM-ODP is accompanied by a viewpoint language, which defines concepts and rules for specifying systems from the corresponding viewpoint.

We turn to the Enterprise Model. The Enterprise Model was the first conceptual framework that seriously raised the issue of motivation in requirements engineering. It includes seven submodels named objectives, concepts, agents or actors, activities and usage, functional requirements, nonfunctional requirements, and information system's submodels. The *objectives submodel* describes the reason or motivation for

Table 6.1
The Information Systems Architecture (ISA) framework (Sowa & Zachman 1992)

	Concepts (What?)	Function (How?)	Network (Where?)	Agents (Who?)	Time (When?)	Motivation (Why?)
Scope	List of things important to the business	List of processes the business performs	List of locations in which the business operates	List of organizational units of the business	List of events significant to the business	List of business goals and strategies
Model of the business	ER-diagram	Business process model (process flow diagram)	Logistics network (nodes and links)	Organization chart with roles, skill sets, and authorizations	Business master schedule	Business plan with objectives and strategies
Model of the information system	Data model (fully normalized)	Data flow diagram; application architecture	Distributed system architecture	Human interface architecture (roles, data, access)	Dependency diagram, entity life history	Business rules' model
Technology model	Data architecture (tables and columns); mapping to legacy data	System design: structure chart, pseudocode	System architecture (hardware, software types)	User interface (how the system will behave); security design	Control flow diagram (control structure)	Business rules' design
Components	Physical data storage design	Detailed program design	Network architecture and protocols	Screens, security architecture (who can see what?)	Timing model	Specification of business rules in program logic
Functioning system	Converted data	Executable programs	Communication facilities	Trained people	Business events	Enforced business rules

the activities, agents, and object types defined by the other submodels. The *concepts submodel* is used to define the set of object types, relationships, and object attributes of the problem domain we are talking about. The *actors or agents submodel* is used to discuss and define the set of agents for each studied activity and the relationships between the agents. In the *activities and usage submodel*, each organizational activity is defined and described, including the existing activities and the activities to be modified or to be developed, as well as the information and material flows between different activities. The four submodels described lay a foundation for the *functional* and *nonfunctional requirements submodels* that elaborate specific functional and quality objectives set for the information system. The *information system's submodel* is a complete, formal specification of the information system—the design model—that supports the activities defined by the activities and usage submodel and the functional and nonfunctional requirements submodels. The Enterprise Model is depicted in figure 6.1.

Finally, we consider the process modeling framework, which originally was created to describe software development processes but has also been more broadly

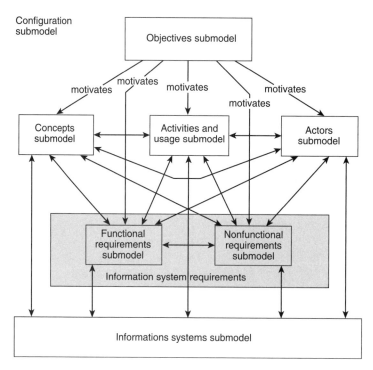

Figure 6.1
The Enterprise Model (Bubenko and Kirikova 1994)

applied to modeling problem domains. The process modeling framework defines functional, behavioral, organizational, and informational modeling perspectives. The *functional perspective* represents activities to be performed, and the flows of conceptual objects relevant to these activities. The *behavioral perspective* represents when the activities are performed, as well as aspects of how they are performed through feedback loops, iteration, complex decision-making conditions, entry and exit criteria, and so forth. The *organizational perspective* represents where and by whom (which agents) in the organization the activities are performed, the physical communication mechanisms used to transfer conceptual objects, and the physical media and locations used for storing conceptual objects. The *informational perspective* represents the conceptual objects produced or manipulated by the activities; this perspective includes both the structure of the conceptual objects and the relationships among them.

Let us now compare the four frameworks. First, we notice that there are differences in abstraction layers covered by the frameworks. Among the four frameworks analyzed, only the ISA framework has six explicit abstraction layers. The process modeling framework does not mention abstraction layers. It puts a strong emphasis on modeling from the designer's and builder's perspectives, but also covers some aspects of the owner's perspective. RM-ODP similarly involves the owner's, designer's, and builder's perspectives. The Enterprise Model emphasizes problem domain modeling and requirements analysis—that is, the owner's perspective—to which it devotes six submodels out of the seven.

Comparing the modeling aspects of the frameworks reveals that all four frameworks agree on the concepts aspect, which RM-ODP and the process modeling framework call the "information viewpoint" and the "informational perspective," respectively. This is natural because information modeling for databases was the first area of modeling that was equipped with systematic methods, such as Entity-Relationship Modeling.

We notice that the motivation aspect of the ISA framework corresponds to the objectives submodel of the Enterprise Model. In contrast, the objectives of the system are addressed by the enterprise viewpoint in RM-ODP. The process modeling framework does not explicitly address motivation modeling, but it emphasizes the importance of asking the question "why?" in process modeling.

Further inspection of the frameworks reveals that some modeling aspects define the functions required of the system. Three frameworks, the ISA framework, the Enterprise Model, and the process modeling framework, define the activities to be performed by the system under the respective function aspect, activities and usage submodel, and functional perspective. RM-ODP defines the functions under the enterprise viewpoint and refines them under the computational viewpoint.

There are modeling aspects dealing with individual components of the system required for fulfilling the functions. The ISA framework and Enterprise Model define human and manmade agents required for performing the activities within their agents modeling aspect, and the process modeling framework does the same within its organizational modeling perspective. RM-ODP describes under its computational viewpoint functional decomposition of the system into components suitable for distribution.

Related to functions of agents or components is their behavior, which can be viewed as consisting of the functions and their timing. In other words, behavior models define *what* activities are to be performed by agents or components and *when* they are to be performed. The process modeling framework has an explicit behavioral perspective for modeling the behavior of agents. The ISA framework addresses agents' behavior within a combination of its function and time modeling aspects, and RM-ODP describes how each component works under its computational viewpoint.

Modeling aspects of yet other kind address interactions between the agents or components and the infrastructure required for that. These issues are dealt with by the network aspect of the ISA framework, the enterprise and engineering viewpoints of RM-ODP, and the organizational perspective of the process modeling framework. The Enterprise Model describes the relationships between the agents within its agents submodel and the interactions between them within its activities and usage submodel.

Table 6.2 compares two of the frameworks that were analyzed previously: the ISA framework and RM-ODP. The table shows how the modeling aspects of the two frameworks correspond to each other.

We are interested in the engineering of potentially open distributed systems that span heterogeneous networks. For example, an intelligent home system involves local area networks, as well as global cable and wireless networks, which are needed, for example, for contacting the homeowner. Because there is currently no conceptual framework for designing and implementing such systems, we have derived one from

Table 6.2
Comparison of frameworks for conceptual modeling

"+": correspondence between concepts		ISA					
		Concepts	Function	Network	Agents	Time	Motivation
RM-ODP	Enterprise		+		+		+
	Information	+					
	Computational		+			+	
	Engineering			+	+		
	Technology	+	+	+	+	+	

the existing conceptual frameworks. Based on the earlier discussion, an *information modeling aspect* should definitely be included in our new conceptual framework. As interactions are crucial for distributed systems, we have merged the modeling aspects related to agents and interactions between them into the *interaction modeling aspect*. Similarly, we have merged the modeling aspects dealing with function and behavior into the *behavior modeling aspect*. Because motivation leads to behaviors, we have also subsumed the motivation aspect under the behavior aspect. The resulting conceptual framework has three vertical modeling aspects—information, interaction, and behavior—as compared to the six aspects of the ISA framework, which is too many for an average person to grasp. We do not finalize our conceptual framework here, but postpone it until section 6.3, after discussing the MDA.

6.2   Model-Driven Architecture

The Model-Driven Architecture (MDA) by the Object Management Group (OMG) is an approach to using models in software development that separates the domain model of a sociotechnical system from its design and implementation models. MDA proposes three types of models: Computation Independent Models (CIMs), Platform-Independent Models (PIMs), and Platform-Specific Models (PSMs). In MDA, a *platform* denotes a set of subsystems and technologies that provide a coherent set of functionalities through interfaces and specified usage patterns. Examples of platforms are CORBA, Java 2 Enterprise Edition, Microsoft.NET, JACK, and JADE. Two of these examples are discussed in chapter 5.

Computation Independent Models describe the requirements for the system and the problem domain of the system, as well as the environment in which the system is to be situated. CIMs play an important role in bridging the gap between domain experts on one hand, and experts in designing and constructing sociotechnical systems on the other. Platform Independent Models (PIMs) show the part of the system design specification that does not change from one platform to another. Platform Specific Models (PSMs) complement PIMs with the details that specify how the system is to be implemented on a particular platform.

Figure 6.2 shows that the three abstraction layers of MDA—CIMs, PIMs, and PSMs—naturally correspond to the motivation, system design, and deployment layers of the conceptual space of chapter 2. The abstraction layers of the conceptual space and the MDA layers also match with the owner's, designer's and builder's perspectives that were discussed in section 1.5. Indeed, motivation is the concern for owners, while designers take care of the design layer and builders situate the system in an environment. These parallels are reassuring about the naturalness of the abstraction layers selected for the conceptual space. The conceptual space is populated with models where each model is a representation of the system at the chosen

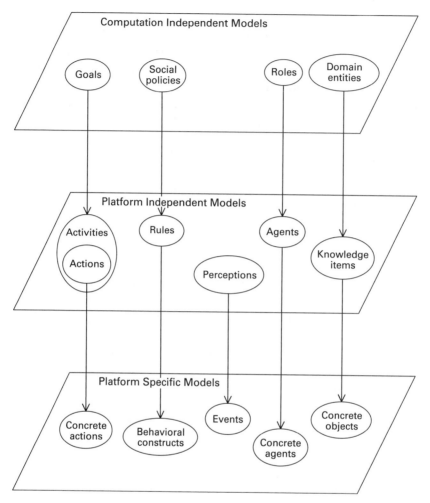

Figure 6.2
The Model-Driven Architecture mapped to the conceptual space

abstraction layer and from the chosen modeling aspect—information, interaction, or behavior. These models reflect the concepts of the conceptual space. The types of agent-oriented models that inhabit the conceptual space were presented in chapter 3.

In section 2.5, we showed how concepts at different layers of the conceptual space are related to each other. In chapter 3, we demonstrated how the models based on these concepts are created. MDA uses the term "model transformation," which is the process of converting one model to another model of the same system. MDA focuses on transformations between PIMs and PSMs, leaving transformations from

CIMs to PIMs aside, probably because of their anticipated complexity. However, this is exactly where agent-oriented modeling can step in by providing an appropriate set of CIM and PIM concepts that can be related to each another. As figure 6.2 reflects, goals, roles, social policies, and domain entities of agent-oriented modeling can often be transformed into the activities, agents, rules, and knowledge items of agent-oriented design. According to figure 6.2, there is also a correspondence between the design and implementation concepts. Using the MDA terminology, transformations between agent-oriented PIMs and PSMs can be specified as mappings between the platform independent types and patterns and the corresponding platform dependent types, as shown in figure 6.2.

6.3   The Viewpoint Framework

We now define a conceptual framework for distributed systems that is based on the modeling perspectives identified in section 6.1, and which is compliant with MDA, overviewed in section 6.2. This conceptual framework, the *viewpoint framework*, is depicted in table 6.3. It consists of a matrix with three rows representing different abstraction layers and three columns representing the viewpoint aspects of interaction, information, and behavior. Each cell in this matrix represents a specific viewpoint (not to be confused with the RM-ODP viewpoints discussed in section 6.1), such as "conceptual interaction modeling," "computational information design," or "behavior implementation." The abstraction layers of the viewpoint framework— "conceptual domain modeling," "platform-independent computational design," and "platform-specific design and implementation"—correspond in the conceptual space to the motivation, system design, and deployment layers, respectively. They have as counterparts the corresponding layers of MDA, CIMs, PIMs, and PSMs.

The models at the two higher abstraction layers of the viewpoint framework are independent of particular software or hardware platforms. Differently, the models

Table 6.3
The viewpoint framework

Viewpoint models	Viewpoint aspect		
Abstraction layer	Interaction	Information	Behaviour
Conceptual domain modeling	Role models and organization models	Domain models	Goal models and motivational scenarios
Platform-independent computational design	Agent models and acquaintance models, interaction models	Knowledge models	Scenarios and behavior models
Platform-specific design and implementation	Agent interface and interaction specifications	Data models and service models	Agent behavior specifications

at the layer of platform-specific design and implementation consider specific tools and platforms with which the system is going to be built. As is pointed out in chapter 5, in addition to being platform-independent, the models at the two higher layers are also *architecture-independent*; that is, they do not prescribe or imply the usage of any specific system or agent architecture.

The models at the lowest layer are *platform-specific*, sometimes also described as *platform-dependent*. For example, if the technology to be used for implementing the design constructs of the computational information design viewpoint is a relational database, the corresponding data models at the layer of platform-specific design and implementation have to be *normalized*. Similarly, if the agents modeled under the computational interaction design viewpoint are to be implemented as having the BDI architecture described in section 5.1, the behavior implementation models to be utilized can be plan diagrams and capability overview diagrams.

There is a particular set of models corresponding to each abstraction layer of the conceptual space. The models for the motivation layer express how the system is motivated. The models for the system design layer express how the system is designed. The models for the deployment layer express how the system is situated in its environment. In the viewpoint framework, the models of each abstraction layer are also categorized vertically according to the viewpoint aspects of interaction, information, and behavior. We next describe how the cells of the viewpoint framework are populated with generic types of models introduced in chapter 3.

In the viewpoint framework represented in table 6.3, goal models and motivational scenarios are located in the cell determined by row 1 and column 3, that is, under the conceptual behavior modeling viewpoint. This is because motivation leads to behaviors. Role models and the models of relationships between roles, organization models, are to be found in the cell determined by row 1 and column 1—that is, under the conceptual interaction modeling viewpoint. Domain models are in the cell determined by row 1 and column 2—that is, under the conceptual information modeling viewpoint. They represent information about the problem domain and about the environment where the system is to be situated.

Agent models and acquaintance models are positioned in the cell determined by row 2 and column 1—that is, under the interaction design viewpoint. Agent and acquaintance models define agent types and interaction pathways between agents of these types. Interaction models, just like agent and acquaintance models, are located in the cell determined by row 2 and column 1—that is, under the interaction design viewpoint. In addition to modeling interactions between agents, interaction models can also capture interactions between agents and their environment. Knowledge models are in the cell determined by row 2 and column 2—that is, under the information design viewpoint. Scenarios and behavior models are positioned in the cell determined by row 2 and column 3. Behavior models include behavioral interface models and agent behavior models.

The models created at the platform-specific design and implementation layer of table 6.3 are agent interface and interaction specifications, data models and service models, and agent behavior specifications. These models are dependent on specific agent or other kinds of architectures and platforms. Some of platform-specific design models are addressed in chapter 7 in the context of specific agent-oriented methodologies.

The viewpoint framework represented in table 6.3 can be populated with different types of models. In other words, there are many ways to fill in the viewpoint framework. We demonstrate some of the ways in chapter 7, where we provide an overview of six agent-oriented methodologies.

6.4   Background

The Information Systems Architecture (ISA) framework was proposed by Zachman (1987). It is one of the earliest conceptual frameworks and is the most extensive. The ISA framework was refined by Sowa and Zachman (1992).

RM-ODP is described by Putman (2001). The main focus of his book is on specifying software architectures.

The Enterprise Model was proposed by Bubenko (1993). It was refined and further described by Bubenko and Kirikova (1994). The Enterprise Model was the first conceptual framework that explicitly addressed goals.

The process modeling framework was proposed by Curtis, Kellner, and Over (1992). Interestingly from our agent-oriented perspective, they claim that the constructs that collectively form the essential basis of a process model are

- agent—an actor (human or machine) who performs a process element;

- role—a coherent set of process elements to be assigned to an agent as a unit of functional responsibility; and

- artifact—a product created or modified by the enactment of a process element.

Several conceptual frameworks have been compared by Kirikova (2000). Taveter (2004a) compares conceptual frameworks in the agent-oriented context and proposes a framework consisting of the following six views of agent-oriented modeling: informational view, functional view, behavioral view, organizational view, interactional view, and motivational view.

The Model-Driven Architecture is described in OMG 2003. It has been applied to agent-oriented modeling by Jayatilleke, Padgham, and Winikoff (2005), Penserini et al. (2006), and Taveter and Sterling (2008). Jayatilleke, Padgham, and Winikoff represent CIMs in terms of agent component types, such as belief, trigger, plan, and step. Penserini et al. (2006) describe agents in CIMs with regard to their capabilities, which are then transformed into plans consisting of activities. Taveter and Sterling (2008) describe in more detail transformations of agent-oriented models between the three layers of the MDA.

The viewpoint framework was first proposed by Taveter and Wagner (2005). It is based on the framework for agent-oriented business modeling proposed by Taveter (2004a), which is in turn rooted in the ideas of the ISA framework. The applications of the viewpoint framework for business process automation and manufacturing simulation have been described by Taveter (2005a, 2006a) and in Taveter 2006b, respectively. Further, Guizzardi (2006) describes the application of the viewpoint framework to agent-oriented knowledge management.

II APPLICATIONS

An underlying belief of this book is that it is important for software developers and students to be exposed to good examples of models and artifacts from the various stages of the software life cycle. By looking at detailed models, a developer might be expected to adapt the models to build their applications. Analogously, an important way to teach programming is to have students read other people's code.

People need guidance to learn to think in a different way. Two ways to encourage others to think differently are to provide a methodology and to show larger examples where all the parts fit together. Both are demonstrated in part II.

Chapter 7 presents a sample of methodologies that have been developed within the agent-oriented software engineering community. The methodologies are demonstrated with a conference management example that has been developed for several of the methodologies. Chapters 8, 9, and 10 show substantive examples from the domains of e-commerce, smart home, and educational software. The examples have been developed using a variety of methodologies and are of varying degrees of detail and maturity. We believe they should be helpful for developers wishing to use agent-oriented concepts in their systems. There are many ways to go about modeling, and we expect the astute reader to critique the models and improve them.

Reading this book will not immediately make someone an expert agent developer. Nonetheless, the reader should receive guidance on how to start developing multi-agent systems. By being exposed to a range of examples and a range of methodologies, a reader will have a useful background for learning more about specific modeling methods.

7 Agent-Oriented Methodologies

In chapter 3, various kinds of models are distinguished for agent-oriented modeling. The process of applying these models is not explicitly described in chapter 3, because processes are defined by particular software engineering methodologies. A *software engineering methodology* is accordingly a process for the organized production of software using a collection of predefined techniques and notational convention. An *agent-oriented software engineering methodology* is a software engineering methodology that uses the notion of agent or actor in all stages of its process.

This chapter describes five agent-oriented methodologies that have been developed within the agent research community to guide agent system development. The five methodologies by no means exhaust the research into appropriate methodologies. Some of the methodologies directly use the models of chapter 3. Other methodologies use different models.

We do not give a complete description of any of the methodologies. Neither do we present a detailed comparison of the methodologies, though we do place all in the viewpoint framework described in chapter 6. We prefer not to be too prescriptive. There are pointers for interested readers to follow for more information in the background section.

We do not strongly advocate any one specific methodology. We believe (and hope) that there will be convergence around the key concepts in the next few years, analogous to the settling of the object-oriented community around UML. In the interim, experience with any of the methodologies described in this chapter will increase one's appreciation of agent-oriented modeling.

The chapter is organized as follows. The first section describes the domain of conference management, which has been used as a point of comparison between agent-oriented methodologies. It is fortunate to have such a comparison, which was fostered by the Agent-Oriented Software Engineering Workshop held in Hawaii in May 2007 in conjunction with the international conference on Autonomous Agents and Multiagent Systems (AAMAS).

The next five sections describe how to develop agent-oriented models for the conference management system using some of the more prominent methodologies Gaia, MaSE, Tropos, Prometheus, and a composite of ROADMAP and RAP/AOR. This last methodology combines the experiences of Leon and Kuldar.

Note that the viewpoint framework presented in the book in chapter 6 did not exist at the time the agent-oriented software engineering methodologies we describe were developed. Consequently, some of the terminology and models do not exactly correspond. We err on the side of using the original descriptions when things do not correspond. Although the software life cycles that the methodologies presume are not identical, they are loosely consistent, envisioning stages of requirements elicitation and analysis, architectural and detailed design, and implementation. We are optimistic that a more unified agent-oriented methodology will emerge, combining the best features of each.

7.1   A Conference Management System

A common example is presented to allow informal comparison between the methodologies we present. The specific common example is a conference management system. The type of conference being managed is an academic one where authors submit papers written for the conference, and a program committee (PC) chooses between the papers based on reviews submitted by its members or reviewers delegated by them. The scope of the common example is only part of conference management—namely, preparation of the technical program. The number of papers typically submitted is in the tens or hundreds.

The process that will be described by the various methodologies reflects what goes on for computer science conferences across the range of computing disciplines. No attempt has been made to generalize to other domains in the sciences or humanities. There are several semiautomated conference management software systems available. At the time the book is being written, the EasyChair system seems to be growing in popularity. In 2006, 150 conferences used the system; in 2007, several hundred conferences used the system.

The technical program consists of a collection of papers presented over several days.[2] Academics and students interested in presenting at the conference submit papers for consideration. The papers must be submitted by a given deadline. The papers are distributed by a program chair to members of the PC, which may be slightly hierarchical for larger conferences, who in turn may delegate to reviewers

---

2. Programs also usually contain invited talks, which are not considered here.

they know and whose opinion they trust. There are some constraints in that reviewers should not review their own papers or those of close colleagues, and there are anonymity concerns.

The reviews are completed by an internal deadline. Some chasing up of reviewers is typically required, and occasionally late reviews need to be requested. Papers are selected based on the reviews. The selection may happen at a meeting or electronically. Usually some mediation is needed between conflicting views. Once the papers are selected, the authors are notified and provided with comments from the reviews. The authors of the chosen papers submit final copies of their papers that are collated for publication.

In principle, using a conference management system as the system for comparing agent-oriented methodologies seems suitable. Conference management is naturally a sociotechnical system involving people, software, and technology. Also, there are high-level goals and roles that agents must fulfil, and important quality goals, such as timeliness of responses by agents, the need for anonymity in reviews, and fairness and transparency in decision making. How well the comparison works we leave the reader to assess. We do note that the designs described in the next five sections are idealized. It would be interesting if practical difficulties in conference management could be linked to the goals and roles.

To conclude this section and give some perspective on the scope of a multiagent system for helping with preparing the technical program, we describe some of the functionality of EasyChair. According to its Web site, the current version supports

- management and monitoring of the PC
- sophisticated and flexible management of the access of PC members and referees to papers and conflicts of interests
- automatic paper submission
- paper assignment based on the preferences of PC members
- list of the latest events
- submission of reviews
- sending emails to PC members, referees, and authors
- monitoring email
- online discussion of papers
- author response (or "rebuttal") phase, when the author can respond to the reviews
- automatic preparation of conference proceedings

and many other features.

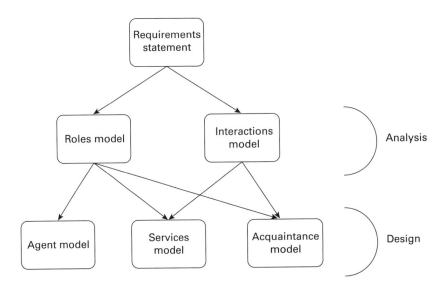

Figure 7.1
The original Gaia models (Wooldridge, Jennings, and Kinny 2000). With kind permission of Springer
Science + Business Media.

7.2   Gaia

Gaia was the first agent-oriented development methodology to gain wide recognition. It promoted the use of organizational abstraction to model computing. It
claimed to be an architecture-independent methodology that covered the requirements analysis and design stages of the software development life cycle. Gaia has
undergone some evolution. In this section, we briefly describe the original Gaia with
its five models, and then the revised Gaia models that were used to model fragments
of a conference management system.

The Gaia methodology models both the macro (social) aspect and the micro
(agent internals) aspect of the multiagent system. Gaia views a system as an organization consisting of interacting roles. Figure 7.1 shows the models produced by using
Gaia as presented in the initial version of Gaia. The methodology is applied after
requirements have been gathered and specified, and covers the analysis and design
phases.

The models can easily be mapped to the viewpoint framework described in chapter
6. The two models from the analysis stage belong in the conceptual domain modeling
layer. The role model corresponds to the behavior viewpoint, and the interaction
model corresponds to the interaction viewpoint. The three models from the design
stage belong in the platform-independent design layer. The agent model corresponds
to the behavior viewpoint, the services model corresponds to the information view-

Table 7.1
Mapping the models of Gaia to the viewpoint framework

Viewpoint models	Viewpoint aspect		
Abstraction layer	Interaction	Information	Behavior
Conceptual domain modeling	Interaction model		Role model
Platform-independent computational design	Acquaintance model	Services model	Agent model
Platform-specific design and implementation			

Role Schema: REVIEWER

Description:
This preliminary role involves receiving papers for review from some conference official, reviewing that paper, and sending back a completed review form.

Protocols and Activities:
ReceivePaper, ReviewPaper, SendReviewForm

Permissions:
reads   *Papers*   // *all the papers it receives*
changes   *ReviewForms*   // *one for each of the papers*

Responsibilities
Liveness:

$$\text{REVIEWER} = (\text{ReceivePaper.ReviewPaper.SendReview})^{maximum\_number}$$

Safety:
- *number_of_papers = number_of_reviewforms*

Figure 7.2
The Gaia role schema for REVIEWER (Zambonelli, Jennings, and Wooldridge 2003). Reprinted with permission by ACM.

point, and the acquaintance model corresponds to the interaction viewpoint. This is summarized in table 7.1.

During analysis, roles in the system are identified, and their interactions are modeled. Roles in Gaia are abstract constructs used to conceptualize and understand the system. They have no realization in the implemented system after the analysis stage. In the initial version of Gaia, all roles are atomic constructs and cannot be defined in terms of other roles. Roles are defined by role schemas, which have the following attributes: responsibilities, permissions, activities, and protocols. Figure 7.2 is the role schema for the role REVIEWER in our conference management example. The model describes the role. It is good practice to sum up a role in a single sentence. The word "preliminary" is used in the description to indicate that it may be refined later in the software development process.

Activities are tasks that a role can assume without interacting with other roles; protocols are tasks a role can take that involve other roles. Two protocols,

ReceivePaper and SendReviewForm, and one activity, ReviewPaper, have been attached to the Reviewer role with obvious intended meanings.

Responsibilities of a role define its functionalities. There are two types of responsibilities: liveness properties and safety properties. Liveness properties describe the general behavior of the role and are represented by a regular expression over the sets of activities and protocols the role processes. The liveness property is represented as (ReceivePaper.ReviewPaper.SendReviewForm)$^{maximum\_number}$, which means that the two activities and one protocol are performed one after the other in the order specified up to *maximum_number* times, where *maximum_number* is the maximum number of papers that the reviewer is requested to review. Safety properties are properties that the agent acting in the role must always preserve. There is a single safety property in figure 7.2—namely, that the number of papers equals the number of review forms.

Permissions limit the resources available to the role, usually expressed as some information that the role can read, write, or create. The permissions specify both what the role can and cannot use. There are two permissions in figure 7.2. The reviewer needs to be able to read the papers and fill in the review forms.

In summary, the role model for a system is a collection of role schemas, each schema detailing the attributes for a role in the system.

An interaction model is developed based on the initial role model. It contains a protocol definition for each protocol of each role in the system. The protocol definition describes the high-level purpose of the protocol, ignoring implementation details such as the sequence of messages exchanged. The protocol definition outlines the initiating role, the responding role, the input and output information, as well as a brief description of the processing the initiator carries out during the execution of this protocol.

Figure 7.3 contains the protocol schema for the ReceivePaper protocol in the role model. The name of this protocol is Receive Paper, the initiating role is PC Chair or PC Member, and the responding role, or partner, is Reviewer. The input in figure 7.3 is the information about the paper, and the output is whether the reviewer agrees to review the paper.

Analysis within Gaia involves refining the role model and the interaction model iteratively. The role and interaction models serve as the initial input to the design stage.

During design, the abstract constructs from the analysis stage, such as roles, are mapped to concrete constructs, such as agent types, that will be realized at runtime. Gaia requires three models to be produced during the design stage. The agent model outlines the agent types in the system. The services model outlines the services indicated by the roles assigned to the agent types. The acquaintance model depicts communication links between agent types.

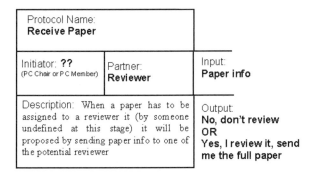

Protocol Name: **Receive Paper**		
Initiator: **??** (PC Chair or PC Member)	Partner: **Reviewer**	Input: **Paper info**
Description: When a paper has to be assigned to a reviewer it (by someone undefined at this stage) it will be proposed by sending paper info to one of the potential reviewer		Output: **No, don't review** **OR** **Yes, I review it, send me the full paper**

Figure 7.3
The Gaia protocol schema for Receive Paper (Zambonelli, Jennings, and Wooldridge 2003). Reprinted with permission by ACM.

Assigning the roles to agent types creates the agent model. Each agent type may be assigned one or more roles. For each agent type, the designer annotates the cardinality of agent instances of that type at runtime.

In Gaia, a service is a coherent block of functionality neutral to implementation details. The service model lists services that agents provide. They are derived from the activities and protocols of the roles. For each service, four attributes must be specified—namely, the inputs, outputs, preconditions, and postconditions. They are easily derived from attributes such as protocol input from the role model and the interaction model. Please note that the concept of service in Gaia is different from the concept of service embodied in the service models described in chapter 3.

The acquaintance model is a directed graph between agent types. An arc from A to B signals the existence of a communication link allowing A to send messages to B. The purpose is to allow the designer to visualize the degree of coupling between agents. In this light, further details such as message types are ignored.

The revised version of Gaia introduced three organizational concepts: organizational rules, organizational structure, and organizational patterns. An explicit environment model was also added into the methodology. The environment model arguably fits into the missing box in the viewpoint framework diagram, table 7.1, as a model at the conceptual domain modeling layer concerned with the information viewpoint. Figure 7.4 shows the revised development models in Gaia, with the implicit process that one starts developing the models at the top of the figure, and proceeds with the models later in the software life cycle.

To conclude this section, we note the relative simplicity of the Gaia models. The simplicity has contributed significantly to its success as perhaps the most cited agent-oriented software engineering methodology. From our experience, students or industry developers have no difficulty understanding Gaia concepts. Anecdotally, it

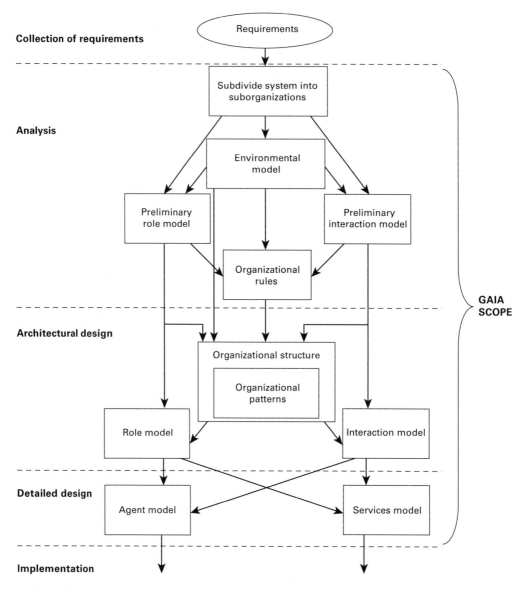

Figure 7.4
The models of Gaia 2 (Zambonelli, Jennings, and Wooldridge 2003). Reprinted with permission by ACM.

has often been used in agent courses. However, there are limited tools—if any—to support Gaia, and its use is being supplanted by other methodologies.

7.3 MaSE

MaSE (Multiagent Systems Engineering) is an architecture-independent methodology that covers the complete development life cycle. MaSE was one of the earlier agent-oriented software engineering methodologies to be developed. It was pioneering in its engineering focus. MaSE has been used to design systems ranging from computer virus immune systems to cooperative robotics systems.

Figure 7.5 outlines the steps and models of the MaSE methodology. It proposes nine classes of models to be developed: a Goal Hierarchy, Use Cases, Sequence Diagrams, Roles, Concurrent Tasks, Agent Classes, Conversations, Agent Architecture, and Deployment Diagrams in the life cycle stages of analysis and design. Analysis in MaSE starts by capturing goals of the system. Use cases are created with sequence diagrams to clarify the system behavior and act as the intermediate step in translating goals into system roles. Roles are created as units of system requirements and the communication between roles is clarified as concurrent tasks. Agent classes are decided based on roles, and conversations are constructed for these agent classes.

We relate the models included in figure 7.5 to the viewpoint framework. Four of the models reflect the interaction viewpoint: sequence diagrams and role models at the conceptual domain modeling layer, and conversation diagrams and agent class models at the platform-independent computational design layer. Role models and agent class models are shared by the interaction and behavior viewpoints. Most of the models are concerned with the behavior viewpoint. As indicated in table 7.2, the models are evenly divided across the three layers of the framework. We observe the lack of emphasis on the information viewpoint. That does not necessarily mean that MaSE ignores the concerns of the information viewpoint. As we shall see in the following conference management example, there is a lot of information about the domain of conference management present. However, an information model is not extracted explicitly.

MaSE has been extended to the Organization-based Multiagent Systems Engineering (O-MaSE) framework. It allows for construction of custom methodologies, using ideas from the Object-oriented Process, Environment and Notation (OPEN) method engineering approach. O-MaSE was used for the comparison exercise at the 2007 Agent-Oriented Software Engineering Workshop, where several groups presented their designs for a conference management system. We give some of the O-MaSE models created for the case study to convey aspects of modeling in MaSE.

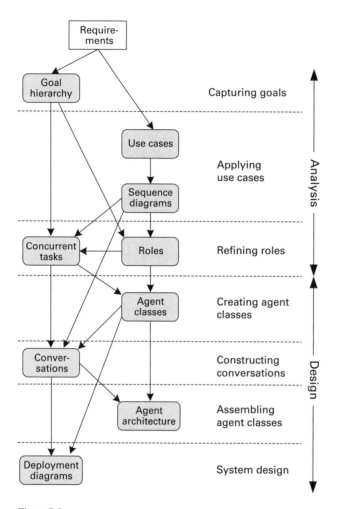

Figure 7.5
The MaSE process diagram (Wood and DeLoach 2001). With kind permission of Springer Science + Business Media.

A tool has been built to support O-MaSE development. The agentTool is a Java-based graphical development environment to help users analyze, design, and implement multiagent systems using the O-MaSE methodology. It has been designed as an Eclipse plug-in. Tool support is essential if agent-oriented methodologies are going to have significant uptake.

The O-MaSE process described at the workshop has seven stages, starting from the system requirements definition. The first stage is a requirements-focused stage in which goals are modeled to produce a requirements goal hierarchy. A goal hierarchy

Table 7.2
Mapping the models of MaSE to the viewpoint framework

Viewpoint models	Viewpoint aspect		
Abstraction layer	Interaction	Information	Behavior
Conceptual domain modeling	Sequence Diagrams		Goal Hierarchy, Use Cases, Role Model
Platform-independent computational design	Conversation Diagrams		Concurrent Tasks, Agent Class Diagrams
Platform-specific design and implementation			Agent Architecture Diagrams, Deployment Diagrams

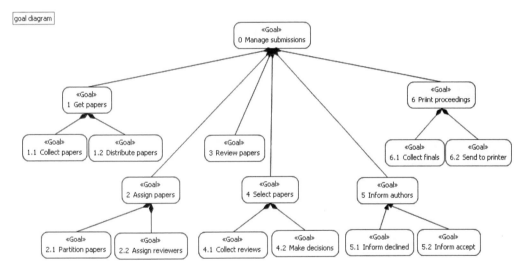

Figure 7.6
A goal tree for the conference management system

for the conference management system is shown in figure 7.6. The top-level Manage submissions goal is split into six subgoals: Get papers, Assign papers, Review papers, Select papers, Inform authors, and Print proceedings. Five of these subgoals are split into two further subgoals. For example, Assign papers is divided into Partition papers and Assign reviewers.

The second stage of the O-MaSE process is also requirements-focused. Goals in the goal hierarchy are refined to produce a Goal Model for Dynamic Systems (GMoDS)—a kind of model not included by the original MaSE methodology. A requirements-refined GMoDS model is shown in figure 7.7. The model expresses some dependencies between goals. For example, one dependency is that collecting

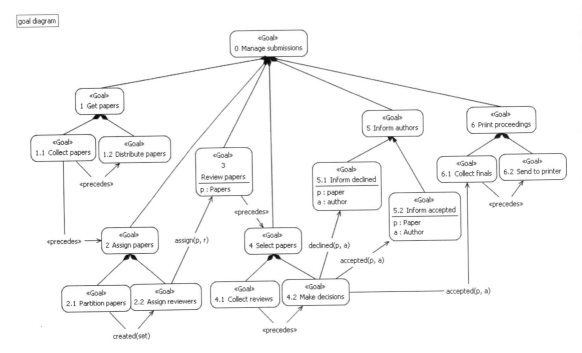

Figure 7.7
A GMoDS model for the conference management system

papers precedes distributing papers. Another dependency is that a decision produced by the "Make decisions" goal has either of the "declined(p,a)" or the "accepted(p,a)" forms, which are communicated to the "Inform declined" and the "Inform accepted" goals, respectively.

The third stage of the O-MaSE process takes the GMoDS model and models the organization to produce an organization model, which is another model type that has been added to MaSE by O-MaSE. An organization model is provided in figure 7.8. The overall organization is a conference management system that achieves the overall goal of managing submissions. The model suggests that four actors are involved: PC Chair, Author, Reviewer, and Printer. It describes some of the activities in which the actors are involved. For example, the PC Chair partitions papers, selects reviewers, and selects papers. The PC Chair actor must interact with the Reviewer actor. The Printer actor is concerned only with printing the proceedings.

The fourth stage of the O-MaSE process models roles using the GMoDS and organization models. The output is a role model, shown in figure 7.9. The figure expands the organization model in a natural way. Roles are different from how they

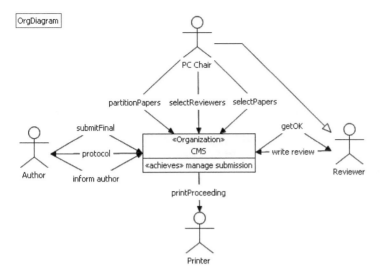

Figure 7.8
An organization model for the conference management system

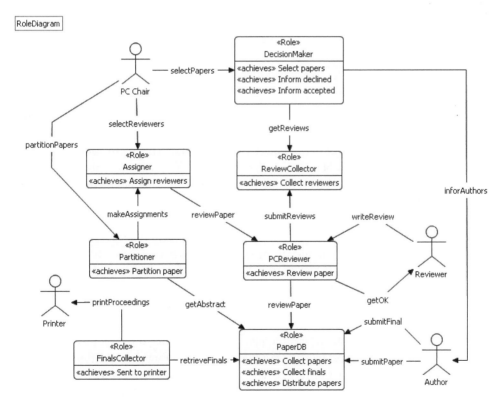

Figure 7.9
A role model for the conference management system

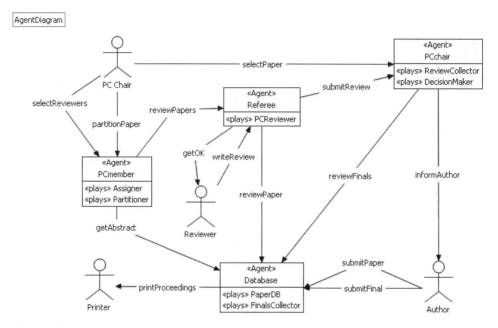

Figure 7.10
An agent class diagram for the conference management system

are described in chapter 3, corresponding to units of functionality in which an actor may be involved. The figure shows seven roles: `DecisionMaker`, `Assigner`, `ReviewCollector`, `Partitioner`, `PCReviewer`, `FinalsCollector`, and `PaperDB`. It also shows interactions between actors and roles. For example, the `Reviewer` actor writes a review and sends it to the `PCReviewer`, and the `PCReviewer` sends a `getOK` to acknowledge the receipt of the review.

The fifth stage switches from analysis to design. Agent classes are modeled, with the role model as input and an agent class model being produced. An agent class diagram for the conference management system is given in figure 7.10. Roles have been assigned to the agents in the system. Four agents have been chosen: a `PCchair` playing the roles of `ReviewCollector` and `DecisionMaker`, a `Referee` playing the role of `PCReviewer`, a `PCmember` playing the roles of `Assigner` and `Partitioner`, and a `Database` playing the roles of `PaperDB` and `FinalsCollector`.

The sixth and seventh stages use the agent class diagram to model protocols and plans, respectively. These stages correspond to constructing conversation in figure 7.5. Protocol diagrams for O-MaSE are similar to Tamagotchi protocols discussed in chapter 3 and to other methodologies. Agent plans use a statechart notation. An example plan is shown in figure 7.11 for a `Referee` agent. The plan for an agent encompasses behavior models from chapter 3.

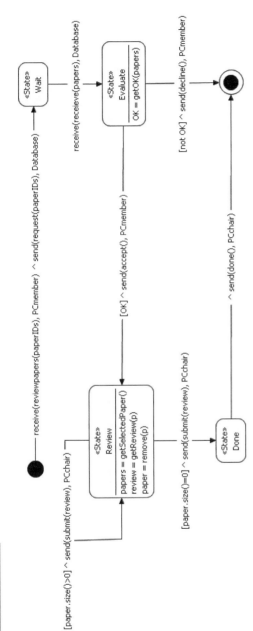

Figure 7.11
A plan diagram for the Referee agent

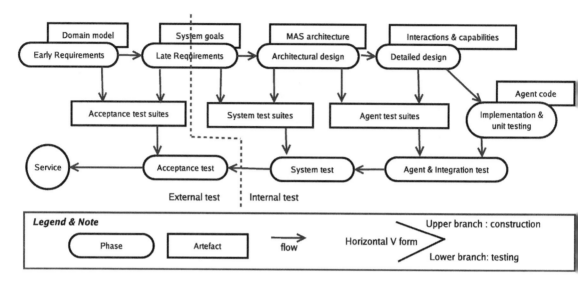

Figure 7.12
The Tropos process diagram (Nguyen, Perini, and Tonella 2008). With kind permission of Springer Science + Business Media.

The strength of MaSE is in its concrete processes that are easy to understand and follow, its tool support, and its architectural independence. There has been steady improvement in both methodology and tool support. More information can be gathered from the references given at the end of the chapter.

7.4 Tropos

Tropos is derived from the Greek τροποσ, which means "way of doing things"; also τροπή, which means "turn" or "change." Tropos is a software development methodology that uses the concepts of actor, goal, and (actor) dependency to model early and late requirements, and architectural and detailed design. It has arguably had the most research effort involved of any agent-oriented software engineering methodology.

The overall process can be seen in figure 7.12. It covers the complete software life cycle. There are stages for early requirements, late requirements, architectural design, detailed design, implementation and unit testing, agent and integration testing, system testing, and acceptance testing. The artifacts produced are a domain model, system goals, a multiagent system architecture, interactions and capabilities, agent code, and test suites at the agent, system, and acceptance levels.

Table 7.3
Mapping the models of Tropos to the viewpoint framework

Viewpoint models	Viewpoint aspect		
Abstraction layer	Interaction	Information	Behavior
Conceptual domain modeling	Actor Diagram	Actor Diagram	Goal Diagrams
Platform-independent computational design			Refined Goal Diagrams
Platform-specific design and implementation	Agent Interaction Diagrams	UML Class Diagrams	Capability Diagrams, Plan Diagrams

The Tropos research team has expended considerable effort in providing tool support. There is a tool support for each of the stages. The tool is called the Tool for Agent Oriented Modeling (TAOM4E) and is an Eclipse plug-in. It is distributed as free software under a General Public Licence (GPL).

We relate the models to the viewpoint framework. The Tropos domain model consists of actor diagrams and goal diagrams. As shown in table 7.3, actor diagrams belong to the interaction viewpoint at the conceptual domain modeling layer, as they model dependencies between actors. Actor diagrams are also concerned with the information viewpoint, because they represent resources used by actors. Goal diagrams deal with individual actors and hence belong to the behavior viewpoint at the same layer. When further refined for the system to be developed, goal diagrams are also concerned with the behavior viewpoint at the layer of platform-independent computational design. As goal diagrams include dependencies between actors of the system, they reflect system architecture.

At the platform-specific design and implementation layer, the dependencies are reflected by interactions between agents, which are modeled as agent interaction diagrams. The other viewpoints at the lowest abstraction layer are covered by UML class diagrams for information modeling and capability diagrams and plan diagrams for behavior modeling.

Table 7.3 reflects that Tropos defers detailed interaction and information modeling until platform-dependent design, when the agent architecture and implementation platform have been decided. Tropos assumes the agent architecture to be BDI.

We show Tropos models developed for the conference management system. In addition, actor and goal diagrams of Tropos are used in section 8.2 for the analysis stage of the manufacturing simulation case study.

The first stage, early requirements analysis, involves the modeling of stakeholder intentions using goals in the context of the organization requiring the system to be developed. Stakeholders are modeled as actors. An actor can be an agent, a role, or a position. Dependencies between actors are modeled with a dependum, which characterizes the nature of the dependency. The dependum can be of type hard

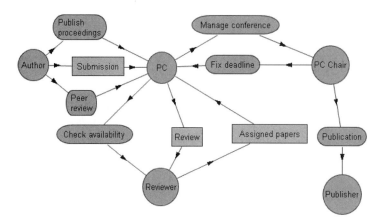

Figure 7.13
An initial actor diagram for the conference management system

goal, soft goal, task, or resource. A soft goal is a goal with no clear-cut criteria to determine satisfaction, usually used to represent nonfunctional requirements. Soft goals correspond to quality goals (described in chapter 4). Tropos suggests four questions to guide the analysis: Which are the main actors? What are their goals? How can they achieve them? Does an actor depend on another actor to achieve its goals?

The result of the first stage is an actor diagram, an example of which is provided in figure 7.13. Five actors are identified: `PC`, `PC Chair`, `Author`, `Reviewer`, and `Publisher`. Six dependencies are modeled as goal dependencies: `Publish proceedings`, `Peer review`, `Manage conference`, `Fix deadline`, `Check availability`, and `Publication`. In a goal dependency, one actor depends on another actor for achieving a goal. Three dependencies are modeled as resource dependencies: `Submission`, `Review`, and `Assigned papers`. In a resource dependency, one actor depends on another for utilizing a resource.

The actor diagram is expanded, taking the perspective of each actor. Goals are decomposed into subgoals. Alternative ways of achieving goals are considered. Soft goals are considered, which may contribute to the achievement of a goal or prevent its achievement. Figure 7.14 shows the resulting goal diagrams for the `PC Chair` and PC actors. Soft goals are represented as clouds in the figure.

In the late requirements analysis stage, Tropos introduces the system into the models as a new actor that contributes to achieving the stakeholder goals. Higher-level goals are decomposed into more concrete ones until sufficient details are captured as requirements. Figure 7.15 shows an expanded actor diagram for the conference management system. Decomposition, means-ends analysis, and contribution analysis are

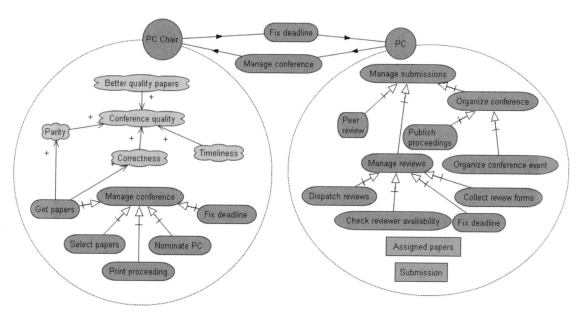

Figure 7.14
The goal diagram for the PC Chair and PC actors

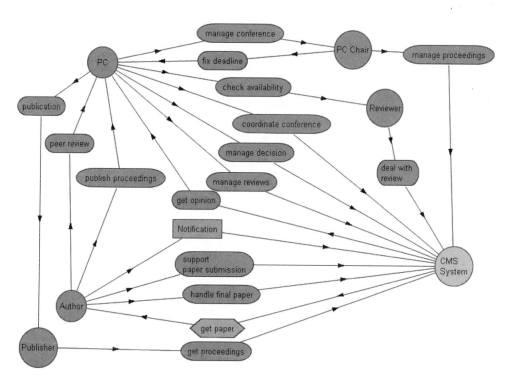

Figure 7.15
An expanded actor diagram for the conference management system

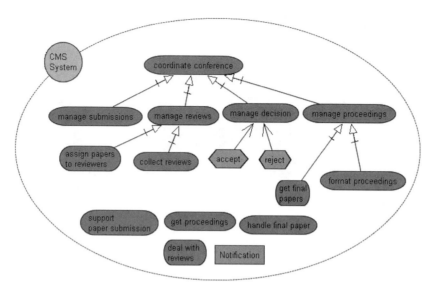

Figure 7.16
The goal diagram for the CMS System actor

performed on the system's goals. The result of these analyses is shown in figure 7.16. The expanded actor diagram shown in figure 7.15 introduces the get paper task dependency between the CMS System and Author actors. Figure 7.16 introduces the tasks accept and reject that are required for achieving the manage decision goal.

Architectural design and detailed design in Tropos involves identifying and adopting appropriate architectural styles and design patterns to implement the goals of the actors.

Architectural design consists of three activities: decomposing and refining the system actor diagram including new actors as a result of various analyses, identifying capabilities, and moving from actors to agents. An example model from the architectural design stage in Tropos is given in figure 7.17. In that model, the CMS System actor has been refined into the Conference Manager, Paper Manager, Review Manager, and Proceedings Manager actors. The goal, task, and resource dependencies between these actors are included in the model.

A further expansion of the goal diagram depicted in figure 7.17 gives us figure 7.18. That goal diagram expresses the goals to be achieved and the tasks to be performed, as well as the resources to be utilized by the Conference Manager, Paper Manager, Review Manager, and Proceedings Manager actors.

Detailed design involves specifying the internal agent behaviors taking into account the implementation platform. Though requirements analysis and architectural design stages of Tropos are architecture-independent, the stage of detailed design is geared toward BDI agent architecture. Four types of diagrams are produced:

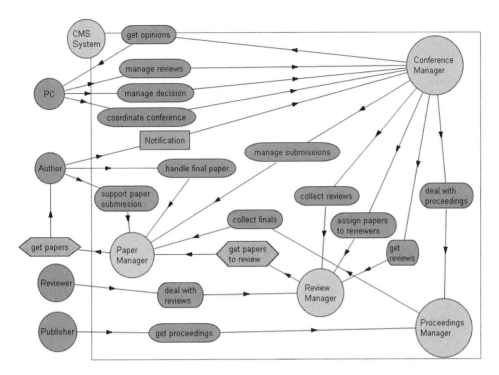

Figure 7.17
A refined goal diagram for the CMS System actor

capability diagrams and plan diagrams, which are similar to the behavior models presented in chapter 3; agent interaction diagrams, which are similar to protocol models presented in chapter 3; and UML class diagrams, for information modeling. We do not give specific examples here, as they are similar to the models of detailed design in other agent-oriented methodologies.

It is straightforward to map the Tropos detailed design models to BDI agents. Some BDI agent platforms were overviewed in chapter 5. Code generation is possible for Jadex, which is a BDI extension to JADE. Tropos has also considered test case generation at the agent level and can produce Jadex and JADE test cases. We do not consider them here.

7.5   Prometheus

The motivation for developing the Prometheus methodology parallels the motivation for this book: "to have a process with associated deliverables which can be taught to industry practitioners and undergraduate students who do not have a background in agents and which they can use to develop intelligent agent systems." Prometheus

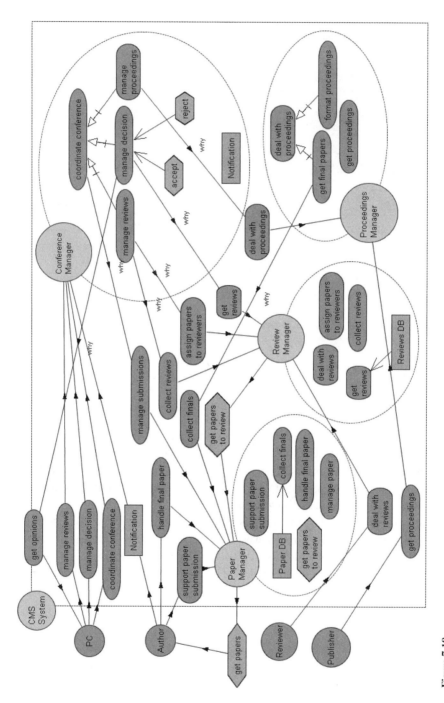

Figure 7.18
A further refined goal diagram for the CMS System actor

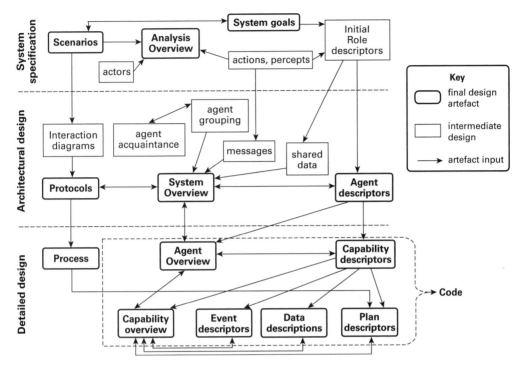

Figure 7.19
The Prometheus process diagram (Padgham and Winikoff 2004)

focuses on three stages of the software life cycle: specification, design, and implementation. It has methods for producing artefacts at each of the three stages. The standard Prometheus process diagram is given in figure 7.19.

The system specification stage corresponds to the motivation layer of the conceptual space described in chapter 2. Several artefacts are produced during the system specification stage. Scenarios describe sequences of activities that the system is supposed to perform and the goals to be achieved by them. They correspond to motivational scenarios from chapter 3. System goals give the overall goals of the system and correspond to goal models from chapter 3. Initial role descriptors are an initial description of functions that may achieve the system goals and loosely correspond to role models from chapter 3. In addition to these three artefacts, percepts and actions are specified as the interface between the system and the external world corresponding to what the system will sense and how it will act, respectively. Prometheus encourages the identification of a system boundary from early on. Determining the actions and percepts is effectively doing some domain modeling.

The architectural design stage also produces several artefacts. The primary decision is what agents will be in the system to deliver the functionalities described to

Table 7.4
Mapping the models of Prometheus to the viewpoint framework

Viewpoint models	Viewpoint aspect		
Abstraction layer	Interaction	Information	Behavior
Conceptual domain modeling	Analysis Overview Diagram, System Roles Diagram		Goal Overview Diagram, Functionalities, Scenarios
Platform-independent computational design	Agent Acquaintance Diagram, Interaction Diagrams, Protocol Diagrams, System Overview Diagram	Data Coupling Diagram	Agent Descriptors
Platform-specific design and implementation	Event Descriptors	Data Descriptors	Agent Overview Diagrams, Process Specifications, Capability Overview Diagrams

meet the system goals. The agents are described by agent descriptors. Agent role grouping diagrams and agent acquaintance diagrams are useful mechanisms to help produce a good design. The overall architecture is summarized in a system overview diagram, which specifies the data that the system will use, as well as protocols between agents. Protocols can be separately refined. Note that a system overview diagram represents a logical architecture, rather than a physical system architecture.

The detailed design stage fleshes out the agent descriptors to a level that they can be easily deployed. Agents are specified in terms of capabilities with appropriate capability descriptors. A capability is described by a capability overview diagram, event descriptors, data descriptions, and plan descriptors. The protocols are used to specify a process. Note that Prometheus intends for the underlying agents to reason through the use of goals and plans.

The major Prometheus artifacts are placed in the viewpoint framework in table 7.4. Although the artifact names given in the Prometheus process diagram are not identical to the artifact names in the table, the reader can see that there is good coverage over all three layers and viewpoints. Placement of the artifacts is somewhat subjective, as several models do not fit neatly in a single cell. The system overview diagram, for example, implies interaction and behavior as well as information.

The system specification and architectural design stages are platform- and architecture-independent. The detailed design stage is architecture-dependent, and develops the agents further in BDI style. Agents are developed in terms of capabilities, which are grouped descriptions of plans that the agent has, data that the agent manipulates, events that the agent responds to, and messages that the agent sends.

We now demonstrate the use of Prometheus for the conference management system. The architectural design stage of Prometheus is also used in sections 9.2 and

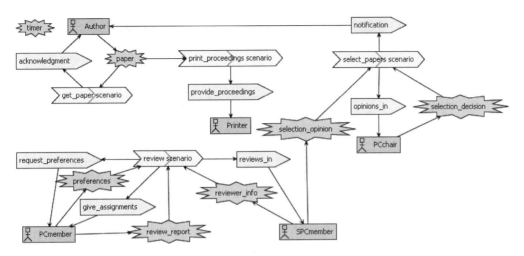

Figure 7.20
An analysis overview diagram for the conference management system

9.3 for the Smart Music Player and Secret Touch examples. Diagrams were drawn with the Prometheus Design Tool (PDT). The Prometheus research team realized from the outset of its project that tool support was essential, and has expended considerable effort in developing and improving PDT. The tool provides some checking capability, for example disallowing references to nonexistent artifacts, barring two artifacts having the same name, and avoiding certain errors. PDT can produce detailed reports about the artifacts created. It has been used successfully by a range of students in agent courses around the world.

We turn now to the conference management example. We follow the practice of the previous two sections and follow the presentation made at the 2007 Agent-Oriented Software Engineering Workshop. The functionality presented there covered paper submission, paper reviews, paper selection and author notification, and final paper collection and printing of the proceedings.

The system specification stage of Prometheus covers four activities: producing an analysis overview, listing scenarios, producing a goal overview diagram, and grouping goals into roles. We cover each of them briefly, and give an example of a model from the conference management domain.

Developing an analysis overview diagram proceeds in two steps. The first step is to identify the external actors and scenarios in which they participate. The second step is to identify for each scenario the percepts that come into the system and the actions that result from it. An analysis overview diagram for the conference management system that has gone through the two steps is given in figure 7.20. There are five external actors: `Author`, `PCmember`, `SPCmember`, `Printer`, and `PCchair`. There are

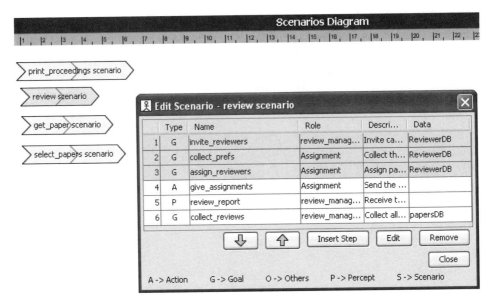

Figure 7.21
The review scenario for the conference management system

four scenarios: print_proceedings, get_paper, review, and select_papers. The get_paper scenario has one percept, namely paper, and performs one action, namely acknowledgment. The select_papers scenario has two percepts— selection_opinion and selection_decision—and two actions: opinions_in and notification.

The next stage is to develop scenarios that the proposed system should enact. A scenario is a sequence of steps. Each step is labeled by its type, name, role, description, and the data it accesses. The type of a step is a goal, action, percept, or subscenario. A sample scenario for reviewing a paper is given in figure 7.21. It has six steps. The first three steps are goals, invite_reviewers, collect_prefs, and assign_reviewers, respectively. The fourth step is an action of giving the assignments. The fifth step is a percept, namely receiving the review report, and the final step is another goal, collect_reviews.

The next stage is to develop a goal overview diagram. It is closely linked to the scenarios developed in the previous step. Figure 7.22 gives a goal overview diagram for the conference management system. It represents twenty goals. The top-level goal is manage_conference, which has four subgoals.

The next stage is to identify roles and associate them with goals. Typically, several goals are associated with an individual role. Appropriate actions and percepts are also attached to the role. Figure 7.23 gives a system roles diagram for the conference

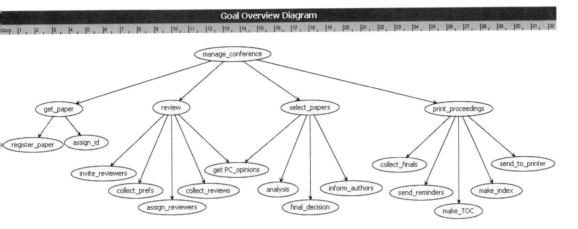

Figure 7.22
A goal overview diagram for the conference management system

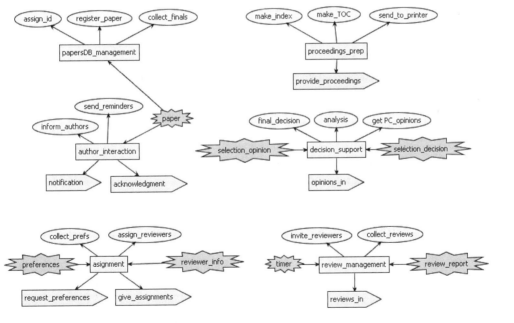

Figure 7.23
A system roles diagram for the conference management system

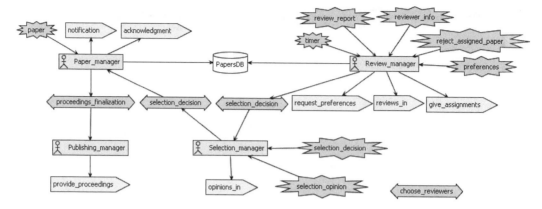

Figure 7.24
A system overview diagram for the conference management system

management system. There are six roles that cover all the goals drawn in the goal overview diagram in figure 7.22. For example, the `assignment` role is responsible for achieving the goals `collect_prefs` and `assign_reviewers`. The percepts perceived by an agent playing that role are `preferences` and `reviewer_info` and the actions performed by it are `request_preferences` and `give_assignments`.

The architectural design stage builds on the artifacts produced in the system specification stage. The initial step is to decide on the agents in the system by looking at how roles might be grouped. The PDT tool provides support for an agent role grouping diagram. Standard software engineering principles of cohesion and coupling are used to help decide the agents. Which roles share data is an important consideration; there is a useful data coupling diagram. In our running example, four agents are chosen: `Review_manager` for the roles `assignment` and `review_management`, `Paper_manager` for the roles `author_interaction` and `papersDB_management`, `Publishing_manager` for the role `proceedings_prep`, and `Selection_manager` for the role `decision_support`. Protocols between agents are described textually and placed automatically in the relevant diagram.

The overall architecture of the system is summarized in a system overview diagram. Figure 7.24 gives a system overview diagram for the conference management system. The four agents are shown. Protocols between agents are depicted; for example, `proceedings_finalization` is a protocol between the `Paper_manager` and the `Publishing_manager` agents. Protocols are defined and edited in PDT via a text editor, using a notation that extends AUML. There are four protocols given in figure 7.24. The shared data store `PapersDB` is shown. Also in the system overview diagram are the percepts sensed by an agent and the actions performed by it. For

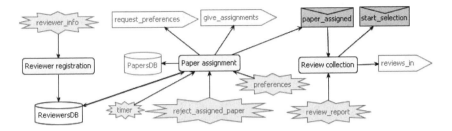

Figure 7.25
The agent overview diagram for `Review_manager`

example, the `Selection_manager` senses two percepts, `selection_opinion` and `selection_decision`, and performs the action `opinions_in`.

Moving on to detailed design, we consider agents and capabilities. Agents are described in terms of capabilities, internal events, plans, and internal data structures. An agent overview diagram depicts capabilities within an agent, events between capabilities, messages, percepts, and actions. Figure 7.25 gives the agent overview diagram for the `Review_manager` agent in the conference management system. It has three capabilities: `Reviewer registration`, `Paper assignment`, and `Review collection`. It has two internal databases: `ReviewersDB` used by two of the capabilities, and `PapersDB` used by the `Paper assignment` capability. The `Paper assignment` capability senses three percepts: `preferences`, `timer`, and `reject_assigned_paper`. It sends a `paper_assigned` message to the `Review collection` capability and performs two actions: `request_preferences` and `give_assignments`.

A capability overview diagram describes the internals of the capability, including plans to handle each input. Plan descriptors consist of a name, description, triggers, context, incoming and outgoing messages, relevant percepts and actions, used and produced data, and the goal it is intended to achieve. Importantly, it contains a procedure and includes failure conditions and steps for failure recovery.

The artifacts produced by the detailed design stage were conceived with the BDI agent architecture in mind. Consequently, it is straightforward to implement the agents in a BDI-oriented agent programming language—indeed, in any of the languages described in chapter 5, though clearly some have greater support than others. There is actually a feature in PDT to generate JACK code. The code generation capability can maintain some level of synchronization between detailed design and code when one or the other changes.

To conclude this section, we note that there is similarity between the methodologies that we have presented so far. They cover similar stages of the software development

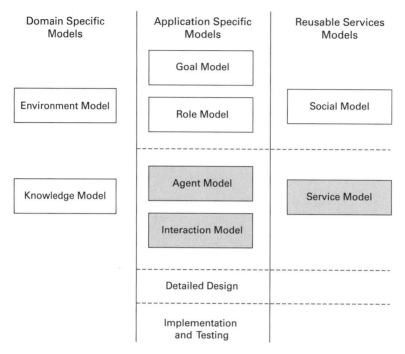

Figure 7.26
ROADMAP analysis and design models

life cycle and give comparable abilities to agents, though there are differences in concepts and models. We believe it would be possible to merge the methodology with a spirit of cooperation between the research groups.

7.6   ROADMAP and RAP/AOR

In this section we describe two agent-oriented methodologies: ROADMAP and RAP/AOR. We have chosen to describe both of them in one section, because the methodologies complement each other well. ROADMAP puts the emphasis on domain and systems analysis, and RAP/AOR is geared toward design. We begin the section by giving a short overview of both methodologies.

The ROADMAP (Role-Oriented Analysis and Design for Multiagent Programming) methodology was originally derived from the Gaia methodology, which was overviewed in section 7.2. Figure 7.26 shows the models of the ROADMAP methodology. In ROADMAP, the models are divided vertically into domain-specific models, application-specific models, and reusable services models. The environment model and knowledge model represent information about a specific domain. The

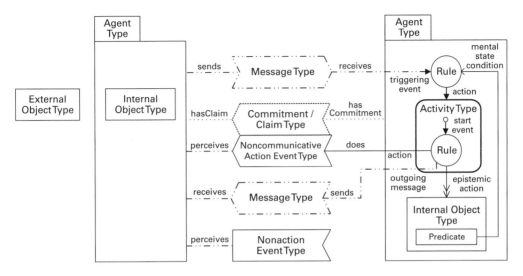

Figure 7.27
The modeling elements of AOR diagrams. This figure appears in Taveter and Wagner 2006. Copyright 2009, IGI Global, www.igi-global.com. Posted by permission of the publisher.

goal model, role model, agent model, and interaction model are tied to the system being modeled. Generic and reusable components in the system are captured by the social model and service model. The models are also split horizontally by dotted horizontal lines according to the domain analysis and design phases, so that the goal model, the role model, and the social model are created in the domain analysis phase, and the agent model, interaction model, and service model belong to the architectural design phase. The environment model and knowledge model are created in the domain analysis phase and refined in the architectural design phase.

The RAP/AOR (Radical Agent-Oriented Process/Agent-Object-Relationship) methodology is aimed at creating distributed organizational information systems, such as business process and supply-chain management systems. To cater for the design needs of such systems, RAP/AOR models the behavior of an agent as founded on its perceptions and on its basic mental state components: beliefs and commitments. The methodology is based on the Agent-Object-Relationship Modeling Language (AORML). In AORML, the agents in a problem domain are distinguished from the nonagentive objects. Event perceptions by the agents and their actions and commitments are explicitly represented in the models.

The basic model type in RAP/AOR is the Agent-Object-Relationship (AOR) diagram specified by figure 7.27. An AOR diagram enables the representation in a single diagram of the types of human and manmade (e.g., software) agents of a sociotechnical system, together with their beliefs and behaviors. An AOR diagram can take various forms. An AOR agent diagram depicts the agent types of a problem domain, together with their internal agent types, the beliefs of agents of these types, and the relationships among them. An AOR interaction-frame diagram provides a static picture of the possible interactions and the evolution of commitments/claims between two or more types of agents without modeling any specific process instance. An AOR interaction-sequence diagram depicts (some part of) a prototypical instance of an interaction process. An AOR behavior diagram is a specification of parameterized behavior of agents of the type in focus that is expressed as a flow of execution via sequencing of subordinate activities whose primitive elements are individual epistemic, communicative, and noncommunicative actions.

The combined process for the ROADMAP and RAP/AOR methodologies is represented in figure 7.28. The figure shows the steps of the modeling process, the resulting models, and how the models are derived from each other.

The best developed and most extensively used models of ROADMAP are the ones focusing on application-specific domain modeling: goal and role models. They define the purpose and goals for the system to be created and the roles needed for achieving the goals. They are complemented with domain models, which have been derived from environment and knowledge models of ROADMAP.

Goal, role, and domain models have been combined with the models of the RAP/ AOR methodology, which provides the strongest support for the abstraction layer of platform-independent computational design. The RAP/AOR methodology also covers platform-dependent computational design, for which it uses certain types of UML models. The combination of models originating in the ROADMAP and RAP/AOR methodologies is represented in table 7.5.

We next show how the process in figure 7.28 can be applied to the development of a conference management system. In addition, the models featured by the combined ROADMAP and RAP/AOR methodology are used in chapters 4 and 9 for the design of a greeting system and intruder detection system in the Intelligent Home case study. In chapter 8, RAP/AOR models form part of the design of e-commerce automation and manufacturing simulation systems.

The purpose and requirements for the conference management system are described by goal models, which were introduced in section 3.2 as high-level behavior models. An overall goal model for the system is represented in figure 7.29. Recall that goals represent functional requirements, while quality goals are nonfunctional requirements. According to the model, the purpose of the system is "Run conference." The quality goal associated with this goal expresses a general requirement to organize and run a high-quality conference. The run conference goal has been decomposed into seven subgoals: "Fix deadlines," "Form PC," "Get papers," "Get reviews," "Select papers," "Organize conference event," and "Publish proceedings," which describe different aspects of running a conference. Attached to the "Fix dead-

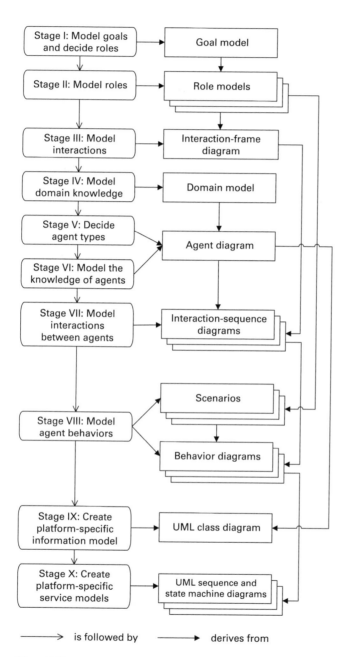

Figure 7.28
The combined modeling process for ROADMAP and RAP/AOR

Table 7.5
The viewpoint framework filled out with the models of the ROADMAP and RAP/AOR methodologies

Viewpoint models	Viewpoint aspect		
Abstraction layer	Interaction	Information	Behavior
Conceptual domain modeling	Role models (ROADMAP) and interaction-frame diagrams (RAP/AOR)	Domain model (ROADMAP)	Goal models (ROADMAP)
Platform-independent computational design	Interaction-sequence diagrams (RAP/AOR)	Agent diagram (RAP/AOR)	Scenarios and AOR behavior diagrams (RAP/AOR)
Platform-specific design and implementation	UML class and sequence diagrams (RAP/AOR)	UML class diagrams (RAP/AOR)	UML class and sequence diagrams (RAP/AOR)

lines" goal is the quality goal "Realistic deadlines." The quality goal "Appropriate conference venue" associated with the "Organize conference event" goal reflects the importance of a well-functioning conference venue for holding the actual conference event.

As seen in section 3.2, goal models include roles, which define capacities or positions with functionalities needed for achieving the goals. Various roles are required for achieving the goals defined in figure 7.29: PC Chair, PC Member Candidate, PC Member, Author, Reviewer, and Publisher.

The goal model represented in figure 7.29 can be further elaborated, but we do not cover this material here.

We next move to the modeling of roles related to the system to be developed using the role models described in section 3.3. As we know, goals in goal models apply to the system as a whole. Differently, role models model the responsibilities that need to be exercised by enactors of individual roles to achieve the goals. Role models also include constraints that restrict role enactors. Role models for the roles Author and PC Chair are shown in tables 7.6 and 7.7, respectively.

The role models represented in tables 7.6 and 7.7 include but do not explicitly model interactions between enactors of the roles. To gain a better understanding of the problem domain that is being analyzed, we sketch interactions between enactors of these roles using interaction-frame diagrams introduced in section 3.6. Figure 7.30 models the types of interactions between agents playing the roles Author, PC Chair, PC Member, and Reviewer. The figure uses the notation that was introduced by figure 7.27. In the figure, interactions that are likely to be performed by the mediation of the system's user interface—submitPaper, submitFinalVersion, and submitReview—are modeled as noncommunicative or physical action event types. The rest of the interactions modeled in figure 7.30 are types of messages sent between agents. Each message type is prefixed by a *function*: two examples are request, by

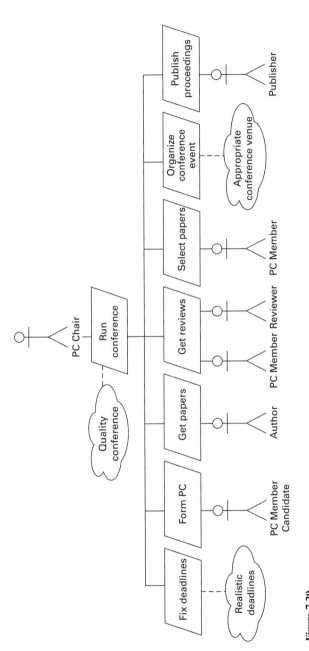

Figure 7.29
An overall goal model for the conference management system

Table 7.6
The role model for Author

Role name	Author
Description	The role of writing and submitting a paper.
Responsibilities	Send his or her paper for the conference to the PC chair.
	Receive the confirmation of paper submission.
	Receive the submission number.
	Receive the acceptance/rejection decision and the reviews of the paper.
	Receive a request from the PC chair to submit the final version of the accepted paper.
	Send the final version of the accepted paper to the PC chair.
Constraints	The paper must be submitted before the submission deadline.
	The final version of the accepted paper must be submitted before the submission deadline for camera-ready papers.

Table 7.7
The role model for PC Chair

Role name	PC Chair
Description	The PC Chair manages the process of determining the technical program for the conference.
Responsibilities	Invite PC members.
	Receive confirmations of acceptance from PC members.
	Register PC members.
	Advertise the conference.
	Decide submission deadlines.
	Decide submission format.
	Receive the papers for the conference.
	• Store the papers.
	• Assign submission numbers to the papers.
	• Confirm paper submissions with the authors.
	Interact with PC members to receive their reviewing preferences.
	Assign the papers to PC members for reviewing.
	Re-distribute the papers rejected for review.
	Receive the reviews done by PC members.
	Negotiate with PC members about borderline or conflicting papers.
	Make acceptance/rejection decisions on the papers.
	Notify the authors of the acceptance/rejection decisions.
	Send the reviews to the authors.
	Request and receive final versions of the accepted papers.
	Request the publisher to print the final versions of the accepted papers as the proceedings of the conference.
	Submit the final proceedings to the publisher according to an agreed deadline.
Constraints	Each paper must be distributed to at least three PC members for reviewing.
	There is a limit to the number of papers that a PC chair can review.
	A PC member cannot review his or her own paper.
	A PC member cannot review a paper with which he/she has a conflict of interest.
	The authors must be notified in a timely manner whether their paper has been accepted or rejected.
	The submissions of final versions of the accepted papers to the publisher must be complete, with all the accepted papers included.

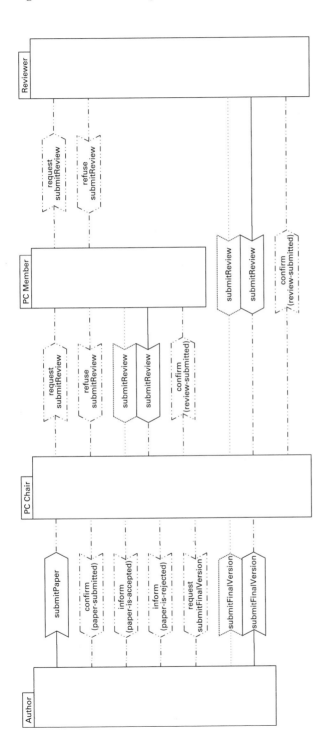

Figure 7.30
An interaction-frame diagram for the conference management system

which the sender requests the receiver to perform an action, and `inform`, with which the sender informs the receiver about something.

Central in the RAP/AOR methodology is the modeling of commitments and claims and their creation and discharging. In the interaction model depicted in figure 7.30, the types of noncommunicative action events `submitFinalVersion` and `submitReview` are coupled with the corresponding commitment/claim types. The `submitReview` commitment occurs in the model twice, because a PC member can delegate the reviewing to an external reviewer, which is reflected by the delegation of the corresponding commitment. The `submitPaper` action event may also be coupled with a commitment/claim. This happens if paper submission is preceded by the submission of an abstract. Please note that a commitment and claim can be viewed as two sides of the same coin: what is a commitment for one agent is a claim for the other agent.

Next, we create a conceptual information model. The purpose of a conceptual information model is to model knowledge of the problem domain that is to be represented in the system and handled by it. As explained in section 3.4, a model of this kind can also be called a domain model. A domain model is a derivation of the environment and knowledge models in the original ROADMAP methodology. The domain model for the conference management system is depicted in figure 7.31. The domain model represents the entities of the problem domain that are relevant for the system to be developed. The model also shows relationships between entities. Figure 7.31 expresses that a conference has a conference program consisting of papers to be presented. Each paper is submitted by its authors. The conference program is decided by the PC, which consists of PC members. Each PC member is responsible for reviewing papers. A PC member may delegate paper reviewing to an external reviewer, who is then responsible for submitting the review. A conference also has proceedings, which are published by the publisher.

So far, we have been talking about roles. At some stage, the types of agents that are to play the roles need to be decided. The ROADMAP and RAP/AOR methodologies share a common feature: they decide agent types relatively late in a modeling process. Both methodologies also allow role information to be preserved and represented at runtime, because different agents can take on the same role. For example, different human agents can play the PC Member role. This implies that the system should provide its functionalities in terms of roles.

In RAP/AOR, a manmade agent can automate a part or all of the activities performed by a human agent enacting his or her role. When deciding which activities should be automated, it may be helpful to analyze responsibilities attributed to the roles of the system and interactions between agents playing the roles.

When analyzing the responsibilities of the roles modeled in tables 7.6 and 7.7, notice that the responsibilities attributed to the roles Author and PC Member are

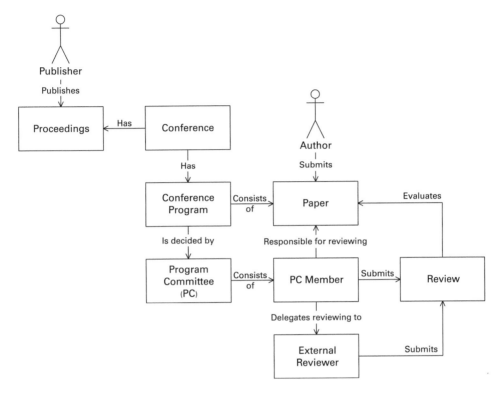

Figure 7.31
The domain model for the conference management system

human-centric, which cannot be easily automated. Indeed, how can you automate writing a paper or review? However, it would certainly help if the human researcher had a manmade helper agent keeping track of the commitments that its human owner has toward other agents, such as a commitment to submit a review or a final version of the paper.

Note that all the represented noncommunicative action event types and the commitment/claim types coupled with them depicted in figure 7.30 are targeted at an agent playing the PC Chair role. Agents playing the Author, PC Member, and Reviewer roles make at various times commitments to an agent playing the PC Chair role to submit a review and to submit a final version of the paper and then perform the corresponding actions. As commitments and claims are like opposite sides of the same coin, it is sufficient if an agent playing the PC Chair role keeps track of the claims that it has against other agents and reminds other agents about any unsatisfied claims. For example, a PC chair can remind a PC member about an overdue review. Consequently, we observe that the system would most benefit from the automation of the activities performed by an enactor of the PC Chair role, which can be done by a manmade agent of type ChairAgent.

Should the activities performed by a ChairAgent be divided among agents of its various subtypes, such as PapersManagerAgent, ReviewsManagerAgent, and DecisionsManagerAgent? It may not be necessary, because the activities that would be performed by agents of the types mentioned are separated in time, as they are triggered by different events. These activities should be modeled separately, but can still be performed by the same agent.

The sociotechnical conference management system is accordingly designed to consist of one manmade agent of type ChairAgent, playing the role of PC Chair, and several human agents of type Person, playing the Author, PC Member, and Reviewer roles. The shorthand for these agent types is ChairAgent/PC Chair, Person/Author, Person/PC Member, and Person/Reviewer.

Having decided the types of agents, the next step is to transform the domain model into the knowledge model. The knowledge model for the conference management system is represented in the agent diagram in figure 7.32. According to the model, general knowledge about the conference, including the submission deadlines and conference dates, is publicly available for all agents of any types. The model also shows that the knowledge about papers and their authors and reviews is shared between agents of several types, and the knowledge about the conference program, PC members, and external reviewers is represented exclusively within an agent of type ChairAgent. Naturally, the PC chair may choose to make a part of its private knowledge public by, for example, by publishing the names, affiliations, and countries (but not email addresses!) of PC members, and later by publishing the conference program. The RAP/AOR methodology provides means for representing partially public or shared knowledge. We do not discuss those means here. It may be necessary to define what parts of shared knowledge are available for which agents more precisely. The knows-association link between the agent type Person/PC Member and the object types Paper and Review in figure 7.32 models that a PC member knows about several papers and reviews.

The relationship between an object and the agent described by it is represented by describes-associations like the association between the object type Author and the agent type Person/Author. The describes-association models that an object of the Author type describes an author.

After having decided the agent types and modeling the knowledge of agents of those types, interactions between human and manmade agents of a sociotechnical system are modeled using interaction-sequence diagrams described in section 3.6.

The next stage is agent behavior modeling. Tables 7.8 and 7.9 give example scenarios for achieving the "Get papers" and "Submit paper" goals of the conference management system. The scenarios are represented in a format derived of goal-based

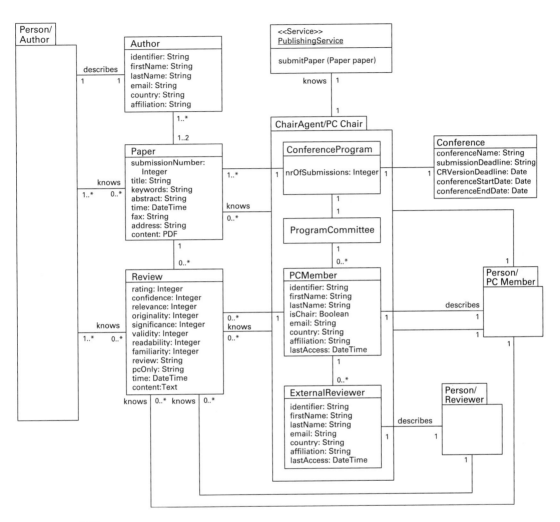

Figure 7.32
The knowledge model for the conference management system

Table 7.8
The scenario for achieving the "Get papers" goal

SCENARIO 1				
Goal		Get papers		
Initiator		ChairAgent/PC Chair		
Trigger				
DESCRIPTION				
Condition	Step	Activity	Agent types / roles	Resources
Interleaved	1	Advertise conference	Person/PC Chair	
	2	Submit paper (**Scenario 2**)	Person/Author, ChairAgent/PC Chair	Paper, Author

Table 7.9
The scenario for achieving the "Submit paper" goal

SCENARIO 2				
Goal		Submit paper		
Initiator		Person/Author		
Trigger		Paper submission by an author		
DESCRIPTION				
Condition	Step	Activity	Agent types / roles	Resources
	1	Send/receive paper	Person/Author, ChairAgent/PC Chair	Paper
	2	Store paper	ChairAgent/PC Chair	Paper, Author
	3	Assign submission number	ChairAgent/PC Chair	Paper
	4	Confirm submission	Person/Author, ChairAgent/PC Chair	Paper

use cases, which were originally used in the RAP/AOR methodology. This format was introduced and explained as an example scenario format in section 3.8.

As we explained earlier in this section, it is feasible to model the conference management system as consisting of one manmade agent type, three human agent types, and one external service, publisher. The automation of human activities occurs within a manmade agent of the ChairAgent type. The activities performed by a ChairAgent largely depend on the activities performed by human agents playing the Author, PC Member, and Reviewer roles. Figure 7.33 is an AOR behavior diagram that models the behavior of a ChairAgent in reaction to submitting a paper by an author. It reflects the scenario represented in table 7.9. Rule R1 in figure 7.33 specifies that in response to receiving a paper submitted along with information

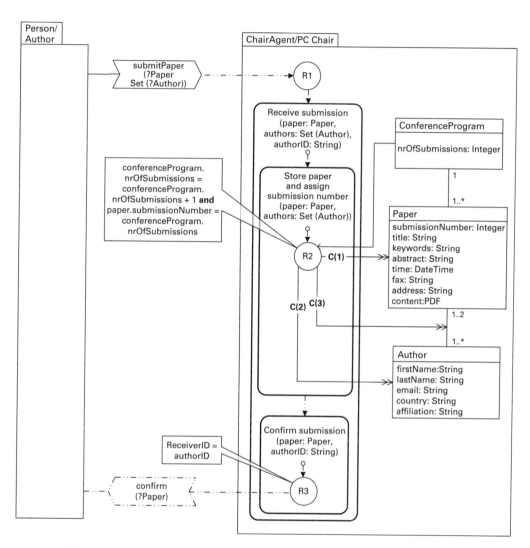

Figure 7.33
The behavior diagram for submitting a paper

about its authors, an activity is started to receive submissions. This activity consists of sequential subactivities of storing a paper and assigning it a submission number, and confirming submission. The former subactivity includes rule R2, which specifies three epistemic actions of the CREATE type. For each epistemic action, its order in the sequence is shown in parentheses. The first epistemic action creates an object of the Paper type. The second epistemic action creates the Author objects for the set of authors and the third epistemic action creates associations between each Author object and the Paper object. Also, according to the Object Constraint Language (OCL) expression attached to rule R1, the value of the nrOfSubmissions attribute of the ConferenceProgram object is incremented by 1. After that, rule R2 assigns this value as the submission number to the corresponding Paper object. Rule R3 in the confirming submission activity is responsible for sending a confirmation message to the author.

We have seen that AOR behavior diagrams enable both an agent's knowledge and its behavior to be modeled. AOR behavior diagrams contain all the necessary information required for generating platform-dependent design models and code. For example, it has been shown by Kuldar that AOR behavior diagrams can be straightforwardly transformed into the implementation constructs of the Java-based JADE agent platform. JADE was one of the agent platforms overviewed in chapter 5. However, the nature of the conference management system modeled does not require a software agent based system for implementation, but should rather be implemented as a client-server system. This has also been done in real life, where conference management systems such as EasyChair have been implemented.

Note that we have not used quality goals in the design. The quality goals in the goal model in figure 7.29 are high-level. A human would determine whether they had been met—for example, whether the conference venue was appropriate. In a more detailed exposition of this case study, it would be natural to require that the reviews should be completed in a timely way, which would have imposed specific timing constraints. A different example would be that the decisions be fair, which would be tricky to quantify.

7.7   Background

The definition of a software engineering methodology given at the outset of the chapter has been provided by Rumbaugh et al. (1991).

The EasyChair conference management system repeatedly mentioned in the chapter is described on its Web site (http://www.easychair.org). Another similar conference management system is OpenConf (http://www.openconf.org). Three of the methodologies described in this chapter—MaSE, Tropos, and Prometheus—have been applied to the case study of conference management. The results from the comparison are reported in the proceedings of the Agent-Oriented Software Engineering Workshop 2007, edited by Luck and Padgham (2008). The applications of the MaSE, Tropos, and Prometheus methodologies to the conference management system case study are respectively described by DeLoach (2008), Morandini et al. (2008), and Padgham, Thangarajah, and Winikoff (2008).

The first methodologies for developing multiagent systems emerged as attempts were made to commercialize agent technology. An early group investigating agent applications was the Australian Artificial Intelligence Institute (AAII), who developed a methodology described by Kinny, Georgeff, and Rao (1996). The experience at AAII was shared with Wooldridge and Jennings, who were very active with agents in the United Kingdom. Their discussions led to the Gaia methodology (Wooldridge, Jennings, and Kinny 2000).

Agent-oriented software engineering (AOSE) emerged as an area in its own right early in the 2000s (Ciancarini and Wooldridge, 2001) and has become an active research area. AOSE methodologies and approaches loosely fall into one of two categories. One approach adds agent extensions to an existing object-oriented notation. The prototypical example is Agent UML, which was first proposed by Odell, Parunak, and Bauer (2001). The second approach has been taken by methodologies that explicitly use agent concepts. The methodologies that have been described in this chapter belong to the second group. Several methodologies have been developed and are maturing. Gaia was updated (Zambonelli, Jennings, and Wooldridge, 2003) and several extensions were proposed (Cernuzzi et al. 2004).

The MaSE methodology is described by DeLoach, Wood, and Sparkman (2001) and by DeLoach and Kumar (2005). The methodology has been extended to environment modeling by DeLoach and Valenzuela (2007). The extension of MaSE— the O-MaSE methodology—was proposed by Garcia-Ojeda et al. (2008). The MaSE methodology is accompanied by the agentTool. More information about the agentTool can be found on http://agenttool.cis.ksu.edu.

Tropos is a software development methodology founded on concepts used to model early requirements, specifically the i^* modeling framework proposed by Yu (1995). The i^* framework uses the concepts of actor, goal, and (actor) dependency to model early and late requirements, and architectural and detailed design. The Tropos methodology was introduced by Bresciani et al. (2001). The methodology is extensively described by Bresciani et al. (2004) and by Giorgini et al. (2005). Tropos models can be created by the TAOM4E tool. More information about the TAOM4E tool can be found at http://sra.itc.it/tools/taom4e.

The Prometheus methodology was introduced by Padgham and Winikoff (2003). The citation describing the motivation for developing the Prometheus methodology in the beginning of section 7.5 is from Padgham and Winikoff 2003 (see p. 174).

The methodology is thoroughly described by Padgham and Winikoff (2004). Prometheus is accompanied by the PDT, which is described by Padgham, Thangarajah, and Winikoff (2005). More information about the PDT tool can be found at http://www.cs.rmit.edu.au/agents/pdt.

The ROADMAP methodology was originally proposed as an extension of the first version of Gaia (Wooldridge, Jennings, and Kinny 2000) for open systems. ROADMAP is the subject of Thomas Juan's Ph.D. thesis at the University of Melbourne (Juan 2008). The ROADMAP methodology was introduced by Juan, Pearce, and Sterling (2002). In comparison with Gaia, it provides explicit models for requirements elicitation and for describing the domain and the execution environment of the system. ROADMAP also extends Gaia by explicit models for representing social aspects. A metamodel for the methodology was introduced by Juan and Sterling (2003). The models evolved over several iterations, led by Thomas in his Ph.D. work. The notation that was developed for goal and role models is described by Kuan, Karunasekera, and Sterling (2005). The modeling aspects that address software quality in ROADMAP are illuminated by Sterling and Juan (2005). A domain model is derived from knowledge and environment models in the original ROADMAP methodology. Knowledge models were proposed by Juan, Pearce, and Sterling (2002). Their constituent parts—knowledge components—were defined by Juan and Sterling (2003). Environment models were introduced by Juan, Pearce, and Sterling (2002). The latest refinement of ROADMAP by Juan (2008) also proposes mechanisms for runtime reflection by software agents. Building goal and role models in ROADMAP is facilitated by the use of the ROADMAP Editor Built for Easy deveLopment (REBEL) tool. The tool can be downloaded from http://www.cs.mu.oz.au/agentlab/rebel.html.

The RAP/AOR methodology is based on AORML by Wagner (2003) and on the Business Agents' Approach by Taveter (2004a). The methodology was introduced by Taveter and Wagner (2005). The modeling concepts used in RAP/AOR have ontological foundations put forward by Guizzardi and Wagner (2005a). As is emphasized by Taveter and Wagner (2005), RAP/AOR is more concerned with distributed agent-based information systems (such as business process automation and supply-chain management systems) for the business domain and not so much with AI systems. The scenarios included by the case study of a conference management system have been derived from goal-based use cases (Cockburn 2001), which were originally used in the RAP/AOR methodology. RAP/AOR has been applied to the automation of business-to-business electronic commerce as reported by Taveter (2005a) and manufacturing simulation as reported by Taveter and Wagner (2006) and Taveter (2006b). The descriptions of those applications have also been included in chapter 8 of this book. The RAP/AOR methodology was supported by the COnceptual Network Ontology Editor (CONE) tool, which is described by Taveter (2005b).

The ROADMAP and RAP/AOR methodologies have been used jointly in Sterling, Taveter, and the Daedalus Team 2006a and in Taveter and Sterling 2008.

Many other agent-oriented software engineering methodologies exist, such as MESSAGE (Caire et al. 2004) and TAO (Silva and Lucena 2004). It is beyond our scope to treat them comprehensively. Many agent-oriented methodologies are described in Henderson-Sellers and Giorgini 2005 and Bergenti, Gleizes, and Zambonelli 2004. More information about the Jadex agent platform can be found at http://vsis-www.informatik.uni-hamburg.de/projects/jadex.

Juan, Sterling, and Winikoff (2002) propose a modular approach enabling developers to build customized project-specific methodologies from AOSE features. An AOSE feature is defined by Juan et al. (2003) to encapsulate software engineering techniques and models, and supporting Computer-Aided Software Engineering (CASE) tools and development knowledge such as design patterns. It is considered a standalone unit to perform part of a development phase, such as analysis or prototyping, while achieving a quality attribute such as privacy. Another method for building customized methodologies—OPEN (Firesmith and Henderson-Sellers 2002)—includes the notions of Work Units, Work Products, Producers, Stages, and Languages. We describe in Sterling, Taveter, and the Daedalus Team 2006a how these notions can be used for feature-based agent-oriented software engineering.

8 Industry-Related Applications

This chapter explores two industry-related applications of agent-oriented modeling undertaken by Kuldar. We show how these applications can be modeled with combinations of the ROADMAP, Tropos, and RAP/AOR methodologies, which were overviewed in chapter 7. Whenever deemed appropriate, we have complemented the set of models included by these methodologies with additional models from chapter 3, such as domain and agent models. The case study presented in section 8.1 demonstrates agent-based automation of business-to-business (B2B) e-commerce. This case study has been modeled using a combination of ROADMAP and RAP/AOR. The case study presented in section 8.2 concerns agent-oriented modeling and simulation of a ceramics factory. This case study has been modeled by a combination of Tropos and RAP/AOR. Section 8.3 gives some background for both case studies.

8.1 Business-to-Business E-Commerce

As pointed out in section 1.3, B2B e-commerce is fundamentally distributed and naturally modeled with agents. A typical activity in B2B e-commerce is procurement by bidding. Suppose that there is a company in need of commodities or services that are provided by other companies. A representative of the buying company sends *requests for quotes* to representative(s) of the selling companies. The representatives of the selling companies respond by *quotes*. Each quote includes a price and possibly other selling conditions, such as pickup or delivery place and time. The buyer then decides to buy the commodity or service from one of the sellers and informs all the bidders of its decision. This is followed by ordering, product delivery, and paying. Procurement by bidding usually happens by email or increasingly by the mediation of e-commerce Web portals.

In B2B e-commerce, the term "automation" is frequently understood to refer to transferring from paper-based information exchange to electronic information exchange. However, with electronic information exchange, human operators essentially continue doing what they did before—except by electronic means. For example, procurement by bidding is now done by email instead of phone. Automation can also refer to the automation of decision making performed by humans. In the bidding example, making most of the decisions can be automated by delegation to software agents. Such systems naturally leave the final say for humans, but still automate a lot of mental work that is usually fully undertaken by humans.

Several computational architectures and environments for B2B e-commerce have been developed since the Internet boom. There is a World Wide Web architecture document that includes services and agents invoking the services. There are standard proposals such as RosettaNet, papiNet, and ebXML (Electronic Business using eXtensible Markup Language) that define frameworks of knowledge required for B2B e-commerce and types of business processes between e-commerce parties. In addition, there are standard proposals for business process modeling, such as BPMN and XML Process Definition Language (XPDL), where XML stands for eXtensible Markup Language. However, these are all disparate approaches that do not provide a straightforward transition from business process modeling to business process automation. To facilitate the integration of business process modeling and business process automation, we need to model business processes so that all the viewpoints of the viewpoint framework, described in chapter 6, are represented. This includes modeling how human and manmade agents representing e-commerce parties make decisions and interact.

We now describe the modeling, design, and implementation of an agent-based procurement system. The system was designed and implemented as a prototype in the Plug-and-Trade B2B and B2B+DM research projects of the Technical Research Centre of Finland–VTT Information Technology. Three Finnish companies participated—two large and one medium-size. The system was modeled and designed using the RAP/AOR methodology, which was described in section 7.6. The procurement system was implemented using the JADE agent platform described in chapter 5.

We now present a complete set of models for the application covering all the cells of the viewpoint framework shown in table 6.2. The models from the original application have been complemented with goal, role, and domain models from the ROADMAP methodology described in section 7.6.

Figure 8.1 models the most generic goals of B2B e-commerce under the *viewpoint of conceptual behavior modeling*. The model shows that the purpose of B2B e-commerce is "Trade," which is characterized by the quality goals "Timely processing" and "Commitments are binding." The lefthand quality goal in the figure expresses that if agents agree on a deal, they should not be allowed to decommit on that deal. The righthand quality goal expresses that trading should be timely, which is an underlying motivatation for the automation of B2B e-commerce. The subgoals of "Trade"—"Procure" and "Sell"—reflect the interests of agents playing two separate roles: Buyer and Seller.

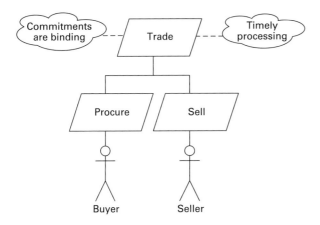

Figure 8.1
The goal model of B2B e-commerce

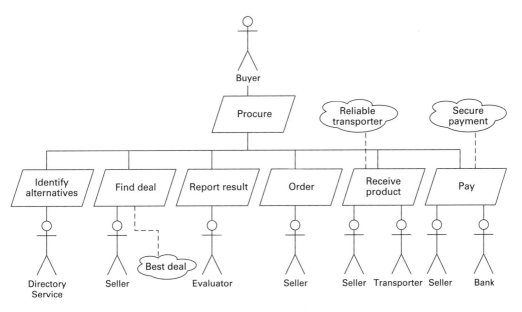

Figure 8.2
The goal model of procuring products

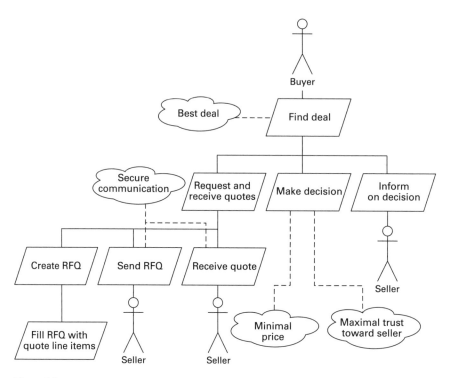

Figure 8.3
The goal model of finding a deal

Figure 8.2 refines the goal "Procure" that was introduced in figure 8.1. According to figure 8.2, procurement consists of identifying alternatives, finding a deal, reporting the result, ordering, receiving the product, and paying. A directory service of some sort enabling businesses to discover each other, such as, for example, UDDI (Universal Description, Discovery and Integration), is used for achieving the subgoal "Identify alternatives"—hence the role Directory Service related to the subgoal. The subgoal "Find deal" is associated with the role Seller and is characterized by the quality goal "Best deal." The "Report result" goal is to be achieved by an enactor of the role Evaluator. It concerns reporting the results of procurement to the relevant stakeholders. The "Receive product" and "Pay" subgoals are associated with the respective roles Transporter and Bank and with the respective quality goals "Reliable transporter" and "Secure payment."

There are many ways of finding a deal. An important one among them is known as a contract net: sending requests for quote (RFQs) to potential sellers and receiving quotes back from them. The goal model for this option is represented in figure 8.3. The goal "Find deal" has been decomposed into three subgoals: "Request and

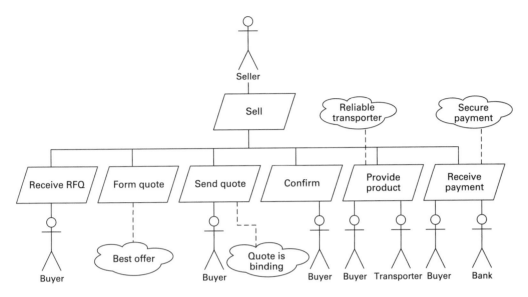

Figure 8.4
The goal model of selling products

receive quotes," "Make decision," and "Inform on decision." The most crucial goal is "Make decision," the achieving of which is influenced by the quality goals "Minimal price" and "Maximal trust toward seller." The subgoal "Request and receive quotes," in turn, has been divided into the subgoals "Create RFQ," "Send RFQ," and "Receive quote." As the RFQ and quotes constitute sensitive business information, the quality goal "Secure communication" pertains to the second and third of these goals. In addition, the goal "Create RFQ" has the subgoal for filling the RFQ with the descriptions of the product items to be procured. The goal "Inform on decision" and the subgoals "Send RFQ" and "Receive quote" are associated with the role Seller. Please note that the order in which the subgoals are presented in figure 8.3 does not imply any chronological order in which they are to be achieved.

The goals of the seller in B2B e-commerce are modeled in figure 8.4. The goal "Sell" has three subgoals—"Receive RFQ," "Form quote," and "Send quote"—which represent different stages of a contract net for a seller. The subgoal "Form quote" is to be achieved in such a manner that the quality goal "Best offer" would be met. The quality goal "Quote is binding" attached to the "Send quote" goal elaborates the "Commitments are binding" quality goal discussed earlier. The "Provide product" and "Receive payment" subgoals are associated with the respective roles Transporter and Bank and with the respective quality goals "Reliable transporter" and "Secure payment."

Table 8.1
The motivational scenario of automated procurement

Scenario name	Automated procurement
Scenario description	The organizations of both the buyer and the sellers are represented by software agents. The buyer organization requires certain commodities to be supplied by seller organizations. In order to buy the commodities, the buyer first identifies potential suppliers. After identifying the alternatives, the buyer delegates the buying process to its software agent, which performs the following activities: (a) create RFQ; (b) send RFQ to the software agents of the sellers; (c) receive quotes from the sellers' agents; (d) decide the seller from which to buy; (e) inform the sellers' agents about the decision; (f) order the commodities; (g) pay for the commodities. The seller organization delegates to its software agent the following matching activities: (a) receive RFQ; (b) form quote; (c) send quote; (d) confirm order; (e) register payment.
Quality description	Quote is binding for the seller. The deal achieved should be the best possible for the buyer. A seller offering the minimal price should be favored. A seller that is most trusted should be favored. Payment should be secure.

Having created the goal models, we describe a motivational scenario for an agent-based system for automated procurement. It includes the technology to be used, which is software agents in the given case study, so that customers and stakeholders can determine how well the proposed system achieves the goals. The motivational scenario of automated procurement is shown in table 8.1.

We now move to the *conceptual interaction modeling viewpoint*, where we first model roles. Tables 8.2 and 8.3 show role schemas created for the roles Buyer and Seller. Because the purpose of the procurement system is to buy commodities on behalf of the buyer, the principal responsibilities in the system are fulfilled by a performer of role Buyer. Some responsibilities are left to the sellers. It is safe to assume that they will be fulfilled because it is in the sellers' interest to sell their commodities.

In addition to role schemas, the conceptual interaction modeling viewpoint is captured by the organization model, which is represented in figure 8.5. In section 2.2, we pointed out that a market is characterized by benevolence relationships between the participating agents. Accordingly, the organization model represented in figure 8.5 shows the isBenevolentTo relationships between the roles Seller and DirectoryService on one hand and Seller and Buyer on the other. This relationship

Table 8.2
The role model for Buyer

Role name	Buyer
Description	The Buyer role is played by a buyer organisation in B2B e-commerce.
Responsibilities	Identify alternative sellers. Create a RFQ. Send the RFQ to the sellers. Receive quotes from the sellers. Decide the seller from which to buy. Inform the sellers on the decision. Order the commodities from the chosen seller. Receive the commodities. Pay for the commodities.
Constraints	The deal achieved should be the best possible for the buyer. A seller offering the minimal price should be favored. A seller that is most trusted should be favored. Payment should be secure. Transporter should be reliable.

Table 8.3
The role model for Seller

Role name	Seller
Description	The Seller role is played by a seller organization in B2B e-commerce.
Responsibilities	Receive a request for quote. Form the quote. Send the quote to the buyer.
Constraints	Quote is binding for the seller. The seller should benefit from the price offered in the quote. Payment should be secure. Transporter should be reliable.

typically appears between the roles of a service provider and requester. It expresses that the service provider performs the service requested if it is able and willing to do so, but the service provider also has an option to refuse the service request. The organization model also represents that some responsibilities of the seller and buyer roles are performed by agents enacting their respective subroles Sales Representative and Procurement Representative.

We next move to the *conceptual information modeling viewpoint*. As explained in section 3.4, a domain model represents the types of domain entities of the problem domain and the relationships between them. The domain model of B2B e-commerce is represented in figure 8.6. The model represents the main domain entities in B2B e-commerce—RFQ, Quote, PurchaseOrder, and Confirmation—and their relationships with each other and with the relevant roles. There may be a

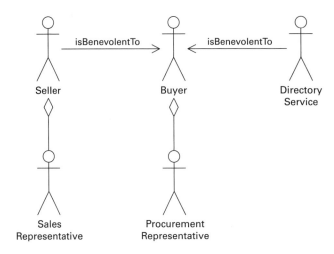

Figure 8.5
The organization model of B2B e-commerce

`PurchaseOrder` associated with an instance of `Quote`. There is always an `Invoice` related to the confirmed `PurchaseOrder`.

Having created the models necessary for the abstraction layer of computation-independent domain modeling, we move to the abstraction layer of platform-independent computational design. From the *viewpoint of computational interaction modeling*, we first map roles to agent types.

Although an agent model belongs to neither the ROADMAP nor RAP/AOR methodology, we present the agent model for the case study. In B2B e-commerce, both of the roles Seller and Buyer are performed by institutional agents—companies. The agent model of B2B e-commerce, which is depicted in figure 8.7, shows that each of the roles Buyer and Seller is mapped to the software agent type `TradeAgent` and human agent type `Person`. Why have these roles been mapped to just one software agent type? As you will see toward the end of this section, our design and implementation principles enable the roles Seller and Buyer both to be played by software agents of the same type. Figure 8.7 also shows that the multiagent system consists of two software agents and two people.

The agent model shown in figure 8.7 is combined with the agent acquaintance model. This model represents that a `TradeAgent` can interact with several other `TradeAgents` and one human agent at a time, whereas any `TradeAgent` can initiate an interaction with other `TradeAgents` and a human agent can initiate an interaction with a `TradeAgent`.

The knowledge model of the case study of B2B e-commerce is shown in figure 8.8, which is known as an *AOR agent diagram*. It reflects the *computational information*

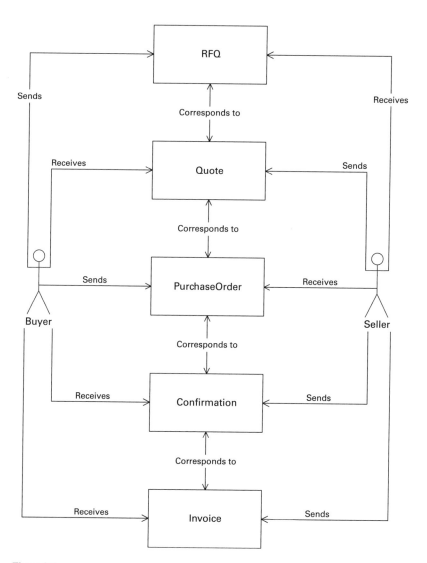

Figure 8.6
The domain model of B2B e-commerce

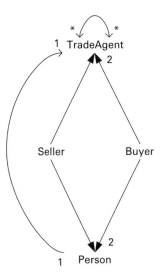

Figure 8.7
The agent and acquaintance models of B2B e-commerce

design viewpoint. The agent diagram first represents the institutional agents whose knowledge is modeled. An institutional agent is denoted by the agent type Organization. The diagram also shows that the institutional agents playing the roles Buyer and Seller contain internal agents of types Person and TradeAgent that act on behalf of the organization. The knowledge of the institutional agents is modeled by representing conceptual object types of the problem domain, as well as their relationships to the agent types and with each other. Objects of these types constitute the agents' common and private knowledge. The conceptual object types included in the knowledge model originate in the RosettaNet standard for B2B e-commerce. Just as in RosettaNet, RFQ and Quote, and PurchaseOrder and Confirmation of the domain model have been combined into single object types. Objects of types PurchaseOrder/Confirmation, RFQ/Quote, and Invoice are *shared* between institutional agents playing the roles Buyer and Seller. In addition to shared object types, there are *private* object types. An institutional agent playing the role Buyer has knowledge about institutional agents performing the role Seller and the product items sold by them. Similarly, an institutional agent playing the role Seller knows about its own product items. The private object types Seller, ProductItemOfSeller, and ProductItem are accordingly represented within agents playing the roles Buyer and Seller.

For some object types modeled in figure 8.8, attributes and predicates are defined. For example, an object of type QuoteLineItem in figure 8.8 satisfies one of the

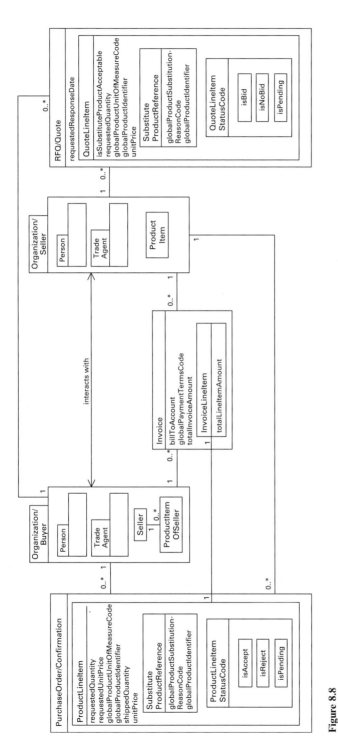

Figure 8.8

The agent diagram of B2B e-commerce. This figure appears in Taveter and Wagner 2005. Copyright 2009, IGI Global, www.igi-global.com. Posted by permission of the publisher.

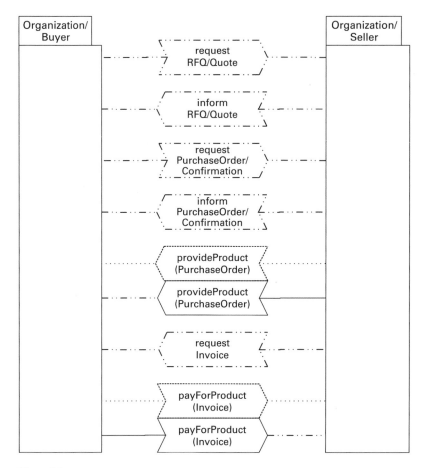

Figure 8.9
An interaction-frame diagram between Buyer and Seller. This figure appears in Taveter and Wagner 2005.
Copyright 2009, IGI Global, www.igi-global.com. Posted by permission of the publisher.

following *status predicates*: isBid, isNoBid, and isPending, and an object of type
ProductLineItem represented in the same figure is characterized by one of the
status predicates isAccept, isReject, and isPending.

We now move to the *computational interaction design viewpoint* where interactions
between agents are modeled. This has been done using AOR interaction-frame and
interaction-sequence diagrams. An interaction-frame diagram modeling the interactions between the institutional agents playing the roles Seller and Buyer is represented in figure 8.9.

An AOR interaction-sequence diagram, like the one shown in figure 8.10, depicts
(some part of) a prototypical instance of an interaction process. Figure 8.10 repre-

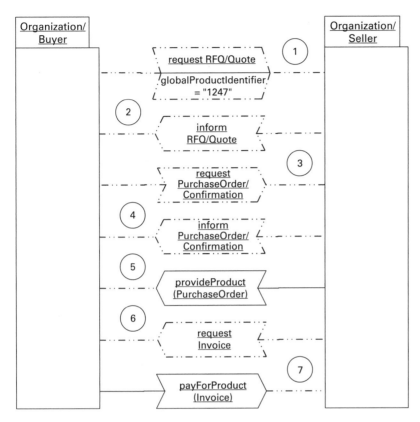

Figure 8.10
An interaction-sequence diagram between institutional agents. This figure appears in Taveter and Wagner 2005. Copyright 2009, IGI Global, www.igi-global.com. Posted by permission of the publisher.

sents the messages sent and actions performed between two concrete institutional agents, where the first agent purchases from the second one a product that is identified by the value "1247" of the attribute globalProductIdentifier.

Next, we present models of the *computational behavior design viewpoint*. In the original project, it was important to create behavior models that could be executed. Two kinds of behavior models have been created for our case study: scenarios and AOR behavior diagrams. As representative examples, we present behavior models for achieving a buyer's goal "Find deal" and a seller's goals "Receive RFQ," "Form quote," and "Send quote." The corresponding scenarios are represented in tables 8.4–8.9. They translate goals into activities, determine for each activity the condition of its performing, and show the agent types and roles, as well as resources involved in performing the activity. The scenarios denote for resources by "R" that the resource is read and by "W" that the resource is written. The scenarios shown in

Table 8.4
The scenario for achieving the "Find deal" goal

SCENARIO 1					
Goal		Find deal			
Initiator		Buyer			
Trigger		A request by an internal human agent			

DESCRIPTION					
Condition	Step	Activity	Agent types and roles	Resources	Quality goals
Repeat for each seller	1	Request and receive quotes (**Scenario 2**)	TradeAgent/Buyer, TradeAgent/Seller	RFQ/Quote (W, R), Seller (R), ProductItemOfSeller (R)	Timely processing
	2	Make decision	TradeAgent/Buyer	RFQ/Quote (R), Seller (R)	Best deal minimal price, maximal trust towards seller, timely processing
	3	Inform the winner	TradeAgent/Buyer, TradeAgent/Seller	RFQ/Quote (R), Seller (R)	Timely processing

Table 8.5
The scenario for achieving the "Request and receive quotes" goal

SCENARIO 2					
Goal		Request and receive quotes			
Initiator					
Trigger					

DESCRIPTION					
Condition	Step	Activity	Agent types and roles	Resources	Quality goals
	1	Create RFQ	TradeAgent/Buyer	RFQ/Quote (W), Seller (R)	Timely processing
	2	Fill RFQ with quote line items (**Scenario 3**)	TradeAgent/Buyer	RFQ/Quote (W), ProductItemOfSeller (R)	Timely processing
	3	Send RFQ	TradeAgent/Buyer, TradeAgent/Seller	RFQ/Quote (R)	Timely processing, secure communication
	4	Receive quote	TradeAgent/Buyer, TradeAgent/Seller	RFQ/Quote (W)	Timely processing, secure communication

Table 8.6
The scenario for achieving the "Insert quote line item into the RFQ" goal

SCENARIO 3					
Goal	Fill RFQ with quote line items				
Initiator					
Trigger					

DESCRIPTION					
Condition	Step	Activity	Agent types and roles	Resources	Quality goals
For each product	1	Insert the quote line item	TradeAgent/Buyer	RFQ/Quote (W), ProductItemOfSeller (R)	Timely processing

Table 8.7
The scenario for achieving the "Sell" goal

SCENARIO 4					
Goal	Sell				
Quality goals					
Initiator	Buyer				
Trigger	RFQ sent by the buyer				

DESCRIPTION					
Condition	Step	Activity	Agent types and roles	Resources	Quality goals
	1	Receive RFQ	TradeAgent/Seller, TradeAgent/Buyer	RFQ/Quote (W)	Timely processing
	2	Form quote (**Scenario 5**)	TradeAgent/Seller	RFQ/Quote (W), ProductItem (R)	Timely processing, best offer
Quote is approved by an internal human agent	3	Send quote	TradeAgent/Seller, TradeAgent/Buyer	RFQ/Quote (R)	Timely processing, quote is binding

Table 8.8
The scenario for achieving the "Form quote" goal

SCENARIO 5					
Goal					
Initiator					
Trigger					

DESCRIPTION					
Condition	Step	Activity	Agent types and roles	Resources	Quality goals
	1	Process product item (**Scenario 6**)	TradeAgent/Seller	RFQ/Quote (W), ProductItem (R)	Timely processing, best offer

Table 8.9
The scenario for processing a product item

SCENARIO 6					
Goal	Form quote				
Initiator					
Trigger					

DESCRIPTION					
Condition	Step	Activity	Agent types and roles	Resources	Quality goals
The product item is available in the quantity requested	1	The product item is to be bid which is registered in the quote	TradeAgent/Seller	RFQ/Quote (W), ProductItem (R)	Timely processing, best offer
The product item is not available in the quantity requested	1a	The product item is not to be bid which is registered in the quote	TradeAgent/Seller	RFQ/Quote (W), ProductItem (R)	Timely processing, best offer

Tables 8.4–8.9 have been derived from goal-based use cases, which were originally used in the research project.

Scenarios are turned into AOR behavior diagrams, which are more precise behavior models. The reader may wonder why we need precise behavior models that are attributed to organizations. The reason is that we chose an implementation approach where executable AOR behavior diagrams were transformed into equivalent XML-based representations that were then interpreted and executed by software agents representing the organizations involved. In our case study of automating B2B processes, machine-interpretable representations for business process types are crucial, because new business process types emerge and old ones frequently change.

As pointed out in section 7.6, AOR behavior diagrams enable the computational behavior modeling viewpoint to be combined in the same diagram with the computational information and interaction modeling viewpoints. This results in a single integrated behavior model. The AOR behavior diagram shown in figure 8.11 models the behavior of an agent performing the role Buyer in a procurement business process. According to the model, rule R1 is triggered by a human agent by performing a physical action of the type issueRFQ(?String ?Integer). This action is performed by mediation of a user interface of some kind. When triggered, rule R1 starts an activity of type "Find deal." This activity achieves the goal "Find deal" represented in the goal model in figure 8.3. A "Find deal" activity consists of a number of sequential subactivities, the types of which correspond to the subgoals modeled in figure 8.3. When this activity is invoked, the String and Integer arguments of the issueRFQ action, which contain the identifier of the product to be procured and the requested quantity, are assigned to the activity's parameters productCode and quantity.

Rule R2 specifies a forEach loop that executes an activity of type "Request and receive quote" for each instance of the object type Seller (not to be confused with the role Seller) satisfying the sellsProduct predicate that is evaluated with the product identifier as the parameter. A "Request and receive quote" activity is thus executed for each seller that sells the product to be procured. The activities in the forEach loop are executed in parallel, meaning that the next activity may be started before the previous ones are finished. This avoids deadlock situations—for example, when a seller does not respond with a quote.

Rule R3 within a subactivity of type "Create RFQ" creates an instance of RFQ/ Quote. This is followed by the creation of an association between the RFQ/Quote created and the corresponding object of type Seller. The association is needed for relating each seller to the quotes to be received.

Rule R4 included in a subsequent "Fill the RFQ" activity first retrieves the instance of ProductItemOfSeller, which describes the requested product item according to the seller's product identification system. It then starts an activity of type "Insert quote line item" with the instance of ProductItemOfSeller as a parameter and with the requested quantity as another parameter. Rule R5 included in the activity creates an instance of QuoteLineItem that describes within the quote the product to be procured. The variable assignments made when creating the QuoteLineItem are specified in the callout attached to the mental effect arrow.

Rule R6 included in an activity of type "Send RFQ" sends the newly created instance of RFQ/Quote to the enactor of the role Seller. As just one RFQ/Quote is sent to each seller, the instance is identified by the seller related to it. Rule R7 included in an activity of type "Receive quote" is triggered by receiving the quote from the enactor of Seller. Finally, rule R8, which is triggered by a nonaction event—time event—of type Timeout, starts an "Inform the winner" activity. Rule

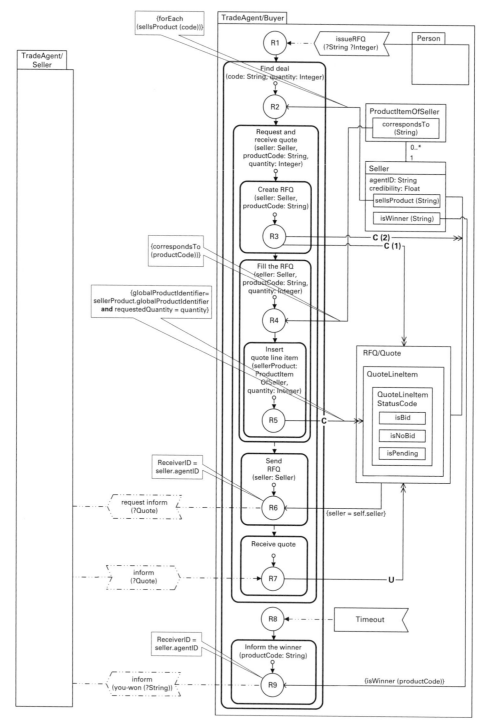

Figure 8.11
The behavior model for Buyer. This figure appears in Taveter and Wagner 2005. Copyright 2009, IGI Global, www.igi-global.com. Posted by permission of the publisher.

R9 included in this activity notifies the winner of the contract net, who is determined by evaluating the predicate isWinner.

The behavior of an agent performing the role Seller in a procurement business process is modeled in figure 8.12. Rule R1 is triggered by receiving the request for quote from an enactor of Buyer. Rule R2 specifies that upon the start of an enclosing activity of type "Form quote," its subactivity of type "Process product item" is performed for the instance of the object type QuoteLineItem belonging to the instance of RFQ/Quote received from the buyer. The subactivity "Process product item" checks the availability of the given product item that is specified by the input parameter item of type QuoteLineItem. If the product item corresponding to the instance of QuoteLineItem is available in the quantity requested, the status of the QuoteLineItem is updated to isBid. In the opposite case, the status of the QuoteLineItem is updated to isNoBid. Rule R4 specifies that, upon the end of an activity of type "Form quote" if the quote is approved by an internal human agent, an activity of type "Send quote" is performed. Rule R5 included in this activity sends the modified by bids instance of RFQ/Quote to the enactor of Buyer.

Quality goals are not explicitly represented in figures 8.11 and 8.12, because it is assumed that they have been *operationalized* by AOR behavior diagrams. For example, the predicate isWinner of the object type Seller modeled in figure 8.11 is required to consider both the price offered by a seller and the trustworthiness of the seller in making an automated decision of choosing from whom to buy a particular product.

In order to facilitate generation of XML-based representations of business process models, we have developed the corresponding XML schema, whose instances describe business process types in a machine-interpretable way. By using the schema, it is possible to represent business process types from different perspectives. For example, the models of the procurement business process type created in our case study are transformed into two XML-based representations that describe the procurement business process type from the perspectives of the roles Seller and Buyer.

In the prototype application, interorganizational business process types were described as AOR behavior diagrams by means of the Integrated Business Process Editor. The latter was developed as an extension to the CONE tool of VTT Information Technology. Figure 8.13 shows a snapshot of the model of the procurement business process type that was created using the editor. The model represented in the figure focuses on modeling the behavior of a Seller. The notation used by the CONE tool is the one that preceded the notation that we currently use for AOR behavior diagrams.

The prototype application is represented in figure 8.14. As figure 8.14 reflects, the XML-based representations of a business process type are automatically generated

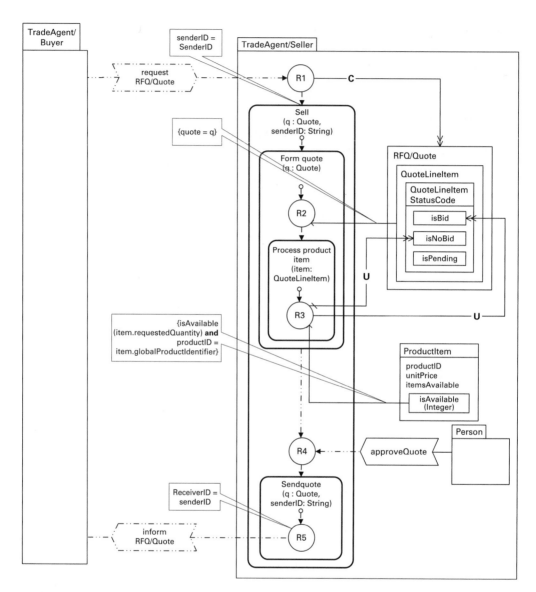

Figure 8.12
The behavior model for Seller. This figure appears in Taveter and Wagner 2005. Copyright 2009, IGI Global, www.igi-global.com. Posted by permission of the publisher.

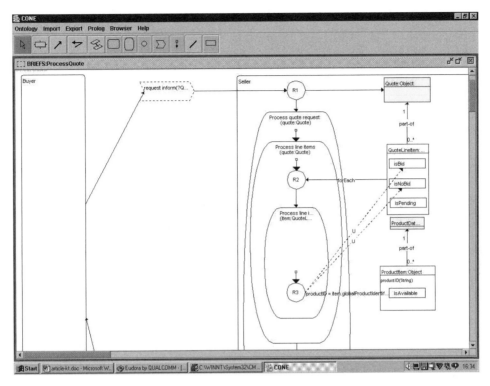

Figure 8.13
A part of the procurement business process type focusing on Seller modeled by the Integrated Business Process Editor. This figure appears in Taveter and Wagner 2005. Copyright 2009, IGI Global, www.igi-global.com. Posted by permission of the publisher.

from AOR behavior diagrams modeled by the Integrated Business Process Editor. Business process models to be executed include accessing enterprise systems of the company. Enterprise systems can include the Enterprise Resource Planning (ERP), Customer Relationship Management (CRM), and Enterprise Application Integration (EAI) systems shown in figure 8.14. Interfaces to them are presented as services to the Business Process Interpreter. The XML-based representation of a business process type is interpreted by the Business Process Interpreter, which works in cooperation with the software agent representing the corresponding party—an instance of `TradeAgent`. The latter has been implemented using the JADE agent platform, which was described in chapter 5.

Agents communicate with each other using messages in the Agent Communication Language (ACL) defined by FIPA. As figure 8.14 illustrates, an agent representing a party first invokes the Business Process Interpreter to read the description of the business process type, as requested by the agent's human user, and to create its

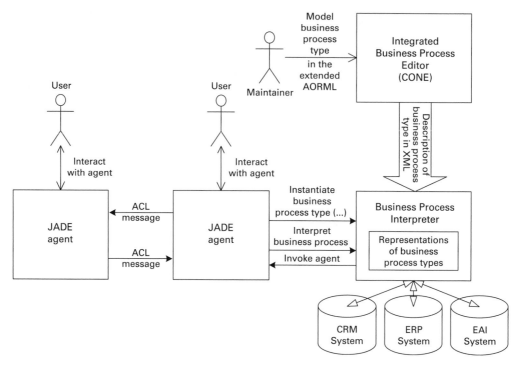

Figure 8.14
The business process automation system. This figure appears in Taveter and Wagner 2005. Copyright 2009, IGI Global, www.igi-global.com. Posted by permission of the publisher.

internal representation of the business process type. Thereafter, when the agent receives a message or "perceives" an input by a human user through the graphical user interface (GUI), the agent invokes the Business Process Interpreter to act according to the process type description. When the Business Process Interpreter acts, it in turn invokes the JADE agent and displays messages through the agent's GUI.

When evaluating quotes, the software agent—an instance of `TradeAgent`—representing the Buyer considers trust as another criterion in addition to price. This is needed to achieve the quality goal "Maximal trust toward seller" that is modeled in figure 8.3. Trust is determined by including in the behavior model of an agent performing the role Buyer in a procurement business process a rule that increases or decreases the weight of trustworthiness of a potential seller by considering its past behavior. A snapshot shown in figure 8.15 illustrates how the trustworthiness of sellers is considered by the prototype application. According to the snapshot, a quote with a higher price offered but whose bidder has a considerably higher credibility ranks better.

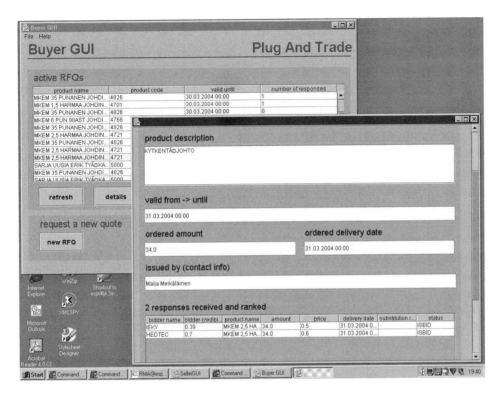

Figure 8.15
A snapshot of the Buyer's GUI of the procurement system (Taveter 2005)

8.2   Manufacturing

The business landscape is changing everywhere. New business models emerge in all areas. They span from offshore manufacturing to the outsourcing of software development and services. Subcontracting is a way that the countries newly admitted to the European Union are able to participate in European manufacturing projects. The case study in this section deals with the Tallinn Ceramics Factory Ltd. located in Tallinn, Estonia. Introducing new business models is already reality at the Tallinn Ceramics Factory, because a large portion of the orders received by it are subcontracted orders for mug handles and stove tiles for fireplaces from Sweden and other countries. To comply with new business models, manufacturing processes in many cases need to be re-engineered. This is facilitated by modeling and especially by simulation of the manufacturing processes.

In this section, a combination of the Tropos and RAP/AOR modeling methodologies is applied to the modeling and simulation of manufacturing processes of

Tallinn Ceramics Factory. An agent-oriented approach was chosen for two reasons. First, primary components of any factory are communicating and interacting agents, such as workers and robots. Second, an agent-oriented modeling approach lends itself easily to simulation. In particular, the models of the problem domain developed by following the RAP/AOR methodology can be quite straightforwardly turned into the implementation constructs of the simulation environment based on the JADE agent platform. Overviews of the Tropos and RAP/AOR methodologies were provided in sections 7.4 and 7.6, respectively. The JADE agent platform was described in chapter 5.

The core of manufacturing processes of any factory lies in the scheduling of production operations. The purpose of applying the scheduling method briefly described below was re-engineering—improving the existing manufacturing processes of the factory.

The job-shop scheduling problem or factory scheduling problem can be defined as one of coordinating sequences of manufacturing operations for multiple orders so as to

• obey the temporal restrictions of production processes and the capacity limitations of a set of shared resources (e.g., machines), and

• achieve a satisfactory compromise with respect to a myriad of conflicting preferential constraints (e.g., meeting due dates, minimizing work-in-progress, and so on).

Two kinds of scheduling can be distinguished:

• *predictive scheduling*, which concerns an ability to effectively predict shop behavior through the generation of production plans that reflect both the full complexity of the factory environment and the stated objectives of the organization, and

• *reactive scheduling*, which concerns an ability to intelligently react to changing circumstances, as the shop floor is a dynamic environment where unexpected events (e.g., machine breakdowns and quality control inspection failures) continually force changes to planned activities.

The simplest reactive methods invoked in response to changed circumstances are the Right Shifter and Left Shifter. The *Right Shifter* implements a reactive method that resolves conflicts by simply pushing the scheduled execution times of designated manufacturing activities forward in time. The *Left Shifter* provides a similar method that pulls manufacturing activities backwards in time (i.e., closer to being performed) to the extent that current resource availability and temporal process constraints will permit.

We next describe modeling of the ceramics factory from the interaction, information, and behavior aspects of the viewpoint framework considering the scheduling principles presented earlier. We distinguish between the abstraction layers of computation-independent domain modeling and platform-independent computational design.

The models of the *conceptual interaction modeling viewpoint* are Tropos actor diagrams, as explained in section 7.4. An actor diagram for the manufacturing case study is depicted in figure 8.16. The actors represented in the diagram are *organizational roles* that are played by institutional agents.

The model reflects that an institutional agent playing the Customer role depends on the institutional agent playing the Sales Department role for achieving its goal `Product set produced`. This dependency is modeled as a goal dependency rather than a task dependency, because the Customer is interested in achieving its goal but does not care *how* the goal is achieved. The Customer also depends on the Sales Department for achieving its `Smooth service` soft goal and for providing the `Proposal` information resource. The Sales Department, in turn, depends on the Customer for the `Payment` resource and for achieving the `Customer happy` soft goal.

The Sales Department depends on the Production Department for performing the `Produce product set` task. This dependency is modeled as a task dependency rather than a goal dependency, because the Sales Department requests the Production Department to produce the product set of a specific type based on its discussions with the Customer. That product type uniquely determines the sequence of production operations required for producing the product set. The Sales Department also depends on the Production Department for information on the predicted due date of accomplishing a product set, which is modeled as a resource dependency.

An institutional agent playing the Factory Management role relies on the Sales Department for achieving the `Market share maintained and increased` soft goal and on the Production Department for achieving the `Orders satisfied on time` soft goal.

An institutional agent playing the Production Department role depends on individual institutional agents playing the Resource Unit role for performing specific production operations. For example, the Production Department depends on the Moldmaking Unit for performing the `Make and provide molds` task and on the Combustion Unit for performing the initial combustion, post-glazing combustion, and post-decoration combustion production operations, which have not been specified in figure 8.16. Moldmaking Unit and Combustion Unit form subclasses of Resource Unit. For optimal scheduling, the Production Department also depends on the Resource Unit for information on the capacities, machine breakdowns, and so forth of manufacturing resources, which is modeled as a resource dependency.

The model shown in figure 8.16 reflects that the Production Department depends on the Completed Production Store, which is another subtype of Resource Unit, for

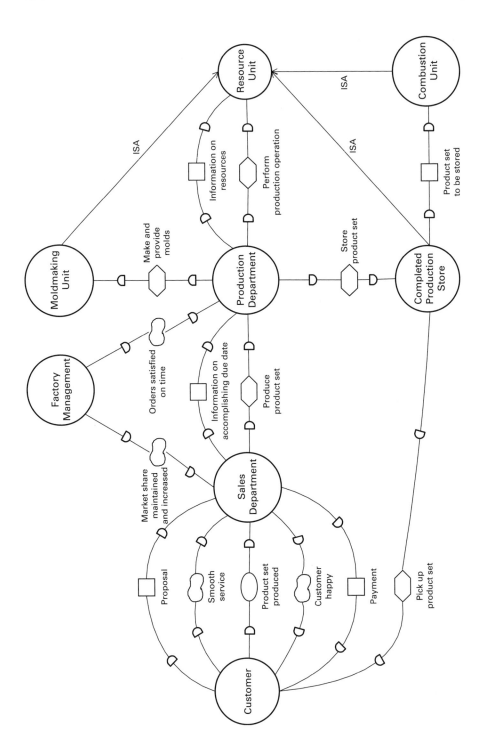

Figure 8.16
An actor diagram for the manufacturing case study

performing the `Store product set` task. The Completed Production Store, in turn, depends on the Customer for the `Pick up product set` task.

The *conceptual behavior modeling viewpoint* is represented by Tropos goal diagrams, which provide the rationale for modeling agent behaviors. An example goal diagram for an institutional agent playing the Production Department role is depicted in figure 8.17.

According to the model, the Production Department satisfies the `Produce product set` task dependency by performing an internal `Have product set produced` task. This task consists of nine subtasks, which have in turn been elaborated into a number of lower-level subtasks. The first five subtasks, `Create product set`, `Instantiate production plan`, `Schedule production order`, `Propose accomplishing due date`, and `Receive confirmation or rejection`, initiate a manufacturing process. A `Propose accomplishing due date` subtask, which is linked with the `Information on accomplishing due date` resource dependency, serves to provide the Sales Department with information on the predicted due date of accomplishing a product set. A `Schedule production order` subtask reflects that the due date of accomplishing the order is found by actually scheduling the order. A `Receive confirmation or rejection` subtask reflects that the order with a proposed due date may be accepted or rejected by the customer. The `Receive rejection` subtask of `Receive confirmation or rejection` express that if the order is rejected, the production operations scheduled for its accomplishment will be canceled.

If the order is accepted, the next four subtasks—`Commit`, `Manage order`, `Have product set stored`, and `Inform on order completion`—will be performed. A `Commit` subtask expresses that the Production Department commits toward the Sales Department to have a product set produced. A `Manage order` subtask is connected with the `Perform production operation` task dependency on the Resource Unit. This generic dependency and the subtasks associated with it are refined for two specific resource units: Moldmaking Unit and Completed Production Store. A `Manage moldmaking` subtask is connected with the `Make and provide molds` task dependency on the Moldmaking Unit. Similarly, a `Have product set stored` subtask is associated with the `Store product set` task dependency on the Completed Production Store. A `Check molds` subtask is linked with the `Information on molds` resource dependency on the Moldmaking Unit to reflect that this kind of information is required for performing the task. Similarly, a `Receive report on storing product set` subtask is related to the `Information on completed product sets` resource dependency on the Completed Production Store.

The model includes a `Schedule production operation` subtask of `Manage order`, which is associated with the `Minimal tardiness` soft goal. This soft goal characterizes the way a production operation should be scheduled. Another

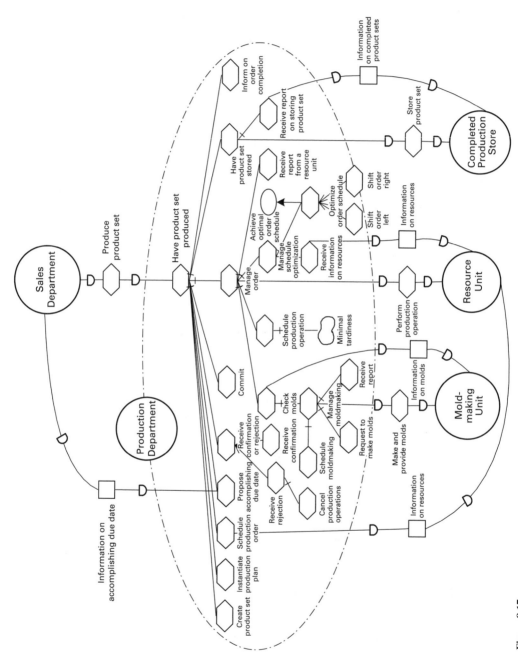

Figure 8.17
A goal diagram for Production Department

important subtask of `Manage order` is `Manage schedule optimization`. It, in turn, consists of `Receive information on resources` and `Optimize order schedule` subtasks. As the information on resources, including their capacity changes, is provided by different institutional agents playing the Resource Unit role, a `Receive information on resources` subtask is connected with the resource dependency `Information on resources`. As the model reflects, an `Optimize order schedule` subtask serves to achieve the `Optimal order schedule` goal. Next-level subtasks of `Optimize order schedule`—namely, `Shift order left` and `Shift order right`—reflect the two basic schedule adjustment methods that were described previously.

The *conceptual information modeling viewpoint* is captured by a conceptual information model. The Tropos methodology represents a conceptual information model as resources in goal models. We now elaborate on Tropos by providing a domain model. The domain model represented in figure 8.18 describes the manufacturing domain of the ceramics factory. Representing the information aspect of the viewpoint framework for the focus organization(s) can be regarded as creating an ontology. The ontology—the conceptual information model—of the ceramics factory has been developed according to the principles of the OZONE (O3 = Object-Oriented OPIS, where OPIS stands for Opportunistic Intelligent Scheduler) scheduling ontology. The OZONE scheduling ontology can be described as a meta-model of the scheduling domain. It uses the notions of `Resource`, `ProductionOrder`, `ProductionOperation`, and `ProductSet` to represent the manufacturing environment in which scheduling takes place. More specifically, scheduling is defined in OZONE as a process of feasibly synchronizing the use of resources by production operations to satisfy production orders over time. A production order is an input request for one or more product sets that designates the commodities or services required. Satisfaction of production orders is accomplished by performing production operations. A production operation is a process that uses resources to produce commodities or provide services. The use of resources and the performing of production operations are restricted by a set of constraints.

Having covered conceptual domain modeling, we next move to platform-independent computational design. We do this by mapping the modeling constructs of the conceptual domain modeling layer to those of the platform-independent computational design layer. The platform-independent computational design uses the models from the RAP/AOR methodology.

The *viewpoint of platform-independent interaction design* addresses interaction modeling. Before interactions can be modeled, agent types need to be decided. The institutional agent `CeramicsFactory` belongs to the agent type `Organization`. The agent `CeramicsFactory` consists of instances of the institutional agent type `OrganizationUnit`, representing departments and other internal units of the

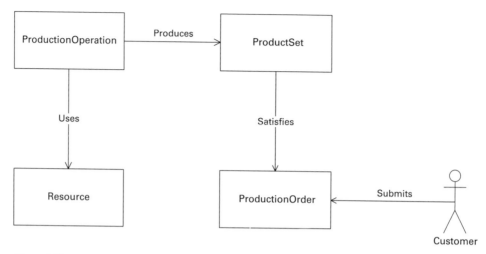

Figure 8.18
The domain model of the ceramics factory

factory. An institutional agent playing the Customer role is also of the `Organiza-tion` type. The type of an agent and the role played by it are jointly represented with the `AgentType/Role` notation.

Interactions between the institutional agents related to the ceramics factory are modeled in the *interaction model* in figure 8.19. Interactions are rooted in dependencies represented by the Tropos actor diagram of conceptual interaction modeling, which is depicted in figure 8.16. A set of interactions realizes a goal dependency as a *goal delegation*, a task dependency as a *task delegation*, and a resource dependency as a *resource acquisition*. For example, the resource dependency between the Customer and Sales Department for the `Proposal` information resource modeled in figure 8.16 becomes the acquisition of that resource by the Customer from the Sales Department.

Most of the communicative action event types represented in the interaction model in figure 8.19 belong to one of two message types: `request`, by which a sender requests the receiver to perform a communicative or physical action or both of them; and `inform`, which identifies a communicative action. In addition, there are messages of types `propose`, `accept-proposal`, and `reject-proposal` with obvious meanings.

The interaction model represented in figure 8.19 consists of several interaction frames. The first interaction frame is between the institutional agents playing the roles Customer and Sales Department. It is based on the `Product set produced` goal dependency shown in figure 8.16 by modeling the delegation of the goal by the Customer to the Sales Department. The interaction frame under discussion starts with a communicative action event type representing a request by the Customer to

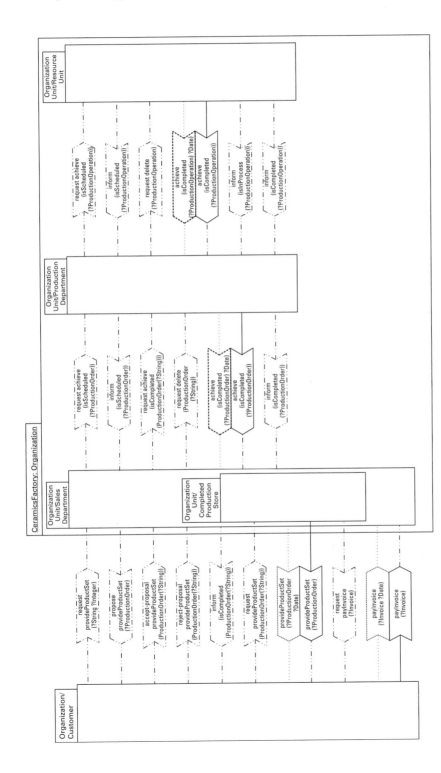

Figure 8.19
The interaction model of the ceramics factory.

provide it with the product set that is identified by the product code (?String) and quantity required (?Integer). The following three communicative action event types of this interaction frame comply with the Proposal resource dependency between the roles Customer and Sales Department in the actor diagram in figure 8.16. They reflect the acquisition of the Proposal resource by the Customer. The acquisition is modeled by a proposal by the Sales Department to provide the Customer with the product set according to the production order created by the Sales Department and its acceptance or rejection by the Customer. The instance of the production order, which includes a specific due date, is described by the ?ProductionOrder data element of the corresponding communicative action event. If the proposal is accepted, the Sales Department commits on behalf of the Ceramics-Factory toward the Customer to provide it by the due date with the product set defined by the production order. A commitment of this type is satisfied by an action event of the type provideProductSet(?ProductionOrder), which is coupled with the corresponding commitment type. As explained in section 7.6, this commitment is viewed as a claim by the Customer. After the product set has been produced, the Sales Department first informs the Customer about the completion and the Customer then issues to the Completed Production Store (an internal institutional agent of the Sales Department) a request to release the product set identified by the corresponding ProductionOrder. The Completed Production Store provides the Customer with the product set in question, which reflects the Pick up product set task dependency and the corresponding task delegation between the Completed Production Store and Customer.

The interactions of the interaction frame remaining to be analyzed are based on the dependency for the Payment resource between the Sales Department and Customer. They realize the acquisition of the Payment resource by the Sales Department. As is reflected by figure 8.19, the Sales Department first sends to the Customer the invoice (?Invoice). This is accompanied by creating a claim for the Sales Department against the Customer that it would pay for the product set according to the invoice by a certain date. The claim is satisfied by paying for the product set by the Customer.

The interaction frame between the Sales Department and Production Department models how the Production Department manufactures the products for the Sales Department. The types of interactions included in the interaction frame realize the Produce product set task dependency between the Sales Department and Production Department, which is modeled in figure 8.16. These interactions reflect the delegation of the Produce product set task by the Sales Department to the Production Department.

The first two communicative action event types of the interaction frame model the acquisition of the Information on accomplishing due date resource by the Sales

Department. The resource dependency between the Sales Department and Production Department involving that type of resource is represented in figure 8.16. The information about the predicted due date of accomplishing a production order is obtained by requesting the Production Department to schedule the production order. Accordingly, the first communicative action event type of the interaction frame models a request by the Sales Department to the Production Department to schedule the production order that is described by the `?ProductionOrder` data element of the action event. Because neither scheduling a production order nor producing a product set according to it can be immediately perceived by the Sales Department, both are modeled as making true the respective status predicates `isScheduled` and `isCompleted` of the corresponding instance of `ProductionOrder`.

After the Production Department has returned the scheduled production order to the Sales Department, it receives from the Sales Department a request to either complete or delete the production order. In the first case, a commitment/claim of the type `(achieve(isCompleted(?ProductionOrder) ?Date)` is formed between the Production Department and Sales Department. The satisfaction of this commitment/claim is expressed by the corresponding `achieve`-construct type which expresses a condition to be achieved.

The interaction frame between the Production Department and the Resource Unit in figure 8.19 is based on the `Information on resources` resource dependency and `Perform production operation` task dependency between the Production Department and Resource Unit roles, as modeled in figure 8.16. By means of interactions of the types included in the interaction frame, the Production Department delegates the tasks of performing production operations to the corresponding resource units and acquires from the resource units information on progress and scheduling conflicts detected.

The first communicative action event type between the Production Department and Resource Unit models a request by the Production Department to schedule the production operation that is described by the `?ProductionOperation` data element of the action event. In addition to initial scheduling of a production operation, a request of this type is also sent if a time conflict in the schedule is detected within the Production Department.[3] The second message type in the interaction frame models the scheduling confirmation by the Resource Unit. The third message type represents a request to delete the scheduled production operation described by `?ProductionOperation`. A message of this type is sent only if the production order including the production operation to be deleted has been rejected by the Customer.

---

3. This situation is represented by the same interaction frame, because interaction-frame diagrams do not model the order in which action events of specified types occur.

Messages of the types inform(isScheduled(?ProductionOperation)), inform(isInProcess (?ProductionOperation)), and inform(isCompleted (?ProductionOperation)) inform the Production Department about the status changes of the production operation described by ?ProductionOperation. A message of the type inform(isCompleted (?ProductionOperation)) may trigger rescheduling of the remaining production operations required to satisfy the production order by pushing them forward or backward in time when the production operation is completed later or earlier than scheduled.

The viewpoint of *platform-independent computational information design* is for representing the knowledge for the agents of the simulation system. The knowledge model of the simulation system is represented as an agent diagram in figure 8.20. The knowledge model refines the domain model for the manufacturing domain represented in figure 8.18. It describes object types of the ceramics factory and their relationships and ascribes them as knowledge items to agents of the corresponding types. In the knowledge model, the concept ProductionOrder of the domain model is represented by the object type ProductionOrder. Knowledge about ProductionOrders is shared between the agent CeramicsFactory and agents of type Organization/Customer. A ProductionOrder is characterized by a number of attributes and the status predicate isCompleted. The most important attributes are releaseTime, dueTime, productCode, and quantity. The attributes releaseTime and dueTime are respectively the earliest and latest time when the production operations for producing the product set defined by the ProductionOrder can start and end. The attributes productCode and quantity respectively specify the type and number of the products in the product set requested. The internal representation of the object type ProductionOrder within the agent CeramicsFactory satisfies one of the following status predicates: isPreliminary, isScheduled, isProposed, isAccepted, isRejected, or isDelivered. The internal representation is required because these status predicates are relevant only from the perspective of the factory.

In addition to the object type ProductionOrder, there is another shared object type Invoice. Knowledge of its instances is shared between the CeramicsFactory and agents of type Organization/Customer. The object type Invoice contains attributes orderID, productCode, quantity, and price, among others. In addition, its internal representation within the OrganizationUnit/Sales Department has the status predicates isPreliminary, isSent, and isPaid, which are relevant only for the Sales Department of the factory.

The type of the product requested by the customer is modeled by the object type ProductType. An instance of ProductType is identified by its attributes productName (e.g., "coffee cup Kirke") and productCode (e.g., "22882"). The internal representation of the object type ProductType within the OrganizationUnit/Production Department differs from its base object type by a number of relation-

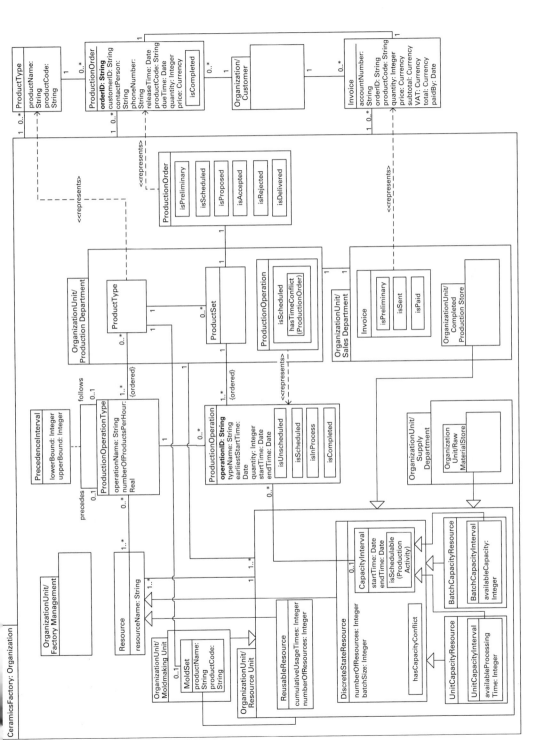

Figure 8.20

The knowledge model of the ceramics factory. This figure appears in Taveter 2006b. Copyright 2009, IGI Global, www.igi-global.com. Posted by permission of the publisher.

ships to other object types. Among them, an ordered sequence of instances of ProductionOperationType associated with a ProductType defines manufacturing operations required for producing products of the corresponding type. An instance of ProductionOperationType is characterized by the name of the manufacturing operation type (operationName) and the average speed of performing an operation of the corresponding type (numberOfProductsPerHour). The latter includes the time required for setting up the resources before a ProductionOperation of the given type can actually start. This attribute is required for predictive scheduling. There are associations of type PrecedenceInterval between instances of ProductionOperationType. Each association specifies the lower bound and upper bound of the temporal separation between production operations of two types. The associations of type PrecedenceInterval are intended to provide a basis for describing generic manufacturing processes, defining sets of possible sequences of manufacturing operations.

Specific sets of products to be produced to satisfy production orders are represented as instances of the object type ProductSet, which corresponds to the concept ProductSet of the domain model. Each ProductSet is associated with an ordered sequence of instances of ProductionOperation, in which each ProductionOperation belongs to the corresponding ProductionOperationType.

The object type ProductionOperation corresponds to the concept ProductionOperation in the domain model. A ProductionOperation can have the status isUnscheduled, isScheduled, isInProcess, or isCompleted. An instance of ProductionOperation is characterized by the following attributes: activityID, typeName, earliestStartTime, quantity, startTime, and endTime. The identifying attribute operationID contains the identifier of the production operation, which is automatically assigned upon creation of the corresponding object. The action of scheduling a ProductionOperation results in determining values for the attributes startTime and endTime. The attribute earliestStartTime indicates the earliest time at which the given ProductionOperation can be started, considering the endTime of the previous production operation scheduled and the releaseTime of the ProductionOrder. The object type ProductionOperation has a specific internal representation within the OrganizationUnit/Production Department. It refines the status predicate isScheduled by the internal predicate hasTimeConflict(ProductionOrder), because a time conflict between scheduled activities can be detected only within the OrganizationUnit/Production Department. The predicate hasTimeConflict (ProductionOrder) can be defined using the OCL.

The notion Resource of the domain model is reflected in the knowledge model by the object type Resource. Each institutional agent of type OrganizationUnit/ Resource Unit has knowledge about objects belonging to at least one of the

Resource's subtypes `ReusableResource` and `DiscreteStateResource`. A `ReusableResource`, like a set of ceramic molds, is a resource whose capacity becomes available for reuse after the `ProductionOperation` to which it has been allocated finishes. As Figure 8.20 reflects, an instance of `ReusableResource` is characterized by two attributes: `cumulativeUsageTimes` and `numberOfResources` with obvious meaning. `DiscreteStateResource` is a resource like a worker or a kiln whose availability is a function of some discrete set of possible state values (e.g., *idle* and *busy*). Each such resource is characterized by the attributes `numberOfResources` and `batchSize`. The latter is the number of products that the resource can process simultaneously.

The capacity of a resource is represented as an ordered sequence of intervals like workshifts. Each interval is represented with the object type `CapacityInterval`. Such an interval indicates the instances of `ProductionOperation` that are anticipated to be consuming capacity within its temporal scope and the capacity that remains available. The specializations of `CapacityInterval`, not shown in the figure, are `WorkMonth`, `WorkWeek`, and `WorkShift`, which were implemented in the simulation environment. Successful scheduling results in attaching a `CapacityInterval` to one or more instances of `ProductionOperation`. In order to determine whether a `CapacityInterval` can be allocated to the given `ProductionOperation`, the object type `CapacityInterval` possesses the predicate `isSchedulable(ProductionOperation)`. There are two versions of this predicate, which are defined for the `CapacityInterval`'s two subtypes `UnitCapacityInterval` and `BatchCapacityInterval`. They are included in the respective two subtypes of `DiscreteStateResource`: `UnitCapacityResource` and `BatchCapacityResource`, where a `UnitCapacityResource`, like a worker, can process only one product at a time; that is, its `batchSize` is 1, but a `BatchCapacityResource`, like a kiln, can process simultaneously up to `batchSize` products. The available capacity of a `UnitCapacityInterval` is characterized by the attribute `availableProcessingTime` (e.g., per work shift); the available capacity of a `BatchCapacityInterval` is represented by the attribute `availableCapacity`, which describes the number of products that the resource is capable of processing at a time. The predicates `isSchedulable(ProductionOperation)` for the object types `UnitCapacityInterval` and `BatchCapacityInterval` are defined using OCL.

The modeling viewpoint of *platform-independent computational behavior design* addresses the modeling of what functions the agent has to perform, as well as modeling when, how, and under what conditions work has to be done. This viewpoint for the manufacturing case study has been captured by AOR behavior diagrams. For example, the AOR behavior diagram for the `OrganizationUnit/ Production Department` agent type represented in figure 8.21 is based on the Tropos goal model depicted in figure 8.17.

In the AOR behavior diagram of figure 8.21, an activity of type "Process production order" is started by rule R19 in response to receiving a message containing a request to schedule a production order. As is shown in the figure, an activity of type "Process production order" consists of sequential subactivities reflecting the corresponding internal tasks modeled in the Tropos goal diagram in figure 8.17. Only the activity type "Schedule production order" is refined in figure 8.21. Rule R23 included in this activity type specifies a forEach loop, where upon the start of an activity of type "Schedule production order," its subactivity of type "Schedule production operation" is performed for each object for which the precondition shown in the callout is true. This precondition makes sure that activities of type "Schedule production operation" are performed only for the production operations associated with the given production order, which is identified by the value of the input parameter order. In addition, the expression isNextActivity(order) ensures the scheduling of production operations in the correct order.

The subactivity "Request scheduling" in figure 8.21 sends an appropriate request while the subactivity "Register scheduling" waits for and registers the scheduling of the production operation. When a time conflict is detected, a production order is rescheduled in a similar way that pushes all the production operations included in it forward in time.

AOR behavior diagrams can be transformed into the programming constructs of the JADE agent platform. This is how a simulation environment for the ceramics factory was designed and implemented.

For performing simulation experiments, an onsite survey was first performed at Tallinn Ceramics Factory. In the survey, the average speeds of performing production operations of different types, as well as the minimal precedence intervals required between the operations, were found and recorded. These values were used in simulation experiments.

The simulation environment lends itself to both predictive and reactive scheduling. Table 8.10 represents a production schedule for producing a product set of type "Molded ceramic product 22882." The production schedule reflects that kilns have a specific work cycle because of the requirements for cleanliness and safety—they are in operation on Mondays, Wednesdays, and Fridays. Table 8.10 shows the start and end times of production operations before and after detecting two time conflicts within the OrganizationUnit/Production Department. As the table reflects, the scheduled execution times of the "Initial elaboration" and "Painting" production operations have been pushed forward in time because their preceding production operations have taken more time than had been initially scheduled. In a similar manner, reactions to the changes in the number of available resources could be simulated. Note that because of the requirement to warrant a homogeneous quality of ceramic products in a product set, a production operation—once started on a product set—should be finished on the same day.

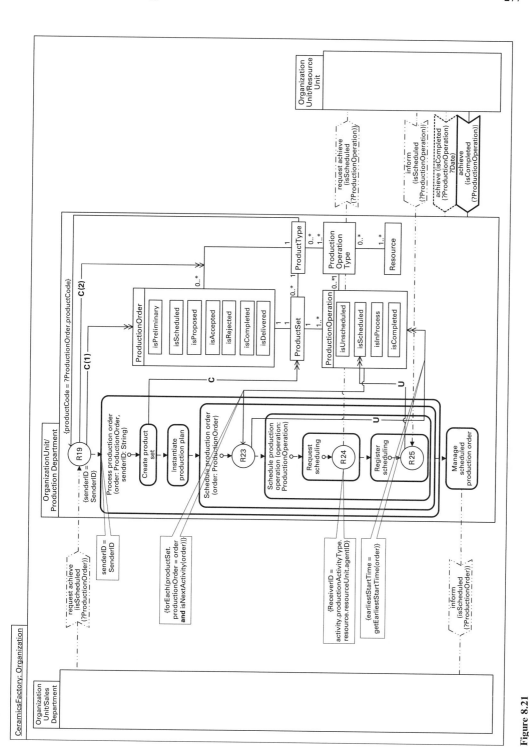

Figure 8.21

Table 8.10
A schedule for the production process of the "Molded ceramic product 22882" product set before and after the right shift (Taveter 2006b)

Production operation	Start time	End time	New start time	New end time
Molding	Mon Aug 29 08:00	Mon Aug 29 12:32	Mon Aug 29 08:00	Mon Aug 29 12:53
Initial elaboration	Tue Aug 30 12:33	Tue Aug 30 13:05	Tue Aug 30 12:54	Tue Aug 30 13:26
Engobe painting	Mon Sep 05 08:00	Mon Sep 05 13:20	Mon Sep 05 08:00	Mon Sep 05 13:42
Initial combustion	Wed Sep 07 08:00	Wed Sep 07 16:00	Wed Sep 07 08:00	Wed Sep 07 16:00
Elaboration	Fri Sep 09 08:00	Fri Sep 09 08:32	Fri Sep 09 08:00	Fri Sep 09 08:37
Painting	Fri Sep 09 08:33	Fri Sep 09 11:53	Fri Sep 09 08:38	Fri Sep 09 11:58
Glazing	Mon Sep 12 08:00	Mon Sep 12 13:20	Mon Sep 12 08:00	Mon Sep 12 13:20
Post-glazing combustion	Wed Sep 14 08:00	Wed Sep 14 16:00	Wed Sep 14 08:00	Wed Sep 14 16:00
Decoration	Fri Sep 16 08:00	Fri Sep 16 10:00	Fri Sep 16 08:00	Fri Sep 16 10:00
Post-decoration combustion	Mon Sep 19 08:00	Mon Sep 19 09:30	Mon Sep 19 08:00	Mon Sep 19 09:30
Packaging	Tue Sep 20 09:31	Tue Sep 20 10:19	Tue Sep 20 09:31	Tue Sep 20 10:19

A snapshot of the simulation environment is given in figure 8.22. The snapshot shows the user interfaces for the agent representing the Customer and the agents of the Production Department and several Resource Units of the factory.

8.3 Background

B2B e-commerce was proposed as an application area for agent technology in 1996 by Jennings et al. (1996). They used agents for negotiating and information sharing between e-commerce parties.

Blake (2002) identifies the following areas where agents can be applied in B2B e-commerce: strategic sourcing (requisition and vendor selection), electronic procurement, supply-chain and workflow automation, and supplier relationship management.

Agent as a generic modeling abstraction also appears in the Architecture of the World Wide Web (WWW) proposed in (W3C 2003). It defines an agent as a person or a piece of software acting on the WWW information space on behalf of a person, entity, or process.

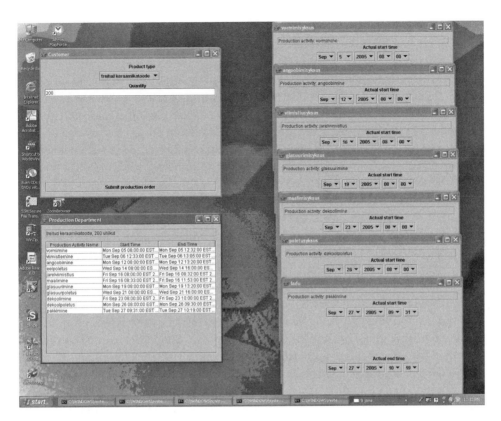

Figure 8.22
A snapshot of the simulation environment. This figure appears in Taveter and Wagner 2006. Copyright 2009, IGI Global, www.igi-global.com. Posted by permission of the publisher.

During the last decade, standards for B2B e-commerce have been proposed for various industry areas, such as RosettaNet (http://www.rosettanet.org) for electronics and information and communication technology industries and papiNet (http://www.papinet.org) for forest and paper industries. An industry-independent standard, ebXML (Electronic Business using eXtensible Markup Language, http://www.ebxml.org) has been proposed by the Organization for the Advancement of Structured Information Standards (OASIS). The same organization has also proposed a standard for dynamic discovery of Web Services—UDDI (http://www.uddi.org). There are also standard proposals for business process modeling, such as BPMN (http://www.bpmn.org) and XPDL (http://wfmc.org/xpdl.html). Even though the standard proposals mentioned do not explicitly employ the notion of agent, they could benefit from agent-oriented modeling.

The Plug-and-Trade Business-to-Business electronic commerce (Plug-and-Trade B2B) project described in section 8.1 was conducted at the Technical Research

Centre of Finland in 2003–2004. Three major Finnish companies participated in the project. An interesting feature of the project not addressed in section 8.1 was the usage of "internal" Web services for providing the software agents with uniform interfaces to enterprise systems of the company.

The case study of B2B e-commerce explained in this chapter was first presented by Taveter (2004b). Two other publications have focused on different aspects of the case study: Taveter 2005a, on representing and reasoning about trust by agents, and Taveter 2006a, on the markup language interpreted by agents. The markup language is represented as an XML Schema (http://www.w3.org/XML/Schema). The modeling aspects of the case study have been treated by Taveter and Wagner (2005). The CONE tool, which forms the basis for the business process modeling tool used in the case study, has been described by Taveter (2005b). Taveter (2005a) complemented the original RAP/AOR models of the B2B e-commerce domain by goal and role models of ROADMAP. The goal models have been influenced by similar goal models presented by Rahwan, Juan, and Sterling (2006).

The subject of the manufacturing case study overviewed in this chapter—Tallinn Ceramics Factory—is described on its Web page http://www.keraamikatehas.ee. The term "modeling by simulation" for manufacturing systems was proposed by Tamm, Puusepp, and Tavast (1987) two decades ago. Simulation can be considered a method for implementing a model over time (Smith 1998). Rothwell and Kazanas (1997) have defined a simulation as an "artificial representation of real conditions." Agent-based simulation of production environments has been applied by, for example, Raffel (2005) for designing Automatically Guided Vehicle (AGV) Transport Systems and by Labarthe et al. (2003) for simulation of supply chains. Tools for simulation of manufacturing processes have been proposed by Parunak, Baker, and Clark (1997) and Vrba (2003).

A general scheduling solution utilized in the manufacturing case study described in this chapter is based on the works by Ow, Smith, and Howie (1988); Smith et al. (1990); and Smith (1995); the method proposed in them can be naturally modeled in an agent-oriented way and simulated by software agents.

The OZONE scheduling ontology, which forms the foundation for the domain model of the ceramics factory modeled and simulated, was proposed by Smith and Becker (1997).

The transformation of goal, task, and resource dependency into the respective goal and task delegation and resource acquisition has been proposed by Guizzardi (2006).

The case study of modeling and simulation of the ceramics factory described in this chapter was introduced by Taveter and Hääl (2002). It was described in more detail by Taveter (2004a and 2006b).

9 Intelligent Lifestyle Applications

The previous chapter showed how agent-oriented modeling could be applied in an industry setting. This chapter looks at agent-oriented modeling in a different context: the intelligent home domain. The case studies in this chapter are less mature, and were developed not in response to a direct demand for a piece of software, but for a variety of research and teaching purposes.

The chapter is organized as follows. Section 9.1 discusses some agent-oriented models that would be suitable for an intelligent home. Leon has found over several years of teaching that a smart home works well as a domain for student projects. The two main examples shown in this section are an agent greeting scenario and an intruder handling scenario, which have been expanded into a set of models. Parts of the greeting and intruder detection scenarios have been prototyped in a software engineering student team project. Section 9.2 discusses agent-oriented models for a device for mediating intimacy, an example arising from a research project. The models facilitated interesting conversations between the members of the research team who had widely varying technical backgrounds. The use of socially oriented quality goals was particularly interesting, and has led to a follow-up research project. The device was not built, however. Section 9.3 discusses an agent-oriented design of an intelligent music player. It was developed as a student project, and is presented in the spirit of encouraging other students and developers to experiment with agent-oriented modeling. Section 9.4 gives some background.

9.1 Intelligent Homes

Chapters 1 and 4 discussed the smart home domain, in which appliances interoperate seamlessly for the benefit of the home occupants. Themes within the intelligent home are ubiquity, communication, and automation. These themes are more general than just the home. We can talk about intelligent cars, intelligent offices, intelligent devices, and we use the overarching term here—namely, intelligent lifestyles. As mentioned in chapter 1, it is easy to envisage an intelligent home with separate agents working in concert to control subsystems such as air conditioning, entertainment, and security. For example, lights might be turned on automatically when the owner came home. They might brighten or dim to fit the occasion or to match the outdoor light. Speakers might be distributed through the house to allow music to follow you from room to room.

Several intelligent homes are already in existence. An example is the home of the billionaire Bill Gates, a very modern twenty-first-century house in the Pacific lodge style, with advanced electronic systems everywhere. Visitors to the Bill Gates house are tracked by a microchip that is given to them upon entrance. This small chip sends signals throughout the house, and a given room's temperature and other conditions will change according to preset visitor preferences.

We believe that agent-oriented modeling is suitable for capturing requirements for an intelligent home, a complicated distributed sociotechnical system. The requirements models can be mapped into designs. We give a set of models for two scenarios. The first is greeting a person arriving at the home in a manner appropriate to the time of day and the person's company. The second is a multiagent security system for tracking people in the house. If a particular person is not recognized by the system, an intruder alert could be initiated whereby the home owner and the police were contacted, complete with photo of the intruder. Any visitors or tradespeople scheduled to visit the house could be warned to stay away. The ROADMAP and RAP/AOR methodologies overviewed in section 7.6 were loosely followed for modeling the intelligent home scenarios.

We present the greeting subsystem as if we were following an agent-oriented methodology. Recall the greeting scenario in an intelligent home briefly discussed in section 4.6. Figure 4.8 is a goal model of a greeting scenario constituting the *conceptual behavior modeling viewpoint*. It includes the roles Greeter and Greetee, which are attached to the top-level goal, "Greet." Additionally, there is the Evaluator role. An agent that performs the role monitors and reports on the satisfaction of the person being greeted.

Next, we move to the *conceptual interaction modeling viewpoint*, where the roles required for achieving the goals are modeled in terms of their responsibilities and constraints. Responsibilities include the interactions required between the agents playing the roles. Responsibilities are rooted in and extend goals. Constraints are typically based on quality goals. Table 9.1 models the Greeter role. The Greetee and Evaluator roles are modeled as tables 9.2 and 9.3.

We next move to the *conceptual information modeling viewpoint*, where we model domain knowledge to be represented in the system. Figure 9.1 depicts the domain model for a greeting scenario. As explained in chapter 3, domain models represent domain entities and roles, and relationships between them. According to the model shown in figure 9.1, an agent playing the Greeter role analyzes a person description,

Table 9.1
The role model for Greeter

Role name	Greeter
Description	The Greeter role is responsible for greeting agents, referred to as greetees, entering the environment.
Responsibilities	Notice greetee. Recognize greetee. Formulate greeting. Articulate greeting. Register response to the greeting.
Constraints	The greetee should be accurately noticed and identified. Greeting should be articulated in a timely manner. Formulation must be appropriate to the greetee and the context.

Table 9.2
The role model for Greetee

Role name	Greetee
Description	The entrant to the environment.
Responsibilities	To be noticed by the greeter. Perceive greeting. Reply to the greeting.
Constraints	—

Table 9.3
The role model for Evaluator

Role name	Evaluator
Description	The Evaluator role is responsible for evaluating the greeting.
Responsibilities	Observe greeting. Evaluate greeting. Issue evaluation report.
Constraints	Evaluation must be impartial.

which may identify a greetee. A person description is modeled as the `Person-Description` domain entity. A greeting, represented as the `Greeting` domain entity, is articulated by the greeter and is perceived by the greetee. The greeting is determined by its context, which is modeled as the `Context` domain entity. An entity of type `Context` describes the current time and the activities in which the greetee is currently participating, such as having a business lunch or family dinner, doing exercises, and so on. Each greeting is paired with a response. The greeter receives the feedback provided by an agent playing the Evaluator role. `Response` and `Feedback` are modeled as the corresponding domain entities.

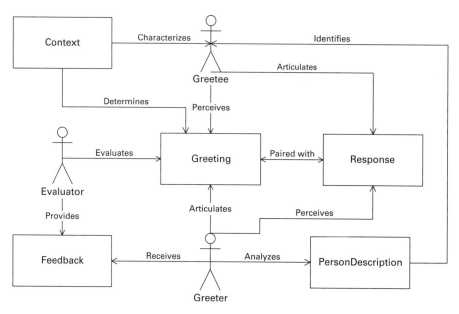

Figure 9.1
The domain model for a greeting scenario

We have now covered all the viewpoints of conceptual domain modeling. The next layer is platform-independent computational design. We first map roles to agent types from the *computational interaction design viewpoint*.

There are the following three roles in a greeting scenario: Greeter, Greetee, and Evaluator. Having an agent greeting itself makes little sense. So we map the Greeter role and the Greetee role to different agent types. We map the Greeter role to the GreeterAgent type. Manmade agents of this type would form part of an intelligent home system. We assume that an agent being greeted is a human agent, although in a really futuristic home we can envision a system that would greet a cleaning robot on duty. We therefore map the Greetee role to the Person agent type. With these assumptions, the only remaining issue is which agent takes on the Evaluator role. One can envisage the agent playing the Greeter role, or the agent playing the Greetee role, also playing the Evaluator role. To warrant impartial evaluation, which was expressed as a constraint for the Evaluator role, we choose to map the Evaluator role to another manmade agent type, EvaluatorAgent. The role mapping for a greeting scenario was simple. In the context of a more complex system, role mapping requires much more consideration.

After having decided the agent types, we next model interactions between agents. Figure 9.2 represents a prototypical interaction sequence between agents of the three

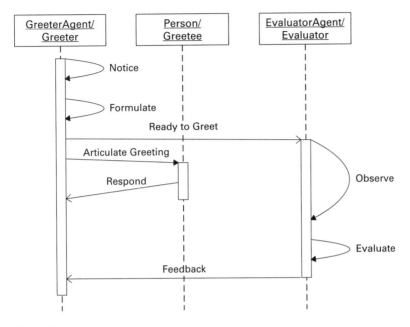

Figure 9.2
Prototypical interactions in a greeting scenario

types, also showing the role being played by each agent. In addition to the inter-actions, the model also includes some behaviors of individual agents. The notation used by the figure is a derivation of UML sequence diagrams.

Next, we move to the *computational information design viewpoint*, where we model knowledge by agents of each of the three types. In other words, we map the global knowledge that was represented from the conceptual information modeling view-point to knowledge held by individual agents. As mentioned in chapter 3, agents can have two kinds of knowledge: shared knowledge and private knowledge. In a greeting scenario, knowledge about particular instances of greeting and response is shared between the two agents of types Person and GreeterAgent involved and the agent of type EvaluatorAgent, who is to evaluate the greeting. Relevant domain entities from the domain model are Greetee, Context, and Feedback. In the computational information design model, the knowledge about Greetee, Context, and Feedback objects is shared between agents of the GreeterAgent and EvaluatorAgent types.

There is a lot of relevant knowledge for the greeting scenario, much of it common sense. It is well known in AI that reasoning about commonsense knowledge is diffi-cult. Indeed expressing all the knowledge that an agent would need to ensure that a greeting is appropriate is challenging, and almost certainly infeasible. The cultural differences alone defy complete and correct expression.

Nonetheless, to give a flavor of how knowledge might be modeled, we give some simple Prolog facts and rules. For example, we can express that different classes of people—for example, family, friends, and visitors—may come to the house. Each class could be listed as greetees, with particular individuals identified as family or friends:

```
greetee(X) :- family(X).
greetee(X) :- friend(X).
greetee(X) :- visitor(X).
family('John').
friend('Alice').
```

We can model different types of family members and friends:

```
family(X) :- parent(X).
family(X) :- sibling(X).
friend(X) :- colleague(X).
```

We might also specify a Prolog rule expressing that a person is a visitor if he or she is not a family member or friend:

```
visitor(X) :- not(family(X)), not(friend(X)).
```

The system is capable of producing greetings using various phrases. The greeting phrases that the system can say need to be listed. The types of greeting should also be listed. The Prolog facts might include

```
greeting_phrase('hello').
greeting_phrase('good day').
greeting_phrase('good morning').
greeting_phrase('welcome').
greeting_type(formal).
greeting_type(informal).
greeting_type(welcome).
greeting_type(insult).
```

The attributes of the greeting could be derived from knowledge of the greetee and her company and from the context. An overly simple example might have a family member be greeted by a friendly phrase, which might be expressed as follows:

```
greeting_greetee(G,P) :-
      family(G), greeting_phrase(P), friendly(P).
```

The following rule expresses that if the time is morning and a family member returns from jogging, the appropriate greeting is articulated:

```
greeting_greetee(G, 'Good morning, hope you feel fresh now') :-
    family(G), time_context(morning), activity_context(jogging).
```

This last rule uses the notion of context, which is not clearly defined, but brings us to our next consideration. We also need to model the interface to a service that provides contextual information to a greeter agent upon request. From the conceptual information modeling viewpoint, we introduced the `Context` domain entity. Without going into any additional details here, we can assume that the contextual knowledge is embodied in an object of type `Context` that is returned by the `getContext(Greetee)` operation of the `ContextGateway` service object.

After having decided upon agent types and knowledge contained by agents of these types, we turn to the *computational behavior design viewpoint* by modeling agent behaviors. We use for coarse-level behavior modeling the RAP/AOR methodology described in section 7.6. Figure 9.3 depicts an AOR diagram modeling the behaviors of agents of types `GreeterAgent` and `EvaluatorAgent`.

Unlike in the previous chapter, we do not describe the behavior diagram in detail, but instead let the reader observe that the greeting activity described in the diagram consists of identifying the person, querying the context, formulating the greeting, articulating the greeting, and registering the response. Communication is needed with the `EvaluatorAgent` to indicate when the greeting has started and to receive feedback.

We now model intruder handling, another scenario of an intelligent home. This example has been used for several years in agent classes at the University of Melbourne, and is universally accessible to a wide audience. It even allows for performance to make a class more entertaining or interactive.

Intruder handling is closely related to greeting. If the person noticed is not recognized as a family member, friend, or visitor, he or she is deemed to be an intruder invoking the following relevant scenario. Suppose that a stranger appears in the house while the homeowner, whom we named Jane in section 4.6, is away. After capturing the image of a person, the security agent first checks the database of the people known by the system to find out that the stranger is neither a family member nor a friend. The security agent may also forward the image to Jane and ask whether she knows the person. If the person is not known, family members and scheduled visitors are warned through the most appropriate channel—for example, a mobile phone or a PC at work—to stay away temporarily. Meanwhile, the security agent cooperates with an agent of the police department to report the incident and provide the image so that the suspect can be identified.

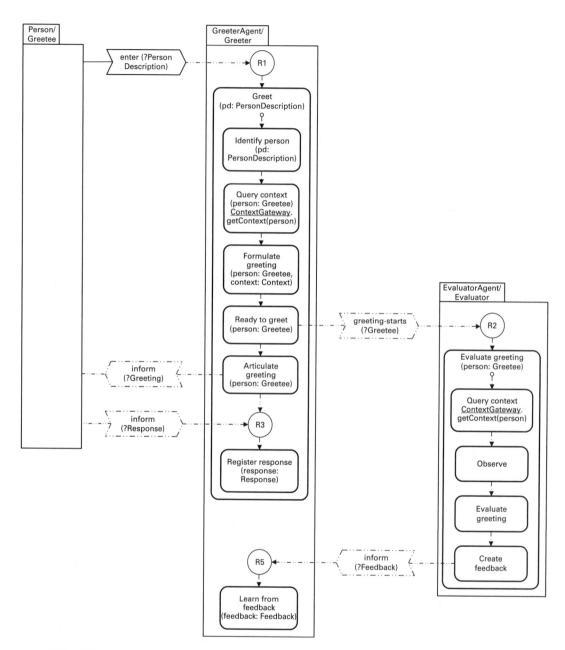

Figure 9.3
A behavior diagram for a greeting scenario

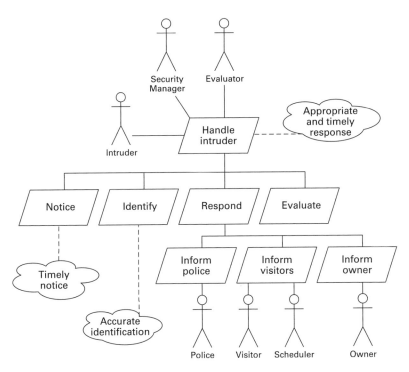

Figure 9.4
A goal model for intruder handling

The *conceptual behavior modeling viewpoint* of the intruder handling scenario is given by a goal model. The goal model in figure 9.4 captures the motivational scenario described previously. We briefly describe the goal model. The overall goal of the subsystem is to handle intruders, expressed by the overall goal "Handle intruder." A quality goal is attached to the root goal to express that the response needs to be appropriate and timely. Three roles are indicated as relevant to the overall goal: Security Manager, Intruder, and Evaluator. The overall goal has been elaborated into four subgoals: "Notice," "Identify," "Respond," and "Evaluate." Two quality goals, "Timely notice" and "Accurate identification," are attached respectively to the "Notice" and "Identify" subgoals. The "Respond" subgoal in turn has been elaborated into three subgoals: "Inform police," "Inform visitors," and "Inform owner." To accomplish these, the additional roles of Police, Visitor, Scheduler, and Owner have been added.

Subsequently, the roles identified by the goal model are described by role models, which belong to the *conceptual interaction design viewpoint*. Table 9.4 represents the role model for the Security Manager role shown in figure 9.4. The model lists the

Table 9.4
The role model for Security Manager

Role name	Security Manager
Description	The Security Manager identifies and responds to an intruder detected in the house.
Responsibilities	Detect the presence of a person in the environment.
	Take an image of the person.
	Compare the image against the database of known people.
	Contact the police and send the image to them.
	Check the house schedule for planned visitors.
	Notify each visitor expected that day to stay away.
	Inform the owner that the police are on their way and the visitors have been warned not to enter the house.
Constraints	Photos of the owner and visitors need to be provided to the system in advance.
	A subject to be detected needs to be seen within the camera's image area.
	To receive messages, the owner and visitors must be accessible by electronic means of communication.

Table 9.5
The role model for Scheduler

Role name	Scheduler
Description	The Scheduler role maintains a schedule for the home.
Responsibilities	Maintain a schedule of events.
	Determine event priorities.
	Detect event conflicts.
	Notify the owner about forthcoming events.
	Notify the owner about event conflicts.
	Answer queries on the schedule.
Constraints	Events can be entered or changed by the owner or by a person authorized by the owner.

responsibilities of an agent playing the Security Manager role and the constraints that apply to the agent exercising these responsibilities. Tables 9.5, 9.6, 9.7, 9.8, and 9.9 similarly contain the role models for the Scheduler, Visitor, Owner, Police, and Evaluator roles.

We next move to the *conceptual information modeling viewpoint*, where we decide and represent the domain entities relevant for an intruder handling scenario. The domain model for an intruder handling scenario is shown in figure 9.5. Central is the PersonDescription domain entity that represents the visual information—and possibly also voice information—captured about the person detected by the security manager. The security manager analyzes a person description. If the person description does not identify a person known by the system, the person is considered to be an intruder. In this case, the person description is forwarded to the police, who may be able to identify a concrete suspect. To find the service people authorized to be in

Table 9.6
The role model for Visitor

Role name	Visitor
Description	The Visitor visits the home.
Responsibilities	Provide the owner with a recent photo. Register a visit with the owner. Update the details of the visit with the owner if necessary. Cancel the visit with the owner if necessary. Receive from the security manager a request to stay away.
Constraints	To receive a request to stay away, the visitor must be accessible by electronic means of communication.

Table 9.7
The role model for Owner

Role name	Owner
Description	The Owner owns the home.
Responsibilities	Insert the photos of the visitors, family members, and himself/herself into the system. Register all scheduled visits with the scheduler. Update the details of a visit with the scheduler if necessary. Cancel the visit with the scheduler if needed. Receive from the security manager a request to stay away.
Constraints	The schedule must be kept up to date. To receive a request to stay away, the owner must be accessible by electronic means of communication.

Table 9.8
The role model for Police

Role name	Police
Description	An institutional role for keeping law and order.
Responsibilities	Receive notification about the intrusion. Notify the staff on duty in the proximity of the intrusion site. Identify the intruder from the database of suspects.
Constraints	The staff on duty must be notified immediately. For identification, notification must be accompanied by a photo.

Table 9.9
The role model for Evaluator

Role name	Evaluator
Description	The Evaluator role evaluates the process of intruder handling.
Responsibilities	Observe intruder handling. Evaluate intruder handling. Issue evaluation report.
Constraints	Evaluation must be impartial.

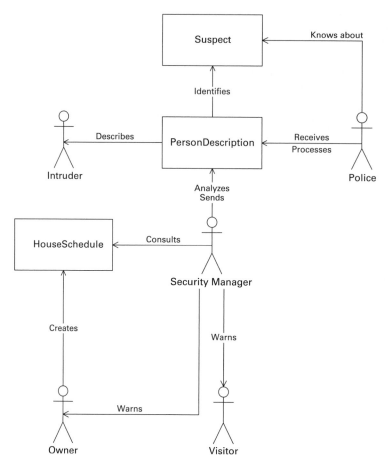

Figure 9.5
The domain model for intruder handling

the house, like plumbers and electricians, and the scheduled visitors to be warned to stay away, the security manager consults the house schedule, which has been modeled as the HouseSchedule domain entity. An entity of the HouseSchedule type contains the start and end times of various activities that are to take place in the house, such as visits by friends and colleagues, family celebrations, and calls by service people. The schedule is created by the owner.

The domain entities related to the evaluation of intruder handling are omitted from the domain model depicted in figure 9.5 and from all the subsequent models, because intruder handling is evaluated in essentially the same way as greeting.

Having covered all the viewpoints of conceptual domain modeling, we move to the abstraction layer of platform-independent computational design. The first modeling activity to be performed here is mapping roles to agent types from the *computational interaction design viewpoint*.

Some roles in an intruder handling scenario are obviously performed by people. Such roles are Intruder, Visitor, and Owner. In particular, we have chosen to map the Visitor and Owner roles to human agent types, because their performing agents are not involved in complex information processing. Therefore, all that is required of a human performing one of these roles is to have a device enabling simple information input and output, such as a Blackberry or mobile phone.

As most of the information processing in the intruder handling scenario is carried out by an agent playing the Security Manager role, this role should undoubtedly be mapped to the manmade agent type `SecurityAgent`. To meet the "appropriate and timely response" quality goal, the Police role should likewise be mapped to the `PoliceAgent` type of automated manmade agents. Our mappings result in human agents of type `Person` playing the Intruder, Visitor, and Owner roles, and manmade agents of types `SecurityAgent` and `PoliceAgent` playing the Security Manager and Police roles, respectively.

Having decided the agent types, one might want to sketch interactions between agents of these types in an intruder handling scenario. This task can be done in the form of an interaction-sequence diagram, as depicted in figure 9.6, which models a prototypical sequence of interactions between agents in an intruder handling scenario. According to the interaction model, an intruder handling scenario starts by a sensor-aided detection of a physical move by an intruder that is perceived as an event by the `SecurityAgent`. This is followed by messages from the `SecurityAgent` to the `PoliceAgent`, visitors, and the owner.

Having modeled from the computational interaction design viewpoint, we need to model from the viewpoints of computational information design and computational behavior design. What modeling from these viewpoints effectively means is filling out the agent boxes shown in figure 9.6 with the knowledge and behavior modeling constructs for the respective agent types. A combined knowledge and behavior model for the intruder handling scenario is given in figure 9.7.

From the *computational information design viewpoint*, we map the domain entities from the domain model given in figure 9.5 to the knowledge items of individual agent types. As shown in figure 9.7, the `PersonDescription` object type is shared between agents of the `SecurityAgent` and `PoliceAgent` types, because the intruder description is the main information exchanged between those agents. However, the notation used in the figure does not imply that all the instances of `PersonDescription` are shared between a `SecurityAgent` and `PoliceAgent`. The figure also shows that both agents have private knowledge of instances of the respective `Subject` and `Suspect` object types.

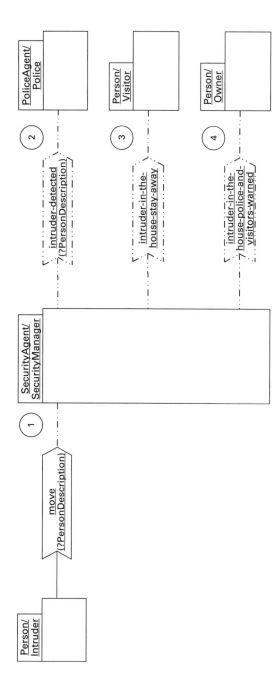

Figure 9.6
Prototypical interactions in intruder handling

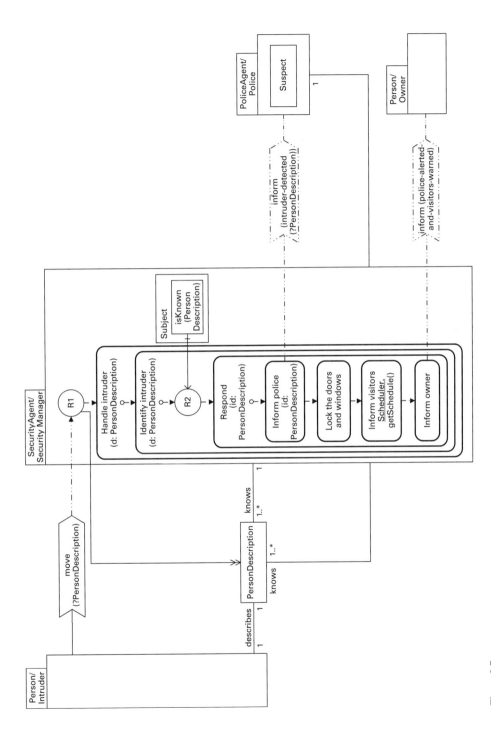

Figure 9.7
A combined knowledge and behavior model of intruder handling

From the same viewpoint, we also model the interface to the `Scheduler` service. The `getSchedule()` operation of that service returns an object of the `HouseSchedule` type, containing the house schedule for the current time. The `HouseSchedule` domain entity was first modeled in the domain model shown in figure 9.5.

Going to the *computational behavior design viewpoint*, figure 9.7 combines the knowledge model with the behavior model of an intruder handling scenario. In the behavior model, the outermost activity is started by rule `R1`, which is triggered by an action event of the `move(?PersonDescription)` type. This modeling construct represents a physical move performed by an intruder that is perceived as an event by the security agent. The precise mechanism of perceiving is of no interest at this stage of a systems engineering process. Rule `R1` also creates an instance of the `PersonDescription` object type within the security agent.

A "Handle intruder" activity starts an "Identify intruder" subactivity that triggers rule `R2`. This rule prescribes checking the Boolean value returned by the `isKnown(PersonDescription)` predicate attached to the `Subject` object type. If the predicate evaluates to *false*—that is, if the person described by the `PersonDescription` is not recognized—an activity of type "Respond" is started. This activity consists of sequential subactivities of types "Inform police," "Lock the doors and windows," "Inform visitors," and "Inform owner" types. These subactivity types have not been further refined in the figure. The subactivity type "Lock the doors and windows" is required to facilitate arrest. The subactivity type "Inform visitors" involves the invocation of the `Scheduler` service.

Note that most activity types modeled in figure 9.7 correspond to the goals represented in the goal model in figure 9.4. In the given case study, an activity of some type achieves a goal of the respective type. For example, an activity of the "Respond" type achieves a "Respond" goal.

A system, whose two features were described in this section, was prototyped in the Intelligent Lifestyle project. The project was conducted in 2004 by a team of final-year undergraduate software engineering students at the University of Melbourne. For *platform-dependent design*, the project team identified two feasible ways for designing the multiagent system. One way is to use a vertical layered architecture where information is passed from low-level input devices to upper layers where that information is converted to a high-level representation format to be used by agents and processed by the agents. The other way is to use a horizontal design where agents provide services relating to their interests to other agents. In this way, agents can access situational context from a variety of agents, each of which deals with a specific kind of context. However, in such a peer-to-peer architecture, there is little control over contextual information, which makes it hard to process conflicting information or achieve information accuracy. It is also difficult to consider the history of information within such a design. In addition, such design cannot handle large numbers of agents—for example, more than a hundred agents—as it is complicated to organize agents with diverse interests in a hierarchy.

Considering the two options, therefore, the project team decided to adopt a vertical, two-tiered architecture consisting of an application tier and a context tier. The context tier provides the application tier with the information gathered from input devices. If needed, that information is further processed by the context tier before being passed to the application tier. The application tier uses that information to provide services to both humans and software agents. Humans interact with the services of the application tier through communication devices.

The agents of the application tier need to communicate with each other. The project team decided that designing a communication mechanism from scratch would be beyond the scale of the project. It was decided to choose an agent framework. To that end, three freely available frameworks—JADE (see section 5.5), Open Agent Architecture (OAA), and 3APL (see section 5.3)—were chosen for detailed evaluation. Out of the three frameworks considered, the JADE agent platform was chosen due to its stability, language features, and simplicity. Also, as pointed out in section 7.6, the modeling constructs of the RAP/AOR methodology, used for the case study of intelligent home in this section, can be transformed in a straightforward manner into the implementation constructs of JADE.

9.2 Secret Touch

The second of the case studies in this chapter comes from a different source than the first. The University of Melbourne was involved in a project entitled "Mediating Intimacy: Strong-Tie Relationships" through its participation in the Smart Internet Technology Cooperative Research Centre in 2004. The project was specifically interested in how couples may use technology and the Internet to mediate intimacy to help them to feel closer while physically apart.

In the project, six couples were studied using ethnographic techniques. Workbooks and diaries produced by the six couples documented interactions the couples had throughout the day. From this data, information systems researchers created scenarios suggesting technological devices to assist in mediating intimacy.

One of the scenarios developed was Secret Touch. Secret Touch was conceived as a software system on a small pocket device that communicated wirelessly over the Internet with a partner's similar device. Partners in an intimate relationship could thus interact discretely, and remotely, through physically moving the device in their pocket, causing their partner's device to move in an identical fashion.

The workbooks and documents produced by the couples and the designs produced by the researchers did not obviously translate into processes and artifacts used in traditional software engineering methodologies. At this stage, a new project was initiated within the Smart Internet Technology Cooperative Research Centre involving agent-oriented modeling. The intent was to see whether agent modeling could be used to capture requirements and design for devices such as the Secret Touch in social settings.

The project started as a series of discussions[4] between an agent-oriented modeling team and information systems researchers. The motivation-level and design-level models presented shortly in this section were developed iteratively interleaved with the discussions. Before presenting the models, we highlight two notable aspects of the discussions.

The first aspect concerns the use of abstract quality goals. From the perspective of the couple who were responsible for the Secret Touch scenario, it was necessary that the use of the Secret Touch device required an element of flirtatiousness. Flirting was duly added as a quality goal. Perhaps unsurprisingly, the discussants did not agree on what constituted flirting behavior. However, after considerable entertaining conversation, it was concluded that in flirting there needed to be an element of both risk and playfulness. Neither of these qualities can be easily quantified, but were noted in the motivation layer models. The proposed design models were assessed, albeit informally, as to whether they maintained a suitable level of risk and play. This use of abstract quality goals was considered useful by the team and was different to other methods of using quality attributes. In the following models, the quality goals are mentioned without the surrounding conversations.

The second notable aspect from the discussions was determining the amount of interaction that should be allowed between the couples. There was diversity of opinion as to whether the device should allow only a simple response or whether complicated sequences of manipulations of a Secret Touch device should be allowed. It was observed that network bandwidth and device design would affect the complexity of the device response. In discussing these trade-offs, it was quickly realized that one could design a range of Secret Touch devices. Four devices were considered during the project. Each of the different devices had different motivational goals.

The simplest of the Secret Touch devices, Flirt, is envisaged as transforming all device movements into *touches*; that is, when one partner moves the device, it is regarded by the other as a touch. The touches are instantaneously sent to the partner's device, as well as immediately transforming all touches received into movements. Simultaneously incoming and outgoing movements would be resolved by the device itself, which then moves in a direction reflecting the vector sum of both

---

4. The discussions were most interesting and have led in fact to ongoing research.

Table 9.10
A motivational scenario for Secret Touch—Discrete Flirt

Scenario name	Secret Touch—Flirt
Scenario description	Both partners of a couple reach in their pockets during work. She feels that he is fiddling with the device. She turns the device in the other direction, engaging in playful activity.
Quality description	Couples want to communicate privately. Feeling each other. Being playful, with an element of risk. Individuals like fiddling with toys.

touches—potentially a real tug-of-war situation examined at some detail in the design discussion.

The discrete version, Discrete Flirt, enables partners to engage in a turn-taking dialogue. It allows a device to be switched off or set to passively receive touches and replay them later—for example, when the important meeting at work is over. Allowing the partner that much control fundamentally changes the motivation.

The third device envisaged, Fiddler's Choice, is an intelligent, learning device. A partner may allow the device to respond if unable to personally engage. Fiddler's Choice can also be used solo, in which the partner is actually a manmade agent.

The final product in the range, Guessing Game, is designed for playing hard and fast in personal relationships. There is no longer a set partnership or connection between two devices. Instead a group of devices is available, which may be shared by an intimate couple or may reflect multiple partners. An open, dynamic system reflects that devices may randomly appear and disappear from the game.

The ROADMAP methodology overviewed in section 7.6 was followed for modeling the Secret Touch case study. A motivational scenario for the case study is presented in table 9.10. We concentrate on the Flirt device here. However there was some discussion of how an overall goal model could cover a range of devices.

We give a goal model corresponding to motivational scenario of table 9.10. The goal model was drawn with the REBEL tool. The notation for the REBEL tool is slightly different than given previously in chapter 7, where the goal models were drawn using Microsoft Visio. Table 9.11 contains the notation. REBEL was also used for the Smart Music Player overviewed in the next section.

The goal model depicted in figure 9.8 is the overall goal model for flirting. Two Partner roles are responsible for the goal "Flirt," which by nature is "Risky" and "Playful," the associated quality goals. The "Flirt" goal has two subgoals: "Initiate flirt" and "Respond to flirt." Initiating the flirt by an agent playing the Touch Giver role involves translation of the device movement into a touch, reflected by the "Translate movement into giving touch" subgoal. Similarly, responding to the flirt

Table 9.11
Notation for goal models in the REBEL tool

Notation	Meaning
Goal (parallelogram shape)	Goal
Quality Goal (cloud shape)	Quality goal
Role (stick figure)	Role
⟶	Relationship between goals
⎯⎯⎯	Relationship between a goal and quality goal or between a goal and role

by an agent playing the Touch Acceptor role involves translation of the device movement into a touch, reflected by the "Translate movement into responding touch" subgoal. The roles associated with both the latter two subgoals are Touch Perceiver and Device Manager.

Figure 9.9 models the Device Manager role described by the REBEL tool, which manages interaction between the software system and the physical device. The Device Manager is responsible for translating touches received into physical movements and vice versa. Constraints include being accurate and having a finite capacity to perceive.

System design layer models were developed using the Prometheus methodology discussed in section 7.5. The design for the Flirt system contains two agents of the respective types `Intimacy Handler` and `Device Handler`. The `Intimacy Handler` agent enacts two roles: Touch Giver and Touch Acceptor. The `Device Handler` agent enacts two roles: Device Manager and Touch Perceiver.

Figure 9.10 shows the Prometheus system overview diagram for the Flirt device that we are describing. Agent coupling is indicated by links between agents via protocols. The "Exchanges" protocol enables the `Intimacy Handler` agent and the `Device Handler` agent to exchange touches bidirectionally as received touches are

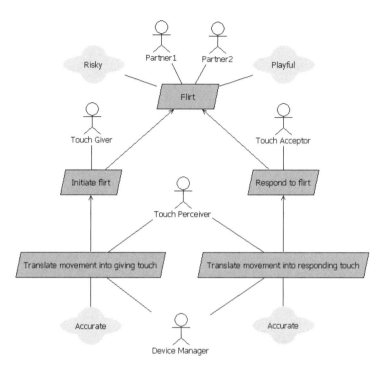

Figure 9.8
The goal model for flirting

passed on to be felt and created touches are passed on and then sent to the paired Secret Touch device. The percepts and actions show the interaction of each agent with the outside world. The `Device Handler` agent perceives the percept "Movement" and also initiates the action "Move Device." The `Intimacy Handler` agent handles two percepts, "Arrival of Touch" and "Touch Returned to Sender." This agent performs one action, "Give a Touch" sent to the paired Secret Touch device.

Figure 9.11 displays the agent overview diagram for the `Intimacy Handler` agent. The "Sending" capability and the "Reception" capability are designed to send or receive touches for the Flirt prototype. A touch to be sent arrives in a "perceivedTouch" or a "proposedTouch" message. The "proposedTouch" message would be sent by the `Resource Handler` agent, which is not modeled here. The "Reception" capability passes the perceived touch on to the `Device Handler` agent to be felt and stores the touch in the knowledge base or alternatively discards the touch.

The agent overview diagram for the `Device Handler` agent is shown in figure 9.12. The "TouchToMovement" plan is triggered by an incoming "feel" message. The plan reads the touch itself, represented by a knowledge base, and executes the

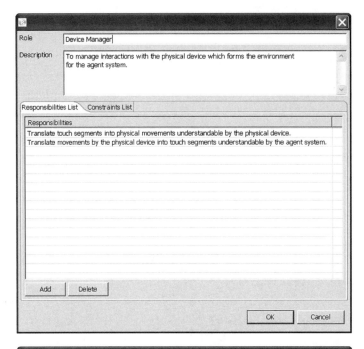

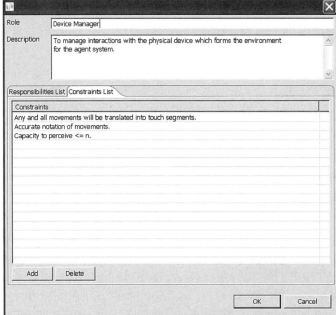

Figure 9.9
The role model for Device Manager

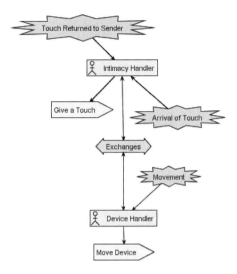

Figure 9.10
The system overview diagram for the Flirt device

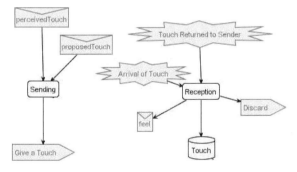

Figure 9.11
The agent overview diagram for `Intimacy Handler`

action "Move Device" accordingly. Similarly the plan "MovementToTouch" would react to the percept "Movement" and create and store a "Touch" sent further via the "recorded" message.

To conclude the section, we reflect on the models produced for the Secret Touch motivational scenario. In presenting the models, Leon has found that they are accessible to a wide range of stakeholders including those without a software background. Several informal surveys of audiences were conducted. The survey results indicated that the models were broadly understood. The project for which the models were produced had the intention to investigate whether data produced from ethnographic

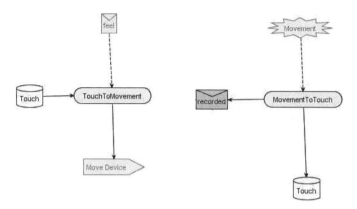

Figure 9.12
The agent overview diagram for `Device Handler`

studies could routinely be translated into software requirements. More research needs to be done for a definitive answer. However the project and follow-up activities do suggest that agent-oriented models can facilitate such a translation.

The role and goal models facilitated real communication with the researchers, who were nontechnical clients. The flexibility and high-level nature of the models enabled the software engineer who developed the models to present very high-level abstractions for feedback. This approach is important for communication with nontechnical people. The usefulness of agent concepts was confirmed by survey results and other feedback. The initial Secret Touch analysis and design was presented and discussed, and a set of questions answered by participants was evaluated. Feedback was immediate, rich, and extremely usable.

The importance of the agent-human analogy was explicitly captured in the survey responses. A survey question about whether the agent paradigm was useful for understanding the proposed system received a unanimously positive response. Quality goals were confirmed to be useful for highlighting intangible requirements, as often encountered in social contexts. The interaction designers reacted very positively to the quality goals. It was noted that the ability to capture quality goals such as playfulness and risky behavior was unusual in software engineering methodologies.

9.3   Smart Music Player

The objective of the case study described in this section was to design an agent-oriented system for controlling a Smart Music Player (SMP). The purpose of the SMP system is to improve the listener's experience by automating most interactions between the music player and the listener and by providing flexible system control. We focus on SMP's main functionalities related to playing music. There are possible additional functionalities that a Smart Music Player may have, such as tuning in to radio stations, playing videos, and showing photos, which we do not consider in this book.

The main functionalities of SMP are as follows:

• *Turn the SMP on or off* The listener can turn the SMP on or off through her mobile phone or PC, by a voice command, or via the SMP's interface. If the listener has set up a playing duration, the SMP will turn off at a particular time.

• *Music selection* If the listener is nearby, the SMP automatically selects and plays the music best suited to the listener's emotions and current activities. If the listener is not nearby, the SMP sets up a playlist based on listener preferences.

• *Volume control* When playing music, the SMP automatically adjusts the volume according to the decibel level of the surrounding environment. Voice commands can override the automatic settings.

• *Track control* The listener can control the music track via voice commands or by means of the SMP interface.

• *Music library management* The SMP can download music files, back up and delete music files, and transfer music files between different devices. Music files are represented in the form of media agents. A media agent is an "intelligent" audio file stored in the system that can copy itself to a suitable device where there are enough music files with similar pieces of music. It can also delete itself when, for example, there is not enough space on the SMP.

The case study makes a series of assumptions. First, a personal computer (PC) is assumed to be available to back up music files from the music player. Second, a sensor package is assumed to be gathering physiological data. Third, a voice recorder is assumed to be available to record audio files. It is also assumed that the listener would have informed the SMP about her music preferences. The listener would also have trained the SMP regarding voice commands. The music player is in an intelligent home environment where wireless communication can occur between a mobile phone, the SMP, and the PC. The ringtone of the phone is recorded before using the SMP. Online music sites are assumed to be set up before a player can download music from the Internet.

For historical reasons, the design was developed using a combination of the Prometheus and ROADMAP methodologies, which are described in sections 7.5 and 7.6, respectively. Requirements elicitation and analysis were supported by the ROADMAP methodology, and system design was supported by the Prometheus methodology.

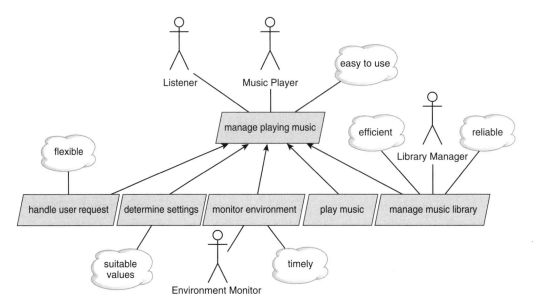

Figure 9.13
The overall goal model for SMP (Luo, Sterling, and Taveter 2007)

The combination of the ROADMAP and Prometheus methodologies took advantage of their tool support. The goal models presented in this section and section 9.2 were originally created with the REBEL tool for ROADMAP but have been subsequently redrawn to improve visual quality. The design models were created with the PDT tool for Prometheus.

Domain analysis involved capturing requirements at a high abstraction level by goal models constituting the *conceptual behavior modeling viewpoint*. Figure 9.13 represents the overall goal model for the SMP system. The purpose of the SMP system, as captured by the root goal "manage playing music" is to manage the SMP. The Music Player role is required for achieving this goal. The "easy to use" quality goal indicates that it should be easy to manage playing music with the system. The "manage playing music" goal is achieved via the following subgoals: "handle user request," "determine settings," "monitor environment," "play music," and "manage music library." These subgoals have corresponding roles and quality goals attached to them.

Parts of the goal tree depicted in figure 9.13 can be refined by separate models. Figure 9.14 shows the refinement of the "manage music library" goal.

Figure 9.15 elaborates three other goals—"determine settings," "monitor environment," and "play music"—to several subgoals with the associated roles and quality goals. According to the model, to achieve the "determine settings" goal, we need to

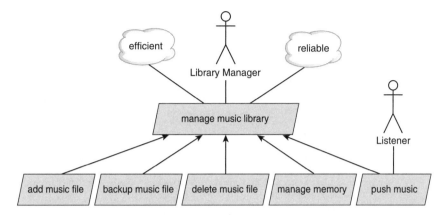

Figure 9.14
The goal model for managing the music library (Luo, Sterling, and Taveter 2007)

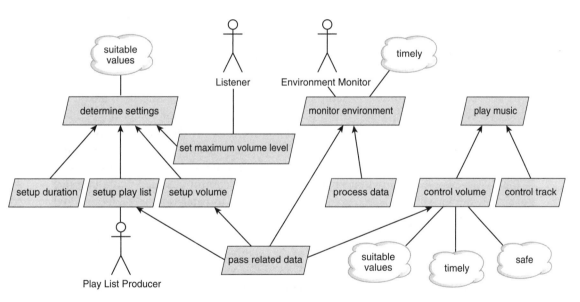

Figure 9.15
The goal model for determining settings, monitoring the environment, and playing music

Table 9.12
The role model for Listener

Role name	Listener
Description	The Listener role controls and monitors the music being played both in content and sound settings.
Responsibilities	Request to play music through the PC, mobile phone, by a voice command, or by the SMP's interface. Control the SMP through the PC, mobile phone, by voice commands, or by the SMP's interface. Provide details of settings (e.g., start time, duration, music selection principles, maximum volume level, and volume) when requesting to play music. Provide predefined information (e.g., ringtone, music ratings, address of an online music store, and the times to download new popular music files from the online music store). Train the SMP. Respond to messages displayed by the SMP. Provide the necessary hardware and ensure it is correctly connected.
Constraints	Must know how to use a PC to control the SMP. Must know how to use a mobile phone to control the SMP. Must know the voice command instructions (e.g., SMP on, SMP off, increase volume, decrease volume, play, pause, stop, next, repeat, and play previous music file). Must know how to connect the hardware.

achieve the "setup duration," "setup play list," "setup volume," and "set maximum volume level" subgoals. The "setup play list" goal is the responsibility of the Play List Producer role and the "set maximum volume level" is the responsibility of the Listener role. The "monitor environment" and "play music" goals have been similarly elaborated. The subgoal "pass related data" is common to several goals, including "setup play list," "monitor environment," and "control volume." Note that the "set maximum volume level" goal has been created to cater for the "safe" quality goal attached to the "control volume" goal.

In a goal model, the achievement of quality goals associated with subgoals does not necessarily ensure the achievement of the quality goal associated with the parent goal. For example, according to figure 9.13, we cannot guarantee that the system is easy to use if the listener's requests are handled flexibly, there is timely monitoring of the environment, suitable values of settings are determined, and music library management is reliable and efficient. Quality goals may conflict. For instance, if the ways for listeners to make requests are too flexible, the system may not be easy to use, because of too many options available, which results in confusion.

We next move to the *conceptual interaction modeling viewpoint* where the roles required for achieving the goals are modeled. As explained in chapter 3, role models are orthogonal to goal models in that they define capacities or positions required for achieving the goals, including the interactions required between the agents playing the roles. The role model in table 9.12 models a listener—a person who requests to

Table 9.13
The role model for Environment Monitor

Role name	Environment Monitor
Description	The Environment Monitor role monitors the environment to recognize and process different signals.
Responsibilities	Detect and receive ring tones and "call finished" signals. Detect the decibel level of the surrounding environment. Detect if the listener is nearby. Monitor physiological data, such as body movements and body heat, of the listener. Update physiological data about the listener. Transmit environment data and physiological data to the play list producer and music player manager.
Constraints	Detect and process a signal within N seconds, where N is a performance requirement.

Table 9.14
The role model for Play List Producer

Role name	Play List Producer
Description	The Play List Producer role selects the music based on listener state and history.
Responsibilities	Receive physiological data from the environment monitor. Learn the listener preferences by storing previous music selections, previous music ratings by the listener, and the physiological data about the listener that was associated with those selections. Determine the average and standard deviations of the values of physiological data obtained from the environment monitor. Determine the current state of the listener based on pre-determined value ranges of physiological data for the listener states *active*, *passive*, and *resting*. Compare the listener's current state and activities to previous music preferences by the listener. Select music files based on the data produced and the listener's proximity.
Constraints	Select a music file within N seconds, where N is a performance requirement. The music files selected to the playlist should fit the listener's emotions and activities.

play music. The Listener role is responsible for making music requests, controlling the SMP, training the player, and determining settings. The Listener role is constrained to know how to use the PC to control the music player, how to use a mobile phone to control the music player, to know voice commands, and to know how to connect hardware.

Table 9.13 includes the responsibilities and constraints for the Environment Monitor role. An environment monitor must detect ring tones, monitor ambient decibel levels, and accept hangup signals. It also analyzes the listener's activities and collects physiological data about the listener when the listener is nearby. An environment monitor has quality constraints related to performance requirements.

Tables 9.14, 9.15, and 9.16 model the respective roles Play List Producer, Library Manager, and Music Player.

Table 9.15
The role model for Library Manager

Role name	Library Manager
Description	The Library Manager role manages the music library.
Responsibilities	Download a new music file from the predefined online music store every N days, where N is a setting by the listener. Record and store music files. Store new music files downloaded by the listener's mobile phone. Receive media agents. Convert a non-media-agent file into a media agent. Copy a newly downloaded music file to the music library. When a new music file is played on the PC, copy the music file to the SMP. Transfer a requested music file from the SMP to the mobile phone. Delete from the SMP a music file with minimum listener preferences when there is not enough space left on the SMP. Double check if a music file is backed up before deleting it. Compare the lists of music files in the music library with those on the SMP whenever the PC and SMP are connected and back up if necessary. Display information to the listener.
Constraints	All music files must be backed up.

Table 9.16
The role model for Music Player

Role name	Music Player
Description	The Music Player role controls music playing.
Responsibilities	Recognize and execute a command by the listener. Turn the SMP on or off. Play a music file based on the settings. Control music track. Receive environment data and physiological data from the environment manager. Control volume according to the listener request or the environment data. Determine the duration of a music file according to the listener's current activities and habits. Record and update the listener preferences as metadata about music files. Display messages to the listener.
Constraints	The music player should have a friendly listener interface. The music player should be able to recognize and process various control signals coming from the listener, environment manager, or other sources. The status of the environment must be recognized and acted upon within N seconds, where N is a performance requirement.

Table 9.17
The music selection scenario

Scenario: music selection

Description: The SMP automatically selects the music files best suited to the listener's current emotions and activities.

Trigger: A request to play music by the listener.

Steps:

#	Type	Description	Data
1	O	A play list is requested	
2	P	The listener is nearby	
3	O	Determine the current state of the listener	Listener data (R, W)
4	G	Set up playlist	Music playing history (R, W)
5	O	Send playlist	Music library (R)

Variation 1: the listener is not nearby.

Description: At step 2, if the listener is not near by, the SMP produces a playlist according to the music preferences by the listener.

Steps:

#	Type	Description	Data
2	P	The listener is not nearby	
3	G	Set up playlist based on the preferences by the listener	Music playing history (R, W)

After having modeled the goals and roles, we revisit the *conceptual behavior modeling viewpoint*, in which we model expected system behavior. We have used Prometheus scenarios. Because the scenarios consider data to be manipulated by the system, they also comprise the *conceptual information modeling viewpoint*. Prometheus scenarios describe system behavior in terms of system goals, system operations, and impact on external data. Each scenario consists of several steps. Each step belongs to one of the five types: Goal (G), Action (A), Percept (P), subScenario(S), or Other (O). For each step, data may be read and/or produced (R: read; W: write). *Actions* represent how the system acts on the external environment and *percepts* represent events/stimuli from the outside world to which the system reacts. Because a scenario captures only a particular sequence of steps, small variations are indicated with brief descriptions. Major variations are presented as separate scenarios.

Table 9.17 represents a scenario of music selection. It describes how the SMP automatically selects and plays music files best suited to the listener's current emotions and activities. Table 9.17 shows two variations for step 2. One of them occurs when the listener is near by. In such a case, the SMP can choose music files to be played

Table 9.18
The scenario of playing music

Scenario: playing music

Description: The SMP plays music files based on the settings by the listener.

Trigger: The SMP is requested to play music.

Steps

#	Type	Description	Data
1	P	The SMP is ready	
2	P	A request to play music is received	
3	G	Set up playing time and duration	Time history (W)
4	O	It is time to start playing	
5	S	Get music selection	
6	O	Determine suitable volume	
7	G	Play a music file	Music library (R)
8	S	Volume control	
9	A	Display music playing information	
10	O	It is time to stop playing	Time history (R)
11	A	Stop playing	
12	A	Turn the SMP off	

Variation 1:

Description: The listener does not set up time and duration.

Steps: Skip the steps 3, 4, 9, and 10.

Variation 2: control track.

Description: The listener can control the track through the PC or mobile phone, by voice commands, or by the SMP's interface. Music playing history will be updated for learning purposes and the metadata about the music file will be updated to change the rating of the corresponding piece of music.

Trigger: A request by the listener to forward, rewind, or repeat the playing of the music file.

Steps: Insert the following steps between the steps 7 and 10 of the main scenario:

#	Type	Description	Data
1	P	A track control request by the listener is received	
2	A	Execute command (forward, rewind, or repeat)	
3	O	Update the music playing history	Music playing history (W)
4	O	Update the metadata about the music file	Music library (W)

Table 9.19
The volume control scenario

Scenario: volume control

Description: When playing music, the SMP automatically adjusts the volume according to the environment. If the phone rings, the SMP turns down the volume for the duration of the conversation and the volume resumes after the hangup.

Trigger: The phone rings while music is being played.

Steps:

#	Type	Description	Data
1	P	Detect ring tone	
2	A	Lower volume	
3	P	Detect that the call is finished	
4	A	Resume volume	

Variation 1: environment changes

Description: During any steps, the decibel level of the environment changes. If the decibel level of the surrounding environment is higher, the SMP accordingly increases the volume and if the decibel level is lower, the SMP accordingly decreases the volume.

Steps:

#	Type	Description	Data
5	P	The decibel level of the surrounding environment changes	
6	A	Adjust volume	

Variation 2: the listener requests to adjust the volume

Description: At any step, the listener can request a change in volume.

Steps:

#	Type	Description	Data
5	P	A request by the listener to change the volume is received	
6	A	Adjust volume	

according to the listener's current state which is based on the physiological data about the listener.

Another scenario takes place when the listener is not near the SMP. In this case, the SMP produces a music list by relying on the music preferences by the listener and also on the physiological data recorded earlier that describes the reactions to different pieces of music by the listener.

Table 9.18 models a scenario of playing a music file; table 9.19 models a volume control scenario. Both of these scenarios have two variations. Table 9.20 represents a scenario of a media agent arrival. This scenario has the "Check space" and "Add music file" subscenarios, which we do not present here. The scenario has one

Table 9.20
The media agent arrival scenario

Scenario: media agent arrival

Description: The SMP receives a media agent music file from another device (for example, from a mobile phone or another SMP). It then checks the available space on the SMP and adds the music file into the music library on the PC.

Trigger: New media agent arrives.

Steps:

#	Type	Description	Data
1	P	"I arrived" message received	File log (W)
2	S	Check space	Music playing history (R)
3	S	Add music file	Music library (W)

Variation 1: not enough space

Description: At step 2, if there is not enough space in the music library for the new media agent music file, the music file that is least preferred by the listener is first backed up on the PC and then destroyed.

Trigger: There is not enough space on the SMP.

Steps:

#	type	Description	Data
1	S	Back up music file	Music library (W) File log (W)
2	S	Destroy music file	Music library (W) File log (W)

variation for the case that there is not enough space on the SMP. The "Back up music file" and "Destroy music file" subscenarios of the variation are not presented here.

We next move to the modeling viewpoint of *computational interaction design*. Here the models produced by requirements analysis are used to determine what agents should exist and how they should interact. Figure 9.16 shows how roles in the SMP system have been mapped onto agent types.

Figure 9.16 reflects that some roles have been mapped to several agent types instead of being mapped to just one agent type. This mapping is necessary, due to the differing concepts of role in Prometheus and ROADMAP. In Prometheus, the concept of "role" is defined at a lower abstraction level. Roles in Prometheus are functionalities. When using Prometheus in design, grouping roles into an agent type is equivalent to grouping similar functionalities to form an agent type. However, in ROADMAP, a problem domain is analyzed in a top-down manner at a higher abstraction level to hide the complexity from customers and stakeholders. In ROAD-MAP, goals are first defined and then the roles that are required for achieving the goals are identified. After that, the responsibilities of each role are defined using a role model. To fulfil a responsibility, a role may need several *diverse* functionalities.

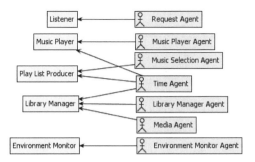

Figure 9.16
The agent-role coupling diagram for SMP (Luo, Sterling, and Taveter 2007). © 2007 IEEE.

Table 9.21
Descriptor of the type `Request Agent`

	Request Agent
Description	An agent of the `Request Agent` type receives a signal from the PC or mobile phone or given by a human voice and translates it into the corresponding instruction.
Goals achieved	Handle user request, determine settings
Creation	First use of the system
Destruction	No

As an agent in Prometheus should provide a set of *similar* functionalities, a role may have to be mapped to different agent types. Therefore, in the hybrid methodology used in this case study, several agents can work jointly to achieve the responsibilities of one role, and one agent can play several roles. Figure 9.16 shows that the responsibilities of the Play List Producer role are fulfilled by agents of types `Time Agent` and `Music Selection Agent`. On the other hand, the `Time Agent` serves three roles: Music Player, Play List Producer, and Library Manager. The newly decided agent types are modeled by the corresponding agent descriptors in tables 9.21–9.26.

After mapping roles to agent types, agent acquaintance diagrams can be used for sketching interaction pathways between agents of these types. The agent acquaintance diagram for the SMP is shown in figure 9.17. It is a variation of an acquaintance diagram explained in chapter 3.

Continuing modeling from the *computational interaction design viewpoint*, scenarios of domain modeling are used to guide the development of interaction diagrams. For the SMP case study, a specific kind of interaction diagram, associated with a scenario, was used. A variation point in this interaction diagram indicates the step at which several variations are possible. An "M" denotes a message passed between agents, a "P" denotes a percept from the external environment, and an arrow with

Table 9.22
Descriptor of the type `Music Selection Agent`

	Music Selection Agent
Description	An agent of the `Music Selection Agent` type makes a well-founded selection of music that best fits the listener's emotions and activities.
Goals achieved	Set up playlist
Creation	A request to play music by the listener is received.
Destruction	A play list has been produced.

Table 9.23
Descriptor of the type `Music Player Agent`

	Music Player Agent
Description	An agent of the `Music Player Agent` type reads the requested music file from the music library and plays it. It also controls the track and volume and displays messages to the listener's mobile phone or PC or to the SMP's interface.
Goals achieved	Determine settings, play music
Creation	A play list is received.
Destruction	The music files included by the play list have been played.

Table 9.24
Descriptor of the type `Library Manager Agent`

	Library Manager Agent
Description	An agent of the `Library Manager Agent` type adds, deletes, and backups music files and transfers files between different devices. It also converts other file formats to the media agent file format that is supported by the SMP system.
Goals achieved	Manage music library
Creation	Initialization
Destruction	No

Table 9.25
Descriptor of the type `Environment Monitor Agent`

	Environment Monitor Agent
Description	An agent of the `Environment Monitor Agent` type monitors the decibel level of the surrounding environment, detects a ring tone of the phone, and determines the state of the listener when the listener is nearby.
Goals achieved	Monitor environment
Creation	Initialization
Destruction	No

Table 9.26
Descriptor of the type Media Agent

	Media Agent
Description	An agent of the Media Agent type is the agent of a music file stored in the system that can make a copy of itself onto a suitable device.
Goals achieved	Push music.
Creation	The file is downloaded/pushed/transferred onto the SMP.
Destruction	The music file has been deleted from the SMP and PC.

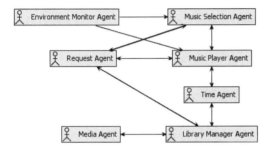

Figure 9.17
The agent acquaintance diagram for SMP

"A" indicates an action executed by the agent on the environment. The abbreviations used for denoting agent types are explained in the "Notes" section of an interaction diagram.

Figure 9.18 represents an interaction diagram for music selection. It has a variation point after the first step, by which the agent of Music Player Agent type requests the agent of Music Selection Agent type to generate a playlist. At that point, the agent of Environment Monitor Agent type checks to see whether the listener is nearby. If the listener is nearby, his or her state is found based on his or her current activities. After that, the agent of type Music Selection Agent proposes to the agent of type Request Agent a number of playlists conforming to the listener's state. The listener then chooses the playlist to be played, which the agent of Music Selection Agent type sends to the agent of Music Player Agent type. The model shown in figure 9.18 reflects that the listener has an option of composing the playlist by selecting music files from among the ones suggested by the music selection agent. A playlist is also proposed if the listener is not nearby. In this case, playlists are proposed based on the previous activities and preferences of the listener.

Figure 9.19 provides an interaction diagram for the scenario of volume control. When the agent of type Environment Monitor Agent accepts one of three percepts, "ring tone," "call finished," or "surrounding environment decibel level changes," it

Scenario: music selection

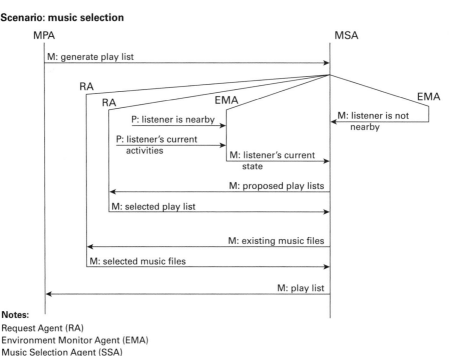

Notes:
Request Agent (RA)
Environment Monitor Agent (EMA)
Music Selection Agent (SSA)
Music Player Agent (MPA)

Figure 9.18
The interaction diagram for music selection

sends the corresponding message to the agent of type `Music Player Agent`, which then accordingly executes one of three actions: "increase or decrease volume," "decrease volume," or "resume." Another variation modeled in figure 9.19 is related to volume adjustment by the listener resulting in a "volume control request" message being sent.

The interaction diagram in figure 9.20 models the interactions related to the arrival of a music file, which is an instance of `Media Agent`. Such an agent copies itself to the SMP only if it finds a suitable environment containing enough music files with pieces of music similar in style. Once a `Media Agent` has arrived on the SMP, it sends an "I arrived" message to the agent of type `Library Manager Agent`, which first checks if there is enough space for the file on the SMP. If there is not enough space on the SMP, another `Media Agent` music file which is least preferred by the listener first backs itself up on the PC, and is then destroyed by the `Library Manager Agent`. After that, the `Media Agent` music file that has arrived is added into the music library on the PC.

Scenario: volume control

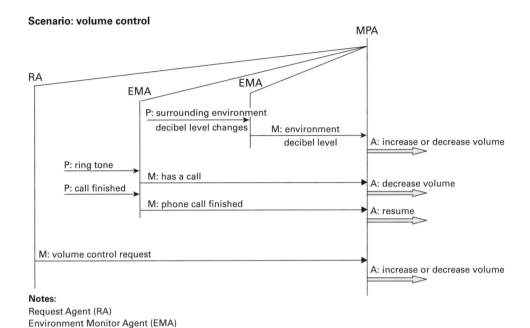

Notes:
Request Agent (RA)
Environment Monitor Agent (EMA)
Music Player Agent (MPA)

Figure 9.19
The interaction diagram for volume control

We now present an overview of the design using a Prometheus system overview diagram. A system overview diagram represents interactions between the agents of the system and interactions between the agents and their environment, as well as manipulation of data sources by the agents. A system overview diagram therefore lies in the *intersection of the computational interaction design and computational information design viewpoints.*

Figure 9.21 shows the system overview diagram for the SMP. Agents interact with each other via protocols, indicated by double-headed arrows. Each protocol contains the messages flowing between agents of the connected types. For instance, the "transfer to environment" protocol between agents of types Library Manager Agent and Media Agent serves to notify the arrival of a new instance of Media Agent and to enable its copying to the SMP. A protocol can be refined into messages of individual types by means of the PDT modeling tool. The percepts and actions modeled in the system overview diagram represent interactions between the system and its external environment. For example, "voice command" is input by the listener for requests, while "turn on/off," "play," and "increase volume" are actions targeted at physical devices.

Scenario: Media Agent arrival

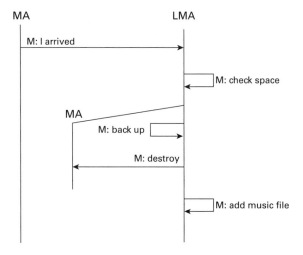

Note:
Library Manager Agent (LMA)
Media Agent (MA)

Figure 9.20
The interaction diagram for Media Agent arrival

We now model the SMP from the *computational behavior design viewpoint* using agent overview diagrams and capability diagrams. An agent overview diagram provides the top-level view of the agent internals. It shows the capabilities of the agent, the task flow between these capabilities, and the data internal to the agent. An agent descriptor, such as the one represented in table 9.24, provides a good initial set of capabilities to be refined by an agent overview diagram. There are two types of messages in agent overview and capability diagrams, *external messages* and *internal messages*, where external and internal messages respectively originate outside and inside of the agent or capability that is being modeled.

Figure 9.22 shows the top-level internal view of an agent of the Library Manager Agent type. Such an agent has the following four capabilities: "add music file," "backup music file," "space management," and "process listener settings." A music file is added into the music library by invoking the "add music file" capability under several circumstances. First, a new music file is downloaded from an online music store when an external "check online music store" message is received. Downloading is modeled as the corresponding percept in figure 9.22. Second, a new music file is added when the listener records a new audio file, for example, by doing some karaoke. This situation is triggered by an internal "record audio file request" message

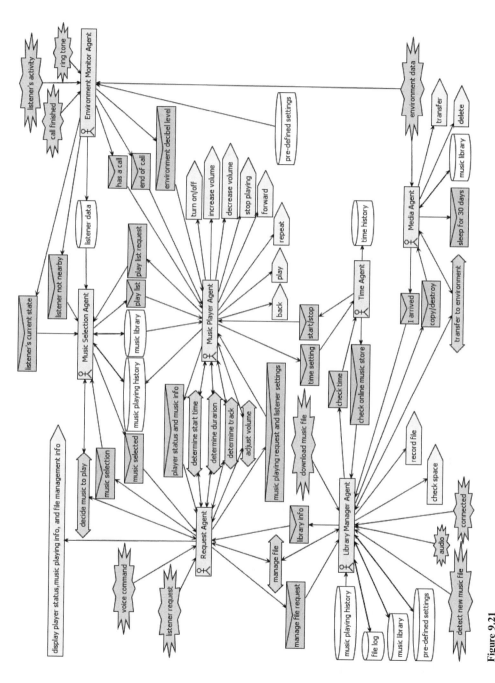

Figure 9.21
The system overview diagram for SMP

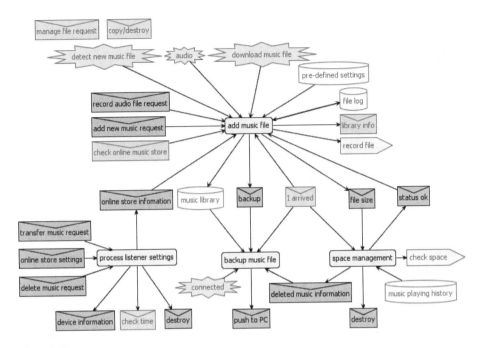

Figure 9.22
The agent overview diagram for Library Manager Agent

and by an "audio" percept. Third, a new music file is added when a new music file is detected on the PC, which is modeled as a "detect new music file" percept. In such a case, adding of the file is triggered by an internal "add new music request" message. The listener may also request to transfer a music file to the PC or to delete a music file, which are triggered by the respective "transfer music request" and "delete music request" internal messages. These messages, as well as the "record audio file request," "add new music request," and "online store settings" internal messages invoke the "process listener settings" capability and elaborate the incoming "manage file request" external message shown in figure 9.22. As can be seen in the system overview diagram in figure 9.21, the "manage file request" external message originates in the Request Agent.

When an external "I arrived" message is received from a Media Agent, the capabilities "backup music file" and "space management" are also triggered, in addition to the "add music file" capability, as is modeled in figure 9.22. These capabilities give rise to the respective internal messages "push to PC" and "destroy" that elaborate the outgoing external "copy/destroy" message targeted at backing up and destroying the least popular with the listener Media Agent.

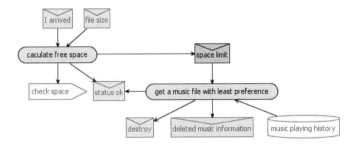

Figure 9.23
The capability diagram for space management

An agent overview diagram can be checked against the system overview diagram in terms of external messages and percepts, data used and produced, and actions. After agent overview diagrams have been created, the design can be checked by comparing goal models and scenarios against each agent overview diagram.

An additional level of agent detail is provided by capability diagrams. A capability diagram describes the internals of a single capability. A capability may include subcapabilities, plans, internal messages, and knowledge. A *plan* represents a subset of functionality that becomes a chunk of code during implementation. Capabilities are refined progressively until all capabilities have been defined.

The capability diagram for the "space management" capability depicted in figure 9.23 consists of two plans. The "calculate free space" plan is triggered when a new `Media Agent` arrives. If there is not enough space left, an internal "space limit" message is sent to another plan, which is "get a music file with least preference." That plan then destroys the music file that is the least popular with the listener to gain more memory space.

A capability diagram can be checked against its enclosing context, which can be either the agent overview diagram or another capability diagram.

As a final step of platform-independent computational design, we sketch data dictionaries from the viewpoint of *platform-independent information design*. Data dictionaries are important for ensuring consistent use of names. Tables 9.27 and 9.28 contain data dictionaries for the respective "music library" and "music playing history" databases, which were introduced by the system overview diagram shown in figure 9.21. The "sleep duration" field of the "music library" database is used when there is not enough memory space on the SMP. In such a case the state of the corresponding `Media Agent` that has been backed up is set to "sleep for 30 days on the PC."

Based on the data dictionary, a database can be designed and implemented either as a relational or an object-oriented database. Characteristics of object-oriented

Table 9.27
The data dictionary for the "music library" database

Field name	Description
Music file ID	Integer (primary key)
Associated MP3 file	MP3 file type
Title	String
Artist	String
Genre	String
Album title	String
Beats-per-minute	Integer
Duration	Time
Preference rate	String
Sleep duration	Time

Table 9.28
The data dictionary for the "music playing history" database

Field name	Description
Music file ID	Integer (primary key)
Play list number	Integer
Played time	Time
Times played	Integer

databases, such as simplicity, extensibility, and support for object-oriented programming, could be advantageous in the design of multiagent systems.

We conclude the discussion of the SMP with three considerations for *platform-independent computational design*. First, we emphasize that while agent overview diagrams and capability diagrams are certainly platform-independent, they are not *architecture-independent*, as they presume the mappings to the BDI agent architecture. The notions of platform-independent and architecture-independent computational design were also considered in chapter 5.

Second, several agents can access the same database, which requires to design and implement a database record locking mechanism of some kind. For example, according to the system overview diagram represented in figure 9.21, the `Music Selection Agent` and `Media Agent` both access the same "music library" database.

We conclude this section with some observations on our experience with the agent-oriented methodologies used in this and the previous two sections. Note that we used two alternative ways of designing intelligent lifestyle applications. The reader may wonder which is the "right" way of designing similar applications. There is no "right" way, as different methodologies emphasize different features.

According to the combination of ROADMAP and RAP/AOR methodologies used in section 9.1, a domain model for a problem domain is expressed in terms of domain entities and relationships between them. After deciding agent types in platform-independent computational design, this information model is refined as private and shared knowledge items of agents of the identified types. In the Prometheus methodology used in sections 9.2 and 9.3, data sources are identified in parallel with the creation of scenarios in conceptual behavior modeling. The elaboration of the internal structure of these data sources is postponed until platform-independent computational design.

In the RAP/AOR methodology, interactions between agents are explicitly modeled in platform-independent interaction design based on role models created in conceptual interaction modeling. The Prometheus methodology represents interactions in platform-independent interaction design as protocols that can be refined into messages of individual types by means of the PDT modeling tool. A substantial difference between the two methodologies lies in the modeling of percepts and actions. In the RAP/AOR methodology, action and percept are often seen as two sides of the same coin, as an action performed by one agent may be perceived as an event by another agent. In contrast, the Prometheus methodology distinguishes between percepts from the environment and actions performed on the environment.

There are also differences related to behavior modeling. The RAP/AOR methodology transforms goals modeled in conceptual domain modeling immediately to activity types of platform-independent computational design and then determines the order of performing activities of these types. Each activity can be modeled in terms of how it changes the agent's knowledge and how it sends messages and performs actions on the environment. In the Prometheus methodology, goal modeling is followed by modeling scenarios for achieving the goals. The scenarios are then elaborated for individual agents as agent overview diagrams and capability diagrams. We reiterate that there is no one "right" way for modeling, and predict that agent methodologies will converge.

9.4 Background

The description of the Bill Gates intelligent home can be found at http://labnol.blogspot.com/2005/05/inside-bill-gates-home.html. In Australia there are several small companies offering consulting services to develop "smart homes" in which there is control of lighting, security, and entertainment and possibly other systems. One such company is Urban Intelligence (http://www.urbanintel.com.au). Also in Estonia, intelligent homes are built and sold (http://www.juurdeveo19.ee/). The design of an intelligent home within the Intelligent Lifestyle project conducted at the University of Melbourne in 2004 has been previously described by Sterling, Taveter, and the Daedalus Team (2006a) and more extensively by Sterling, Taveter, and the Daedalus Team (2006b).

The Secret Touch system was developed by Anne Boettcher in her work for the Smart Internet Cooperative Research Centre. Another case study performed within the same project has been described by Vetere et al. (2005).

The Smart Music Player example is courtesy of Yuxiu Luo, who investigated predicted variations in product lines using music players as an example. She developed the design for the software agents subject taught by Sterling. The requirements engineering and early design of a system controlling a Smart Music Player has been described by Luo, Sterling, and Taveter (2007) and more extensively by Luo and Sterling (2007).

The Smart Music Player was informed by the XPOD device, a prototype of a human activity and emotion-aware music player, which was proposed by Dornbush et al. 2005. That work mainly deals with the player's capabilities to sense the listener's activities and emotions. The Push!Music technology that the SMP design assumes to be utilized has been explained by Jacobsson et al. (2005).

10 An E-Learning Application

This chapter continues our exploration of applying agent models in designing, building, and enhancing systems. We describe a system developed within the Department of Computer Science and Software Engineering at the University of Melbourne. The system, described in section 10.1, involves assessing student learning when interacting with a piece of educational software for animation of algorithms manipulating data structures. The software was written initially without agents in mind. Subsequently agents were added and have added to the system the capability of evaluating whether the software meets its educational objectives.

Thinking in terms of agents expanded the possibilities of what the educational software might do and suggested how the extra capability could be designed and implemented. The idea of agents adding to software was also applied to three other educational software programs as part of a project between Monash University and the University of Melbourne. These other programs are not described here, but thinking about them encouraged us in our advocacy of agent models.

The style of this chapter is different in that it places less emphasis on the viewpoint framework and more emphasis on the software. Some goal models are given, though admittedly they were developed after the fact rather than to guide the agent development. Nonetheless, we include this chapter as a reminder that agent-oriented modeling can take many forms rather than just being the use of a narrow set of models.

10.1 Supporting the Teaching of Algorithms with Animations

Consider teaching within a modern university. Lecturers and students interact so that students can learn the material that the teachers wish to impart within a university subject.[5] Even such an abstract description can be captured in a goal model, as has

---

5. We use the Australian term "subject" rather than "course," the more usual term in America. In any case, the context of educational software is general, and we rely on the reader to adapt terms to their own context.

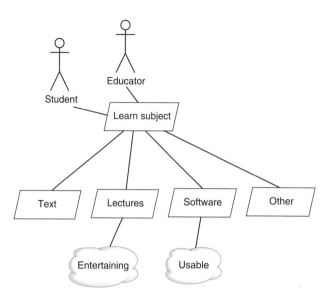

Figure 10.1
A high-level goal model for educating

been done in figure 10.1. An educator and a student involved in a subject have a common goal of the student learning the subject. Subgoals may include a text that describes the material to be learned. There are lectures—which need to be entertaining, these days—and hopefully software, which has to be usable by the student. There are, in principle, other subgoals, not explored here, but captured in the "Other" subgoal.

The diagram in figure 10.1 does not contain much information, but can be a useful starting point for discussion. For example, the way the overall learning goal is decomposed into subgoals is different from decomposing the learning goal into learning activities. We are not advocating one view or other, but are showing how conversations can be started.

Note that the notation for goals and roles is a little different from the notation used elsewhere in the book. The reason is historical. The goal model was drawn by Leon using a different drawing package on the Mac, prior to the existence of an appropriate tool such as REBEL. We decided to leave the diagram to underscore that we are not pedantic about a particular notation and also that we support the principle that models can and often should be interpreted broadly.

Let us move onto the goals and roles surrounding educational software. Once it is decided that a program is to be used in a subject, there are several roles that must be considered. The Educator and Student roles are obvious. Less obvious roles are Developer (to write the program) and Administrator (to oversee deployment in a

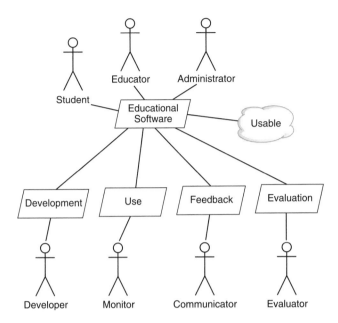

Figure 10.2
A high-level view of educational software

lab or over a network). To elaborate the overall goal: the program needs to be developed and used, with the roles Developer and Monitor responsible, and its use should be evaluated. This last subgoal is the responsibility of the Evaluator role. Ideally feedback is given to the students while using the program, with a Communicator role responsible. The previous description is illustrated by figure 10.2. Note that we have retained the "Usable" quality goal.

In reality, subjects are not developed in a pure top-down manner. Usually, subjects are developed individually and specifically rather than generically. Software is typically added to existing subject material, rather than being an integral part of the subject design. How could agents, goals, and roles relate to subject design, implementation, and teaching?

We turn to a particular software system which has been enhanced by software agents. The system is a modified version of a software tool entitled Algorithms in Action (AIA) for teaching algorithms to second-year computer science students. The AIA software uses multimedia animations of algorithms as a pedagogical tool for teaching computing algorithms. We present some background on the subject and the program.

Here are the objectives of the subject in which AIA is used, as described in the material distributed to students. At the end of the subject, the student should be able to

- explain key algorithms

- describe a range of approaches to algorithmic problem solving

- apply algorithm analysis techniques

- implement algorithms in the C programming language.

- apply skills in new situations—for example, by comparing and contrasting algorithms with respect to a range of properties, and evaluating the appropriateness of algorithms for solving problems

- expose students to concepts, algorithms, and learning opportunities, and to provide support

In fact, the software was not developed to cover any of these objectives, but to help students to learn about algorithms. More pragmatically, AIA was developed to reduce load on teaching staff during a period of burgeoning student numbers. It was hoped that by having a program available for self-study and review, students would need less interaction with heavily overloaded teaching staff. This observation highlights that the software needs to be viewed as part of a complex sociotechnical multi-agent system that includes teachers and students as well as the software.

To be more explicit, the overall educational goal in developing AIA was to assist students in understanding the standard algorithms that are typically learned by a second-year computer science subject. This overall goal encompassed a number of concrete objectives. The objectives included ensuring that students would be able to

- use the software in a remedial sense—to obtain demonstrations (through animation) and explanations of algorithms not understood thoroughly through lectures and textbooks;

- be supported in learning activities that would deepen their understanding of algorithms through exploration; and

- use AIA to review the material independently and at their own pace.

Note that one remedial sense is learning from scratch, in which lectures were not attended at all. The design of the AIA software was motivated by a goal to provide students with a rich and flexible learning environment in which they could undertake learning activities to suit their needs. This has been summarized in the goal diagram in figure 10.3 developed by the ROADMAP methodology. Recall that the ROADMAP methodology was overviewed in section 7.6.

We now describe the AIA software that was built. A rich and flexible environment was provided by giving students considerable control and multiple ways to view an algorithm. The presentation of AIA consists of a coordinated display of animation, pseudocode (a universal computer language), and textual explanation, as shown

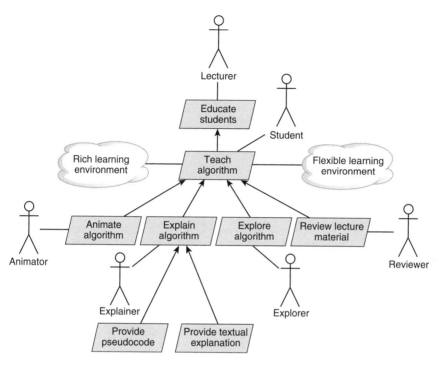

Figure 10.3
The goal model for teaching algorithms

in figure 10.4. Thirty different modules are available within the software: one for each algorithm covered. Execution of each algorithm is traced with a cursor that progresses through the pseudocode, while the animation displays a conceptual representation of the steps in the pseudocode. Textual explanation for each line of pseudocode is available to the student "on request" by a mouse-click. Figure 10.4 shows, from left to right, the explanation window, the pseudocode window, and the animation window for a search structure known as a *multiway radix trie*.

Students have a great deal of control over how they use AIA. Students are able to choose the level of detail at which the algorithm is displayed by expanding or contracting lines of pseudocode to find a level of detail appropriate to their current learning needs. The levels of detail in the animation and in the explanation expand and contract in concert with the level of detail the student chooses for the pseudocode, so that the three views are always synchronized. Students also have a high degree of control over the direction they take when using AIA: they can single-step through the algorithm or run in continuous mode, tailoring the pace precisely to their needs; they can step backwards to replay previous steps; and they can explore the

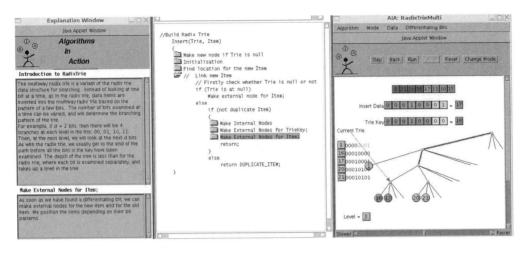

Figure 10.4
A view of the multiway radix trie module of AIA, as it appears to students (Stern and Sterling 2006). Copyright 2009 by the Association for the Advancement of Computing in Education (AACE), http://www.aace.org.

effects of using data of their own choosing and alternate coding of the algorithm, to name but a few.

Educational objectives were not explicitly taken into consideration. It was assumed that students would choose appropriate learning activities and carry them out effectively if they were given the right environment. Subsequent reflection has suggested that such assumptions should have been tested. It is worth noting that challenging such assumptions may have happened if our agent-oriented perspective would have been adopted at the outset. The agent concepts and perspectives described in this section have been articulated subsequently to AIA's initial deployment.

We have partially reconstructed an agent-oriented perspective of the sociotechnical system of students, teachers, and agents using AIA. Figure 10.3 is a part of this reconstruction. Basically, an explicit high-level learning objective has been added to the motivation layer as "Educate students" and "Teach algorithm" goals shown in figure 10.3, and several learning activities have been added to the design layer as we describe shortly. At the deployment layer, concrete objects and concrete actions, subsequently referred to as simply actions, and events caused by concrete actions have been made explicit. Notable events that have been represented are low-level actions of students, including mouse-clicks, data input, and other keystroke operations that control the level of detail displayed, the view available, and the execution of the algorithm. Currently the accuracy of the learning activities and concepts that have been introduced is being evaluated.

The relatively unstructured nature of AIA as originally implemented has allowed it to be used for a variety of learning activities, including set tasks, remedial work, general review, and advanced exploration. Although this versatility is an asset for supporting learning, the virtually limitless number of paths a student can take in any given AIA session makes evaluation a complex task. We posit that students undertake a variety of learning activities that have the potential to lead to under-standing of an algorithm—for example, intensive learning, exploration, and reading explanations.

In order to use agents in the evaluation of the use of AIA, the software framework was extended to record key student actions in a log file, along with relevant parame-ters. Actions to be logged were classified according to which view of the algorithm they pertained.

The Control class of actions determines the animation presentation. Actions in this class control the basic running of all algorithms. The following key control actions common to all algorithms are currently logged:

- run/pause animation
- change speed of animation
- single-step through animation
- back up (all the way to the beginning of the session, if desired)

The following algorithm-specific control actions are also logged:

- input different data
- use different pseudocode for a part of the algorithm
- select different parameters

Data input is considered algorithm-specific, even though all algorithms allow data input, because the range of suggested data for each algorithm is different, having been designed to show particular features of that specific algorithm. All modules allow the student to input data of their own design. The use of alternative coding is appropriate for only some algorithms, and is specific to the algorithm, as is the choice of parameters. An example of an algorithm-specific control parameter is "Differentiating Bits," seen in the animation window of figure 10.4; this parameter chooses the number of bits used in branching in the multiway trie (set to 2 in the fig-ure), but would be meaningless for other algorithms.

The Pseudocode class of actions consists of requests to expand and contract the pseudocode, which in turn affect the level of detail in the animation and explana-tions. The Explanation class of actions consists of requests for textual explanation.

A start time is recorded for every action. Relevant parameters for the Run action are the speed of the animation at the start of the run and at the end of the run, the start line in the pseudocode, the exit mode, and the degree of detail being presented. Parameters for the Step and Backup actions are the location in the pseudocode of the cursor.

Log files are written in XML. XML was chosen for its flexible structure and the availability of Java parsing libraries. There is one log file for each AIA session—where a session is defined as a single access to a particular module by a single student. An example log file shown in figure 10.5 records a student's actions when using AIA to study an insertion algorithm for the multiway radix trie data structure. The log shows that this session was dominated by requests for explanations, most of them prior to running the animation. This is a typical pattern, in which a student uses textual explanations to orient him- or herself to the algorithm before viewing the animation.

Agents have been developed to monitor the use of the software by students as captured by the log files. The agents use the log files as input, and infer which, if any, of the associated sessions were consistent with our models of learning activities. The learning activities that have been investigated are those considered likely to lead to the understanding of the algorithm. Prototype models have been developed for three learning activities. The prototype model for Intensive Learning is based on a view of a student who is using AIA to learn an algorithm that he or she does not comprehend. In our model, this student would be likely to iterate over the material that he or she does not understand, using either the backup or the reset facility of AIA. A minimum number of backups or resets is required in order for a session to be classified as Intensive Learning.

The prototype model for an Exploration learning activity captures sessions in which the student explored an algorithm supported by the AIA facilities for using alternative code or using a variety of user-defined data. A minimum threshold of exploratory actions is set by the person responsible for evaluation.

The model for the use of Explanation in learning was developed after students were observed using the textual explanations more frequently than anticipated. The prototype model for the Explanation learning activity detects sessions where the number of requests for textual explanations exceeds a threshold set by the evaluator.

Software agents have been developed to detect sessions conforming to the models for the Intensive Learning, Exploration, and Explanation learning activities. Inputs to the agent are a collection of log files and the user-defined parameters, such as thresholds. There is an independent agent for each learning activity. The output from the agent is a list of log files of student sessions in which the sequence of actions is consistent with our model(s) for the specified classification(s) and the user-determined parameters. Additional information, such as the counts of particular actions, are also available as output.

```
<session>
<algorithm>AIA: RadixTrieMulti</algorithm>
<starttime>2006-03-31 10:37:00</starttime>
<endtime>2006-03-31 10:38:32</endtime>
<action>
<name>Explanation</name>
<tclass>Explanation</tclass>
<time>2006-03-31 10:37:11</time>
<param name="linenumber" value="3.1"/>
<param name="option" value="Make new node if Trie is null"/>
</action>
<action>
<name>Explanation</name>
<tclass>Explanation</tclass>
<time>2006-03-31 10:37:14</time>
<param name="linenumber" value="3.2"/>
<param name="option" value="Initialisation"/>
</action>
<action><name>Explanation</name>
<tclass>Explanation</tclass>
<time>2006-03-31 10:37:16</time>
<param name="linenumber" value="3.3"/>
<param name="option" value="Find location for the new Item"/>
</action>
<action>
<name>Run Button</name>
<tclass>Control</tclass>
<time>2006-03-31 10:37:19</time>
<param name="startspeed" value="50"/>
<param name="endspeed" value="23"/>
</action>
<action>
<name>Explanation</name>
<tclass>Explanation</tclass>
<time>2006-03-31 10:38:28</time>
<param name="linenumber" value="3.4"/>
<param name="option" value="Link new Item"/>
</action>
</session>
```

Figure 10.5
A log file for an AIA session (Stern and Sterling 2006). Copyright 2009 by the Association for the
Advancement of Computing in Education (AACE), http://www.aace.org.

An external framework has also been implemented to allow the agents to work together, so student sessions can be identified where multiple learning activities are carried out. Sessions that combine a number of learning activities are relatively common. For example, a student might start session learning largely through Explanation, then fill in more detailed understanding using an Intensive Learning mode, and end the session with Exploration. The current framework supports classification based on single models, multiple models, and any subset of a set of models. These agents will identify files associated with student sessions where it has been inferred that the algorithm being studied has been mastered. Models for mastery have not yet been fully defined. In a simplistic sense, a model for mastery might require the student to engage in some exploratory learning activities, as a way of demonstrating mastery. Such a model might not, however, capture all sessions where the student has mastered the material. For example, an able student might be capable of exploring some of the more elementary algorithms mentally, without using the AIA exploration facilities, and such a session would be missed. Similarly, a student who has already mastered an algorithm might use AIA to quickly refresh his or her knowledge. Currently, research is underway to identify such sessions and to distinguish them from perfunctory sessions in which students are learning little.

To summarize the case study, adopting agent concepts has resulted in an expansion of a piece of educational software, and has suggested ways of improving the development of educational software in the future. Matching teacher models of learning activities with actual student behavior extracted from log files gives powerful information to teachers, to software developers, and potentially to students, to increase their understanding of AIA in particular and learning in general.

10.2   Background

The computer animation program Algorithms in Action (AIA) is described by Stern, Naish, and Sondergaard (1999) and by Stern and Naish (2002). More details of the initial program can be found therein. The agent-oriented extensions came about through the PEDANT (Pedagogical Agents for Modeling On-Line and Computer-Interactive Learning) project, a joint project between four schools and faculties across Monash University and the University of Melbourne under a collaborative funding scheme between the institutions. The project is reported in Markham et al. 2003. The main aim of the project was to develop a collection of software agents to investigate the relationship between the way students use on-line and interactive educational tools and the quality of their learning experience. An account of the agent extensions has been provided by Stern and Sterling (2006) and Stern and Lam (2007).

Beyond the project described in some detail in section 10.1, there have been several efforts to adapt agents for educational software. Baylor (2001) was an early advocate for the concept. Jafari (2002) presents scenarios where digital agents would help in the delivery of subjects and courses. Chan and Sterling (2003b) describe an agent framework for assisting in online course environments. One of the agents from their framework automatically built links from exam questions set by the course coordinator to the online course material, which provided feedback for students making mistakes while taking the online exam associated with the course.

Glossary

Accident   an *event* that results in harm, injury, or loss.

Achievement goal   a kind of *goal* targeted at achieving a certain *state of affairs*.

Action   something that an *agent* does; an elementary *activity*.

Action event   a kind of *event* that is caused by the *action* of an *agent*.

Activity or activity occurrence   an execution of *actions* constituting the *activity* situated in a specific *context* that takes time, effort, and application of *knowledge*.

Activity context   a kind of *context* that is characterized by the time and space of performing the *activity*, as well as by other contextual *activities* that enclose the given *activity*.

Activity type   a prototypical job function that specifies a particular way of doing by performing elementary *epistemic actions*, *physical actions*, and *communicative actions*.

Agent   a kind of *physical object* that can act in the *environment*, perceive *events*, and reason.

Agent acquaintance model   a kind of *model* that complements the *agent model* by outlining interaction pathways between the *agents* of the *sociotechnical system*.

Agent architecture   blueprint for *manmade agents* that models the arrangement of *agent* components and the connections between the components.

Agent behavior model   a kind of *model* that describes the behavior of an *agent* of the given *agent type*.

Agent model   a kind of *model* that transforms *roles* from the analysis stage to *agent types* that will be realized at runtime.

Agent-oriented software engineering methodology   a kind of *software engineering methodology* that uses the notion of *agent* or actor in all stages of its *software engineering process*.

Agent type   *type* whose instances are individual *agents*.

Aggregation   a binary *formal relation* between *types* of *entities* that defines how an *entity* of one *type* consists of or contains *entities* of another *type*.

Antirigid type   a *type* whose every instance is not necessarily its instance, that is, can change its *type*.

Architecture-dependent model   a kind of *model* that is expressed in terms of specific *agent architecture* for implementing *manmade agents*.

Architecture-independent model   a kind of *model* that does not prescribe or imply the usage of any specific *agent architecture* for implementing *manmade agents*.

Asynchronous communication performing of *communicative actions* by *agents* so that sending of a message is temporally separated from responding to it.

Atomic event a kind of *event* that is modeled as happening instantaneously.

Attribute a characterization of a *physical agent* or *physical object* in one or more *quality dimensions*.

Authorization relationship a kind of *relation* between *agents* in which an *agent* playing a *role* needs to be empowered to fulfil its *responsibilities* by an *agent* playing another *role*.

Autonomous agent a kind of *agent* that creates and pursues its own agenda as opposed to functioning under the control of another *agent*.

Avoidance goal a kind of *goal* aimed at avoiding a certain *state of affairs*.

Behavioral construct a modeling construct that determines how certain *states of affairs* are related to *concrete actions* performed by a particular *concrete agent*.

Behavioral interface model a kind of *model* that defines an interface for a *behavioral unit* of an *agent*.

Behavioral unit a set of *behavioral constructs* that are applied as a whole.

Beliefs the *knowledge* possessed by an *agent*.

Benevolence relationship a kind of *relation* between self-interested *roles* where an *agent* performing a *role* offers to fulfil *responsibilities* for an *agent* performing another *role* whenever it appears beneficial to the offering agent.

Cease goal a kind of *goal* targeted at ceasing a certain *state of affairs*.

Claim a kind of *social relator* whereby one *physical agent* is entitled to expect that another *physical agent* will perform a certain *action* or bring about a certain *state of affairs*.

Collective activity a kind of *activity* involving *agents* performing two or more *roles*.

Commitment a kind of *social relator* whereby one *physical agent* obliges toward another *physical agent* to perform a certain *action* or bring about a certain *state of affairs*.

Communicative action a kind of *physical action* where an *agent* sends a message to another *agent*.

Communicative action event a kind of *action event* that is caused by sending a message by the sending *agent* that is perceived by the receiving *agent*.

Computational environment a kind of *environment* that *software agents* can access.

Conceptual object a kind of *knowledge item* used for representing a *mental moment*.

Conceptual space an open concept space for systems engineering.

Concrete action something that a *physical agent* does and that may be perceived as an *event* by another *physical agent*.

Constraint an assertion that must be satisfied in all evolving *states* and *state* transition histories of the *sociotechnical system*.

Constraints components of a *role* that specify conditions that an *agent* enacting the *role* must take into consideration when performing its *responsibilities*.

Context the interrelated conditions in which an *entity* exists.

Control relationship a kind of *relation* between a parent *role* and its children *roles* where the enactor of the parent role can delegate its responsibilities to the enactors of its children *roles*.

Controlled autonomy   the notion of autonomy where an *agent* acts autonomously only to the extent it is beneficial to the *physical agent* controlling it.

Controller   the component of an *agent* that performs *actions* affecting the *environment*, including messages sent to other *agents*, through the *agent*'s actuators based on the input *knowledge* it receives from the *agent*'s knowledge base and from its sensors.

Deployment layer   the lower layer of the *conceptual space*, consisting of the *sociotechnical system* situated in its *environment*.

Derivation   a statement of *knowledge* that is derived from other *knowledge* by an inference or a mathematical calculation.

Domain entity   a modular unit of *knowledge* handled by a *sociotechnical system*.

Domain model   a kind of *model* that represents the *knowledge* that the *sociotechnical system* is supposed to handle; represents the *environments*, the *types* of *resources* produced and stored by them, and the *relations* between the *roles*, *environments*, and *resources*.

Endurant   a kind of *particular* that persists in time while keeping its identity.

Entity   anything perceivable or conceivable.

Environment   a first-class abstraction that provides the surrounding conditions for *agents* to exist and that mediates both the interaction among *agents* and the access to *resources*.

Epistemic action or mental action   a kind of *action* performed by an *agent* that is targeted at changing the *agent*'s *knowledge*.

Event   a kind of *perdurant* that is related to the *states of affairs* before and after it has occurred, respectively, and may be perceived by an *agent*.

External action   a kind of *action* performed by an *agent* that is targeted at changing an *environment* in which the *agent* operates.

Formal relation   a kind of *relation* that holds between two or more *entities* directly, without any intermediating *entity*.

Generalization   a taxonomic *formal relation* between more general and more specific *types* of *entities*.

Goal   a set of *states of affairs* intended by one or more *agents*.

Goal decomposition   a kind of *goal formal relation* between *goals* that groups several subgoals related to the same supergoal.

Goal formal relation   a kind of *formal relation* between two or more *goals*.

Goal model   a kind of *model* representing *goals* set for the *sociotechnical system* and the *goal formal relations* between them.

Hazard   a potentially harmful *state of affairs*, where an *accident* is possible.

Hazard analysis   an analysis of a *sociotechnical system* and its *environment* to identify potential *hazards*.

Hierarchy   a kind of *organization* where the enactor of a parent *role* delegates some of its *responsibilities* to the enactors of its children *roles*.

Human role   a kind of *role* that is enacted by a human *agent*.

Individual activity   an *activity* involving an *agent* performing one *role*.

Institutional agent   an aggregate consisting of internal human and *manmade agents*, which share collective *knowledge*, and that acts, perceives and communicates through them.

Intelligent agent   a kind of *agent* that is required to be reactive, proactive, and social.

Interaction diagram   a kind of *interaction model* representing (some part of) a prototypical interaction *process* between *agents* of the *sociotechnical system*.

Interaction model   a kind of *model* that represents an interaction pattern between *agents* of the *sociotechnical system*.

Interaction-frame diagram   a kind of *interaction model* that represents possible interactions between *agents* belonging to two or more *agent types* as *types* of *action events*.

Interaction-sequence diagram   a kind of *interaction diagram* that models prototypical interactions as *action events*.

Intrinsic moment   a kind of *moment* that is existentially dependent on one single *physical object*.

Knowledge   information that may change an *agent* either by becoming grounds for *actions*, or by making an *agent* capable of different or more effective *action*.

Knowledge attribute   a kind of *knowledge item* used for representing an *intrinsic moment* of a *physical agent*.

Knowledge item   a modeling element that is used for representing a *moment* of a *physical agent*.

Knowledge model   a kind of *model* that represents private and shared *knowledge* that the *agents* need for functioning in the *sociotechnical system*.

Logic goal   the postcondition to be achieved by the *activity* in the tradition of the logic approach to the formalization of artificial intelligence.

Maintaining goal   a *goal* aimed at preserving a certain *state of affairs*.

Manmade agent   a kind of *agent* that has been implemented by humans physically or in software or as a combination of both.

Market   a kind of *organization* where each *agent* can choose its *responsibilities* so that they best fit the *goals* and *quality goals* applying to the *agent*.

Material relation   a kind of *relation* that is founded on the existence of an intermediating *entity* termed as *relator*.

Mental moment   a kind of *intrinsic moment* referring to the *mental state* of a *physical agent*.

Mental state   the *state* of an *agent* that is described in terms of anthropomorphic *qualities* like beliefs, responsibilities, expectations, capabilities, goals, desires, and intentions, and *social relators*, such as *commitments* and *claims*.

Model   a hypothetical simplified description of a complex *entity* or *process*.

Moment   a kind of *endurant* that is existentially dependent on another *endurant*, which is named its bearer.

Motivation layer   the upper layer of the *conceptual space* containing abstract modeling concepts needed for defining requirements and purposes of a *sociotechnical system*.

Motivational scenario   a kind of *model* that describes in an informal and loose narrative manner how *goals* are to be achieved by *agents* enacting the corresponding *roles*.

Multiagent system   a kind of *system* where several, perhaps all, of the connected *entities* are *agents*.

Network   a kind of *organization* with *peer relationships* among its *roles*.

Nonaction event   a kind of *event* that is not caused by an *action*.

Nonnumeric attribute   a kind of *attribute* that represents one or more *quality dimensions* qualitatively, for example, as an enumeration value.

Numeric attribute   a kind of *attribute* that represents one *quality dimension* quantitatively as a numerical value.

Object   a kind of *endurant* that satisfies a condition of unity and for which certain parts can change without affecting its identity.

Ontology (sense 1)   the study of existence and modes of existence.

Ontology (sense 2)   a framework of *knowledge* for the *agents* of the problem domain.

Operation   a procedure or transformation performed by a *physical object*.

Optimization goal   a kind of *goal* that strives for maximizing or minimizing a specific optimization function.

Organization   an organized body of *agents* with a particular purpose.

Organization model   a kind of *model* that represents the *relations* between the *roles* of the *sociotechnical system*.

Organizational role   a kind of *role* that is enacted by an *institutional agent*.

Particular   a kind of *entity* that exist in reality possessing a unique identity, an *entity* that exists at least in time.

Peer relationship   a kind of *relation* between *roles* where a *responsibility* can either be delegated by the enactor of a parent *role* or requested by the enactor of a child *role* meaning that the *roles* have equal status.

Perceptions   the information an *agent* receives from its sensors.

Perdurant   a kind of *particular* whose all temporal parts are not present at the same time.

Phases   *antirigid types* that constitute possible stages in the history of a *type* instance.

Physical action   a kind of *action* performed by an *agent* that may be perceived by another *agent*.

Physical environment   a kind of *environment* that is inhabited by *physical entities*.

Physical agent   a kind of *physical object* that can act in the *environment*, perceive *events*, and reason.

Physical entity   a kind of *particular* that exists in both time and space.

Physical object   a kind of *endurant* that satisfies a condition of unity and for which certain parts can change without affecting its identity.

Plan   the means to achieve a *logic goal* by performing a set of *actions*.

Platform   a set of subsystems and technologies that provide a coherent set of functionalities through interfaces and specified usage patterns.

Platform-dependent model   a kind of *model* that describes the design in terms of a particular programming language or *platform*.

Platform-independent model   a kind of *model* that describes the design independently of any particular programming language or *platform*.

Private activity   a kind of *activity* that is performed solely by an *agent* playing a particular *role*.

Proactive agent   a kind of *agent* that does not simply act in response to its *environment*, but is able to exhibit opportunistic, *goal*-directed behavior and take the initiative where appropriate.

Process   a complex *event* that consists of two or more possibly parallel occurrences of *events*.

Protocol   a kind of *interaction model* that represents an interaction pattern between *agents* of two or more *agent types* along with the aspects of the *agents'* behavior.

Quality   a kind of *moment* that inheres in exactly one *endurant* and can be represented in several *quality dimensions*.

Quality attribute   a characterization of the quality of performing an *activity* with respect to some *quality goal*.

Quality dimension   a perceivable or conceivable characterization of a *quality* in human cognition.

Quality goal   a nonfunctional or *quality requirement* of the *sociotechnical system*.

Quality requirement   any requirement about the quality of the software as opposed to its functionality.

Reactive agent   an *agent* that is able to perceive its *environment* and respond in a timely fashion to changes occurring in it.

Relation, also known as association   a kind of *type* whose instances are tuples connected by the relation *entities*.

Relational moment or relator   a kind of *moment* that is existentially dependent on more than one *physical object*.

Relator type   the *type* whose instances are individual *relators*.

Resource   a *physical object* used by a *physical agent* for achieving the *goals* defined for the *sociotechnical system*; a *physical object* produced and stored by an *environment* to be accessed and used by *agents*.

Responsibilities   components of a *role* that determine what an *agent* enacting the *role* must do in order for a set of *goals* and *quality goals* to be achieved.

Rigid type   a *type* whose every instance is necessarily its instance, that is, cannot change its *type*.

Role   an anti-rigid *type*, representing some capacity or position, where *agents* playing the *role* need to contribute to achieving certain *goals* set for the *sociotechnical system*.

Role model   a kind of *model* representing the *responsibilities* and *constraints* pertaining to a *role* that are required for achieving the *goals* set for the *sociotechnical system*.

Routine activity   a kind of *activity* that is not modeled as a *scenario*.

Rule   a kind of *relator type* between the *agent type* to which it is attached and *types* of *mental moments*, *events*, *activities*, and *actions*, representing when an *activity* is created and for how long is stays active, as well as what *actions* are performed in its course.

Safe system   a *sociotechnical system* where the likelihood of the *sociotechnical system* causing an *accident* is acceptably low.

Safety-critical role   a *role* where the *responsibilities* attached to the *role* will affect the safety of the *sociotechnical system*.

Safety-critical system   a *sociotechnical system* where safety is a critical concern.

Scenario   a kind of *model* that describes how the *goals* set for the *sociotechnical system* can be achieved by *agents* of the *sociotechnical system*; a *collective activity* that models how a particular *goal* is achieved by *agents* enacting particular *roles*; a specification of a purposeful sequence of *activities* by the *agents* involved.

Service   a *physical object* that provides functionality to the *agents*.

Service model a kind of *model* that reflects the view of a *multiagent system* as consisting of *agents* and *services*, where *services* make up a *computational environment* for the *multiagent system*.

Signature the definition of the *types* of arguments taken by an *operation* and the *type* of the return value.

Social agent an *agent* that is able to interact, when appropriate, with other *agents* in order to complete its own *activities* and to help others with their *activities*.

Social policy a constraint set by an *organization* on the achievement of *goals*, and on the formation and satisfaction of sets of *commitments* and *claims* by *agents* within the *organization*; defines the *actions* that *agent*(s) subject to the policy may, should not, or must perform on target *agent*(s) when specific relevant *events* occur.

Social relator a kind of *relator* that appears between two or more *physical agents*.

Social relator type the *type* whose instances are *social relators*.

Social role a kind of *role* that is characterized by a set of *responsibilities* toward other *agents* by an *agent* playing the *role*.

Sociotechnical system a kind of *multiagent system* that includes hardware and software, has defined operational *processes*, and offers an interface, implemented in software, to human *agents*.

Software agent a kind of *physical agent* that is implemented as software.

Software architecture the definition of the structures of the *system* that is implemented in software, composed of architectural elements and the *relations* between the elements.

Software engineering methodology a kind of *software engineering process* for the organized production of software using a collection of predefined techniques and notational convention.

Software engineering process a kind of *process* involving *activities*, *roles*, and *resources* that produces intended software of some kind.

Start event a kind of *event* that occurs once per each execution cycle of abstract *agent architecture*.

State (of an entity) a kind of *perdurant* characterizing the *entity* whose imagined elementary temporal parts, snapshots, belong to the same *type* of *perdurants*.

Stateless service a kind of *service* that does not maintain information about its *state* between its invocations.

State of affairs collective *state* of the *entities* of an *environment*.

Subkind a *type* that inherits the principle of identity of its parent *type* and represents its parent *type*'s subset of instances.

System a set of *entities* connected together to make a complex whole or perform a complex function.

System design layer the middle layer of the *conceptual space* consisting of the notions required for modeling and designing a *sociotechnical system*.

Task a kind of *activity* where the *logic goal* to be achieved by the *activity* has been defined explicitly before the *activity* is started and where the *actions* performed by an *agent* are defined in terms of *plans*.

Test action a kind of *action* that checks whether a logical formula is derivable from the *agent*'s *beliefs*.

Type a *universal* that carries a principle of identity for its instances and whose every instance maintains its identity in every circumstance considered by the *model*.

Universals patterns of features, which can be realized in a number of different *particulars*; *entities* that exist neither in space nor in time, that is they cannot be localized.

Use cases   a means for specifying required usages of a *system*.

Viewpoint framework   a matrix with three rows representing different abstraction layers and three columns representing the viewpoint aspects interaction, information, and behavior.

Virtual entities   a kind of *particulars* that exist merely in time.

Virtual environment   a kind of *environment* that is inhabited by *virtual entities*.

List of Acronyms

3APL	Artificial Autonomous Agents Programming Language
AAII	Australian Artificial Intelligence Institute
AAMAS	Autonomous Agents and Multiagent Systems
ACL	Agent Communication Language
AGV	Automatically Guided Vehicle
AHAZOP	Agent Hazard and Operability Analysis
AI	Artificial Intelligence
AIA	Algorithms in Action
AOR	Agent-Object-Relationship
AORML	Agent-Object-Relationship Modeling Language
AOSE	Agent-Oriented Software Engineering
AUML	Agent Unified Modeling Language
BDI	Belief Desire Intention
BPMN	Business Process Modeling Notation
B2B	Business-to-Business
CAD	Computer-Aided Design
CASE	Computer-Aided Software Engineering
CIM	Computation Independent Model
CONE	Conceptual Network Ontology Editor
CORBA	Common Object Request Broker Architecture
CRM	Customer Relationship Management
dMARS	Distributed Multiagent Reasoning System
DSTO	Australian Defense Science and Technology Organisation
EAI	Enterprise Application Integration

ebXML	Electronic Business using eXtensible Markup Language
e-commerce	Electronic Commerce
EDI	Electronic Data Interchange
ER	Entity-Relationship
ERP	Enterprise Resource Planning
FIPA	Foundation for Intelligent Physical Agents
GPL	General Public Licence
GUI	Graphical User Interface
HAZOP	Hazard and Operability Studies
IDE	Integrated Development Environment
ISA	Information Systems Architecture
JACK	Java Agent Compiler and Kernel
JADE	Java Agent Development Environment
KQML	Knowledge Query and Manipulation Language
MaSE	Multiagent Systems Engineering
MDA	Model-Driven Architecture
NASA	The National Aeronautics and Space Administration
OAA	Open Agent Architecture
OASIS	Organization for the Advancement of Structured Information Standards
OCL	Object Constraint Language
O-MaSE	Organization-based Multiagent Systems Engineering
OMG	Object Management Group
OPEN	Object-oriented Process, Environment and Notation
OPIS	Opportunistic Intelligent Scheduler
OZONE	O3 = Object-Oriented OPIS
PC	Program Committee or Personal Computer
PDT	Prometheus Design Tool
PEDANT	Pedagogical Agents for Modeling On-Line and Computer-Interactive Learning
PIM	Platform Independent Model
PRS	Procedural Reasoning System
PSM	Platform Specific Model

RAP/AOR	Radical Agent-Oriented Process / Agent-Object-Relationship
REBEL	Roadmap Editor Built for Easy deveLopment
RFQ	Request For Quote
RM-ODP	Reference Model for Open Distributed Processing
ROADMAP	Role-Oriented Analysis and Design for Multiagent Programming
SMART	Structured and Modular Agents and Relationship Types
SMP	Smart Music Player
STOW	Synthetic Theater of War
STRIPS	Stanford Research Institute Problem Solver
SWARMM	Smart Whole Air Mission Model
TAOM4E	Tool for Agent-Oriented Modeling
UAV	Unmanned Aerial Vehicle
UDDI	Universal Description, Discovery, and Integration
UML	Unified Modeling Language
WWW	World Wide Web
XML	eXtensible Markup Language
XPDL	XML Process Definition Language

References

Arnold, K., Gosling, J., and Holmes, D. 2005. *The Java Programming Language*. 4th edition. Reading, MA: Addison-Wesley.

Asimov, I. 1950. *I, Robot*. New York: Gnome Press.

Bauer, B., and J. Odell. 2005. UML 2.0 and agents: How to build agent-based systems with the new UML standard. *Journal of Engineering Applications of Artificial Intelligence, 18*(2), 141–157.

Baylor, A. L. 2001. Investigating multiple pedagogical perspectives through MIMIC (Multiple Intelligent Mentors Instructing Collaboratively). In J. D. Moore, C. L. Redfield, and W. L. Johnson (eds.), *Artificial Intelligence in Education: AI-ED in the Wired and Wireless Future*. Amsterdam, The Netherlands: IOS Press.

Bellifemine, F., G. Caire, and D. Greenwood. 2005. *Developing multiagent systems with JADE*. Chichester, UK: John Wiley and Sons.

Bellifemine, F., A. Poggi, and G. Rimassa. 2001. Developing multiagent systems with a FIPA-compliant agent framework. *Software—Practice and Experience, 31*(2), 103–128.

Bergenti, F., M.-P. Gleizes, and F. Zambonelli. 2004. *Methodologies and Software Engineering for Agent Systems: The Agent-Oriented Software Engineering Handbook*. Norwell, MA: Kluwer Publishing.

Blaha, M., and J. Rumbaugh. 2005. *Object-Oriented Modeling and Design with UML*. Upper Saddle River, NJ: Prentice Hall.

Blake, M. B. 2002. B2B electronic commerce: Where do agents fit in? In M. B. Blake (ed.), *Agent-Based Technologies for B2B Electronic Commerce: Papers from the AAAI Workshop, Technical Report WS-02-01* (1–8). Menlo Park, CA: American Association for Artificial Intelligence.

Bordini, R. H., J. F. Hübner, and R. Vieira. 2005. Jason and the golden fleece of agent-oriented programming. In R. H. Bordini, M. Dastani, J. Dix, and A. E. F. Seghrouchni (eds.), *Multiagent Programming: Languages, Platforms, and Applications* (3–37). Berlin, Germany: Springer-Verlag.

Bratman, M. E. 1987. *Intentions, Plans, and Practical Reason*. Stanford, CA: CSLI Publications.

Bresciani, P., A. Perini, P. Giorgini, F. Giunchiglia, and J. Mylopoulos. 2001. A knowledge level software engineering methodology for agent oriented programming. In *Proceedings of the Fifth International Conference on Autonomous Agents*, May 28–June 1, Montreal, Quebec, Canada (648–655). New York: ACM.

Bresciani, P., A. Perini, P. Giorgini, F. Giunchiglia, and J. Mylopoulos. 2004. Tropos: An agent-oriented software development methodology. *Autonomous Agents and Multiagent Systems, 8*(3), 203–236.

Brooks, R. 1991. Intelligence without representation. *Artificial Intelligence, 47*(1–3), 139–159.

Bubenko, J. A. 1993. Extending the scope of information modelling. In A. Olivé (ed.), *Fourth International Workshop on the Deductive Approach to Information Systems and Databases, September 20–22, Lloret de Mar, Catalonia, Proceedings* (DAISD 1993). Report de recerca, LSI/93-25-R, Departament de Llenguatges i Sistemes Informatics (73–97). Barcelona, Spain: Universitat Politecnica de Catalunya (UPC).

Bubenko, J. A., Jr., and M. Kirikova. 1994. "Worlds" in requirements acquisition and modelling. In H. Kangassalo and B. Wangler (eds.), *Proceedings of the 4th European–Japanese Seminar on Information*

Modelling and Knowledge Bases, May 31–June 3, Stockholm, Sweden (159–174). Amsterdam, The Netherlands: IOS Press.

Caire, G., W. Coulier, F. Garijo, J. Gómez-Sanz, J. Pavón, P. Kearney, and P. Massonet. 2004. The MESSAGE methodology. In F. Bergenti, M.-P. Gleizes, and F. Zambonelli (eds.), *Methodologies and Software Engineering for Agent Systems: The Agent-Oriented Software Engineering Handbook* (177–194). Norwell, MA: Kluwer Publishing.

Cernuzzi, L., T. Juan, L. Sterling, and F. Zambonelli. 2004. The GAIA methodology: Basic concepts and extensions. In F. Bergenti, M.-P. Gleizes, and F. Zambonelli (eds.), *Methodologies and Software Engineering for Agent Systems: The Agent-Oriented Software Engineering Handbook* (69–88). Norwell, MA: Kluwer Publishing.

Chan, K., and L. Sterling. 2003a. Specifying roles within agent-oriented software engineering. In *Proceedings of the 10th Asia-Pacific Software Engineering Conference* (APSEC 2003), December 10–12, Chiang Mai, Thailand (390–395). Washington, DC: IEEE Computer Society.

Chan, K., and L. Sterling. 2003b. Light-weight agents for e-learning environments. In N. Zhong, Z. W. Ras, S. Tsumoto, and E. Suzuki (eds.), *Foundations of Intelligent Systems, 14th International Symposium, ISMIS 2003, Maebashi City, Japan, October 28–31, Proceedings* (LNAI 2871, 197–205). Berlin, Germany: Springer-Verlag.

Chen, P. P. 1976. The Entity-Relationship Model: Toward a unified view of data. *ACM Transactions on Database Systems*, *1*(1), 9–36.

Chung, L., B. Nixon, E. Yu, and J. Mylopoulos. 2000. *Non-functional Requirements in Software Engineering*. Norwell, MA: Kluwer Publishing.

Ciancarini, P., and M. Wooldridge. 2001. Agent-based software engineering: Guest editors' introduction. *International Journal of Software Engineering and Knowledge Engineering*, *11*(3), 205–206.

Clancey, W. J. 2002. Simulating activities: Relating motives, deliberation, and attentive coordination. *Cognitive Systems Research*, *3*(3), 471–499.

Cockburn, A. 2001. *Writing Effective Use Cases*. Reading, MA: Addison-Wesley.

Cossentino, M. 2005. From requirements to code with the PASSI methodology. In B. Henderson-Sellers and P. Giorgini (eds.), *Agent-Oriented Methodologies* (79–106). Hershey, PA: Idea Group.

Curtis, W., M. I. Kellner, and J. Over. 1992. Process modelling. *Communications of the ACM*, *35*(9), 75–90.

Dardenne, A., A. van Lamsweerde, and S. Fickas. 1993. Goal-directed requirements acquisition. *Science of Computer Programming*, *20*(1–2), 3–50.

Dastani, M., M. B. van Riemsdijk, and J.-J. Ch. Meyer. 2005. Programming multiagent systems in 3APL. In R. H. Bordini, M. Dastani, J. Dix, and A. E. F. Seghrouchni (eds.), *Multiagent Programming: Languages, Platforms, and Applications* (39–67). Berlin, Germany: Springer-Verlag.

DeLoach, S. A. 2008. Developing a multiagent conference management system using the O-MaSE process framework. In M. Luck and L. Padgham (eds.), *Agent-Oriented Software Engineering VIII: The 8th International Workshop on Agent Oriented Software Engineering, AOSE 2007, Honolulu, HI, May 14, 2007, Revised Selected Papers* (LNCS 4951, 168–181). Berlin, Germany: Springer-Verlag.

DeLoach, S. A., and M. Kumar. 2005. Multiagent systems engineering: An overview and case study. In B. Henderson-Sellers and P. Giorgini (eds.), *Agent-Oriented Methodologies* (317–340). Hershey, PA: Idea Group.

DeLoach, S. A., and J. L. Valenzuela. 2007. An agent-environment interaction model. In L. Padgham and F. Zambonelli (eds.), *Agent-Oriented Software Engineering VII: 7th International Workshop, AOSE 2006, Hakodate, Japan, May 8, 2006, Revised and Invited Papers* (LNCS 4405, 1–8). Berlin, Germany: Springer-Verlag.

DeLoach, S. A., M. F. Wood, and C. H. Sparkman. 2001. Multiagent systems engineering. *International Journal of Software Engineering and Knowledge Engineering*, *11*(3), 231–258.

De Wolf, T., and T. Holvoet. 2005. Emergence versus self-organisation: Different concepts but promising when combined. In S. Brueckner, G. Di Marzo Serugendo, A. Karageorgos, and R. Nagpal (eds.), *Engineering Self Organising Systems: Methodologies and Applications* (LNCS 3464, 1–15). Berlin, Germany: Springer-Verlag.

Dignum, V. 2004. A model for organizational interaction: Based on agents, founded in logic. Ph.D. thesis, Utrecht University, The Netherlands.

d'Inverno, M., and M. Luck. 2001. *Understanding Agent Systems*. Berlin, Germany: Springer-Verlag.

d'Inverno, M., M. Luck, M. Georgeff, D. Kinny, and M. Wooldridge. 2004. The dMARS architecture: A specification of the distributed multiagent reasoning system. *Journal of Autonomous Agents and Multiagent Systems*, 9(1–2), 5–53.

Dornbush, S., K. Fisher, K. McKay, A. Prikhodko, and Z. Segall. 2005. XPOD: A human activity and emotion aware mobile music player. In *2nd International Conference on Mobile Technology, Applications and Systems*, November 15–17 (1–6). Washington, DC: IEEE Computer Society.

Farber, Barry. 2003. *Diamond Power: Gems of Wisdom from America's Greatest Marketer*. Franklin Lakes, NJ/Career Press.

Fielding, R. T. 2000. Architectural styles and the design of network-based software architectures. Ph.D. thesis, University of California, Irvine, CA.

FIPA ACL. 2002. *FIPA Agent Communication Language (ACL) Message Structure Specification*. Foundation for Intelligent Physical Agents (FIPA), Standard, December 3, 2002. Retrieved January 13, 2008, from http://www.fipa.org/specs/fipa00061/.

Firesmith, D. G., and B. Henderson-Sellers. 2002. *The OPEN Process Framework: An Introduction*. London, UK: Addison-Wesley.

Franklin, S., and A. Graesser. 1997. Is it an agent, or just a program? A taxonomy for autonomous agents. In J. P. Müller, M. J. Wooldridge, and N. R. Jennings (eds.), *Proceedings of the ECAI '96 Workshop on Agent Theories, Architectures, and Languages: Intelligent Agents III, Heidelberg, Germany, August 12–13, 1996* (LNAI 1193, 21–36). Berlin, Germany: Springer-Verlag.

Garcia-Ojeda, J. C., S. A. DeLoach, Robby, W. H. Oyenan, and J. Valenzuela. 2008. O-MaSE: A customizable approach to developing multiagent development processes. In M. Luck and L. Padgham (eds.), *Agent-Oriented Software Engineering VIII: The 8th International Workshop on Agent Oriented Software Engineering, AOSE 2007, Honolulu, HI, May 14, Revised Selected Papers* (LNCS 4951, 1–15). Berlin, Germany: Springer-Verlag.

Genesereth, M. R., and S. P. Ketchpel. 1994. Software agents. *Communication of the ACM*, 37(7), 48–53.

Giorgini, P., Kolp, M., Mylopoulos, J., and Castro, J. 2005. Tropos: A requirements-driven methodology for agent-oriented software. In B. Henderson-Sellers and P. Giorgini (eds.), *Agent-Oriented Methodologies* (20–45). Hershey, PA: Idea Group.

Guarino, N., and Welty, C. A. 2001. A formal ontology of properties. In R. Dieng and O. Corby (eds.), *Knowledge Acquisition, Modelling and Management, 12th International Conference, EKAW 2000, Juan-les-Pins, France, October 2–6, Proceedings* (LNCS 1937, 97–112). Berlin, Germany: Springer-Verlag.

Guizzardi, G. 2005. *Ontological foundations for structural conceptual models*. Telematica Instituut Fundamental Research Series, No. 15. Enschede, The Netherlands.

Guizzardi, G., R. Falbo, and R. S. S. Guizzardi. 2008. Grounding software domain ontologies in the Unified Foundational Ontology (UFO): The case of the ODE Software Process Ontology. In *Proceedings of the XI Iberoamerican Workshop on Requirements Engineering and Software Environments (IDEAS 2008)*, February 11–15, Recife, Brazil (electronic edition).

Guizzardi, G., and G. Wagner. 2005a. Towards ontological foundations for agent modeling concepts using the Unified Foundational Ontology (UFO). In P. Bresciani, P. Giorgini, B. Henderson-Sellers, G. Low, and M. Winikoff (eds.), *Agent-Oriented Information Systems II, 6th International Bi-Conference Workshop, AOIS 2004, Riga, Latvia, June 8, 2004, and New York, NY, July 20, 2004, Revised Selected Papers* (LNAI 3508, 110–124). Berlin, Germany: Springer-Verlag.

Guizzardi, G., and G. Wagner. 2005b. Some applications of a unified foundational ontology in business modeling. In P. Green and M. Rosemann (eds.), *Business Systems Analysis with Ontologies* (345–376). Hershey, PA: Idea Group.

Guizzardi, G., G. Wagner, N. Guarino, and M. van Sinderen. 2004. An ontologically well-founded profile for UML conceptual models. In A. Persson and J. Stirna (eds.), *Advanced Information Systems Engineering, 16th International Conference, CAiSE 2004, Riga, Latvia, June 7–11* (LNCS 4408, 148–164). Berlin, Germany: Springer-Verlag.

Guizzardi, R. S. S. 2006. Agent-oriented constructivist knowledge management. Ph.D. thesis, Centre For Telematics and Information Technology, University of Twente, The Netherlands.

Guizzardi, R. S. S., and G. Guizzardi. 2008. Ontology-based transformation framework from Tropos to AORML. In P. Giorgini, N. Maiden, J. Mylopoulos, and E. Yu (eds.), *Tropos/i*: Applications, Variations and Extensions*, Cooperative Information Systems Series. Cambridge, MA, and London, England: MIT Press.

Guizzardi, R. S. S., G. Guizzardi, A. Perini, and J. Mylopoulos. 2007. Towards an ontological account of agent oriented goals. In R. Choren, A. Garcia, H. Giese, H. Leung, C. Lucena, and A. Romanovsky (eds.), *Software Engineering for Multiagent Systems V: Research Issues and Practical Applications* (LNCS 4408, 148–164). Berlin, Germany: Springer-Verlag.

Heinze, C., M. Cross, S. Goss, T. Josefsson, I. Lloyd, G. Murray, M. Papasimeon, and M. Turner. 2002. Agents of change: The impact of intelligent agent technology on the analysis of air operations. In L. Jain, N. Ichalkaranje, and G. Tonfoni (eds.), *Advances in Intelligent Systems for Defense*, Series on Innovative Intelligence (Volume 2, 229–264). River Edge, NJ: World Scientific.

Henderson-Sellers, B., and P. Giorgini. 2005. *Agent-Oriented Methodologies*. Hershey, PA: Idea Group.

Høydalsvik, G. M., and G. Sindre. 1993. On the purpose of object-oriented analysis. *ACM SIGPLAN Notices*, 28(10), 240–255.

Huhns, M. N., and L. M. Stephens. 1999. Multiagent systems and societies of agents. In G. Weiss (ed.), *Multiagent Systems: A Modern Approach to Distributed Artificial Intelligence* (79–120). Cambridge, MA, and London, England: MIT Press.

Iglesias, C. A., and M. Garijo. 2005. The agent-oriented methodology MAS-CommonKADS. In B. Henderson-Sellers and P. Giorgini (eds.), *Agent-Oriented Methodologies* (46–78). Hershey, PA: Idea Group.

Ingrand, F., M. Georgeff, and A. Rao. 1992. An architecture for real-time reasoning and system control. *IEEE Expert*, 7(6), 34–44.

Jacobsson, M., M. Rost, M. Håkansson, and L. E. Holmquist. 2005. Push!Music: Intelligent music sharing on mobile devices. In *Adjunct Proceedings of the Seventh International Conference on Ubiquitous Computing* (UbiComp 2005), September 11–14, Tokyo, Japan (electronic edition).

Jafari, A. 2002. Conceptualizing intelligent agents for teaching and learning. *EDUCAUSE Quarterly*, 25(3), 28–34.

Jayatilleke, G. B., L. Padgham, and M. Winikoff. 2005. A model driven component-based development framework for agents. *Computer Systems Science and Engineering*, 20(4), 273–282.

Jennings, N. R. 2000. On agent-based software engineering. *Artificial Intelligence*, 117(2), 277–296.

Jennings, N. R., P. Faratin, M. J. Johnson, T. J. Norman, P. O'Brien, and M. E. Wiegand. 1996. Agent-based business process management. *International Journal of Cooperative Information Systems*, 5(2–3), 105–130.

Jennings, N. R., K. Sycara, and M. Wooldridge. 1998. A roadmap of agent research and development. *Autonomous Agents and Multiagent Systems*, 1(1), 7–38.

Juan, T. 2008. ROADMAP: Agent oriented software engineering for intelligent systems. Ph.D. thesis, The University of Melbourne, Australia.

Juan, T., A. R. Pearce, and L. Sterling. 2002. ROADMAP: Extending the Gaia methodology for complex open systems. In *The First International Joint Conference on Autonomous Agents and Multiagent Systems, AAMAS 2002, July 15–19, Bologna, Italy, Proceedings* (3–10). New York: ACM.

Juan, T., and L. Sterling. 2003. The ROADMAP meta-model for intelligent adaptive multiagent systems in open environments. In P. Giorgini, J. Muller, and J. Odell (eds.), *Agent-Oriented Software Engineering IV, 4th International Workshop, AOSE 2003, Melbourne, Australia, July 15, Revised Papers* (LNCS 2935, 53–68). Berlin, Germany: Springer-Verlag.

Juan, T., L. Sterling, M. Martelli, and V. Mascardi. 2003. Customizing AOSE methodologies by reusing AOSE features. In J. S. Rosenschein, T. Sandholm, M. Wooldridge, and M. Yokoo (eds.), *Proceedings of the Second International Joint Conference on Autonomous Agents and Multiagent Systems (AAMAS-03), Melbourne, Australia, July 14–18* (113–120). New York: ACM.

Juan, T., L. Sterling, and M. Winikoff. 2002. Assembling agent oriented software engineering methodologies from features. In F. Giunchiglia, J. Odell, and G. Weiss (eds.), *Agent-Oriented Software Engineering III, Third International Workshop, AOSE 2002, Bologna, Italy, July 15, Revised Papers and Invited Contributions* (LNCS 2585, 198–209). Berlin, Germany: Springer-Verlag.

Kagal, L., T. Finin, and A. Joshi. 2003. A policy based approach to security for the Semantic Web. In D. Fensel, K. P. Sycara, and J. Mylopoulos (eds.), *The Semantic Web—ISWC 2003, Second International Semantic Web Conference, Sanibel Island, FL, October 20–23, Proceedings* (LNCS 2870, 402–418). Berlin, Germany: Springer-Verlag.

Kasinger, H., and B. Bauer. 2005. Towards a model-driven software engineering methodology for organic computing systems. In M. H. Hamza (ed.), *Computational Intelligence: IASTED International Conference on Computational Intelligence*, July 4–6, Calgary, Alberta, Canada (141–146). Calgary, Alberta, Canada: IASTED/ACTA Press.

Kavakli, V., and P. Loucopoulos. 1998. Goal-driven business process analysis–application in electricity deregulation. In B. Pernici and C. Thanos (eds.), *Advanced Information Systems Engineering, 10th International Conference CAiSE '98, Pisa, Italy, June 8–12, Proceedings* (LNCS 1413, 305–324). Berlin, Germany: Springer-Verlag.

Kendall, E. A. 1999. Agent roles and role models: New abstractions for intelligent agent system analysis and design. In A. Holsten, G. Joeris, C. Klauck, M. Klusch, H.-J. Müller, and J. P. Müller (eds.), *International Workshop on Intelligent Agents in Information and Process Management, TZI-Report No. 9*. Bremen, Germany: University of Bremen.

Kinny, D., M. Georgeff, and A. Rao. 1996. A methodology and modelling technique for systems of BDI agents. In W. Van de Velde and J. W. Perram (eds.), *Agents Breaking Away, 7th European Workshop on Modelling Autonomous Agents in a Multiagent World (MAAMAW), Eindhoven, The Netherlands, January 22–25, Proceedings* (LNAI 1038, 56–71). Berlin, Germany: Springer-Verlag.

Kirikova, M. 2000. Explanatory capability of enterprise models. *Data and Knowledge Engineering*, *33*(2), 119–136.

Kuan, P. P., S. Karunasakera, and L. Sterling. 2005. Improving goal and role oriented analysis for agent based systems. In *16th Australian Software Engineering Conference (ASWEC 2005), March 31–April 1, Brisbane, Australia* (40–47). Washington, DC: IEEE Computer Society.

Labarthe, O., E. Tranvouez, A. Ferrarini, B. Espinasse, and B. Montreuil. 2003. A heterogeneous multiagent modelling for distributed simulation of supply chains. In V. Marik, D. C. McFarlane, and P. Valckenaers (eds.), *Holonic and Multiagent Systems for Manufacturing, First International Conference on Industrial Applications of Holonic and Multiagent Systems, HoloMAS 2003, Prague, Czech Republic, September 1–3, Proceedings* (LNCS 2744, 134–145). Berlin, Germany: Springer-Verlag.

Labrou, Y., and T. Finin. 1997. A proposal for a new KQML specification. TR CS-97-03, February, Computer Science and Electrical Engineering Department. Baltimore, MD: University of Maryland.

Laird, J. E., K. J. Coulter, R. M. Jones, P. G. Kenny, F. V. Koss, and P. E. Nielsen. 1998. Integrating intelligent computer generated forces in distributed simulation: TacAir-Soar in STOW-97. In *Proceedings of the 1998 Simulation Interoperability Workshop*. Orlando, FL.

Leontief, A. N. 1979. The problem of activity in psychology. In Wertsch, J. V. (ed.), *The concept of activity in soviet psychology* (37–71). Armonk, NY: M. E. Sharpe.

Lister, K., and L. Sterling. 2003. Tasks as context for intelligent agents. In *Proceedings of the 2003 IEEE/WIC International Conference on Intelligent Agent Technology* (IAT 2003), October 13–17, Halifax, Canada (154–160). Washington, DC: IEEE Computer Society.

Luck, M., and L. Padgham, eds. 2008. *Agent-Oriented Software Engineering VIII: The 8th International Workshop on Agent Oriented Software Engineering, AOSE 2007, Honolulu, HI, May 14, Revised Selected Papers* (LNCS 4951). Berlin, Germany: Springer-Verlag.

Luo, Y., G. Antoniou, and L. Sterling. 2007. Incorporating security requirements into communication protocols in multiagent software systems. In *Proceedings of the Eighth International Conference on Parallel and Distributed Computing, Applications and Technologies* (PDCAT '07), December 3–6, Adelaide, Australia (159–160). Washington, DC: IEEE Computer Society.

Luo, Y., and L. Sterling. 2007. *Modelling a Smart Music Player with a Hybrid Agent-Oriented Methodology*. Agentlab Technical Report, Department of Computer Science and Software Engineering. Melbourne, Australia: The University of Melbourne.

Luo, Y., L. Sterling, and K. Taveter. 2007. Modeling a smart music player with a hybrid agent-oriented methodology. In *Proceedings of the 15th IEEE International Requirements Engineering Conference*, October 15–19, Delhi, India (281–286). Washington, DC: IEEE Computer Society.

Markham, S., J. Ceddia, J. Sheard, C. Burvill, J. Weir, B. Field, L. Sterling, and L. Stern. 2003. Applying agent technology to evaluation tasks in e-learning environments. In *Proceedings of the Exploring Educational Technologies Conference*. Melbourne, Australia: Monash University.

Martin, D., and I. Sommerville. 2004. Patterns of cooperative interaction: Linking ethnomethodology and design. *ACM Transactions on Computer-Human Interaction, 11*(1), 59–89.

Marchewka, J. T. 2006. *Information Technology Project Management: Providing Measurable Organizational Value*. 2nd edition. Chichester, UK: John Wiley and Sons.

Masolo, C., S. Borgo, A. Gangemi, N. Guarino, and A. Oltramari. 2003. Ontology library. *EU IST Project 2001-33052 WonderWeb: Ontology Infrastructure for the Semantic Web, Deliverable D18*.

Medina-Mora, R., T. Winograd, R. Flores, and F. Flores. 1992. The action workflow approach to workflow management technology. In *Proceedings of the Conference on Computer Supported Cooperative Work (CSCW), October 31–November 4, Toronto, Canada* (281–288). New York: ACM.

Metsker, S. J. 1997. Thinking over objects. *Object Magazine, 7*(3), 56–59.

Morandini, M., D. C. Nguyen, A. Perini, A. Siena, and A. Susi, 2008. Tool-supported development with Tropos: The conference management system case study. In M. Luck and L. Padgham (eds.), *Agent-Oriented Software Engineering VIII: The 8th International Workshop on Agent-Oriented Software Engineering, AOSE 2007, Honolulu, HI, May 14, Revised Selected Papers* (LNCS 4951, 182–196). Berlin, Germany: Springer-Verlag.

Nguyen, D. C., Perini, A., and Tonella, P. 2008. A goal-oriented software testing methodology. In M. Luck and L. Padgham (eds.), *Agent-Oriented Software Engineering VIII: The 8th International Workshop on Agent-Oriented Software Engineering, AOSE 2007, Honolulu, HI, May 14, Revised Selected Papers* (LNCS 4951, 58–72). Berlin, Germany: Springer-Verlag.

Nwana, H. S. 1995. Software agents: An overview. *Knowledge Engineering Review, 11*(2), 205–244.

Odell, J. 2002. Objects and agents compared. *Journal of Object Technology, 1*(1), 41–53.

Odell, J., H. Van Dyke Parunak, and B. Bauer. 2001. Representing agent interaction protocols in UML. In P. Ciancarini and M. Wooldridge (eds.), *Agent-Oriented Software Engineering, First International Workshop, AOSE 2000, Limerick, Ireland, June 10, Revised Papers* (LNCS 1957, 121–140). Berlin, Germany: Springer-Verlag.

Oja, M., B. Tamm, and K. Taveter. 2001. Agent-based software design. *Proceedings of the Estonian Academy of Sciences: Engineering, 7*(1), 5–21.

OMG. 2003. MDA Guide Version 1.0.1. June 12, 2003. Retrieved June 28, 2007, from http://www.omg .org/cgi-bin/doc?omg/03-06-01.

OMG. 2006. Business Process Modeling Notation (BPMN) Specification. Final Adopted Specification, February 6, 2006. Retrieved February 10, 2008, from http://www.omg.org/bpmn/.

OMG. 2007. Unified Modeling Language: Superstructure. Version 2.1.1, February 2007. Retrieved June 28, 2007, from http://www.omg.org/cgi-bin/doc?formal/07-02-05.

Ow, S. P., S. F. Smith, and R. A. Howie. 1998. CSS: A cooperative scheduling system. In M. D. Oliff (ed.), *Proceedings of the 2nd International Conference on Expert Systems and the Leading Edge in Production Planning and Control*, May 3–5, Charleston, SC (43–56). New York: North-Holland.

Padgham, L., and M. Winikoff. 2003. Prometheus: A methodology for developing intelligent agents. In F. Giunchiglia, J. Odell, and G. Weiss (eds.), *Agent-Oriented Software Engineering III, Third International Workshop, AOSE 2002, Bologna, Italy, July 15, Revised Papers and Invited Contributions* (LNCS 2585, 174–185). Berlin, Germany: Springer-Verlag.

Padgham, L., and M. Winikoff. 2004. *Developing intelligent agent systems: A practical guide*. Chichester, UK: John Wiley and Sons.

Padgham, L., J. Thangarajah, and M. Winikoff. 2005. Tool support for agent development using the Prometheus methodology. In *Proceedings of the 2005 NASA/DoD Conference on Evolvable Hardware* (EH 2005), June 29–July 1, Washington, DC (383–388). Washington, DC: IEEE Computer Society.

Padgham, L., J. Thangarajah, and M. Winikoff. 2008. The Prometheus Design Tool—A conference management system case study. In M. Luck and L. Padgham (eds.), *Agent-Oriented Software Engineering VIII: The 8th International Workshop on Agent-Oriented Software Engineering, AOSE 2007, Honolulu, HI, May 14, 2007, Revised Selected Papers* (LNCS 4951, 197–211). Berlin, Germany: Springer-Verlag.

Parunak, H. Van Dyke. 2000. *International Journal of Cooperative Information Systems, 9*(3), 209–227.

Parunak, H. Van Dyke, A. D. Baker, and S. J. Clark. 1997. The AARIA agent architecture: An example of requirements-driven agent-based system design. In *Proceedings of the First International Conference on Autonomous Agents*, February 5–8, Marina del Rey, CA (482–483). New York: ACM.

Pavón, J., J. J. Gómez-Sanz, and R. Fuentes. 2005. The INGENIAS methodology and tools. In B. Henderson-Sellers and P. Giorgini (eds.), *Agent-Oriented Methodologies* (236–276). Hershey, PA: Idea Group.

Peirce, C. S. 1935. *Scientific Metaphysics, Vol. VI of the Collected Papers.* Cambridge, MA: Harvard University Press.

Penserini, L., A. Perini, A. Susi, and J. Mylopoulos. 2006. From stakeholder intentions to software agent implementations. In E. Dubois and K. Pohl (eds.), *Advanced Information Systems Engineering, 18th International Conference, CAiSE 2006, Luxembourg, Luxembourg, June 5–9, Proceedings* (LNCS 4001, 465–479). Berlin, Germany: Springer-Verlag.

Perugini, D. 2007. Agents for logistics: A provisional agreement approach. Ph.D. thesis, The University of Melbourne, Australia.

Picard, G., and M.-P. Gleizes. 2004. The ADELFE methodology. In F. Bergenti, M.-P. Gleizes, and F. Zambonelli (eds.), *Methodologies and Software Engineering for Agent Systems: The Agent-Oriented Software Engineering Handbook* (157–175). Norwell, MA: Kluwer Publishing.

Putman, J., R. 2001. *Architecting with RM-ODP.* Upper Saddle River, NJ: Prentice Hall.

Raffel, W.-U. 2005. Agentenbasierte Simulation als Verfeinerung der Diskreten-Ereignis-Simulation unter besonderer Berücksichtigung des Beispiels Fahrerloser Transportsysteme. Ph.D. thesis, Institut für Informatik, FU Berlin, Germany.

Rahwan, I., T. Juan, and L. Sterling. 2006. Integrating social modelling and agent interaction through goal-oriented analysis. *International Journal of Computer Systems Science and Engineering, 21*(2), 87–98.

Rao, A. S., and M. P. Georgeff. 1991. Modeling rational agents within a BDI architecture. In J. Allen, R. Fikes, and E. Sandewall (eds.), *Proceedings of Knowledge Representation 91* (KR-91) (473–484). San Francisco, CA: Morgan Kaufmann.

Rothwell, W. J., and H. C. Kazanas. 1997. *Mastering the Instructional Design Process: A Systematic Approach.* San Francisco, CA: Jossey-Bass.

Rumbaugh, J., M. Blaha, W. Premerlani, F. Eddy, and W. Lorensen. 1991. *Object Oriented Modeling and Design.* Englewood Cliffs, NJ: Prentice-Hall.

Russell, S. J., and P. Norvig. 2002. *Artificial Intelligence: A Modern Approach.* 2nd edition. Upper Saddle River, NJ: Prentice Hall.

Shoham, Y. 1993. Agent-oriented programming. *Artificial Intelligence, 60*(1), 51–92.

Sierhuis, M., W. J. Clancey, and R. van Hoof. 2003. Brahms: A multiagent modeling environment for simulating social phenomena. In *Proceedings of the First Conference of the European Social Simulation Association* (SIMSOC VI), September 18–21, Groningen, The Netherlands.

Silva, V., and C. Lucena. 2004. From a conceptual framework for agents and objects to a multiagent system modeling language. *Journal of Autonomous Agents and Multiagent Systems, 9*(1–2), 145–189. Norwell, MA: Kluwer Publishing.

Singh, M. P. 1999. An ontology for commitments in multiagent systems: Toward a unification of normative concepts. *Artificial Intelligence and Law, 7*(1), 97–113.

Smith, R. D. 1998. Essential techniques for military modeling and simulation. In D. J. Medeiros, E. F. Watson, J. S. Carson, and M. S. Manivannan (eds.), *Proceedings of the 30th Conference on Winter Simulation*, December 13–16, Washington, DC (805–812). New York: ACM.

Smith, S. 1995. Reactive scheduling systems. In D. E. Brown and W. T Scherer (eds.), *Intelligent Scheduling Systems* (155–192). Norwell, MA: Kluwer Publishing.

Smith, S. F., and M. A. Becker. 1997. An ontology for constructing scheduling systems. In *Working Notes of the 1997 AAAI Spring Symposium on Ontological Engineering* (120–129), Stanford, CA.

Smith, S., P. S. Ow, N. Muscettola, J. Y. Potvin, and D. Matthys. 1990. OPIS: An opportunistic factory scheduling system. In *Proceedings of the 3rd International Conference on Industrial and Engineering Applications of Artificial Intelligence and Expert Systems* (IEA/AIE '90), July 15–18, Charleston, SC (Vol. 1, 268–274).

Sommerville, I. 2007. *Software Engineering*. 8th edition. Reading, MA: Addison-Wesley.

Sowa, J. F., and J. A. Zachman. 1992. Extending and formalizing the framework for information systems architecture. *IBM Systems Journal*, *31*(3), 590–616.

Sterling, L., and T. Juan. 2005. The software engineering of agent-based intelligent adaptive systems. In G.-C. Roman, W. G. Griswold, and B. Nuseibeh (eds.), *27th International Conference on Software Engineering (ICSE 2005), May 15–21, St. Louis, Missouri, Proceedings* (704–705). New York: ACM.

Sterling, L., and E. Shapiro. 1994. *The Art of Prolog: Advanced Programming Techniques*. 2nd edition. Cambridge, MA, and London, England: MIT Press.

Sterling, L., K. Taveter, and the Daedalus Team. 2006a. Building agent-based appliances with complementary methodologies. In E. Tyugu and T. Yamaguchi (eds.), *Knowledge-Based Software Engineering, Proceedings of the Seventh Joint Conference on Knowledge-Based Software Engineering* (JCKBSE '06), August 28–31, Tallinn, Estonia (223–232). Amsterdam, The Netherlands: IOS Press.

Sterling, L., K. Taveter, and the Daedalus Team. 2006b. Experience from building industry strength agent-based appliances. *An Industry Experience Report at the Australian Software Engineering Conference* (ASWEC 2006), April 18–21, Sydney, Australia. Retrieved June 7, 2008, from http://www.cs.mu.oz.au/~kuldar/Daedalus-paper.pdf.

Stern, L., and K. Lam. 2007. A framework for evaluating multimedia software: Modeling student learning strategies. In *ED-MEDIA 2007: World Conference on Educational Multimedia, Hypermedia and Telecommunications*, Vancouver, BC, Canada, June 25–29 (3301–3309). Chesapeake, VA: Association for the Advancement of Computing in Education.

Stern, L., and L. Naish. 2002. Visual representation for recursive algorithms. In *SIGCSE '02: Proceedings of the 33rd SIGCSE Technical Symposium on Computer Science Education*, Cincinnati, OH (196–200). New York: ACM.

Stern, L., L. Naish, and H. Sondergaard. 1999. A strategy for managing content complexity in algorithm animation. In B. Manaris (ed.), *Proceedings of the Fourth Annual SIGCSE/SIGCUE Conference on Innovation and Technology in Computer Science Education* (ITiCSE99), Cracow, Poland (127–130). New York: ACM.

Stern, L., and L. Sterling. 2006. Towards agents for educational software. In *ED-MEDIA 2006: World Conference on Educational Multimedia, Hypermedia and Telecommunications*, Orlando, FL, June 26–30 (2040–2047). Chesapeake, VA: Association for the Advancement of Computing in Education.

Tamm, B. G., R. Puusepp, and R. Tavast. 1987. *Analiz i modelirovanije proizvodstvennyh sistem (Analysis and modeling of production systems)*. Moscow: Finansy i Statistika.

Taveter, K. 1997. From object-oriented programming towards agent-oriented programming. In G. Grahne (ed.), *Proceeedings of the Sixth Scandinavian Conference on Artificial Intelligence* (SCAI '97), August 18–20, Helsinki, Finland (288). Amsterdam, The Netherlands: IOS Press.

Taveter, K. 2004a. A multi-perspective methodology for agent-oriented business modeling and simulation. Ph.D. thesis, Tallinn University of Technology, Estonia.

Taveter, K. 2004b. From business process modeling to business process automation. In J. Cordeiro and J. Filipe (eds.), *Computer Supported Activity. Coordination, Proceedings of the 1st International Workshop on Computer Supported Activity Coordination* (CSAC 2004). In conjunction with ICEIS 2004, April, Porto, Portugal (198–210). Porto, Portugal: INSTICC Press.

Taveter, K. 2005a. Business process automation with representing and reasoning on trust. In *Proceedings of the 3rd International IEEE Conference on Industrial Informatics* (INDIN '05), August 10–12, Perth, Western Australia (electronic edition). Washington, DC: IEEE Computer Society.

Taveter, K. 2005b. CONE: Improving human-computer interaction by integrated ontological models. In *Proceedings of the 11th International Conference on Human-Computer Interaction*, July 22–27, Las Vegas, Nevada (electronic edition). Las Vegas, NV: Mira Digital Publishing.

Taveter, K. 2006a. A technique and markup language for business process automation. In *Proceedings of the Workshop on Vocabularies, Ontologies, and Rules for the Enterprise* (VORTE 2006). In conjunction with the Tenth IEEE International EDOC (The Enterprise Computing) Conference, October 16–20, Hong Kong (electronic edition). Washington, DC: IEEE Computer Society.

Taveter, K. 2006b. Application of RAP/AOR to the modeling and simulation of a ceramic factory. In J.-P. Rennard (ed.), *Handbook of Research on Nature-Inspired Computing for Economy and Management* (541–556). Hershey, PA: Idea Group.

Taveter, K., and R. Hääl. 2002. Agent-oriented modelling and simulation of a ceramic factory. In E. Juuso and L. Yliniemi (eds.), *Proceedings of the 43rd Conference of Simulation and Modelling* (SIMS 2002), September 26–27, Oulu, Finland (102–110). Helsinki, Finland: Finnish Society of Automation and Scandinavian Simulation Society.

Taveter, K., and L. Sterling. 2008. An expressway from agent-oriented models to prototype systems. In M. Luck and L. Padgham (eds.), *Agent-Oriented Software Engineering VIII: The 8th International Workshop on Agent-Oriented Software Engineering, AOSE 2007, Honolulu, HI, May 14, Revised Selected Papers* (LNCS 4951, 147–163). Berlin, Germany: Springer-Verlag.

Taveter, K., and G. Wagner. 2006. Agent-oriented modeling and simulation of distributed manufacturing. In J.-P. Rennard (ed.), *Handbook of Research on Nature Inspired Computing for Economy and Management* (527–540). Hershey, PA: Idea Group.

Taveter, K., and G. Wagner. 2001. Agent-oriented enterprise modeling based on business rules. In H. S. Kunii, S. Jajodia, and A. Sølvberg (eds.), *Conceptual Modeling—ER 2001, 20th International Conference on Conceptual Modeling, Yokohama, Japan, November 27–30, Proceedings* (LNCS 2224, 527–540). Berlin, Germany: Springer-Verlag.

Taveter, K., and G. Wagner. 2005. Towards radical agent-oriented software engineering processes based on AOR modelling. In B. Henderson-Sellers and P. Giorgini (eds.), *Agent-Oriented Methodologies* (277–316). Hershey, PA: Idea Group.

Tamagotchi. 2008. *Tamagotchi Connection*. Retrieved February 5, 2008, from http://www.tamagotchi .com.

Vetere, F., M. R. Gibbs, J. Kjeldskov, S. Howard, F. Mueller, S. Pedell, K. I. Mecoles, and M. Bunyan. 2005. Mediating intimacy: Designing technologies to support strong-tie relationships. In G. C. van der Veer and C. Gale (eds.), *Proceedings of the 2005 Conference on Human Factors in Computing Systems* (CHI 2005), April 2–7, Portland, OR (471–480). New York: ACM.

Vrba, P. 2003. MAST: manufacturing agent simulation tool. In *Emerging Technologies and Factory Automation, 2003, Proceedings, ETFA '03, IEEE Conference*, September 16–19 (Volume 1, 282–287). Washington, DC: IEEE Computer Society.

Wagner, G. 2003. The agent-object-relationship meta-model: Towards a unified view of state and behavior. *Information Systems, 28*(5), 475–504.

Weyns, D., Omicini, A., and Odell, J. 2007. Environment as a first class abstraction in multiagent systems. *Autonomous Agents and Multiagent Systems, 14*(1), 5–30.

Wikipedia. 2006a. *Electronic Commerce*. Retrieved October 11, 2006, from http://en.wikipedia.org/wiki/ E-commerce.

Wikipedia. 2006b. *Home Automation*. Retrieved October 11, 2006, from http://en.wikipedia.org/wiki/ Intelligent_home.

Wikipedia. 2006c. *Computer Virus*. Retrieved December 17, 2006, from http://en.wikipedia.org/wiki/ Software_virus.

Wikipedia. 2008a. *Tamagotchi*. Retrieved February 5, 2008, from http://en.wikipedia.org/wiki/ Tamagotchi.

Wikipedia. 2008b. *Procedural Reasoning System*. Retrieved February 25, 2008, from http://en.wikipedia .org/wiki/Procedural_Reasoning_System.

Winikoff, M. 2005. JACK™ intelligent agents: An industrial strength platform. In R. H. Bordini, M. Dastani, J. Dix, and A. E. F. Seghrouchni (eds.), *Multiagent Programming: Languages, Platforms, and Applications* (175–193). Berlin, Germany: Springer-Verlag.

Winograd, T., and F. Flores. 1986. *Understanding Computers and Cognition: A New Foundation for Design*. Reading, MA: Addison-Wesley.

Wood, M. F., and S. A. DeLoach. 2001. An overview of the multiagent systems engineering methodology. In P. Ciancarini and W. Wooldridge (eds.), *Agent-Oriented Software Engineering, First International Workshop, AOSE 2000, Limerick, Ireland, June 10, 2000, Revised Papers* (LNCS 1957, 207–221). Berlin, Germany: Springer-Verlag.

Wooldridge, M. 1999. Intelligent agents. In G. Weiss (ed.), *Multiagent Systems: A Modern Approach to Distributed Artificial Intelligence* (27–78). Cambridge, MA, and London, England: MIT Press.

Wooldridge, M. 2002. *An Introduction to Multiagent Systems*. Chichester, UK: John Wiley and Sons.

Wooldridge, M., and N. R. Jennings. 1995. Intelligent agents: Theory and practice. *Knowledge Engineering Review*, *10*(2), 115–152.

Wooldridge, M., N. R. Jennings, and D. Kinny. 2000. The Gaia methodology for agent-oriented analysis and design. *Autonomous Agents and Multiagent Systems*, *3*(3), 285–312.

W3C. 2003. Architecture of the World Wide Web, First Edition. W3C Working Draft, 9 December 2003. Retrieved July 30, 2007, from http://www.w3.org/TR/2003/WD-webarch-20031209/.

W3C. 2007. Web Services Description Language (WSDL) Version 2.0 Part 1: Core Language. W3C Recommendation, June 26, 2007. Retrieved July 31, 2007, from http://www.w3.org/TR/wsdl20/.

Yu, E. 1995. Modeling strategic relationships for process reengineering. Ph.D. thesis, Department of Computer Science, University of Toronto, Canada.

Zachman, J. A. 1987. A framework for information systems architecture. *IBM Systems Journal*, *26*(3), 276–292.

Zambonelli, F., N. R. Jennings, and M. Wooldridge. 2001. Organizational abstractions for the analysis and design of multiagent systems. In P. Ciancarini and M. Wooldridge (eds.), *Agent-Oriented Software Engineering, First International Workshop, AOSE 2000, Limerick, Ireland, June 10, 2000, Revised Papers* (LNCS 1957, 235–251). Berlin, Germany: Springer-Verlag.

Zambonelli, F., N. R. Jennings, and M. Wooldridge. 2003. Developing multiagent systems: The Gaia methodology. *ACM Transactions on Software Engineering and Methodology*, *12*(3), 317–370.

Index